Mental States
Volume 2: Language and cognitive structure

Studies in Language Companion Series (SLCS)

This series has been established as a companion series to the periodical *Studies in Language*.

Editors

Werner Abraham
University of Vienna

Michael Noonan
University of Wisconsin-Milwaukee USA

Editorial Board

Joan Bybee
University of New Mexico

Ulrike Claudi
University of Cologne

Bernard Comrie
Max Planck Institute, Leipzig

William Croft
University of New Mexico

Östen Dahl
University of Stockholm

Gerrit J. Dimmendaal
University of Cologne

Ekkehard König
Free University of Berlin

Christian Lehmann
University of Erfurt

Robert E. Longacre
University of Texas, Arlington

Brian MacWhinney
Carnegie-Mellon University

Marianne Mithun
University of California, Santa Barbara

Edith Moravcsik
University of Wisconsin, Milwaukee

Masayoshi Shibatani
Rice University and Kobe University

Russell S. Tomlin
University of Oregon

John W.M. Verhaar
The Hague

Volume 93

Mental States. Volume 2: Language and cognitive structure
Edited by Andrea C. Schalley and Drew Khlentzos

Mental States

Volume 2: Language and cognitive structure

Edited by

Andrea C. Schalley and Drew Khlentzos
University of New England

John Benjamins Publishing Company
Amsterdam / Philadelphia

∞™ The paper used in this publication meets the minimum requirements of American National Standard for Information Sciences – Permanence of Paper for Printed Library Materials, ANSI Z39.48-1984.

Library of Congress Cataloging-in-Publication Data

Mental states / edited by Andrea C. Schalley and Drew Khlentzos.
    v. cm. -- (Studies in Language Companion Series, ISSN 0165-7763 ; v. 92-93)
Includes bibliographical references and index.
Contents: 1: Evolution, function, nature -- v. 2. Language and cognitive structure.
1. Psycholinguistics. I. Schalley, Andrea C., 1972- II. Khlentzos, Drew.
P37.M363   2007
401'.9--dc22   2007033516
ISBN 978 90 272 3105 5 (hb : set : alk. paper)
ISBN 978 90 272 3102 4 (hb : v. 1 : alk. paper)
ISBN 978 90 272 3103 1 (hb : v. 2 : alk. paper)

© 2007 – John Benjamins B.V.
No part of this book may be reproduced in any form, by print, photoprint, microfilm, or any other means, without written permission from the publisher.

John Benjamins Publishing Co. · P.O. Box 36224 · 1020 ME Amsterdam · The Netherlands
John Benjamins North America · P.O. Box 27519 · Philadelphia PA 19118-0519 · USA

Table of contents

Preface		VII
List of contributors		IX
1.	Mental categories in natural languages *Drew Khlentzos and Andrea C. Schalley*	1
2.	A culture-neutral metalanguage for mental state concepts *Cliff Goddard*	11
3.	Shape and colour in language and thought *Anna Wierzbicka*	37
4.	Universal and language-specific aspects of "propositional attitudes": Russian vs. English *Anna Gladkova*	61
5.	Mental states reflected in cognitive lexemes related to memory: A case in Korean *Kyung-Joo Yoon*	85
6.	Taste as a gateway to Chinese cognition *Zhengdao Ye*	109
7.	"Then I'll huff and I'll puff or I'll go on the roff!" thinks the wolf: Spontaneous written narratives by a child with autism *Lesley Stirling and Graham Barrington*	133
8.	Interaction between language and cognition in language development *Heather Winskel*	173
9.	What figurative language development reveals about the mind *Herbert L. Colston*	191

10. Would you rather 'embert a cudsert' or 'cudsert an embert'?
    How spelling patterns at the beginning of English disyllables can cue
    grammatical category   213
    Joanne Arciuli and Linda Cupples

11. Ethnobiological classification and the environment in Northern Australia   239
    Brett Baker

12. Events masquerading as entities: Pseudorelative perception verb
    complements in Mawng (Australian) and Romance languages   267
    Ruth Singer

13. Word and construction as units of categorization: The case of change
    predicates in Estonian   289
    Renate Pajusalu and Ilona Tragel

14. Categories and concepts in phonology: Theory and practice   311
    Helen Fraser

15. You can run, but: Another look at linguistic relativity   331
    Roger Wales

Name index   351

Language index   355

Subject index   357

Table of contents of Volume 1   361

Preface

This volume is the second of a two-volume collection on mental states. The contributions to this volume focus on the question what language and language use reveals about cognitive structure and underlying cognitive categories, whereas the first volume is concerned with evolutionary and functional aspects of certain mental states in an effort to understand their nature.

The contributions to this volume address the question what insights conceptual categorisation can give us into the organisation and structure of the mind and thus of mental states. Topics and linguistic phenomena investigated under this view include narratives and story telling, language development, figurative language, questions of linguistic categorisation, linguistic relativity, and more generally the linguistic coding of mental states (such as perceptions and attitudes).

The volume comprises contributions from psychologists and linguists who explore the interaction between language and cognition. This reflects the provenance of the chapters, versions of which were presented at the *International Language and Cognition Conference*, held in September 2004 at Pacific Bay Resort in Coffs Harbour, Australia.

We would like to express our gratitude to the reviewers from the diverse areas represented in these volumes. Without their expertise we could not have put together such a broad-ranging, interdisciplinary compilation. We would also particularly like to thank Vicki Knox and Michael Roberts for their tireless work in the preparation of the manuscripts, and the Language and Cognition Research Centre of the University of New England for its financial support.

Andrea C. Schalley and Drew Khlentzos

List of contributors

Joanne Arciuli
Department of Psychology
Charles Sturt University
Panorama Ave
Bathurst NSW 2795
Australia
jarciuli@csu.edu.au

Brett Baker
Language and Cognition Research Centre
School of Behavioural, Cognitive and Social Sciences
University of New England
Armidale NSW 2351
Australia
brett.baker@une.edu.au

Graham Barrington
Royal Children's Hospital
Flemington Road
Parkville VIC 3052
Australia
gbarring@bigpond.net.au

Herbert L. Colston
Psychology Department
University of Wisconsin-Parkside
Kenosha WI 53141–2000
United States of America
herbert.colston@uwp.edu

Linda Cupples
Department of Linguistics
Speech Hearing and Language Research Centre
Division of Linguistics and Psychology
Macquarie University
Sydney NSW 2109
Australia
linda.cupples@mq.edu.au

Helen Fraser
Language and Cognition Research Centre
School of Behavioural, Cognitive and Social Sciences
University of New England
Armidale NSW 2351
Australia
hfraser@une.edu.au

Anna Gladkova
School of Language Studies
Linguistics Program
The Australian National University
Canberra ACT 0200
Australia
Anna.Gladkova@anu.edu.au

Cliff Goddard
Language and Cognition Research Centre
School of Behavioural, Cognitive and Social Sciences
University of New England
Armidale NSW 2351
Australia
cgoddard@une.edu.au

Drew Khlentzos
Language and Cognition Research Centre
School of Behavioural, Cognitive and Social Sciences
University of New England
Armidale NSW 2351
Australia
dkhlentz@une.edu.au

Renate Pajusalu
Institute of Estonian and General Linguistics
University of Tartu
Ülikooli 18
Tartu 50900
Estonia
renate.pajusalu@ut.ee

Andrea C. Schalley
Language and Cognition Research Centre
School of Behavioural, Cognitive and Social Sciences
University of New England
Armidale NSW 2351
Australia
andrea.schalley@une.edu.au

Ruth Singer
Linguistics department, Radboud University &
Max Planck Institute for Psycholinguistics
Radboud Universiteit Nijmegen
Faculteit der Letteren Taalwetenschap
Postbus 9103
6500 HD Nijmegen
The Netherlands
ruth.singer@gmail.com

Lesley Stirling
School of Languages and Linguistics
University of Melbourne
Parkville VIC 3010
Australia
lesleyfs@unimelb.edu.au

Ilona Tragel
Language Centre
University of Tartu
Ülikooli 18
Tartu 50090
Estonia
Ilona.Tragel@ut.ee

Roger Wales
Faculty of Humanities and Social Sciences
La Trobe University
Bundoora VIC 3083
Australia
r.wales@latrobe.edu.au

Anna Wierzbicka
School of Language Studies
Linguistics Program
The Australian National University
Canberra ACT 0200
Australia
Anna.Wierzbicka@anu.edu.au

Heather Winskel
MARC Auditory Laboratories
University of Western Sydney
Penrith South DC NSW 1797
Australia
h.winskel@uws.edu.au

Zhengdao Ye
School of Language Studies
Linguistics Program
The Australian National University
Canberra ACT 0200
Australia
Zhengdao.Ye@anu.edu.au

Kyung-Joo Yoon
School of Language Studies
Linguistics Program
The Australian National University
Canberra ACT 0200
Australia
kyoon@hufs.ac.kr
Kyung-Joo.Yoon@anu.edu.au

CHAPTER 1

Mental categories in natural languages

Drew Khlentzos and Andrea C. Schalley

Is the way we conceive of the mind an artefact of the culture in which we happen to live? A recurrent question in the study of languages and cultures concerns the extent to which language and culture shape thought. No one doubts that important conceptual categories are derived from our native tongue but how deep is the impression language makes on thought? Is the way we classify the various phenomena we experience language-and-culture relative in some strong sense?

Consider the following thesis: *But for the language we speak and the culture in which we live we would not conceive of the world in just the way we do.* This is presumably true. However thus stated it is also a very weak claim. For it amounts to little more than the truism above – that many of our conceptual categories are derived from our specific linguistic-cultural context. To be sure, the thesis becomes more interesting once we discover that certain classifications such as those of colour are not the universals we might have expected them to be. Yet even then the thesis falls well short in logical strength of the famous Sapir-Whorf hypothesis that the language we speak determines what we perceive. That hypothesis implies that the XYXYs do not see that the ripe tomato is red, the weaker hypothesis only entails that they do not remark upon it.

The question is not whether different cultures conceptually classify the world in different ways (they surely do), it is whether the specific ways in which each culture classifies the world are accessible to those from other cultures, whether their languages are *genuinely* inter-translatable.

A major concern of the authors of this volume is the nature of conceptual classifications of mental states and, in particular, the relation of any such classification to the particular language in which it is framed. Suppose it could be shown that some languages lacked any means for verbally identifying certain mental states that English speakers regarded as fundamental. What should we infer from this?

According to supporters of the Natural Semantic Metalanguage (NSM) program in linguistics we should infer that these English words are "ethnocentric" and that the mental states they denote are thereby unfit to discharge any serious explanatory role in cognitive science. Thus Cliff Goddard contends in his essay "A culture-neutral metalanguage for mental state concepts":

> [M]any key terms in the discourse of mainstream Western psychology, cognitive science and philosophy are language-specific, including ... *fear*, *sadness* and *surprise* ... *belief* and the construct of *mind* itself.

This is a rather dramatic-sounding claim – could there be a culture where no one is ever sad or fearful or surprised, one where no one ever believes anything or, most striking of all, where the idea of mind had gained no traction at all within folk consciousness?

However this is not what is meant by the NSM ethnocentricity thesis. It is not that no one is ever sad or ever believes anything (as eliminative materialists in cognitive science aver), it is just that the English-language concepts of sadness or belief are highly parochial ones that English speakers mistakenly presume to be universal and primitive. Whence, if our goal is to describe basic human psychology rather than Anglocentric accretions to it, we should not invoke culturally-distilled descriptions of mental states such as "belief" and "sadness" or even "mind" as theoretical primitives suited to explain the workings of human cognition or emotion. Belief and sadness are (culturally) derivative concepts, not primitive ones, according to NSM.

Following Goddard's NSM essay and one by Anna Wierzbicka, the linguist who first propounded NSM, the next three chapters in this volume apply the techniques of NSM to the meanings of words for mental states in various languages. Anna Gladkova compares Russian and English propositional attitude verbs, Kyung-Joo Yoon focuses on the meanings of three Korean words *kiekna-* 'memory comes, remember', *kiekha-* 'remember', and *chwuekha-* 'reminisce', Zhengdao Ye discusses the meanings of Chinese 'taste'-related words that describe various mental states.

NSM is a bold and ambitious program in semantics. Its claim to have discovered sixty or so universal human concepts is, if true, of the utmost significance in understanding human categorisation. The crucial NSM thesis that an acceptable semantic theory must effect a conceptual analysis of words can be challenged. In defending the conceptual analysis requirement, Wierzbicka in her contribution "Shape and colour in language and thought" takes her lead from Leibniz who stressed that there can be no understanding anything without conceptual decomposition into parts "which can be understood in themselves". Formal semantic theories are of no use according to Wierzbicka because their technical concepts are not accessible to ordinary speakers, yet "ordinary English" is of no use either since it contains too many hidden ethnocentric assumptions. The solution is to develop an informal metalanguage built from semantic primes common to all languages.

In her study, she presents a case for Leibniz's thesis that language is the mirror of the mind. Where Leibniz merely dreamt of a future wherein, as he put it, "a precise analysis of the signification of words would tell us more than anything else about the operations of the understanding", through NSM his dream has today become a reality, according to Wierzbicka. For NSM's semantic analyses of different languages has resulted in the identification of "a rich set of empirical linguistic universals" that represent "a set of sixty or so universal human concepts – conceptual primes, which correspond to Leibniz's notion of 'the alphabet of human thoughts', and a universal grammar, which corresponds, to some extent, to his notion of a universal 'philosophical grammar'".

Until quite recently Eleanor Rosch's conjecture that the eleven basic colour categories of English might represent universal and innate human categories seemed empirically plausible. But recent ethnological studies of colour classification in various languages has cast doubt upon it. Thus neither the Berinmo people who inhabit dense tropical rain forest in Papua New Guinea nor the nomadic Himba who wander the arid land on the border of Angola and Namibia are sensitive to the English green/blue boundary. Wierzbicka observes from her study of Burarra-speaking Australian Aboriginals in Arnhem land that it can be extremely difficult to even fit some indigenous colour classifications into the English colour framework. Even more striking is her claim that basic metrical and shape predicates such as 'long' and 'round' are not the common linguistic currency of speakers of other languages such as Polish!

We should be careful to distinguish the question of whether people from a given culture have a certain concept from the question of whether the language they speak has a specific term that expresses that concept. Polish speakers clearly can perceptually discriminate round things from non-round things. To the extent that perceptual discrimination requires concepts they have the concept of roundness. Whether the concept of roundness for Polish speakers is primitive or complex is a matter for further investigation. The mere absence of a dedicated term denoting that concept does not decide this issue.

In her contribution "Universal and language-specific aspects of 'propositional attitudes': Russian vs. English", Anna Gladkova argues that English is not the only language to promulgate ethnocentricity under the mantle of cognitive science. Just as for the English word *belief* the Russian word *sčitat* is touted as denoting a primitive mental state where it is nothing of the sort, Gladkova contends. *Sčitat* represents a considered opinion, one arrived at through a process of weighing evidence or reflecting on one's store of information and knowledge. To that extent it has some affinity with the English *belief* and is often rendered as 'believe' in translation.

Gladkova compares the NSM approach to linguistic meaning with that of the Moscow School of Semantics (MSS). Both are committed to the existence of semantic primitives. Both seek to explicate the semantics of natural languages by means of a metalanguage containing such primitives or primes. However where MSS allows that the metalanguage might be a formal one, it is important to NSM that the metalanguage be a natural language or at least be constructed from those natural language expressions identified as semantic primes.

In her "Mental states reflected in cognitive lexemes related to memory: A case in Korean", Kyung-Joo Yoon promotes NSM as a semantic metalanguage that is ideally poised to avoid ethnocentrism by consisting of words denoting universal conceptual primes. Yoon sees ethnocentrism at work in the way English speakers and scientists conceive of memory, leading them to expect every language to have a word denoting memory. Korean doesn't. Yoon uses the resources of NSM to offer neutral semantic explications of the key Korean terms associated with recollection: *kiekna-*, *kiekha-*, and *chwuekha-*.

Finally, in "Taste as a gateway to Chinese cognition", Zhengdao Ye outlines the central role taste plays in the Chinese conceptual scheme arguing that the Western philosophical tradition that shapes Western ways of thinking sees the sense of taste as inferior to vision and hearing. Indeed, Ye offers the intriguing proposal that the mind/body problem that so bedevils Western philosophy has no counterpart in "the peculiarly Chinese 'embodied' way of thinking, knowing and feeling". Ye's chapter comprises a contribution to the NSM program by providing NSM explications of Chinese words associated with taste.

We have been considering a semantic theory that makes interesting predictions about the cognitive structure of competent speakers of a language. We might wonder whether markedly atypical linguistic performance is a reliable indicator of specific cognitive deficits? In the chapter "'Then I'll huff and I'll puff or I'll go on the roff!' thinks the wolf: Spontaneous written narratives by a child with autism", Lesley Stirling and Graham Barrington examine the written and oral re-tellings of familiar fairy tales by a high-functioning seven-year old boy with autism, Lincoln.

Stirling and Barrington focus on the aspects of perspective marking and episodic macrostructure in story-telling. While approximately half of all autistic children never acquire functional language, "higher-functioning" individuals are those of normal intelligence who possess functional language. Story-telling involves the understanding and occupation of a variety of differing perspectives – those of the narrator, the audience and the characters within the story. It is thus ideally suited to test some of the competing theories about the nature of autism.

Stirling and Barrington consider three major theories of autism: (1) mind-blindness, (2) executive control, and (3) weak central coherence. According to the "mind-blindness" account, autistic individuals lack a theory of the minds of others. They therefore have severe difficulties comprehending another person's perspective. Executive control theory conjectures that autistic children are deficient in skills of planning and inhibition of immediate desires subserving long-term goals. These executive control functions are somehow impaired. The central coherence theory posits an inability to identify the local detail that captures the gist of a higher-level meaning as the key cognitive anomaly of the autistic mind.

Stories are hierarchically arranged into episodes. Stirling and Barrington report that apart from being shorter and containing fewer episodes than usual, Lincoln's re-tellings revealed he had a very clear idea of what it was to tell a story and a keen grasp of episodic macrostructure. He represents the characters' mental states using predicates such as *think* and *worry*, even imputing to characters mental states not explicitly ascribed in the original story. Lincoln is clearly not "mind-blind". So does this exercise reveal any cognitive deficits in Lincoln?

Stirling and Barrington identify Lincoln's difficulty with knowledge state management as the most serious one. Lincoln has the mother pig tell the three little pigs of the imminent threat of the wolf. He has the wolf divulge to the little pigs his plan to climb onto the roof. The high-functioning autistic individual's problem is not that of comprehending the very idea of mental states other than one's own but instead appears to be a difficulty with grasping how nested mental states are to be represented and how they interact, Stirling and Barrington aver.

Heather Winskel also examines narratives in an effort to understand the relation between language and cognition in normal language development in her chapter "Interaction between language and cognition in language development". Focusing on temporal vocabulary, Winskel investigates Thai childrens' narratives. Early use of temporal connectives to express temporal relations declines in adult speech with relative clauses and causal connectives supplanting the connectives. Aspectual marking, optional in Thai, is easily accessible to the child and as a result invariably appears in the early language-user's temporal vocabulary.

Winskel's conclusion is that language clearly influences the child's cognitive development during the early phase of acquiring a language in order to express thoughts (thinking-for-speaking). In this phase "it can be seen that early caretaker-child interactions, and the input that the child is exposed to, is critical in the formation of language-specific semantic categories", Winskel maintains.

Herbert L. Colston's contribution "What figurative language development reveals about the mind" is the last chapter in this volume addressing the development of mental states and abilities. Colston empirically studies the naturalistic production of figurative language in children and adults – specifically of hyperbole, which often functions as a means of complaining. His findings suggest that children develop the ability to produce hyperbole much earlier than generally thought so far, and that their production of hyperbole is remarkably similar to the hyperbole production of adults. This poses a challenge to the "late development" view, according to which children do not show adult competency at comprehending or producing figurative language until they are roughly 7 or 8 years old. However, the study presented here provides support for the claim that at least simple figurative language cognition is in place early.

The author provides several alternative possible explanations for why the production of the figurative form of hyperbole appears at or prior to comprehension of other figurative forms, but especially argues that a Theory of Mind – in contrast to claims by the proponents of the late development view – strongly supports that children are fully capable of using figurative language at near adult capacities much earlier than generally thought. He presents arguments that Theory of Mind is indeed a requirement of all language functioning, based on the view of "Language as Sensation/Perception of Others' Minds" (LASPOM): In order to communicate successfully, speakers have to be able to mutually "sense" or "perceive" each other's mind, and this reflexive property *is* in Colston's view Theory of Mind and makes language cognition possible. The fact that very young children communicate – and that they, for instance, communicate with people but do not try to engage inanimate objects in conversation – is a strong indication that they do have knowledge that other people have minds. Therefore, the conclusion is, they have to have Theory of Mind from very early on, and it is not surprising that they also produce hyperbole as an instance of figurative language much earlier than generally thought. Theory of Mind and hence mental capabilities are presented as prerequisites for language development.

This contribution thus highlights and explicitly argues for the relevance of the existence of particular cognitive states for a person to achieve linguistic competence. Cognition is seen as a necessity for language development. This might appear as contradicting those contributions that see language as heavily influencing categorisation and thought; however, we have to distinguish language development as an instance of ontogenesis from the development of a language's lexicon, which corresponds to phylogenetic development.

Leaving the question of narrative and figurative language production, the volume turns to the theoretical question of how children learn to assign words to syntactic or grammatical categories. It is argued that children need to learn this ability to categorise words in order to master the grammatical rules that govern word combinations, which in turn is imperative for any full-fledged language acquisition. Joanne Arciuli and Linda Cupples' contribution "Would you rather 'embert a cudsert' or 'cudsert an embert'? How spelling patterns at the beginning of English disyllables can cue grammatical category" addresses this issue of how speakers categorise words into grammatical categories and thence how their mind processes linguistic structure and meta-linguistic information.

In contrast to the natural hypothesis that the representation and processing of grammatical category information is syntactic, previous research has shown that the classification surfaces at different levels of representation. Arciuli and Cupples give an overview of which cues have been confirmed as facilitating this process of categorisation so far: mainly semantic and phonological ones. They pose the obvious question whether another cue might be found in orthography. Having studied the relevance of word-endings, they embark on the empirical investigation of word-beginnings in English disyllables. The study comprises two stages: a dictionary analysis and an experiment involving native speakers. The dictionary analysis was carried out to confirm that word-beginnings can be associated in a statistically significant way to grammatical categories. Having successfully demonstrated this association, in order to address the motivational question outlined above, the authors then set out to test whether skilled native English readers are sensitive to this correlation. Their experiments – including tasks with non-words – show that speakers are indeed sensitive to this correlation and thus that there appear to be orthographical cues for the assignment of grammatical categories, which in turn might cue lexical stress. The results lend support to multi-layered approaches to language and cognition and show that cues on different levels of language representation exist for the relationship between language and cognitive structure, that is, for the present study, between orthography as a representational system for language and mental categories linked to meta-linguistic information.

The next contribution, Brett Baker's "Ethnobiological classification and the environment in Northern Australia", focuses on the cognitive structures underlying ethnobiological classification systems of two Australian Aboriginal languages, Ngalakgan and Wubuy (both spoken in Arnhem Land in the Northern Territory). These structures – the folk taxonomic systems – are extracted via an analysis of names and lexemes for flora and fauna. Baker highlights two characteristics as typical of Indigenous Australian folk taxonomies: (i) the majority of botanical names refer to species, with genera remaining unnamed, and (ii) most names for biological taxa are "monomial" or monomorphemic. In addition, the linguistic structure of the discussed languages does not allow the creation of compound names for biological taxa.

Both (i) and (ii) are counter to the hitherto widely accepted claims about ethnobiological classifications systems by Brent Berlin. In particular, the importance of species names and unimportance of genera in the presented systems conflicts with Berlin's position that generics are a universal category (and correspond to Rosch's basic level categories), and that they form the starting points of taxonomic classifications. Baker argues that this non-conformance with Berlin's system is rooted in the unique structure of the Australian flora, where species belong to large, internally diversified genera, i.e. because the biological discontinuities are perceived at the level of species rather than – as Berlin's universals predict – at the level of genera.

This indicates that we are dealing with an example where human perception of the biological environment heavily impacts on cognitive structuring – on the folk taxonomy or more broadly folk ontology – and that these structures show up in linguistic coding in a way which makes the coding structurally different from the coding of other classificatory systems that arose in other environments – due to the differences in mental categorisation based on perceptual experience. It might be worth noting that the Australian environment has also affected the taxonomy of Eucalypts as coded by Australian English, as Baker elaborates, which is a further argument in favour of his claims. Last but not least, another feature of the Aboriginal classification systems should not remain unmentioned: The superordinate terms that do exist are almost always related to function or use rather than (biological) taxonomic classification, and therefore functional classificatory terms intermingle with taxonomic terms.

Perception and common function also play a central role in Ruth Singer's contribution "Events masquerading as entities: Pseudorelative perception verb complements in Mawng (Australian) and Romance languages". Singer in particular discusses one verb complement construction of perception verbs – the pseudorelative – and uncovers an unexpected convergence in the expression of perception in the Australian Aboriginal language Mawng and some Romance languages. This is rather unusual given that Mawng and the Romance languages are not related in any way – why, then, does such an unusual structure as the pseudorelative occur in unrelated languages?

The answer, she asserts, can be found in the common function of the construction in discourse – which, she argues, has led to a convergence in form and function in the different languages. More specifically, the pseudorelative's function is to introduce a new referent into the discourse while at the same time making a predication of it, which in principle violates Lambrecht's "Principle of the separation of reference and relation". This principle posits that there is a cognitive constraint on introducing new referents and simultaneously making new predications of them. Universal cognitive tendencies or constraints and their deliberate circumvention can thus lead to the development of rather unusual grammatical structures in unrelated languages. In addition, the mere fact that this rare construction occurs in unrelated languages is itself an indication of how cognitive structure impacts on linguistic coding and language.

In their essay "Word and construction as units of categorization: The case of change predicates in Estonian", Renate Pajusalu and Ilona Tragel describe the relation between some common Estonian words describing change and the conceptual categories they represent. The four words on which they focus, *jääma*, *saama*, *minema* and *tulema*, are all highly polysemous. Choice of each verb depends upon the type of change the speaker has in mind. Moreover, a specific meaning of each predicate is tightly linked to the particular construction in which it occurs, and whilst it is possible to give "change-of-state" meanings for all four verbs, these are not the primary meanings for them, Pajusalu and Tragel observe. The change-of-state meanings for *jääma, saama, minema* and *tulema* are, respectively, 'remain', 'get', 'go', and 'come'.

Pajusalu and Tragel note the complexity of the principles governing selection of the appropriate change verb – which of the four verbs to use depends on whether the change in question is conceived of as a negative or positive one quantitatively as well as whether it is positive or negative from the evaluative perspective of the one experiencing the change (where this is relevant). If the change is a positive one, a further distinction is drawn between active and passive change.

In "Categories and concepts in phonology: Theory and practice", Helen Fraser argues against what she regards as a naïve realism that equates the meaning of a word with the thing to which it refers. As against naïve realism, words refer not to things but concepts, she contends. This being so, cognitive science requires a theory of concepts and the theory she favours is a phenomenological one that brackets the external reality behind concepts (what the concepts are concepts of) and studies concepts directly.

Concepts are abstract entities as are words and it is very easy to confuse the two especially when the object of study is words. Fraser sees this bimodal confusion of words with concepts and concepts with objects in the world vitiating phonology both in theory and also in practice. Literacy merely requires the appreciation that letters represent sounds. However naïve realism (the "Natural Attitude") impels ordinary speakers to think that the sounds in question are physical acoustic phenomena. In fact they represent abstractions from physical sounds – that is concepts of sounds – Fraser contends.

Let us conclude this introduction as we began – with the question of conceptual relativity. Roger Wales in his essay "You can run, but: Another look at linguistic relativity" looks at the psychological processing involved in linguistic comprehension by comparing descriptions of verbs of motion made by English and Spanish speakers. He argues that linguistic relativity is primarily concerned with conceptual processes rather than the products of those processes in mental representations together with the words expressing them that linguists have studied. To study processing in using verbs of motion requires taking into account a speaker's perception, memory and task construal, according to Wales.

Path-dominant verbs of motion such as *enter* and *ascend* are manner-independent. Such verbs predominate in Spanish and other Romance languages. English contains many motion verbs where manner is a determinant of application together with path which is a separate determinant – verbs such as *ran to*. By asking people to act out verbs of motion, recording their movements with point-light displays, participating observers were asked to make forced choice decisions as to the verb best describing the acted movement.

The target set of English verbs included *hop, walk, stroll, shuffle, shamble, run, jog* and *sprint*. 'Walk' and 'run' sets of verbs are distinguished by two factors: relative speed of movement and whether the agent's feet are typically on the ground at the same time or not. Participants' judgments clustered around two sets – the 'walk' verbs and the 'run' verbs in the case of English-speaking participants.

Wales' finding is that this result is robust across the two languages of English and Spanish in spite of the inclusion of path information and suppression of manner information in the Spanish verbs of motion. He infers that English and Spanish perceivers of action see the relevant actions in precisely the same way. Although this is exactly the result we would expect from a biological perspective it does not sit well with the more extreme versions of linguistic relativity promulgated by Sapir and Whorf.

CHAPTER 2

A culture-neutral metalanguage for mental state concepts

Cliff Goddard

In contemporary cognitive science, mental state concepts from diverse cultures are typically described via English-specific words for emotions, cognitive processes, and the like. This is terminological ethnocentrism and it produces inaccurate representations of indigenous meanings. The problem can be overcome by employing a metalanguage of conceptual analysis which is based on simple meanings such as KNOW, THINK, WANT and FEEL. Cross-linguistic semantic research suggests that these and other semantic primes are shared across all languages and cultures (Goddard & Wierzbicka 2002; cf. Wierzbicka 1999; Harkins & Wierzbicka 2001). After summarising this research, the chapter shows how complex mental state concepts from English, Malay, Swedish, and Korean can be revealingly analysed into terms which are simple, clear and transposable across languages.

1 Introduction

Taking a global perspective, there is tremendous variation in the lexicon of mental states. Most words in the English lexicon of cognition, including apparently "basic" ones, are language and culture-specific (Harkins & Wierzbicka 2001; Palmer, Goddard & Lee 2003; Wierzbicka 1999). This applies, *inter alia*, to words for emotional and attitudinal states (such as *angry*, *happy*, *surprised*, *love*, *anxiety*, *grief*, and so on), for epistemic states and cognitive processes (such as *believe*, *doubt*, *remember*), and for psychological constructs (such as *mind*, *psyche*, *memory*, and so on). As amply demonstrated in many studies in cross-linguistic semantics and linguistic anthropology, such words rarely have exact meaning equivalents in other languages. Many social scientists, unfortunately, seem to regard the "problem of translation" simply as a methodological hindrance – as something to be "gotten around" so that they can move on to implementing familiar research techniques. Indigenous concepts are typically tagged with English glosses, and the crude technique of back-translation (see Section 6) is taken as a guarantee of semantic equivalence. In effect, this amounts to treating the English lexicon of emotion and cognition as if it were a neutral descriptive metalanguage for the mental states of people in other languages and cultures. There are profound theoretical and methodological costs attached to this widespread practice.

First, it accords a kind of epistemological superiority to the language of the investigators, as if it can be taken for granted that the culture-specific categories of the English language represent objective psychological realities, whereas those of other languages do not. Second, explicating the concepts of one language and culture in terms of the alien concepts of another language and culture is to give way to an insidious terminological ethnocentrism. It inevitably leads to a distorted and inaccurate picture, due to the epistemological "spin" imparted by the culture-specific categories. Over half a century ago Edward Sapir warned: "The philosopher needs to understand language if only to protect himself against his own language habits" (Sapir 1949: 165). Sapir's warning is just as relevant for today's psychologists and cognitive scientists.

Third, a description framed in terms which are inaccessible and unrecognisable to the people whose mental lives are being described can never open up an "insider perspective", in the anthropological sense. On the contrary, it prevents us from seeing emotional and mental life as the people concerned see it. Yet as Fehr and Russell (1984: 483) have put it: "Part of the psychologist's job in such cases is to understand emotion concepts as people use them in everyday life". Without access to an insider perspective, it will be difficult, if not impossible, to appreciate how folk psychology helps to shape people's experience and to inform their interpersonal interactions (cf. Bruner 1990). Finally, framing representations of mental concepts in foreign terms closes off the description to the people concerned, which in turn closes off important sources of verification and evidence.

But how can mental states be described at all, if not in terms of some lexicon of cognition, drawn from some particular language? Fortunately, empirical evidence from cross-linguistic semantics indicates that, despite the tremendous variation, a very small number of cognitive meanings are shared across languages, namely (to list them using English exponents) KNOW, THINK, WANT and FEEL, and furthermore, that these meanings share a set of grammatical potentials. KNOW, THINK, WANT and FEEL are among the 63 universal semantic primes which have been identified over the past twenty years of cross-linguistic research by Anna Wierzbicka and colleagues in the Natural Semantic Metalanguage framework (Goddard & Wierzbicka 1994, 2002; Wierzbicka 1996). In Section 2, I will provide an overview of NSM research and findings, then look in more detail at the four cognitive semantic primes just mentioned, with a view to delineating the lexicogrammatical profile of each. In Sections 3 to 5, I will show how, using the metalanguage of semantic primes, complex and culture-specific meanings from any language can be "unpacked" into terms which are readily transposable across languages. We will look at contrastive examples of emotion terms, epistemic verbs and ethnopsychological constructs in several languages. It will emerge that many key terms in the discourse of mainstream Western psychology, cognitive science and philosophy are language-specific, including so-called "basic emotion" concepts such as *fear*, *sadness* and *surprise*, epistemic verbs and categories such as *believe* and *belief*, and the construct of *mind* itself. Section 6 gives concluding remarks.

2. Semantic primes for mental states

The NSM metalanguage is described in considerable detail in various publications, especially in Goddard and Wierzbicka (2002), which also contains six studies demonstrating that the posited semantic primes and their basic syntactic frames exist in a set of typologically and genetically diverse languages. Detailed studies of a range of other individual languages have also been carried out over the past 15 or so years, so that there is now a substantial body of cross-linguistic work on the realisations of semantic primes, and on associated matters of semantic typology generally.[1] Figure 1 displays some of the locations of languages which have been studied from this point of view.

Figure 1. Sample of languages other than English studied in the NSM framework

---

1. More references are listed at the NSM Homepage: http://www.une.edu.au/lcl/nsm/index.php.

The full NSM lexicon of universal semantic primes is set out in summary form in the Appendix, using English exponents. For the purposes of this chapter, we will concentrate on the four semantic primes which can be seen as preeminently "cognitive" in character – namely, KNOW, THINK, WANT and FEEL (we will not consider SEE and HEAR, though these too are, in a sense, mental and/or experiential in character). Any metalanguage, of course, comprises not only a vocabulary but also a grammar, and the NSM metalanguage is no exception. The grammar of the NSM metalanguage includes combinatorics (how primes can combine with one another), valency options (different syntactic frames which are available for particular primes), and complementation (how some primes can combine with whole sentences). I will shortly illustrate these notions by reviewing the lexicogrammatical profiles of semantic primes KNOW, THINK, WANT and FEEL. Before that, however, consider Table 1. It shows lexical exponents of these primes in a range of languages from five language families: Indo-European (Spanish, Polish), Tai-Kadai (Lao), Austronesian (Malay, Mbula), Niger-Congo (Ewe), Sinitic (Mandarin Chinese). In most of these languages, most of the primes are encoded by a monomorphemic item. In several languages, however, some of the exponents are formally complex.

Table 1. Exponents of cognitive primes in seven languages*

	Malay	Spanish	Lao	Ewe	Chinese	Mbula	Polish
KNOW	tahu	saber	huu4	nyá	zhīdao	-ute	wiedzić
THINK	fikir	pensar	khùt1	súsú	xiăng	-kam=ŋgar	myśleć
WANT	mahu	querer	jaak5	dí	yào	lele-=be/=pa	chcieć
FEEL	rasa	sentir	huu4.sùk2	se le lāme	gănjué	-yamaana	czuć

* Sources for the data in Table 1 are as follows: Goddard (2002), Travis (2002), Enfield (2002), Ameka (1994), Chappell (2002), Bugenhagen (2002), Wierzbicka (2002).

They include the Lao and Ewe exponents of FEEL *huu4.sùk2* and *se le lāme*, respectively; and the Mbula exponent of THINK *-kam=ŋgar*. Though these words are morphologically complex, the claim is that their meanings are unitary and cannot be composed from the (apparent) meanings of the constituent items. For example, the Lao exponent of FEEL *huu4.sùk2* contains the form *huu4*, which as an independent word is the exponent of KNOW; but as Enfield (2002: 176) says: "the expression is not semantically analysable into 'know' plus something else". In the Lao case, the putative "extra" morpheme *sùk2* does not occur elsewhere. The situation is somewhat different in Ewe, because each element of the composite expression *se le lāme*, is meaningful if taken separately. By itself, *se* means 'hear' and *le lāme* is a prepositional phrase meaning literally 'in (the) body'. Nonetheless, the expression as a whole cannot be interpreted as 'hear in the body': It means simply FEEL (nor is the expression confined exclusively to bodily feelings) (Ameka 1994). Examples of this kind, i.e. expressions which are formally analysable but semantically unitary, crop up sporadically across languages.

The sample of words in Table 1 can be used to illustrate another point, namely that, like other common words, exponents of semantic primes are often polysemous, and that they may be polysemous in different ways in different languages. For example, the exponent of FEEL in Malay, namely *rasa*, can also mean 'taste'; the exponent of WANT in Spanish, namely *querer*, can also mean 'like, love'; the exponent of THINK in Chinese, namely *xiǎng*, can also mean something like 'intend'. After some 15 years of cross-linguistic research into the realisations of primes across languages, it is known that polysemic patterns like these are quite frequent.

I will now give a thumbnail lexicogrammatical sketch of each of the cognitive primes, touching also on questions concerning the cross-linguistic identification of exponents.

Exponents of semantic prime KNOW are generally easy to identify across languages. Sometimes there are portmanteaus with negation, e.g. Yankunytjatjara *ninti* 'know', *ngurpa* 'don't know'. It is not uncommon for languages to have two exponents of KNOW, one for sentential complements and one for noun-phrase complements, as with German *wissen* and *kennen*, and Polish *wiedzić* and *znać*. An unresolved issue in NSM semantics concerns "knowing a person".[2] Leaving this aside, the basic syntactic frames for KNOW can be stated in a summary fashion as follows. The first two frames have KNOW with a substantive complement alone, as in (1), or with this complement plus an additional "topic" valency option (realised in English by a prepositional phrase introduced with *about*), as in (2). In a third frame, KNOW can take a sentential complement (a so-called *that*-complement), as in (3). Finally, there are a set of "ignorative" frames focusing on the category of knowledge, including those illustrated in (4a)–(4c). In these contexts, *who, what*

---

2. Wierzbicka (2002: 92–96) argues that the two Polish verbs are syntactically conditioned allolexes, i.e. variants, notwithstanding the fact that *wiedzić* tends to be associated with "propositional knowledge" and *znać* with "personal knowledge". It is true that from an intuitive point of view knowing a person is something quite different from knowing a fact, but it is also true that the verb *znać* can be used with noun-phrase complements other than those designating persons; for example, *Ja znam okoliczności* 'I know the circumstances' or *Ja znam fakty* 'I know the facts'. Such sentences imply that *znać* at least involves or includes *wiedzić* KNOW, and hence that it cannot be semantically primitive. After considering and rejecting a number of possible paraphrases for *znać* in terms of *wiedzić* KNOW and other elements, Wierzbicka concludes that none are satisfactory, and that *znać* and *wiedzić* are combinatorial allolexes. On this account, the difference between 'knowing someone' and 'knowing something' is inherent in the two different combinations, i.e. whether the complement is 'someone' or 'something', and cannot be "factored out" via paraphrasing one or other uses of 'know'.

and *where* can be regarded as variants of the primes SOMEONE/PERSON, SOMETHING/THING, and WHERE/PLACE, respectively. Though presented here in English, all these frames are claimed to represent cross-linguistically universal construction types, realisable in all languages.

(1) someone knows something

(2) someone knows something about someone/something

(3) someone knows that [——]_s

(4) a. someone knows who did it
    b. someone knows what happened
    c. someone knows where it happened

Exponents of semantic prime THINK commonly have polysemic meanings such as 'worry', 'long for', 'count' and 'intend' (cf. Goddard 2003a). These recurrent polysemies can complicate the identification of exponents of THINK somewhat, but not nearly as much as the fact that the English verb *think* has several language-specific peculiarities in its usage and polysemic extensions (cf. Goddard & Karlsson 2004; Wierzbicka 1998). The minimal frame for THINK is simply 'someone thinks about Y', i.e. with a "topic" argument but without any accompanying substantive complement, as in (5). A substantive complement can be added however, as in (6). In a third frame, THINK can take a "quasi-quotational" complement introduced by 'like this', i.e. 'someone thinks like this: - -', as in (7). Finally, a *that*-complement is also possible, but (unlike as with KNOW) only if the verb is accompanied by a temporal expression, such as 'at this time' or 'now', tying it to a particular time. English, of course, permits the use of *think* in a general "opinion" sense (as in *I think that oranges are the best fruit*), but this is a peculiarity of English, not shared by many other languages of the world. In cross-linguistic perspective it seems that a *that*-complement of THINK has to represent a real "occurrent" thought, not a generalised opinion.

(5) someone thinks about something/someone

(6) someone thinks something (good/bad) about something/someone

(7) someone thinks like this: " – – "

(8) at this time (or: now), someone thinks that [——]_s

Exponents of semantic prime WANT often have polysemic extensions to meanings such as 'like' and 'love' (as mentioned earlier, in relation to Spanish). Another well attested extension is to 'seek', as in Ewe and Ulwa (Ameka 1994; Hale 1994). The simplest frame has a substantive complement, as in (9). The most interesting and distinctive property of WANT is the difference between "equi" complements, as in (10), and "non-equi" complements, such as those in (11a) and (11b). Many languages employ different morphosyntax in the two types of clausal complements (cf. Travis 2003) and some, such as Japanese and Samoan, employ different lexical verbs (allolexes) in these contexts (Harkins 1995).

(9) someone wants something

(10) someone wants to do (know, say, ...) something

(11) a. someone wants someone else to do (know, say, ...) something
     b. someone wants something to happen

Exponents of semantic prime FEEL commonly have polysemic extensions to meanings such as 'taste' and 'smell', and to 'hold an opinion', as in Malay, French, and Mandarin (Chappell 2002; Goddard 2002; Peeters 1994). Sometimes the exponents of FEEL and HEAR are identical in form, or else the exponent of FEEL is formally related to 'hear' in some other way. The example of Ewe *se le lāme* [hear in. body] has already been mentioned. Another interesting example is *dhäkay-ŋänha* FEEL [taste-hear], from the Gumatj dialect of Yolngu Matha (Australia) (Michael Cooke p.c.). Sometimes the exponent of FEEL is identical to a body-part word, typically the word for 'liver', 'heart', or 'stomach', or less commonly a more general term for 'insides'. Three basic frames are posited for FEEL, as shown in (12)–(14).

(12) someone feels like this

(13) someone feels something good/bad

(14) someone feels something good/bad towards someone else

FEEL is the semantic foundation for both emotion words (*sad*, *angry*, *excited*, etc.) and sensation words (*hungry*, *thirsty*, *hot*, *cold*, etc.). The meanings of emotion words also involve cognitive primes such as THINK and WANT, while the meanings of sensation words involve these and additionally the prime BODY.

This concludes our outline of the four cognitive semantic primes: KNOW, THINK, WANT and FEEL. A common reaction of those encountering the NSM system for the first time is surprise at the small size of the posited metalanguage and scepticism that such a restricted set of terms would be sufficient to explicate the numerous mental state terms in the world's many languages, and to capture the subtle differences between them. In the remainder of the chapter I want to go some way towards answering these doubts, while at the same time showing that many English terms which are regarded as unproblematical in the conventional discourse of cognitive science are in fact semantically complex and deeply culture-specific.

3 Explicating emotion terms: "Surprise" in English and Malay

Following Paul Ekman and colleagues (cf. Ekman 1992; Ekman & Davidson 1994; among other works), many psychologists believe in the existence of a small set of biologically in-built human emotions, such as *happiness, sadness, fear, anger* and *surprise*. The claim is often made that these basic emotions are named in all languages, and that each is associated with a biologically pre-programmed facial expression. Against these claims, there is a large body of contrary evidence from linguistic anthropology, psychological anthropology and cultural psychology, which demonstrates the cultural variability of emotional experience (cf. Briggs 1970; Harré 1986; Holland & Quinn 1987; Kitayama & Markus 1994; Levy 1973; Lutz 1988; Rosaldo 1980; Schwartz, White & Lutz 1992; Shore 1996; Shweder 1991, 1993, 2003; White & Kirkpatrick 1985). A substantial literature in cross-linguistic semantics demonstrates that even supposedly basic emotions have no manifestations in certain languages (for example, there is no counterpart to *sadness* in Tahitian, no counterpart to *disgust* in Polish); and that apparent translation equivalents in particular languages are in fact substantially different (for example, that German *Angst* is substantially different to English *fear*, that French *bonheur* is substantially different from English *happiness*), cf. Wierzbicka (1999), Harkins and Wierzbicka (2001), Enfield and Wierzbicka (2002). Using the NSM metalanguage, it is possible to pin down the precise similarities and differences between the emotion terms of different languages, as I will now attempt to show by way of comparing "surprise" terms in English and Malay (Bahasa Melayu, the national language of Malaysia), cf. Goddard (1997). It will not be possible to provide full justification for the content of each and every explication, but this is not necessary for the purpose at hand.

Consider the following set of explications for the English terms: *surprised, amazed* and *shocked*. They follow a format which has proved itself valuable in many studies. Essentially this depends on linking a feeling with a certain characteristic "cognitive scenario". For example, *surprise* is explicated in [A] as a feeling that can be linked with a thought like "something happened now, I didn't think that this would happen". A "stronger" kind of surprise, namely *amazement*, is explicated in [B]. It can be linked with a characteristic thought like: "something happened now, I didn't think that something like this could happen".

[A] X was surprised
  X felt something at that time
  like people can feel when they think like this:
    "something happened now
    I didn't think that this would happen"

[B]   *X was amazed*
X felt something at that time
like people can feel when they think like this:
   "something happened now
   I didn't think that something like this could happen"

Coming now to *shocked*, it is a reaction to coming face to face with the realisation that something very bad has happened, something which one would have thought could not happen. It induces a sense of confusion or mental paralysis: 'I can't think now'. Furthermore, the feeling is unpleasant; i.e. the experiencer does not simply 'feel something', but 'feels something bad'. (Note that *to be shocked*, which is the expression explicated in [C], is not identical to *to get a shock* or *to have a shock*. Though related, these expressions have somewhat different meanings and require somewhat different explications.)

[C]   *X was shocked*
X felt something bad at that time
like people can feel when they think like this:
   "I now know that something very bad happened
   I didn't think that something like this could happen
   I can't think now"

The Malay language has two words – *terkjut* and *terperanjat* – which are glossed as 'surprised' in Malaysian bilingual dictionaries, such as the *Kamus Lengkap* 'Comprehensive Dictionary'. Both are also glossed as 'startled' and as 'shocked'. On closer examination (Goddard 1997), it can be seen that neither exactly matches any word in English.[3] *Terkejut* is a reaction to a sudden stimulus – a noise, being touched, seeing something unexpected, or hearing something unexpected. The experience is momentarily disruptive, and is thought to be mildly harmful. These points are illustrated by the textual examples below.

(15)   *Tiba-tiba Zarof <u>terkejut</u> dari lamunannya bila bahunya ditepuk dan orang itu terus berdiri di sisinya.*
   'Suddenly Zarof was <u>startled</u> from his reveries when a hand landed on his shoulder. Someone was standing beside him.'

---

3.   The difficulty of finding a suitable Malay match for English *surprise* has been noted even by psychologists working in the basic emotions paradigm, such as Boucher (1983) and Heider (1991). Boucher (1983: 409) chose another word *hairan* (Goddard 1997: 169–171), but explains: "it connotes more of the 'astonishment' meaning of surprise than the English term does". Heider (1991: 56–57) opted for *terkejut*, while recognising that it (and *terperanjat*, which he regards as synonymous) has a consistently 'negative tone', compared with English *surprise*.

(16) *Dia terdengar Muhamad Jusuh berkata, "Habis pokok getah Lebai Dahaman." "Kenapa?" tanya Siti Munah seperti <u>terkejut</u>.*
'He heard Muhamad Jusuh say, "Something got at Lebai Dahaman's rubber trees." "What?" asked Siti Munah <u>in surprise</u> (lit. as if *terkejut*).'

Explication [D] presents *terkejut* as the reaction one has to an unsettling thought: "Something happened now, I don't know what". The momentarily disruptive effect is depicted both as cognitive ('for a short time X couldn't think') and physical ('for a short time X couldn't move'). The final component acknowledges the professed "folk belief" that the *terkejut* experience is not good for a person. There is no reference to X 'feeling something', because one cannot speak, in Malay, of 'feeling' *terkejut*, i.e. the expression **rasa terkejut* is anomalous.[4]

[D] X *terkejut*
    X thought like this at that time:
        "something happened now
         I don't know what"
    because of this, something happened to X
    because it happened, for a short time X couldn't think, for a short time X couldn't move
    when this happens to someone, it is not good for this someone

Terperanjat is a stronger reaction to something totally unexpected. It is much more unpleasant than *terkejut*. Malay consultants say that it is a bit like 'getting a scare' or 'getting a fright'. Translation equivalents include 'stunned' and 'taken aback', as well as 'startled' and 'surprised'. In some cases, a physical description is provided, emphasising the debilitating effect. The stimulus for *terperanjat* is usually (though not necessarily) a communicative act with some content, for example, bad news, but the information doesn't have to be bad. It could just be very unexpected. For example, one could *terperanjat* on hearing that one has been promoted or that one has won the lottery, or in a situation like (17).

(17) *Tiket-tiket habis dijual. Ketika Pak Su melangkah masuk ke dewan dia sendiri agak <u>terperanjat</u> dan kurang percaya dengan sambutan itu.*
'The show was sold out. When Pak Su entered the hall, he <u>was taken aback</u> and could not believe the reception.'

Terperanjat is thought to be potentially harmful. A person who *terperanjat* will often put a hand to his or her heart. It is believed that children should not be *buat*

---

4. The interpretation of *terkejut* as something that 'happens to' someone is consistent with the prefix *ter-*, which is found in the verb *terjadi* 'happen' itself, and in many verbs depicting involuntary or accidental 'happenings', cf. Goddard (2003b).

terperanjat 'made to *terperanjat*' because their *semangat* 'spirit' is not strong enough to withstand it. It is even possible to speak of a person literally dying of *terperanjat* (e.g. *Dia mati terperanjat sebab anaknya masuk penjara* 'He died of shock because his son went to prison'). Naturally then, people are supposed to be mindful of the possibility of making others *terperanjat*, to avoid it if possible, or otherwise to soften the impact with some kind of forewarning.

These examples are consistent with explication [E]. Once again the event is depicted as something that happens to a person in response to a prototypical thought, in this case: "I now know that something happened, I didn't think that something like this could happen". In response to this thought, the experiencer is mentally thrown off balance for some time. Notice that the vague time-period attributed to this disruptive effect ('for some time') contrasts with the short-term disruption of *terkejut* ('for a short time'). As with *terkejut*, there is no reference in the explication to the subject 'feeling something', in accord with the fact that in Malay the phrase **rasa terperanjat* (lit. feel *terperanjat)* is anomalous.

[E] X *terperanjat*
     X thought like this at that time:
        "I now know that something happened
         I didn't think that something like this could happen"
     because of this something happened to X
     because it happened, for some time X could not think
     when this happens to someone, something bad happens inside this someone

It may have occurred to the reader that *terkejut* and *terperanjat* are closer to English *to be startled* and *to get a shock* than to *surprised*. But if this is so, there is no equivalent to *surprised* as such in Malay. Similar demonstrations could be adduced for many other languages and for many other areas of the emotion lexicon (Wierzbicka 1999). The truth is that from a semantic point of view, the notion that there are any universal "basic emotions" is an illusion – let alone the notion that such putative universals just happen to correspond to words of the English language, while being inexplicably missing from other languages. Emotion concepts are semantically complex and culture-specific. They represent local interpretations of how people can feel in response to particular cognitive and social scenarios. This does not mean, however, that these different local ways of thinking about emotions are incommensurable – far from it. The innumerable culture-specific ways of thinking about emotions, embodied in the emotion vocabularies of the world's languages, are constructed from and can be explicated in terms of a small set of shared conceptual universals (semantic primes), including KNOW, THINK, WANT and FEEL.

4 Explicating epistemic verbs: English vs. Swedish

The term "epistemic verb" refers to verbs such as English *believe, doubt, assume, suppose*, and so on. No doubt the most important member of the English set is *believe* (with its related noun *belief*). Especially in philosophy, its importance can hardly be overestimated, given the pervasive discourses about "belief states", the distinction between *knowledge* and *belief*, and so on. What often goes unrecognised is that *believe* is a highly English-specific word, which lacks precise equivalents even in other European languages. I will demonstrate this by comparing English with Swedish (cf. Goddard & Karlsson 2004); for a detailed study of Russian, see Gladkova (this volume).

English *believe* is a polysemous word and it occurs in several frames, e.g. *to believe someone, to believe in someone*, which are not considered here. We will confine ourselves to *to believe that ...*, as in the examples in (18). The analysis presented here is drawn from Wierzbicka (2006: Chapter 5). Roughly speaking, *to believe that* conveys a considered conviction or commitment. It also conveys a certain gravitas, as shown by the fact that it can collocate with adverbs like *strongly* (e.g. *I strongly believe that ...*). It corresponds with the noun *belief*.[5]

(18) a. *I believe that they shouldn't have the vote, erm expats I mean.*
 b. *I believe that ultimately we're going to have to get ourselves into a position where we ...*
 c. *I believe that that is the key factor to being successful in this particular HEO role.*

According to Wierzbicka (2006: 218), the relevant sense of *believe* can be explicated as in [F]. The first component expresses something like a considered thought, using a *that*-complement of semantic prime THINK. Then follows acknowledgement or awareness of the possible existence of another point of view ('I know that someone else can think not like this'). Subsequent components express the speaker's apparent confidence that he or she can provide some kind of justification for thinking this way (for example, evidence that the proposition is true, that it has been vouched for by a reliable source, etc.), and finally, the speaker's apparent confidence that he or she can explain or defend the value of thinking like this. The final component is intended to capture the intuition that one's beliefs are "valued".

---

5. There is also another distinct use of *believe* in the "parenthetical" formula *I believe*, which has a "lighter" meaning. This usage cannot combine with *strongly* or other similar adverbs, nor can it be matched with any talk of *beliefs*. For example, I could say, using the parenthetical formula *I believe*, something like: *Oh, I believe the Library has a copy*; but one would hardly expect me to add any adverbs such as *strongly* to such a statement, nor could I refer to *my belief* that the Library has a copy.

[F]   *I believe that – –*
   when I think about it, I think that – –
   I know that someone else can think not like this
   I can say why I think like this
   I can say why it is good if someone thinks like this

The epistemic verbs of Swedish present a quite different picture. As well as the semantic prime THINK *tänka*, the language has two common epistemic verbs, *tro* and *tycka*, which dictionaries and native speakers tend to gloss as 'believe' and as 'think (that), be of the opinion', respectively. Viberg (1980) and Fortescue (2001) point out that *tro* is used "in relation to verifiable states of affairs", while *tycka* is used "to express judgements based on private experiences or subjective evaluation". They are illustrated in (19)–(21) below. The contrast shown in (21a) and (21b) is particularly revealing: With *tro*, the speaker backs up his or her assessment with a known fact, whereas with *tycka*, the backup relies on a sensory experience.

(19)   *Jag tror att det blir soligt i morgon.*
   'I think it's going to be sunny tomorrow.'

(20)   *Jag tycker att hon är söt/trevlig.*
   'I think she's pretty/nice.'

(21)   a.   *Jag tror att potatisen är färdig nu. Den har kokat i tjugo minuter.*
      'I think the potatoes are done now. They've been cooking for twenty minutes.'
   b.   *Jag tycker att potatisen är färdig nu. Den känns mjuk.*
      'I think the potatoes are done now. They feel soft.'

Like English *believe*, *tro* seems to allow that others might not share the speaker's view, but it does not imply the same degree of personal conviction as *to believe that*. Statements with *jag tror* can in most cases be challenged by interlocutors without any resultant bad feelings on either part.

(22)   a.   *Jag tror att det blir soligt i morgon.*
      'I think it's going to be sunny tomorrow.'
   b.   *Nej, på radion sade de att det skulle regna.*
      'No, on the radio they said it's going to rain.'

Goddard and Karlsson (2004) have proposed the explication in [G], in a first-person frame. As one can see, as well as voicing the speaker's view ('I now think like this: – –'), it contains an "epistemic disclaimer" ('I don't say I know it'), an evidential component referring to an item of the speaker's knowledge ('I think like this because I know something'), and allowance for a contrary point of view ('I know that someone else can think not like this').

[G] *Jag tror att – –* [Swedish]
I now think like this: – –
I don't say I know it
I think like this because I know something
I know that someone else can think not like this

The same authors argue that *tycka* can be assigned the explication in [H]. Comparing the two explications, it can be seen that the critical difference resides in the nature of the evidential component. With *tro* this is based on something the speaker KNOWS, while with *tycka* it is based on something the speaker FEELS. The proposal that *tycka* is grounded in the speaker's feeling not only enables us to capture the intuition that this verb is more "personal" than *tro*, it is also compatible with its broad range of use. Just like semantic prime FEEL, *tycka* can be used equally about emotional, aesthetic and sensory matters.

[H] *Jag tycker att – –*
I now think like this: – –
I don't say I know it
I think like this because I feel something
I know that someone else can think not like this

This brief exploration shows again that the apparently basic terminology of one's home language (words like *believe* in English, like *tro* and *tycka* in Swedish) are frequently "false friends" when it comes to trying to understand the conceptual viewpoint of people from another language and culture. From the point of view of the native speaker (especially one who is monolingual), such words seem so simple and transparent that they are easily mistaken for simple and universal categories of experience.

5   Explicating ethnopsychological constructs: English, Malay and Korean

Most languages – perhaps all – have some kind of nominal expressions designating non-physical parts of a person, akin to English *mind, heart, soul,* and *spirit*. This seems natural enough, given that the semantic prime BODY provides a kind of conceptual reference point or counterpoint. That is, given that a person has a body, but that there is evidently more to a person than a body alone, the question naturally arises: what else is there? There is a significant NSM literature on the cross-linguistic semantics of ethnopsychological constructs. Perhaps the single most discussed example is Russian *duša* (roughly) 'soul' (cf. Wierzbicka 1992, 2005), but other work has examined English *heart*, Malay *hati* (Goddard 2001), Japanese *kokoro* (Hasada 2000: 115–116), and Korean *maum* and *kasum* (Yoon 2003, 2004). There is also a literature on such concepts in the fields of cultural studies (e.g. Pesmen 2000) and cognitive linguistics.

It is perfectly clear from this literature that *mind* is an English-specific construct, without precise equivalents even in European languages such as German and Russian. To date, however, this fact has had a negligible impact on academic discourse, and *mind* continues to be a key word in the discourses of philosophy, psychology, and cognitive science, as one can see from the countless journals and books with titles such as *Mind, Language and Mind, Philosophy of Mind, How the Mind Works, Mind and Brain, Psychology: Mind, Brain and Culture*, and so on. From a cross-linguistic point of view, one unusual thing about English *mind* is its "rationalistic" character, i.e. it is focused on thinking and knowing, to the exclusion of feeling. Feelings, especially feelings towards other people, are allocated to another ethnopsychological location, namely, the *heart*. (Compare the implication of the expressions *a good mind* and *a good heart*.) The explication in [I] for English *mind* is closely based on Wierzbicka (1992, 2005). According to this explication, the term suggests a dualistic way of thinking about a person, in which the *mind* is an invisible counterpart of a person's body on account of which a person can think and can know things, and in which something happens when a person thinks.[6]

[I]   *mind* (a person's *mind*)
    one of two parts of someone (one part is the body, this is the other part)
    people cannot see this part
    because someone has this part, this someone can think about things
    because someone has this part, this someone can know things
    when someone thinks about something, something happens in this part

I will now look briefly into comparable ethnopsychological constructs in Malay and in Korean. Malay *hati* is undoubtedly one of the cultural "key words" of Malay culture (Goddard 2001). It is extremely common both as an independent item, and in numerous fixed expressions for emotions, moods, attitudes, and personal traits. The nearest English gloss is *heart* (in its emotional-moral sense) but the two words are not semantically identical, because the Malay *hati* is more dynamic and more cognitive. Occasionally it has to be translated as *mind*, rather than as *heart*, e.g. in an expression like *senang hati* 'peace of mind' (*senang* 'easy, calm'). Or

---

6.   The final component in explication [I] has been added recently, to depict the dynamic aspect of the *mind* concept, reflected in common expressions such as *What's going on in his mind?*, and in phrases such as *the workings of the mind*.

consider an example such as (23) below: It would hardly be possible to say, in English, that one's *heart* was filled with troubles or with memories – one's *mind*, perhaps, not one's *heart*.

(23)   ... *seribu satu masalah memenuhi hatinya. Ingatannya pada ibunya di kampung, ingat adik-adiknya yang masih kecil-kecil, ingat pula pesanan ibunya.*
'... a thousand and one troubles filled her *hati*. Memories of her mother in the village, of her brothers and sisters who were still little, memories also of her mother's exhortations.'

Like *heart*, however, Malay *hati* can also refer to a particular organ of the human body (in this case, to the liver), and more importantly, it is the realm of feelings, especially sustained feelings about other people, such as *cinta* 'romantic love', *cemburu* 'jealousy, envy', and *sedih* 'sorrow'. The expression *perasaan hati* (where *perasaan* 'feelings' is a nominalisation of *rasa* 'feel') designates feelings which are relatively longstanding, involve evaluation, and are directed toward another person. Also like English *heart*, the *hati* is by nature a private, inner realm. Others cannot know the *isi hati* 'contents of the *hati*' unless the subject chooses to *luahkan* 'let it out' or to *mencurahkan* 'pour it out'.

Some of the numerous fixed verbal expressions involving *hati* are as follows. Taken together, they illustrate the rich nature of the *hati*, which combines aspects of feeling, wanting, and thinking.

jaga hati [lit. watch over *hati*] 'to be protective of (someone's) feelings', *ambil hati* [lit. get *hati*] 'to charm (someone), win over', *suka hati* [lit. please *hati*] 'do as you please, do whatever you feel like', *tidak sampai hati* [lit. not reach *hati*] 'can't stand to (do something)', *cuba hati* [lit. try *hati*] 'test (someone's) honesty or commitment', *ubah hati* [lit. change *hati*] 'change attitude, switch allegiances'.

Goddard (2001) has proposed explication [J], presented here in a slightly modified form. The early components state that the *hati* is a part of a person, that sustained thought about another person can be associated with an event ('something happening') in this part, and that such internal events can give rise to feelings which can be either good or bad. These feelings in turn have motivational consequences, i.e. they can lead to the person wanting to do something, which can again be either good or bad. The *hati* is indeed, in the Malay view, the wellspring of interpersonal feelings and intentions. The fact that these feelings and intentions can be either good or bad imbues the *hati* with a moral ambivalence which is much dwelt upon in Malay folk culture. The next component characterises an important aspect of the phenomenology of the *hati*, not mentioned until now, which is the experience of the *hati* 'saying something' to a person, typically, urging some course of action. The penultimate component specifies that the workings of the *hati* are inaccessible to other people, unless the experiencer wishes other people to know of them. The final component registers the analogy with a part of a person's body, more specifically, with a large internal organ in the middle of the body.

[J] *hati* (a person's *hati*) [Malay]
    a part of someone
    when someone thinks about someone else for some time, something can happen in this part
    when this happens, this someone can feel something because of it
        sometimes it is something good, sometimes it is something bad
    because of this, this someone can want to do something
        sometimes it is something good, sometimes it is something bad
    when something happens in this part of someone, sometimes this someone can think
        about it like this: "something inside me is saying something to me"
    other people can't know what happens in this part of someone if this someone doesn't
        want them to know
    people think about this part like this:
        "it is like a part of someone's body, like a big part inside the middle of the body"

The Korean word *maum* (Yoon 2003, 2004) is one of the widely used basic words in the ordinary life of Koreans. Like Malay *hati*, it is usually rendered into English as either 'mind' or 'heart', but we will see that it differs semantically from both of these, and also from *hati*. Dictionaries indicate that the meaning is a broad one, but are of little help in pinning it down with any precision. Yoon (2004) cites one Korean-English dictionary as follows:

> *maum*: 1. an entity for all kinds of mental activities including thinking, feeling, etc. 2. a personality 3. a mental activity for judging right and wrong 4. an inner thought that is not expressed 5. some feeling that can be changed according to the situation 6. a thoughtful attitude towards other people 7. an interest in something

Unlike *hati* but like *mind* (in this respect), *maum* is often counterposed with *mom* 'body', both in everyday colloquial use, and in scholarly and general literature. For example, there are numerous book titles such as: *Thunthunhan mom kenkanghan maum* 'The healthy body and the healthy *maum*', *Maumkwa momuy pyeng* 'Diseases of body and *maum*', *Momkwa maumuy kwankye* 'The relationship between the *maum* and the body'. The symmetry of *mom* (body) and *maum* suggests that Koreans think of the *maum* as one of the two parts of a human being. While the *mom* 'body' belongs to the physical, material world, the *maum* is an invisible and intangible psychological entity. Nevertheless, paradoxical as it may seem, the *maum* is conceptualised as located somewhere inside one's chest area (like English *heart*, in this respect). Also, in Korean belief, *maum* exists exclusively in human beings, not in other living creatures.

The importance of the *maum* concept is reflected in the existence of a very large number of collocations and set phrases. Yoon (2003, 2004) cites the following metaphorical expressions which highlight the role of the *maum* in intention and attention.

> *maumi kata* [lit. *maum* goes] 'tend to be attracted', *maumi nata* [lit. *maum* comes up] 'want to do something', *maumul ssuta* [lit. use *maum* for someone/something] 'pay attention to someone/something', *maumul mekta* [lit. eat *maum*] 'decide to do something', *maumul colita* [lit. troubles one's *maum*] 'be anxious about or be concerned about'.

It would not be right, however, to regard the *maum* as a figurative "organ of thinking", in the way that English *mind* can be so regarded, because in Korean ethnopsychology this function is actually ascribed to the *meli* (lit. head). It is perfectly possible to think without using the *maum*, but such thinking is or can be morally suspect. To think using the *maum* implies something like altruism or virtue. The importance of the *maum* to a moral life is highlighted by the proverb *Maum-ul calkacimyen cwuketo olhun kwisini toynta* 'One can be a good ghost after death if one has lived with a good *maum*'. A large number of attributive combinations with *maum* imply evaluation of a person's morality or character. For example, the expression 'with a warm *maum*' means something like 'warm-heartedly' and 'with a beautiful *maum*' means something like 'kind-heartedly' or 'tender-heartedly'. A person's *maum* can be good at times and bad at other times. When one's *maum* is good, one tends to do good things for other people. When it is bad, one would behave in the opposite fashion (thus the expressions 'a good *maum*' and 'a bad *maum*' can mean something like 'with good intentions' and 'with bad intentions', respectively). Koreans believe that they can act with *maum* when carrying out various activities, including occupational duties, craft, or even daily routines.

On the basis of this and a range of other evidence, Yoon (2004) proposes the following explication, presented here in a somewhat modified form.[7]

> [K] *maum* (a person's *maum*) [Korean]
>   one of two parts of someone (one part is the body, this is the other part)
>   people cannot see this part
>   because someone has this part, this someone is not like other living things
>   because someone has this part, this someone can feel many things when this someone
>   thinks about something
>   because someone has this part, this someone can do many good things
>   when this part of someone is good, this someone wants to do good things

---

7. The status in the NSM metalanguage of the locution 'think with' is unclear. Research is needed to ascertain whether comparable expressions exist across a wide a range of languages.

> when this part of someone is bad, this someone wants to do bad things
> when someone thinks about something, it is good if this someone thinks with this part
> when someone does something, it is good if this someone thinks with this part like this:
> "I want to do this thing well"

It should be amply apparent at this point that the ethnopsychological constructs of individual languages, when appropriately analysed, are revelatory of widely differing folk models of mental experience. Because they are embodied in the words and phrases of everyday talk and because they represent "experience-near" concepts, such models find their way into people's self-understandings and into their narratives of life experience. There can be little hope of understanding the subjective quality of mental experience of people from other languages and cultures unless we can "crack into" such ethnopsychological constructs and come to appreciate them. At the same time, however, it is equally important to "crack into" the ethnopsychological categories of the English language (categories such as *mind*, *emotion*, and *memory*; cf. Amberber In press), which are taken for granted in much mainstream cognitive science. Analysis into semantic primes provides a new and powerful technique to achieve these ends.

6 Implications and conclusions

Upon first hearing about NSM semantic primes, a typical and understandable reaction is to doubt whether such a small metalanguage is up to the job. Hopefully this study has served in part to answer these doubts, at least in the realm of mental concepts. I believe I have shown that the four cognitive semantic primes KNOW, THINK, WANT and FEEL, in combination with the other elements of the NSM metalanguage, are capable of explicating a diversity of mental state concepts across languages and that they can capture subtle meaning differences with precision. Though one cannot be absolutely sure, because many languages of the world remain to be examined from this point of view, studies to date appear to justify a high degree of confidence that lexical exponents of the semantic primes KNOW, THINK, WANT and FEEL exist in all languages, and that they share certain essential combinatorial properties. I also hope to have shown that other words from the English lexicon of mental states are not universal, but represent contingent culture-specific items; in particular, emotion terms (such as *surprise*, and others), epistemic verbs (such as *believe*, and others) and ethnopsychological constructs (such as *mind*, and others).

If these conclusions are correct, their epistemological and methodological implications are far-reaching, because ultimately all data on other people's mental states relies on self-reports, and self-reports require a language. Even facial expressions, behavioural observations, and other nonverbal data cannot be correlated with particular mental states without some kind of subjective attribution, and such attributions must be made using language. When interpreting the self-reports of people whose native language is not English, if we simply convert their words and conceptual categories into their assumed English counterparts, we are in effect "recoding" those reports, and in the process altering them.

This is a routine practice in cross-cultural studies of emotion. For example, Klaus Scherer and his collaborators (Scherer, Wallbott & Summerfield 1986) administered a questionnaire in eight European countries with the aim of assessing the frequency and quality of emotional experience. Information was sought on four supposedly universal categories, each characterised by a pair of English words: *joy/happiness, sadness/grief, fear/fright, anger/rage*. The technique of translation and back-translation[8] was used "to guarantee equivalence across languages" (Aebischer & Wallbott 1986: 32). But as shown by the semantic studies summarised in this chapter and by numerous others, the procedure of translation and back-translation cannot guarantee equivalence of meaning at all. At best, it merely assures us that the terms being used are the nearest single-word equivalents available in the various languages. In the German version of the questionnaire, for example, one of the words used for the assumed category *fear/fright*, with the sanction of the translation and back-translation procedure, was *Angst* (Scherer 1986: 177); but it is well-known that the meaning of *Angst* is quite different from that of either *fear* or *fright* (cf. Wierzbicka 1999). To take another example, the new field of "happiness studies" seems to be more or less oblivious to the problems of translation. In one collection of 14 psychological studies, titled *Culture and Subjective Well-being* (Diener & Suh 2000), problems of translation occupy but a single paragraph, yet semantic analysis has shown that words such as German *glücklich*, French *heureux*, Chinese *lè* and English *happy* are not semantically equivalent (Wierzbicka 2004).

In my view, it is time to abandon this kind of flawed translation methodology. We can continue to gather self-reports about mental states in indigenous categories (indeed, there can be great value in doing so), but what we cannot do any longer is to assume that the content of these categories can be matched in a simple fashion with the categories of the English language. In order to render such data into a commensurable form, the conceptual concept of the various sets of language-specific

---

8. Back-translation refers to the procedure whereby a translated document is "checked" by being translated back into the original language, preferably by an independent translator.

categories must be carefully analysed and explicated into configurations of semantic primes, which can be transposed without distortion across languages.[9]

None of this means that analysts have to give up using English as a descriptive language. But for our theoretical formulations to be safe from the dangers of ethnocentrism we should ideally confine ourselves to that small part of English which we know to be shared with other languages. At the very least we must handle with great care any expressions which are known to be English-specific.[10]

Taking a broader perspective, I believe that the extensive and growing corpus of NSM descriptions of mental state concepts across different languages opens up new possibilities for the scientific understanding of subjectivity and psychological experience. Explicating mental state concepts in terms of semantic primes can articulate very subtle meaning differences while at the same time freeing the analyses from terminological ethnocentrism and from the epistemological "spin" of English-specific categories. It opens up an "insider perspective" on the mental state concepts of other languages (as well as our own), and in the process can help us develop an improved understanding of how ways of thinking and ways of feeling can be culturally-shaped.

Acknowledgments

I would like to thank Andrea Schalley, Anna Wierzbicka, Kyung-Joo Yoon, and two anonymous reviewers, for comments which have helped improve this chapter.

[9.] On a further methodological note, there can be great value in investigating mental states using scenarios and reporting protocols framed directly in terms of semantic primes. For example, rather than asking people how often and in what circumstances they 'feel angry', we can ask about how often and what circumstances they think something like 'someone did something bad to me, I don't want this'; and about how often and in what circumstances they think something like 'I want to do something bad to this someone because of it'. Framing the reporting protocols in semantic primes makes them cross-translatable and, at the same time, more fine-grained.

[10.] In principle, a language-specific concept such as English *mind*, Malay *hati* or Korean *maum* could provide a useful conceptual tool for cognitive science without it necessarily being lexicalised in other languages. Nonetheless, in order to minimise the risk of everyday understandings of any such term influencing the way it is used in cognitive science, and in the interests of conceptual clarity, it would remain highly advisable to decompose it into a configuration of semantic primes. As Lutz (1988), among others, has pointed out, the semantic content of the English word *mind* (with its focus on knowing and thinking, to the exclusion of feeling) was an important contributing factor to the relative marginalisation of emotions in the discourse of cognitive science over many years. If cognitive science had evolved with Malay or Korean as its intellectual lingua franca, rather than English, one would imagine that emotional and moral concerns would have enjoyed a higher profile from the onset.

References

Aebischer, Verena & Harald G. Wallbott. 1986. Measuring emotional experiences: Questionnaire design and procedure, and the nature of the sample. In Scherer, Wallbott & Summerfield (eds.), 28–38.

Amberber, Mengistu (ed.). In press. *The language of memory from a cross-linguistic perspective.* Amsterdam: John Benjamins.

Ameka, Felix, 1994. Ewe. In Goddard & Wierzbicka (eds.), 57–86.

Boucher, Jerry D. 1983. Antecedents to emotions across cultures. In Sydney H. Irvine & John W. Berry (eds.), *Human assessment and cultural factors*, 407–420. New York, NY: Plenum Press.

Briggs, Jean L. 1970. *Never in anger: Portrait of an Eskimo family.* Cambridge, MA: Harvard University Press.

Bruner, Jerome. 1990. *Acts of meaning.* Cambridge, MA: Harvard University Press.

Bugenhagen, Robert D. 2002. The syntax of semantic primes in Mangaaba-Mbula. In Goddard & Wierzbicka (eds.), Vol. 2, 1–64.

Chappell, Hilary. 2002. The universal syntax of semantic primes in Mandarin Chinese. In Goddard & Wierzbicka (eds.), Vol. 1, 243–322.

Diener, Ed & Eunkook M. Suh (eds.). 2000. *Culture and subjective well-being.* Cambridge, MA: The MIT Press.

Ekman, Paul. 1992. An argument for basic emotions. *Cognition and Emotion* 6(3/4). 169–200.

Ekman, Paul & Richard J. Davidson (eds.). 1994. *The nature of emotion: Fundamental questions.* Oxford: OUP.

Enfield, N. J. 2002. Combinatoric properties of Natural Semantic Metalanguage expressions in Lao. In Goddard & Wierzbicka (eds.), Vol. 2, 145–256.

Enfield, N. J. & Anna Wierzbicka (eds.). 2002. *The body in the description of emotion.* Special issue of *Pragmatics & Cognition* 10(1/2).

Fehr, Beverley & James A. Russell. 1984. Concept of emotion viewed from a prototype perspective. *Journal of Experimental Psychology: General* 113(3). 464–486.

Fortescue, Michael. 2001. Thoughts about thought. *Cognitive Linguistics* 12(1). 15–46.

Gladkova, Anna. This volume. Universal and language-specific aspects of "propositional attitudes".

Goddard, Cliff. 1997. Contrastive semantics and cultural psychology: 'Surprise' in Malay and English. *Culture & Psychology* 3(2). 153–181.

Goddard, Cliff. 2001. *Hati*: A key word in the Malay vocabulary of emotion. In Jean Harkins & Anna Wierzbicka (eds.), *Emotions in crosslinguistic perspective*, 167–196. Berlin: Mouton de Gruyter.

Goddard, Cliff. 2002. Semantic primes and universal grammar in Malay (Bahasa Melayu). In Goddard and Wierzbicka (eds.), Vol. 1, 87–172.

Goddard, Cliff. 2003a. 'Thinking' across languages and cultures: Six dimensions of variation. *Cognitive Linguistics* 14(2/3). 109–140.

Goddard, Cliff. 2003b. Dynamic *ter-* in Malay (Bahasa Melayu): A study in grammatical polysemy. *Studies in Language* 27(2). 287–322.

Goddard, Cliff. In press. Natural Semantic Metalanguage: The state of the art. In Cliff Goddard (ed.), *Cross-linguistic semantics.* Amsterdam. John Benjamins.

Goddard, Cliff & Susanna Karlsson. 2004. Re-thinking 'think': Contrastive semantics of Swedish and English. In Christo Moskovsky (ed.), *Proceedings of the 2003 Conference of the Australian Linguistic Society.* http://www.als.asn.au.

Goddard, Cliff & Anna Wierzbicka (eds.). 1994. *Semantic and lexical universals: Theory and empirical findings*. Amsterdam: John Benjamins.

Goddard, Cliff & Anna Wierzbicka (eds.). 2002. *Meaning and universal grammar: Theory and empirical findings*, Vols. 1 & 2. Amsterdam: John Benjamins.

Hale, Ken. 1994. Preliminary observations on lexical and semantic primitives in the Misumalpan languages of Nicaragua. In Goddard & Wierzbicka (eds.), 263–284.

Harkins, Jean. 1995. Desire in language and thought: A study in crosscultural semantics. Canberra, ACT: Australian National University PhD dissertation.

Harkins, Jean & Anna Wierzbicka (eds.). 2001. *Emotions in crosslinguistic perspective*. Berlin: Mouton de Gruyter.

Harré, Rom (ed.). 1986. *The social construction of emotions*. Oxford: Basil Blackwell.

Hasada, Rie. 2000. An exploratory study of expression of emotions in Japanese: Towards a semantic interpretation. Canberra, ACT: Australian National University PhD dissertation.

Heider, Karl G. 1991. *Landscapes of emotion. Mapping three cultures of emotion in Indonesia*. Cambridge: CUP.

Holland, Nancy & Naomi Quinn (eds.). 1987. *Cultural models in language and thought*. New York, NY: OUP.

Kamus Lengkap. 1990. Edited by Awang Sudjai Hairul & Yusoff Khan. Petaling Jaya: Pustaka Zaman.

Kitayama, Shinobu & Hazel Rose Markus (eds.). 1994. *Emotion and culture: Empirical studies of mutual influence*. Washington, DC: American Psychological Association.

Levy, Robert I. 1973. *Tahitians: Mind and experience in the Society Islands*. Chicago, IL: The University of Chicago Press.

Lutz, Catherine A. 1988. *Unnatural emotions: Everyday sentiments on a Micronesian Atoll and their challenge to western theory*. Chicago, IL: The Chicago University Press.

Palmer, Gary, Cliff Goddard & Penny Lee (eds.). 2003. Talking about 'thinking'. Special Issue of *Cognitive Linguistics* 14(2/3).

Peeters, Bert. 1994. Semantic and lexical universals in French. In Goddard & Wierzbicka (eds.), 423–444.

Pesmen, Dale. 2000. *Russia and soul: An exploration*. Ithaca, NY: Cornell University Press.

Rosaldo, Michelle Z. 1980. *Knowledge and passion: Ilongot notions of self and social life*. Cambridge: CUP.

Sapir, Edward. 1949. *Selected writings of Edward Sapir in language, culture and personality*. Edited by David Mandelbaum. Berkeley, CA: University of California Press.

Scherer, Klaus R. 1986. Emotion experiences across European cultures: A summary statement. In Scherer, Wallbot & Summerfield (eds.), 173–189.

Scherer, Klaus R., Harald G. Wallbott & Angela B. Summerfield (eds.). 1986. *Experiencing emotion. A cross-cultural study*. Cambridge: CUP.

Schwartz, Theodore, Geoffrey M. White & Catherine A. Lutz (eds.). 1992. *New directions in psychological anthropology*. Cambridge: CUP.

Shore, Bradd. 1996. *Culture in mind: Cognition, culture and the problem of meaning*. New York, NY: OUP.

Shweder, Richard A. 1991. *Thinking through cultures: Expeditions in cultural psychology*. Cambridge, MA: Harvard University Press.

Shweder, Richard A. 1993. The cultural psychology of the emotions. In Michael Lewis & Jeannette M. Haviland (eds.), *Handbook of emotions*, 417–431. New York, NY: The Guilford Press.

Shweder, Richard A. 2003. Deconstructing the emotions for the sake of comparative research. In Antony S. R. Manstead, Agneta H. Fischer, & Nico H. Frijda (eds.), *Feeling and emotion* [Studies in Emotion and Social Interaction, Series 2], 81–97. Oxford: OUP.

Travis, Catherine. 2002. La metalengua semántica natural: The natural semantic metalanguage of Spanish. In Goddard & Wierzbicka (eds), Vol. 1, 173–242.

Travis, Catherine. 2003. The semantics of the Spanish subjunctive: Its use in the natural semantic metalanguage. *Cognitive Linguistics* 14(1). 47–70.

Viberg, Åke. 1980. *Tre semantiska fält i svenskan och några andra språk* (Three semantic fields in Swedish and some other languages) [SSM Report 7]. Stockholm: Stockholms universitet, Department of Linguistics.

White, Geoffrey M. & John Kirkpatrick (eds.). 1985. *Person, self and experience*. Berkeley, CA: University of California Press.

Wierzbicka, Anna. 1992. *Semantics: Culture and cognition*. Oxford: OUP.

Wierzbicka, Anna. 1996. *Semantics: Primes and universals*. Oxford: OUP.

Wierzbicka, Anna. 1998. THINK – A universal human concept and a conceptual primitive. In Jacek Juliusz Jadacki & Witold Strawiński (eds.), *In the world of signs. Essays in honour of Professor Jerzy Pelc* [Poznań Studies in the Philosophy of the Sciences and the Humanities 62], 297–308. Amsterdam: Rodopi.

Wierzbicka, Anna. 1999. *Emotions across languages and cultures*. Cambridge: CUP.

Wierzbicka, Anna. 2002. Semantic primes and universal grammar in Polish. In Goddard & Wierzbicka (eds.), Vol. 2, 65–144.

Wierzbicka, Anna. 2004. 'Happiness' in cross-linguistic and cross-cultural perspective. *Daedalus* Spring 2004. 34–43.

Wierzbicka, Anna. 2005. Empirical universals of language as a basis for the study of other human universals and as a tool for exploring cross-cultural differences. *Ethos* 33(2). 256–291.

Wierzbicka, Anna. 2006. *English: Meaning and culture*. New York, NY: OUP.

Yoon, Kyung-Joo. 2003. Constructing a Korean Natural Semantic Metalanguage. Canberra ACT: Australian National University PhD dissertation.

Yoon, Kyung-Joo. 2004. Korean *maum* vs. English *heart* and *mind*: Contrastive semantics of cultural concepts. In Christo Moskovsky (ed.), *Proceedings of the 2003 Conference of the Australian Linguistic Society*. http://www.als.asn.au.

Yoon, Kyung-Joo. 2006. *Constructing a Korean National Semantic Metalanguage*. Seoul: Hankook Publishers.

Appendix

Semantic primes.[†] English exponents (after Goddard In press)

Substantives:	I, YOU, SOMEONE, SOMETHING/THING, PEOPLE, BODY
Relational substantives:	KIND, PART
Determiners:	THIS, THE SAME, OTHER/ELSE
Quantifiers:	ONE, TWO, SOME, ALL, MUCH/MANY
Evaluators:	GOOD, BAD
Descriptors:	BIG, SMALL
Mental predicates:	THINK, KNOW, WANT, FEEL, SEE, HEAR
Speech:	SAY, WORDS, TRUE
Actions, events, movement, contact:	DO, HAPPEN, MOVE, TOUCH
Location, existence, possession, specification:	BE (SOMEWHERE), THERE IS, HAVE, BE (SOMEONE, SOMETHING)
Life and death:	LIVE, DIE
Time:	WHEN/TIME, NOW, BEFORE, AFTER, A LONG TIME, A SHORT TIME, FOR SOME TIME, MOMENT
Space:	WHERE/PLACE, HERE, ABOVE, BELOW, FAR, NEAR, SIDE, INSIDE
Logical concepts:	NOT, MAYBE, CAN, BECAUSE, IF
Intensifier, augmentor:	VERY, MORE
Similarity:	LIKE/WAY

† • primes exist as the meanings of lexical units (not at the level of lexemes) • exponents of primes may be words, bound morphemes, or phrasemes • they can be formally, i.e. morphologically, complex • they can have different morphosyntactic properties in different languages • they can have combinatorial variants (allolexes) • each prime has well-specified syntactic (combinatorial) properties

CHAPTER 3

Shape and colour in language and thought

Anna Wierzbicka

"Colour" and "shape" are concepts important to the speakers of English and of many other languages. They are not, however, universal: There are many languages which have no words corresponding to the English words *colour* and *shape*, and in which questions like "what colour is it?" or "what shape is it?" cannot be asked at all. Clearly, speakers of such languages do not think about the world in terms of "colour" and "shape". How do they think about it, then?

This study shows that by using an empirically discovered set of universal semantic primes which includes SEE and TOUCH we can effectively explore ways of construal of the visual and tangible world different from those embedded in, and encouraged by, English.

1   Languages as the mirror of the mind – and as mirrors of different, culturally shaped, "minds"

I will start with two puzzles, both to do with categorisation.[1]

First, I'd like to invite the reader to imagine two sets of objects. One set includes objects (e.g. sheets of paper or plastic) which in English could be described as dazzling white, sunny yellow, bright red, and silver. The other set includes objects (again, sheets of paper or plastic) which in English would be described as off-white, brownish yellow, blue, green, and black. In the Australian Aboriginal language Burarra, in Arnhem land, the objects in the first set can be described as *-gungaltja*, and those in the other set, as *-gungundja*. These words are the two most basic words that Burarra speakers use to describe the visual world. The question is: What do these words mean? Obviously, they don't mean 'white' and 'black', or 'red' and 'blue'. So what do they mean? There can be no doubt that the speakers of Burarra interpret the world they see largely through the prism of the concepts

---

[1]   The analyses presented in this study owe a great deal to extensive discussions with Cliff Goddard and in most cases have been arrived at jointly.

embodied in these two words. Thus, to understand their interpretation of the visual world we need to understand the meaning of these two words.

Second, I'd like to ask the reader to imagine a set of three small boxes: A round one, a rectangular one (say 15cm by 10cm by 3cm) and a long one (say 20cm by 4cm by 2cm). When asked to describe these boxes, native speakers of English say that one of them is *round*, and another is *long*. As for the third, they are divided, but no one says that it is *round*, and no one says that it is *long*. But when you show the same boxes to native speakers of Polish (which is my native language) the result is different. Here, there is a consensus that one box is *okrągłe* and the other two, *podłużne*. From this, the reader might guess – and rightly so – that *okrągłe* means 'round', but what does the other word, *podłużne* mean?

To native speakers of English, it may seem very natural to describe some objects as *round* and some other ones as *long*, and it might seem to them that "being *round*" or "being *long*" are physical properties of the objects themselves. But native speakers of Polish have a different conceptual grid, and to them, it seems equally natural to describe some objects as *okrągłe* and some others, as *podłużne* (or *podłużny*). Thus, neither "being *long*" nor "being *podłużne*" are simple physical properties of the objects themselves. Rather, they are certain mental constructs, suggested to us by our native languages. So if we want to understand how speakers of Polish conceptualise the world, we have to look into the meaning of *podłużny*. We also need to look into the meaning of *long* – first, to understand how speakers of English conceptualise the world, and second, to get used to the idea that English words like *round* and *long* are not some neutral analytical tools for studying human cognition, but rather, language-specific conceptual constructs just like *podłużny* or *-gungaltja*.

Cognitive studies are concerned with something hidden and invisible: The workings of the human mind. How can scholars find out about these things, given that they are not accessible to direct observation? One answer to this question was put forward three hundred years ago, by the great precursor of modern cognitive studies, Leibniz. Among many profound insights which Leibniz's intellectual legacy holds for us, few are, I believe, more important than that expressed in his words about languages: "I really believe that languages are the best mirror of the human mind, and that a precise analysis of the significations of words would tell us more than anything else about the operations of the understanding" (Leibniz 1996: 333).

Leibniz's insight that languages are the best mirror of the mind is the foundation on which the "NSM" theory of language and thought is built (that is, the theory in which this study is based). But what for Leibniz was a project for the future, three centuries later has become a fact: Empirical, comparative study of many diverse languages of the world is now a reality. The work done over the last three decades or so has led to the emergence and cross-linguistic verification of a rich set of empirical linguistic universals. These universals include a set of sixty or so universal human concepts – conceptual primes, which correspond to Leibniz's notion of "the alphabet of human thoughts", and a universal grammar, which corresponds to some extent to his notion of a universal "philosophical grammar".

To give a few simple examples, innate conceptual primes posited by the NSM theory include concepts like GOOD and BAD, SOMEONE and SOMETHING, BEFORE and AFTER, and IF, BECAUSE and NOT (negation), which we find as tangible words or word-like elements, with a shared set of combinatorial properties, in languages as diverse as Japanese and Russian, Malay and Ewe (West Africa), Lao and Mbula (New Guinea), Yankunytjatjara (Australia) and Spanish, Chinese and Amharic (Ethiopia). The full set of universal human concepts, established through empirical cross-linguistic investigations, is given in the table below, presented here in two versions, English and Polish.

Table 1. Universal human concepts – English version* (cf. Goddard In press)

Substantives:	I, YOU, SOMEONE, SOMETHING/THING, PEOPLE, BODY
Relational substantives:	KIND, PART
Determiners:	THIS, THE SAME, OTHER/ELSE
Quantifiers:	ONE, TWO, SOME, MANY/MUCH, ALL
Evaluators:	GOOD, BAD
Descriptors:	BIG, SMALL
Mental predicates:	THINK, KNOW, WANT, FEEL, SEE, HEAR
Speech:	SAY, WORDS, TRUE
Actions, events, movement, contact:	DO, HAPPEN, MOVE, TOUCH
Location, existence, possession, specification:	BE (SOMEWHERE), BE/EXIST, HAVE, BE (SOMEONE/SOMETHING)
Life and death:	LIVE, DIE
Time:	WHEN/TIME, NOW, AFTER, BEFORE, A LONG TIME, A SHORT TIME, FOR SOME TIME, MOMENT/IN ONE MOMENT
Space:	WHERE/PLACE, HERE, ABOVE, BELOW, FAR, NEAR, SIDE, INSIDE
Logical concepts:	NOT, MAYBE, CAN, BECAUSE, IF
Intensifier, augmentor:	VERY, MORE
Similarity:	LIKE/AS

The Natural Semantic Metalanguage (NSM) which uses these sixty or so universal concepts as its primes is a formal system, described in detail in *Meaning and Universal Grammar* (Goddard & Wierzbicka 2002; see also Goddard 1998; Wierzbicka 1996). It is not a natural language, but an analogue of a subset of natural language (any natural language). It is sufficiently close to natural languages, however, to be inherently intelligible to speakers of all natural languages.

Table 2. Universal semantic primes – Polish version* (Wierzbicka 2002; Goddard & Wierzbicka In press)

Substantives:	JA, TY, KTOŚ, COŚ, LUDZIE, CIAŁO
Relational substantives:	RODZAJ, CZĘŚĆ
Determiners:	TEN, TEN SAM, INNY
Quantifiers:	JEDEN, DWA, NIEKTÓRZY/NIEKTÓRE, DUŻO, WSZYSCY/WSZYSTKO
Evaluators:	DOBRY, ZŁY
Descriptors:	DUŻY, MAŁY
Mental predicates:	MYŚLEĆ, WIEDZIEĆ/ZNAĆ, CHCIEĆ, CZUĆ, WIDZIEĆ, SŁYSZEĆ
Speech:	POWIEDZIEĆ/MÓWIĆ, SŁOWO, PRAWDA
Actions, events, movement, contact:	ROBIĆ, DZIAĆ SIĘ/STAĆ SIĘ RUSZAĆ SIĘ, DOTYKAĆ
Location, existence, possession, specification:	BYĆ (GDZIEŚ), BYĆ/ISTNIEĆ, MIEĆ, BYĆ (CZYMŚ/KIMŚ)
Life and death:	ŻYĆ, UMRZEĆ
Time:	KIEDY/CZAS, TERAZ, PO, PRZED, DŁUGO, KRÓTKO, PRZEZ PEWIEN CZAS, CHWILA/W JEDNEJ CHWILI
Space:	GDZIE/MIEJSCE, TUTAJ, NAD, POD, DALEKO, BLISKO, STRONA, WEWNĄTRZ/W
Logical concepts:	NIE, BYĆ MOŻE, MÓC, BO/Z POWODU, JEŻELI
Intensifier, augmentor:	BARDZO, WIĘCEJ
Similarity:	TAK/TAKJAK

* • exponents of primes may be words, bound morphemes, or phrasemes • they can be formally, i.e. morphologically, complex • they can have different morphosyntactic properties (including word-class) in different languages • they can have combinatorial variants (allolexes) • each semantic prime has a well-specified set of grammatical (combinatorial) properties.

The NSM theory of language and thought can be seen as a partial realisation of Leibniz's program. I think that the sixty or so conceptual primes, discovered through empirical comparative study of diverse languages, provide a rich, substantive set of hypotheses about the innate inner code "written" on the slate of the human mind; and that they give us a powerful tool for analysing human cognition, as well as human languages and cultures. They allow us to explore both the "human mind" reflected in the shared core of all languages, and the culturally shaped "minds" reflected in language-specific conceptual systems.

2. The importance of studying the meaning of words

As Benjamin Lee Whorf (1956: 252) observed decades ago, it is often assumed that "thinking is an obvious, straightforward activity, the same for all rational human beings". In fact, Whorf pointed out, "thinking is most mysterious, and by far the greatest light upon it that we have is thrown by the study of language" (by which he meant "languages"). If we want to understand thinking, we need to study languages. Above all, we need to study the meaning of words, because thinking is done largely with concepts, and concepts are embodied in words. It is astonishing to what extent this basic point has been ignored in the majority of recent writings on "language and mind".

For example, in the Chomskyan tradition in linguistics there has been a constant talk of "the mind", but hardly any attention at all has been given to the meaning of words. Chomsky himself has either dismissed the subject as belonging to lexicographers, not linguists (cf. e.g. Chomsky 1987), or presented it as unfathomable (cf. e.g. Chomsky 2000).

The most semantically oriented linguist working in the Chomskyan tradition, Ray Jackendoff (1994: 17), admitted after decades of semantic research that he had not been able to determine, to his own satisfaction, the meaning of a single word. In his more recent work, he still maintains that at best, linguistics as he understands it can offer *partial* analyses of word meanings and that the goal of stating the full meaning of a single word is currently unattainable (see e.g. Jackendoff 2002: Chapter 11). In my view, these acknowledgments illustrate the semantic sterility of the whole generative enterprise.

In contrast to Chomskyan and post-Chomskyan approaches, the NSM linguistic theory has led, over the years, to hundreds of detailed analyses of the meanings of words. Since these words were drawn from a wide range of languages, and from many different semantic domains, as a result, a great deal has been discovered about the structure of many individual concepts, and, even more importantly, about the organisation of the mental lexicon as a whole. In this study, I am going to report on some of these findings.

To study the meaning of the word in which a given concept is embodied we need to be able to analyse this meaning into its semantic elements. If this analysis is to lead to any real understanding, the elements which we arrive at cannot be invented ad hoc but should be taken from a list of independently justified simple and self-explanatory human concepts. To quote Leibniz again:

> If nothing could be understood in itself nothing at all could be understood. Because what can only be understood via something else can be understood only to the extent to which that other thing can be understood, and so on; accordingly, we

can say that we have understood something only when we have broken it down into parts which can be understood in themselves. (Couturat 1903/1961: 430)

If one tries to analyse the meaning of words into components by relying on some technical or "learned" words which are far from self-explanatory to "ordinary people" then no real understanding is achieved. But as Whorf clearly saw, if one tries to rely in one's analysis on some sort of "plain English" or "basic English" this will not necessarily help one either. The only words which can help us to uncover, and to understand, the structure of concepts embodied in human languages are words which are themselves self-explanatory – self-explanatory not only to speakers of English but to human beings in general, that is, to speakers of all natural languages. On this point, too, it is worth quoting Whorf's words:

It is the "plainest" English which contains the greatest number of unconscious assumptions about nature. This is the trouble with schemes like Basic English, in which an eviscerated British English, with its concealed premises working harder than ever, is to be fobbed off on an unsuspecting world as the substance of pure Reason itself. We handle even our plain English with much greater effect if we direct it from the vantage point of a multilingual awareness. (Whorf 1956: 244)

It is this multilingual awareness which allows us to identify the words (and other expressions) that can be regarded as maximally self-explanatory to all human beings, and out of which all meaningful explanations can be built. The concepts encoded in these self-explanatory words which have equivalent words or word-like elements in all languages can be regarded as the innate building blocks of human thought.

The elementary, self-explanatory, and presumably innate human concepts give us a tool by means of which we can investigate the structure of concepts embodied in words (as well as those embodied in grammatical constructions). Using this tool, we can also compare complex concepts with one another, and by doing so, we can show that there are different types of concepts associated with different levels of complexity, as well as different kinds of structure; and we can make important generalisations about the nature of human thinking.

The first generalisation emerging from the NSM work on the lexicon of many natural languages is that some types of concepts are much more complex than some others, and that, generally speaking, the structure of abstract concepts is much simpler than that of concrete ones. (By "abstract" I mean, essentially, those which do not refer to seeing or touching, and by "concrete" those which do.) This generalisation can be made at all only because the NSM set of semantic primes gives us a common measure. The NSM work done over the last three decades shows that abstract concepts, such as those to do with emotions, values, speech acts and interpersonal relations, and concrete concepts, such as those to do with animals and plants, human artefacts, the environment, and human bodily activities, can be analysed in terms of the same minimal set of universal semantic primes. For example, "concrete" words like *tiger, salt, milk, umbrella* or *boomerang* can be analysed, or "explicated", in terms of the same primes as "abstract" words like *envy, compassion, threat* and *warning*. The generalisation that the semantic structure of the "concrete" lexicon is, on the whole, more complex than that of abstract words, and that this applies to all languages, crucially depends on the existence of this common measure. (For an earlier discussion of this generalisation, see Wierzbicka 1991).

The second generalisation has to do with different types of semantic structure. The extensive explorations of the vocabularies of different languages done over the years within the NSM framework reveal that some concepts can be explicated directly in terms of the semantic primes (or "semantic atoms"), whereas others can only be explicated in stages, that is, via concepts which themselves need to be explicated. If the primes can be likened to atoms, these more complex building blocks can be seen as "semantic molecules". These two different methods of explication – directly through the primes or via the semantic molecules – are not a matter of arbitrary decision but rather follow from the different structures of the concepts themselves. Importantly, the primes or "atoms" are universal, the same in all languages, whereas the "molecules" – as we will see – can be language-specific.

3   Explicating abstract concepts and concrete concepts

Roughly speaking, speech act words like *threat* or *warn* can be explicated along the following lines:

[A]   *person X threatened person Y =*
    X said to Y something like this about something (Z):
        "if you do Z I will do something bad to you"
    X said this because X wanted Y not to do Z

[B]   *person X warned person Y about something =*
    X said to Y something like this about something:
        "I want you to know that something bad can happen to you
        it will be good for you to know it
        if you know it you can do something because of this"
    X said this because X wanted Y to know it

These explications could be elaborated and fine-tuned further, but there is no need to do so here. Importantly, they could be tested against a wide range of examples and against native speakers' intuitions. Such testing is possible because these explications have been formulated in intuitively intelligible natural language.

As mentioned earlier, what applies to words for speech acts applies also to words for emotions. For example, the concepts encoded in the English words *envy* and *compassion* can be explicated (in the same set of primes) along the following lines:

[C] *person X envied person Y* =
 X thought like this about Y:
  "something good happened to Y
  it didn't happen to me
  this is bad
  I want things like this to happen to me"
 when X thought like this X felt something
 like people can feel when they think like this

[D] *person X felt compassion for person Y* =
 X thought like this about Y:
  "something bad happened to Y
  Y feels something bad because of this
  I want to do something good for Y because of this"
 when X thought like this X felt something
 like people can feel when they think like this

If we try, however, to explicate "concrete" lexicon along the same lines, we usually get explications which are so long and complicated as to be practically incomprehensible. This suggests that the internal structure of concepts like 'umbrella' or 'mice' is different from that of concepts like 'threat' and 'warning' or 'envy' and 'compassion'.

Let us try to explore, as an example, the concept encoded in the English word *umbrella*. If we try to explicate this concept in accordance with native speakers' intuitions, we will soon discover that while some aspects of it can be readily captured in semantic primes, others appear to call for the use of concepts other than primes, that is "semantic molecules". As a first approximation, then, I would propose the following explication of *umbrella*, in which "semantic molecules" have been marked as [M]:

[E] *umbrella*
 things of one kind
 things of this kind exist because people make [M] them
 people make [M] them because many people want to do something with them
  at times when it is raining [M] in places where they are
  because they don't want water [M] to touch their bodies
 they have two parts

one part is round [M]
this part is above the other part
this part can be above someone's body on all sides of the body
the other part is long [M]
someone's hand [M] can touch this part on all sides at the same time
because of this when this someone moves, this thing can move at the same time
because of this when this someone moves for some time
the round [M] part of this thing can be above this someone's body for this time

Quite apart from questions as to the accuracy of this explication, it might be asked: What is the point?

To reiterate what was said earlier, the point is to understand the nature of human concepts, and of the thinking that is done with them. What the elucidation of the concept of 'umbrella' undertaken here suggests is that at least one category of concepts – those standing for human artefacts – is very complex and that this complexity is handled by the human mind by means of a "layered" structure involving some "semantic molecules" as well as semantic primes. As I have discussed in earlier work (cf. Wierzbicka 1985, 1996), this is not the only semantic domain which exhibits this kind of structure. At the same time, further exploration of concepts across different semantic domains shows that not all "concrete" concepts are similarly complex in their structure; and also, that some "concrete" concepts can be analysed directly in terms of primes, whereas others may involve two, three or even more levels of complexity.

4   Exploring the concept of shape

Shape, like colour, appears to be an aspect of human cognition which is so intimately bound with perception that any attempt to understand it analytically may seem perverse. This applies to words like *long*, *round*, *blue* or *green* as much as it does to the more general words *shape* and *colour* themselves: To anyone other than a semanticist, words of this kind are likely to seem to be basic, non-decomposable. While it requires an effort to identify the key differences between *threaten* and *warn*, or between *envy* and *compassion*, the task does not seem impossible to a native speaker of English. An attempt to comprehend, analytically, the meaning of *umbrella* may seem bizarre, but not impossible either. But *shape* and *colour*?

These reactions of native speakers are instructive: They indicate that the meaning of words like *shape* and *colour*, or *long* and *blue*, lies deeper under the surface of consciousness than that of abstract words like *threat* and *envy* or concrete words like *umbrella*.

But hidden as the meanings of the words *colour* and *shape* are, we must acknowledge that these words, too, stand for concepts with a complex internal structure, and that with effort, the structure of these concepts, too, can be identified. The very fact that not all languages have words for *shape* and *colour* shows that these are culture-specific conceptual artefacts rather than innate elementary concepts. In this study, I want to focus, above all, on shape, with only a very sketchy discussion of colour, which I have discussed more extensively elsewhere. In particular, I would like to unravel the meaning of the English words *long* and *round*.

Building on the ideas of Leibniz and Locke, I would suggest that so-called physical properties are conceptualised in many languages in terms of the senses by means of which they are perceived (Goddard & Wierzbicka 2007). For example, the concept of "colour" relies on purely visual information, whereas "softness" and "smoothness" rely on touch but not on sight. Shape, in contrast to colour, softness and smoothness, can be established by either touch or sight: People can come to know that something is round either by seeing or by touching it. Roughly speaking, then, the shape of an object is what can be found out about it by either sight or touch. More precisely, "shape" is a kind of knowledge about things which can be obtained by either seeing them or touching them comprehensively, on all sides. It is true that the word *shape* can also be applied to some objects which can't be explored by touch, for example, a rainbow. But in such cases, too, if the word *shape* is used, the information obtained by sight is categorised as a kind of knowledge which, generally speaking, can be obtained by either sight or touch. For example, the shape of a rainbow is likened to that of a bow – an object whose shape could be established during the day by sight, and at night, by touch.

If both "see" and "touch" were universal semantic primes our definitions of "shape" and related words could be relatively simple. In fact, however, this is not quite the case. While SEE is indeed a universal semantic prime, "touch" as a verb of perception is not. On the other hand, we do find in all languages a word or expression for the concept of "touching" in the sense of contact: In all languages, one can say that someone's hand was touching something.

Assuming that the concept of "shape" relies on the primes SEE and TOUCHING (contact), Cliff Goddard and I have arrived at the following explication of this concept:

[F] *shape*
    one kind of thing
    people can know things of many kinds about many things
    this is one of these kinds
    when someone sees something
        this someone can know something of this kind about this thing because of this

> if someone's hands [M] can touch this thing everywhere on all sides
> this someone can know the same because of this

This explication is, essentially, very simple, but it is not framed exclusively in terms of semantic primes, since it includes the word *hands*. The idea of "handling" things of different shapes makes a good deal of intuitive sense. My hypothesis is that this idea is so important to our conceptualisation of the world that it enters the concept of "shape" itself.

5 The importance of hands in the conceptualisation of the world

In my 1985 book *Lexicography and conceptual analysis* I proposed several dozens of explications for various artefacts as well as "natural kinds", pointing out the crucial role of "hands" in the conceptual structure of these concepts. For example, it is essential for the concept of a "cup" (as in a *teacup*) that a person can hold it in one hand. Cliff Goddard (1998) has made a similar point in relation to languages with classifier systems, which often distinguish long things (e.g. bananas) from round things (e.g. oranges) and from flat things (e.g. mats) and which also draw a distinction between rigid and flexible things.

As noted by Goddard, grammatical distinctions of this kind can be very plausibly linked with different ways for "handling" things, that is, doing things to them with one's hands (cf. also Denny 1976).

The idea that the concept of "hands" may be more fundamental in human thinking than that of "long" or "round" may at first seem implausible. But the fact is that the concept of "hands" can be explicated in functional terms, without any reference to shape, while the concepts "long" and "round" – like "shape" itself – do require a reference to hands. So here is an explication of "hands", couched exclusively in semantic primes (cf. Wierzbicka 2007):

[G] *hands*
> two parts of someone's body
> they are on two sides of the body
> these two parts of someone's body can move as this someone wants
> these two parts of someone's body have many parts
> if this someone wants it, all the parts on one side of one of these two parts can touch
>   all the parts on one side of the other at the same time
> because people's bodies have these two parts, people can do many things with many
>   things as they want
> because people's bodies have these two parts, people can touch many things as they want

Given that we do not need any shape-related concepts to explicate "hands", we can freely use "hands" to explicate concepts like those encoded in the English words *long* and *round*. Before presenting these explications, I must emphasise that these words are polysemous in English, and that, to begin with, the explication of *long* is not meant to apply to expressions like *a long time* or *a long way*. The expression *a long time* is semantically indivisible and has nothing to do with shape, and the expression *a long way* is a substitute for the semantically indivisible element FAR.

The polysemy of *long* which I want to discuss in this study is that between *long* as a shape word (roughly, elongated) and *long* as a word of dimension (e.g. 10cm long). *Long* as a shape word occurs in expressions like *something long* (that is, something long in shape) whereas *long* as a dimension word occurs in expressions like *a long tail* or *a long stick*.

The use of *long* in expressions like *a long tail* ($long_2$) is semantically related to the sense of *long* as in *something long* ($long_1$), but it is not identical with it. Roughly speaking, one sense of *long* has to do with shape, whereas the other has to do with dimensions. *Long* as a shape word ($long_1$) can be contrasted with *round*. It is comparable to concepts which play a role in languages with classifiers, where, for example, bananas may take a different classifier than oranges. On the other hand, *long* as a dimension word ($long_2$) has an opposite in the word *short*, and is related to other dimension words such as *wide* and *narrow*, *high* and *low*, and *deep* and *shallow*.

To appreciate the difference between *long* as a shape word ($long_1$) and *long* as a dimension word ($long_2$) it is helpful to pay attention to expressions like *something long*, *something round* and *something flat*, which categorise objects according to shape (e.g. a stick, an orange and a doormat). There are no corresponding expressions based on words for dimensions: **something short*, **something wide*, **something narrow*. In contrast to other dimension words, however, *long* can be used also as a shape word, and so it can also be used in expressions like *something long* or *a long part of the body*. For instance, in Example (1) one can say (a) and (c) but not (b) and (d):

(1) a. *There was something long in the basket.*
    b. **There was something short in the basket.*
    c. *A tail is a long part of the body (...)*
    d. **A nose is a short part of the body (...)*

Consider also words for body parts like *legs*, *arms*, and *fingers*. People's legs can be long or short, but they are always "long" in the sense of shape. Similarly, sticks can be long or short but even a short stick is "long" in shape.

According to my hypothesis, the reason is that a stick has two distinct parts – so called "ends" – which are not like any other parts because they are very far from one another. Relatively speaking, those two special parts are "a long way from one another" – where "a long way" is another way of saying "far". This relatively large distance between the two ends of a stick can be detected both with one's eyes and with one's hands. So here is the proposed explication:

[H] *long₁* (something long, e.g. a stick, a tail, a cucumber)
    when someone sees this thing this someone can think about it like this:
        "two parts of this thing are not like any other parts
         because one of these two parts is very far from the other"
    if someone's hands [M] touch this thing everywhere on all sides
    this someone can think about it in the same way

Having explicated the English word *long₁* (as a shape word) we are now in a position to solve one of the two puzzles with which we have started: The Polish conceptualisation of the visible and tangible world reflected in the word *podłużny* (or *podłużne*). One of the two rectangular boxes can be described in English as *long₁* because in proportion to the other parts, two parts of this box can be regarded as being "very far" from one another. At the same time, both these boxes can be described as *podłużne*, because in proportion to the other parts, two parts of each box can be regarded as being far from one another – not "very far" but "far".

This is, then, the difference between the two conceptualisations, one English and one Polish, that is that of *long₁* and that of *podłużne*: "very far" vs. simply "far". Everything that is "very far" can also be seen as "far", but not everything that is "far" can be seen as "very far". This explains why the Polish category of *podłużny* has a wider scope than the English category of *long₁*.

[I] *podłużny* (a tail, a cucumber, a rectangular box)
    when someone sees this thing this someone can think about it like this:
        "two parts of this thing are not like any other parts
         because one of these two parts is far from the other"
    if someone's hands [M] touch this thing everywhere on all sides
    this someone can think about it in the same way

It is interesting to note that despite the conceptual difference between *long₁* and *podłużny*, they can both be contrasted with 'round' (in Polish *okrągły*, a word equivalent in meaning to the English *round*). This curious fact can be accounted for once we have explicated 'round'. This can be done as follows:

[J] *round* (e.g. an orange)
    when someone sees this thing, this someone can think about it like this:
        "I can't say: 'some parts are not like some other parts
         because some parts are far from some other parts'"
    if someone's hands [M] can touch this thing everywhere on all sides
    this someone can think about it in the same way

As this explication shows, 'round' is as it were an opposite of both *long₁* and *podłużny*. Small wonder, then, that it can be contrasted with both.

Arguably, the same explication of *round* which has been posited here for spherical objects like oranges is also applicable to non-spherical ones, like "round tables" or "round boxes". Of course the shape of an orange is different from that of a round table or a round box, but this can be explained without positing any polysemy for *round*. The point is that if an object has a stable position and is thought of as having a "top" and a "bottom", the subcomponent "on all sides" can be interpreted by the speakers as applying only to the "lateral" sides. Thus the same conceptualisation spelled out in the explication can be applied by the speakers to objects which from an objective, physical point of view are quite different from one another.

It is interesting to note that in some languages, e.g. the West African language Ewe, concepts like "round" and "long" are expressed by means of ideophones, that is, "picture words" whose very form is perceived as iconically depicting their meaning; and that in speech such ideophones are regularly accompanied by gestures. For example, the Ewe word for "round", *nogoo*, is regularly accompanied by a gesture of both hands slightly rounded (with the fingers spread), moving in the air as if clasping a coconut on all sides. The word for "long", *legbee*, is accompanied by a gesture of the two hands moving apart, with each thumb touching the index, as if with an explicit reference to two ends of the object in question (Felix Ameka, pers. com). Such habitual use of gestures to accompany shape words highlights the role of hands in the human conceptualisation of shape.

It is worth noting that, directly or indirectly, all the shape concepts discussed here refer to the *parts* of the objects in question, and, more specifically, to the relationship between the parts – a relationship which can be discovered both by the eye and by the touching hand. In other words, shape is a matter of structure, a structure which is both visible and tangible.

Other physical properties, for example, texture, softness, smoothness and flexibility, are different from shape in some respects but similar in others. Apart from colour, which is purely visual, most other physical properties, too, involve the image of a hand touching something. For example, if a hand touches something "soft", this person can feel something in this part and as a result can think that the object touched "gives way", so that some of its parts move. If a hand touches something "smooth", and moves while touching it, the person can feel something in this part, and as a result can think that there are no tiny parts sticking out on the surface of the object. If the hand touches something hot, the person can feel something in this part because of this and as a result the person can think that it has been near fire.

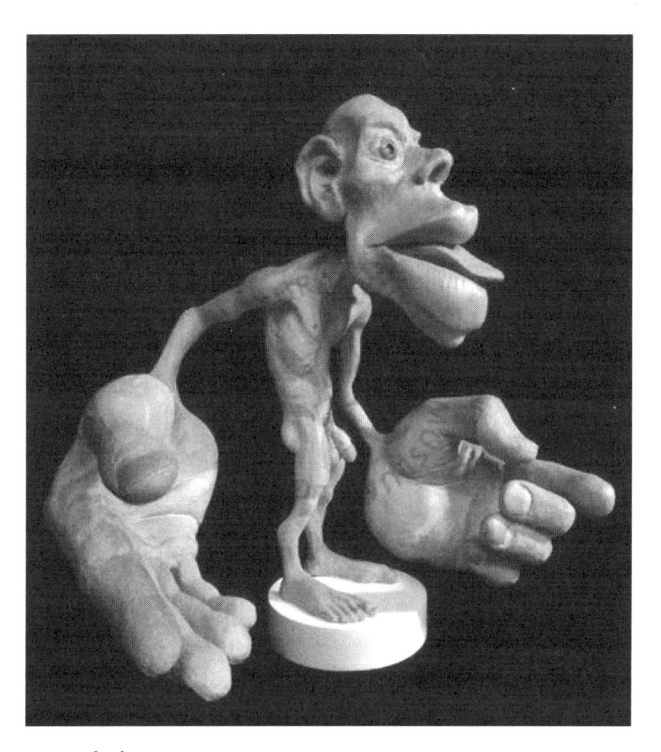

Chapter 3. Shape and colour in language and thought 51

Figure 1. 'Homunculus'

Thus, what might seem to be objective properties of the physical world are in fact often projections of tactile experiences onto the world of objects. The experience of "handling" things, of touching them with one's hands and moving the hands in an exploratory way plays a crucial role in making sense of the physical world. The metaphor of "grasping" in the sense of understanding is revealing in this respect: Human thinking is done, to a considerable extent, with the help of the hands. The use of the hands in counting and in arithmetical operations is only one example of this, though a particularly clear one. The reference to hands hidden in concepts like "long" and "round" is buried deeper under the surface of consciousness than that implicit in, for example, concepts like "smooth" and "rough", not to mention those like "handful" or "pinch" (*a pinch of salt*). But this very hiddenness of "hands" in some of our most basic everyday concepts – such as "long" and "round" – is a witness to its fundamental importance in human cognition: Human hands mediate, to a large extent, between the world and the human mind.

This importance of hands in the human conceptualisation of the world can be illustrated with two Figures. Figure 1 shows the "homunculus" with huge hands, the size of which shows just how much information the human brain is receiving from the hands (in proportion to other body parts). Figure 2 shows that the concept "hands" functions in human thinking as an important semantic molecule, which is actually included in the meaning of apparently simple words such as, for example, *long* and *round*. So "umbrella" includes the molecules "long" and "round", "long" and "round" include the molecule "hands", and the molecule "hands" is built directly out of universal semantic primes.

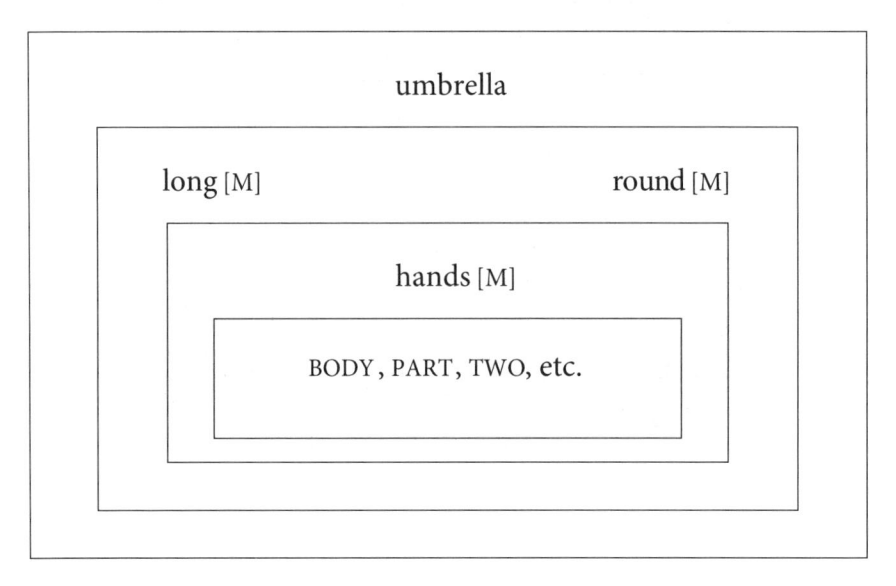

```
┌─────────────────────────────────────────────────────────┐
│                       umbrella                          │
│  ┌───────────────────────────────────────────────────┐  │
│   long [M]                              round [M]      │
│     ┌───────────────────────────────────────────┐      │
│                      hands [M]                         │
│        ┌───────────────────────────────────┐           │
│              BODY, PART, TWO, etc.                     │
│        └───────────────────────────────────┘           │
│     └───────────────────────────────────────────┘      │
│  └───────────────────────────────────────────────────┘  │
└─────────────────────────────────────────────────────────┘
```

Figure 2. Concept "hands" as important semantic molecule in human thinking

6   Shape vs. dimensions

As already mentioned, *long* as a shape word (*long₁*) has an opposite, of sorts, in *round*, whereas *long* as a dimension word (*long₂*) has its opposite in *short*. As discussed, *long₁* implies the perceived presence of two parts which are very far from one another – as compared with the distances between all the other parts of the same thing. *Long* as a dimension word also involves a comparison, but in this case, it is a comparison between different objects of the same kind. Thus, in one case, it is different parts of the same thing, in the other, different things of the same kind.

For example, the expression *a long stick* is implicitly comparing a particular stick with other sticks: While all sticks are "long in shape" (*long₁*), this particular stick is also long (*long₂*) in comparison with other sticks. Similarly, the expression *a short stick* is comparing a particular stick with other sticks: While all sticks, including this one, are "long in shape", in comparison with other sticks this par-

Chapter 3. Shape and colour in language and thought   53

ticular stick is short. Both in the case of *long* and in the case of *short*, what matters is the distance between the stick's two ends. In a short stick, one end is near the other end, in a long stick, one end is far from the other.

The concept of "two ends" sums up, as it were, the meaning of *long₁* and functions as a semantic molecule in the meaning of *long₂*, as well as in that of *short*:

[K]   *long₂* (e.g. a long stick)
   [people can think about this thing like this: "it has two ends [M]"]
   if someone thinks about other things of the same kind at the same time
   this someone can think about this thing (this stick) like this:
      "one end [M] is far from the other end [M]"

[L]   *short* (e.g. a short stick)
   [people can think about this thing like this: "it has two ends [M]"]
   if someone thinks about other things of the same kind at the same time
   this someone can think about this thing (this stick) like this:
      "one end [M] is near the other end"

Other dimension words can be explicated along similar lines. For example, the word *high* implies a considerable distance between the top and the bottom, whereas the word *low* implies the opposite.

[M]   *high* (e.g. a high tower; incomplete explication)
   [people can think about this thing like this: "it has a top [M] part, it has a bottom [M] part"]
   if someone thinks about other things of the same kind at the same time
   this someone can think about this thing (this tower) like this:
      "the top [M] part is far from the bottom [M] part"

[N]   *low* (e.g. a low tower; incomplete explication)
   [people can think about this thing like this: "it has a top [M] part, it has a bottom [M] part"]
   if someone thinks about other things of the same kind at the same time
   this someone can think about this thing (this tower) like this:
      "the top [M] part is near the bottom [M] part"

Although the semantics of *high* and *low* is not as simple as it looks (Wierzbicka 2005a), the complexities involved cannot be discussed here. For the present purposes we can say that all these explications are sound as far as they go. As signalled by the symbol "M", however, they all include some words which are not on the list of semantic primes. In the case of *high* and *low*, these words are *top* and *bottom*, and in the case of *long* and *short* – *ends*. For the explications of the dimension words to work, the semantic molecules in question have to be explicated, too. Simplifying things somewhat, this can be done as follows:

[O] *the top of something*
    a part of something
    people can think about this part like this:
        "this part is above all the other parts"

[P] *the bottom of something*
    a part of something
    people can think about this part like this:
        "this part is below all the other parts"

[Q] *the ends of something*
    two parts of something
    people can think about these two parts like this:
        "these two parts are not like any other parts
        because one of these two parts is very far from the other"
    at the same time they can think about one of these two parts like this:
        "on one side of this part there are many other parts of the same thing
        on the other there are no more parts of the same thing"
    they can think about the other one of these two parts in the same way
    people can't think about these two parts like this:
        "one of these two parts is above all the other parts"

The explication of *the ends* given here explains, inter alia, why an adult human being cannot be called *long* whereas a newborn baby can. The body of an adult is not thought of as having "two ends", because while the head of a tall person is indeed far from the feet the head is thought of as being, normally, above all the other parts of the body. On the other hand, newborn babies are thought of as lying rather than standing, so their bodies can be described as *long*: A baby's head is not conceptualised as being, usually, above the rest of the body.

As these explications show, dimension concepts are closely related to shape concepts, but they are more complex: Shape concepts are built directly out of semantic primes, whereas dimension concepts are based on semantic molecules. As we have seen, shape concepts themselves can function as semantic molecules, for example, in the meaning of words like *umbrella*. We have also seen that such molecules – for example *long₁* – are to some extent language-specific. The same applies to some molecules on which dimension concepts are based, (cf. e.g. Brotherson In press), but I can't demonstrate this within the confines of this study.

A complication which I have to mention in the present context is that *long* as a dimension word also has at least one other meaning, *long₃*, which is used in particular for describing some body parts. For example, a person's fingernails or a person's nose can be described as *long*, without being conceptualised as having "two ends", but rather as having a "beginning" and an "end". This can be explicated as follows:[2]

[R] *long₃ (e.g. a long nose)*
    people can think about this part of the body like this:
        "it has a beginning [M], it has an end [M]"
    if someone thinks about this part of other people's bodies at the same time
        this someone can think about it like this:
        "the end [M] is far from the beginning [M]"

The words *beginning* and *end* (in the relevant sense) can be explicated as follows:

[S] *the beginning of something*
    a part of something
    people can think about this part like this:
        "this part is not like many other parts
          because it is far from another part"
    at the same time they can think about it like this:
        "on one side of this part there are no other parts of the same thing
        on the other side there are many more parts of the same thing"

[T] *the end of something*
    a part of something
    people can think about this part like this:
        "this part is not like many other parts
          because it is far from another part"
    at the same time they can think about it like this:
        "on one side of this part there are many other parts of the same thing
        on the other side there are no more parts of the same thing"

In contrast to *long₂*, *long₃* does not preclude a vertical position. Thus, while an adult person cannot be described as "long", a person's hair or nose can be so described. Furthermore, the shape of something *long₃* doesn't have to be *long₁*: For example, someone's fingernails can be called "long" (*long₃*) even though their shape would not be described as "long" (*long₁*).

Roughly speaking, the concept encoded in *long₃* is as it were "unidirectional" – as if the observer's eyes were moving from one part ("the beginning") to another ("the end"). "The end" is as it were "the last part" – there are no more parts after that part; "the beginning", on the other hand, is as it were "the first part": There are

---

2. Although *long₃* is most common in combination with body parts it does occur in some other contexts as well (cf. for example expressions like *long-stemmed roses*, or sentences like *a long rope was hanging from the window*). The matter requires further investigation.

no other parts before it, but there can be many more parts after it. This "incremental", unidirectional character of *long*$_3$ links it with the concepts of "beginning" and "end" in a temporal sense, which can't be discussed in the confines of this study.

Finally, let me mention the use of *long* (*long*$_4$) in collocations like *a long shirt* or *long trousers*, which are similar to *long fingernails* or *long hair* but which apply to kinds of things rather than body parts, and also the use of *long* in the description of places, as in *a long road* or *a long river*. I will not discuss such collocations here any further, apart from saying that they, too, involve the notions of a "beginning" and an "end" rather than "two ends".

7   What the two Burarra terms mean and why they are not "colour" terms

Let us now return to the question of colour and to the puzzle with which we have started, that is, to the meaning of the two Burarra words *-gungaltja* and *-gungundja*. The referential range of these words has been described by Jones and Meehan (1978: 27) as follows:

> *-gungaltja*: refers to light, brilliant and white colours, and also to highly saturated red;
> *-gungundja*: refers to all other colours, namely dark, dull, and black colours.

Jones and Meehan keep using in relation to the words *-gungaltja* and *-gungundja* the word *colour*, but in fact their own observations show that the distinction is not based on colour at all. Rather, it is based on factors like brightness, lightness and visibility, or on what they themselves have called "brilliance and animation".

Berlin and Kay (1969) glossed words in a "two-term system" like that of Burarra as "white" and "black". In more recent work (cf. e.g. Kay et al. 1997), they replaced "white" and "black" with "white, red, and yellow" and "black", with "black, green, and blue". It is clear, however, that *-gungaltja* doesn't mean "white, red, and yellow". According to Jones and Meehan's key informant, Gurmanamana, the best example of this category is silver foil shining in the sun. Clearly, then, it is not a "colour" category at all, but a more global visual category, for which brilliance is at least as important as hue.

As I see it, to formulate a viable hypothesis about the meanings of the two Burarra terms we must identify a set of conceptual components which will account accurately for each word's range of use. At the same time, we need to look for a common factor linking the different components. Finally, we need to formulate the semantic components that we posit as constituting a given word's meaning in words which would be readily translatable into Burarra itself.

So here is a hypothesis, phrased first in colloquial English, and then, in an NSM explication: *-gungaltja* means, essentially, "eye-catching", and *-gungundja*, "not eye-catching". In addition, there is a triple prototype: fire, sun, and blood – all highly "eye-catching".

[U]   X is *-gungaltja* =
    some things are like this:
        when people see a place where these things are they can always see these things
    the sun [M] is always like this
    fire [M] is always like this
    at some times, blood [M] is like this
    X is like this

There is a great deal of evidence which I could adduce in support of this explication, and which I cannot discuss here (see Wierzbicka 2005b, 2006). Instead, I want to emphasise two points which I see as particularly important from a theoretical point of view. The first point is that an identical explication can be formulated in Burarra itself (the explication and the glosses are due to Margaret Carew and Lester Hiatt).[3] The second point is that this explication makes clear why *-gungaltja* is not a "colour term" at all. The fact that this explication could be phrased in Burarra itself makes it, in my view, a plausible hypothesis about how Burarra people themselves think about the visual world.

[V]   X is *-gungarlcha* =
   a. *gun-nerranga gun-anngiya gu-yinanga:*
      some *gun*-thing it-does like this:
      'some things are like this:'
   b. *jimarna gu-galiya yerrcha rrawa gu-nacha gun-narda gun-anngiya gu-ninyarra*
      suppose people place they see it (where) that thing mentioned earlier is
      gu-galiya yerrcha gu-nacha a-workiya gun-anngiya, gu-gata gun-anngiya
      people always see that thing
      'when people see a place where these things are they can always see these things'
   c. *marn.nga jiny-yinanga jinyi-ninyarra jiny-yorkiya*
      sun she always is like this
      'the sun [M] is always like this'
   d. *bol gu-yinanga gu-ninyarra gu-workiya*
      fire it always is like this
      'fire [M] is always like this'

---

3.   My consultants, Margaret Carew and Lester Hiatt, use different spelling conventions for Burarra words than those that were used by Jones and Meehan (e.g. *-gungaltja* and *-gungarlcha*). I have preserved these different spellings here.

e. *wolawola maningan mu-yinanga mu-ninyarra*
sometimes blood it is like this
'at some times, blood [M] is like this'

f. *gun-narda gu-yininga*
this thing does/is-thus
'X is like this'

The concept of "colour", which is so important in English and of course in many other languages, has no place in Burarra semantics. It is a concept which separates some aspects of people's visual experience (such as those associated with the term *hue*) from some others (such as those associated with the term *brightness*). But Burarra doesn't separate those two aspects. It has no word for "colour" and the question "what colour is it?" doesn't arise (it is never asked). Burarra speakers just don't think in those terms.

To show more clearly why the Burarra words are not colour words I will present an NSM explication of the word *colour* (for further discussion and justification, see Wierzbicka 2006):

[W] *colour*
one kind of thing
people can know things of many kinds about many things
this is one of these kinds
when someone sees something at a time when people can see things well
   this someone can know something of this kind about this thing because of this
if someone wants someone else to know the same kind of thing about it
   this someone can say something like this:
   "people can see something like this when they see something else
   I can say what"

As this explication predicts, usually colours can't be seen in the dark – generally speaking, they can only be seen at times when people can see things well. But things which are *-gungaltja* are conceptualised by Burarra speakers as similar to fire – which is its own source of light and which can be very well seen in the dark. Thus, *-gungaltja* does not dissociate colour from light; it means, above all, that something is visually conspicuous (like, for example, fire is).

People who habitually look at the world in terms of colours can find it difficult to believe that those from other cultures may have a profoundly different perspective on the visible world – for example, that they may habitually distinguish between things of high visibility (like sun, fire and blood) and those of low visibility, rather than things of different colours. The temptation to reject linguistic evidence and to go on assuming that everyone must have a concept of colour ("just like us"), even if they have no word for it, is natural and understandable. It is, however, a temptation that must be resisted. To quote Whorf once more:

> Western culture has made, through language, a provisional analysis of reality and, without correctives, holds resolutely to that analysis as final. The only correctives lie in all those other tongues which by aeons of independent evolution have arrived at different, but equally logical, provisional analyses. (Whorf 1956: 244)

If we want to explore the *human* mind and *human* cognition, rather than the *Anglo* mind and *Anglo* cognition, we need to take seriously evidence from diverse languages of the world.

As NSM researchers have tried to demonstrate for many years, the empirically discovered universal human concepts give us an effective tool with the help of which this evidence can be impartially analysed and reliably made sense of.

References

Berlin, Brent & Paul Kay. 1969. *Basic color terms: Their universality and evolution*. Berkeley, CA: University of California Press.
Brotherson, Anna. In press. The ethnogeometry of Makasai: A linguistic analysis. In Cliff Goddard (ed.), *Cross-linguistic semantics*. Amsterdam: John Benjamins.
Chomsky, Noam. 1987. Language in a psychological setting. *Sophia Linguistica* 22. 1–73.
Chomsky, Noam. 2000. *New horizons in the study of language and mind*. Cambridge: CUP.
Couturat, Louis. 1903. *Opuscules et fragments inédit de Leibniz*. Paris. Reprinted in 1961, Hildesheim: Georg Olms.
Denny, J. Peter. 1976. What are noun classifiers good for? *Chicago Linguistic Society* (CLS) 12. 122–132.
Goddard, Cliff. 1998. *Semantic analysis: A practical introduction*. Oxford: OUP.
Goddard, Cliff. In press. Natural semantic metalanguage: The state of the art. In Cliff Goddard (ed.), *Cross-linguistic semantics*. Amsterdam. John Benjamins.
Goddard, Cliff & Anna Wierzbicka (eds.). 2002. *Meaning and universal grammar: Theory and empirical findings*, Vols. 1 & 2. Amsterdam: John Benjamins.
Goddard, Cliff & Anna Wierzbicka. 2007. NSM analyses of the semantics of physical qualities: *Sweet, hot, hard, heavy, rough, sharp* in cross-linguistic perspective. *Studies in Language* 31(4).
Goddard, Cliff & Anna Wierzbicka. In press. Towards a semantic typology of physical activity verbs: 'cutting' and 'chopping' in English, Polish, and Japanese. *Language Sciences*.
Jackendoff, Ray. 1994. X-Bar semantics. In James Pustejovsky (ed.), *Semantics and the lexicon*, 15–26. Dordrecht: Kluwer.
Jackendoff, Ray. 2002. *Foundations of language: Brain, meaning, grammar, evolution*. Oxford: OUP.
Jones, Rhys & Betty Meehan. 1978. Anbarra concept of colour. In Lester R. Hiatt (ed.), *Australian Aboriginal concepts*, 20–29. Canberra: Australian Institute of Aboriginal Studies.

Kay, Paul, Brent Berlin, Luisa Maffi & William Merrifield. 1997. Color naming across languages. In Clyde L. Hardin & Luisa Maffi (eds.), *Color categories in thought and language*, 21–58. Cambridge: CUP.

Leibniz, Gottfried Wilhelm. 1996. *New essays on human understanding*. Translated & edited by Peter Remnant & Jonathon Bennett. Cambridge: CUP.

Locke, John. (1976 [1690]). *An essay concerning human understanding*. London: Everyman's Library.

Whorf, Benjamin Lee. 1956. *Language, thought and reality: Selected writings of Benjamin Lee Whorf*. Edited by John B. Carroll. New York, NY: Wiley.

Wierzbicka, Anna. 1985. *Lexicography and conceptual analysis*. Ann Arbor, MI: Karoma.

Wierzbicka, Anna. 1991. Semantic complexity: Conceptual primes and the principle of substitutability. *Theoretical Linguistics* 17. 75–97.

Wierzbicka, Anna. 1996. *Semantics: Primes and universals*. Oxford: OUP.

Wierzbicka, Anna. 2002. Semantic primes and universal grammar in Polish. In Goddard & Wierzbicka (eds.), 65–144.

Wierzbicka, Anna. 2005a. Shape in grammar revisited. *Studies in Language* 30(1). 115–117.

Wierzbicka, Anna. 2005b. There are no colour universals, but there are universals of visual semantics. *Anthropological Linguistics* 47(2). 217–244.

Wierzbicka, Anna. 2006. The semantics of colour: A new paradigm. In Carol Biggam & Christian Kay (eds.), *Progress in colour studies*, Vol. 1, 1–24. Amsterdam: John Benjamins.

Wierzbicka, Anna. 2007. Bodies and their parts: An NSM approach to semantic typology. *Language Sciences* 29. 14–65.

CHAPTER 4

Universal and language-specific aspects of "propositional attitudes"
Russian vs. English

Anna Gladkova

> ... the town's Russians would gather to parade, exchange gossip, court, borrow money and lecture each other, as only Russians can, about what was right and what was outrageously wrong with the world.
> Robert Dessaix (2004) *Twilight of Love. Travels with Turgenev.*

In the linguistic literature inspired by the philosophical tradition, it is often assumed that the key distinction in the area of "propositional attitude" is that between "know" and "believe". The Natural Semantic Metalanguage theory of language and thought argues that while KNOW is a universal conceptual prime, "believe" is not. It posits THINK, not "believe" as a universal counterpart of KNOW. The Moscow Semantic School posits primitives ZNAT' (KNOW) and SČITAT' (which has no exact English equivalent). This chapter argues that the use of "sčitat'" and "believe" as putative primes is unjustified. It supports THINK/DUMAT' as a universal conceptual prime and it shows that the use of this element as a prime leads to much better results than the use of "sčitat'".

1. Introduction

The question of "propositional attitude" is crucial to the semantic analysis of natural language. In the cognitive sciences there exists a tradition dating back to ancient times which distinguishes the concepts "knowledge" and "belief" as basic constituents of human cognition. Together with some principles of ancient philosophy, linguistics inherited and accepted this dichotomy as basic and universal. Yet how universal are these concepts? By universal here I mean concepts that are encoded in all languages and have the same meaning.

Contemporary methods of semantic analysis have shown that 'to know' is indeed semantically simple; it cannot be explicated further and can be found in a large number of unrelated languages (Goddard & Wierzbicka 1994, 2002; Wierzbicka 1996). However, 'to believe' is semantically complex and reflects important Anglo-Saxon values of personal autonomy and not imposing one's opinion on others, as was recently demonstrated by Anna Wierzbicka (2006). Therefore, when 'to believe' is used to describe universal tendencies of human cognition, it brings in Anglo cultural understandings which obscure the analysis. Nevertheless, 'to believe' is very frequently used by scholars of different disciplines as a basic unit in talking about cognitive processes. In fact, the salience of 'to believe' led Robert Solomon to call it "a catch-all term in cognitive science" (Solomon 2003: 7), which definitely casts doubt on its suitability as a reliable research tool.[1]

A similar situation exists in the Russian humanities, where scholars treat the word *sčitat'* (a verb that is presumed to be the equivalent of 'to believe') as basic in capturing human thinking. This study argues that, firstly, the meaning of *sčitat'* is complex and, therefore, it cannot be considered an elementary building block in cognitive analysis. Secondly, it demonstrates that *sčitat'* in Russian, like 'to believe' in English, reflects certain cultural norms and, hence, it is a language-biased tool of research.

These issues are addressed in the light of two semantic theories – the Natural Semantic Metalanguage (NSM), developed in Australia, and the Moscow School of Semantics (MSS) theory, developed in Russia. Both schools propose sets of semantic primitives – words which cannot be defined further and which can be used to explicate more complex notions. There exists disagreement between these schools regarding the choice of primitives in the cognitive domain, that is, the words 'to believe'/*sčitat'* and 'think'/*dumat'*. Resolving this controversy is an important theoretical and methodological task because it will answer the question of what words should be regarded as essential and basic in explicating other more complex concepts.

Before turning to the discussion of this matter, a brief comment is needed on the theoretical assumptions of the NSM and MSS approaches in order to explain the existing differences between them in the treatment of primitives relating to mental states.

---

1. I am thankful to Cliff Goddard for referring me to this quote.

2. Theories of the Natural Semantic Metalanguage and the Moscow School of Semantics compared

To begin with, both schools rely on the idea that description of linguistic meaning is possible with a metalanguage which has its own vocabulary and syntax. However, the metalanguages of the two schools are not fully identical. NSM authors claim that the metalanguage of semantic description should be "natural" or "seminatural" (that is use words and their possible combinations from natural languages) and "universal" (these constructions should be identical in meaning in all languages).[2] Development of the MSS theory of metalanguage started with the assumption that this should be a formal metalanguage with artificial syntax, which allowed its authors to claim that it was universal.[3] However, in more recent times, according to Jurij Apresjan, the MSS "metalanguage moves closer to the metalanguage of Anna Wierzbicka" (2000: 218) in terms of naturalness. MSS authors do not accept universality as a factor and believe that the language-specificity of a metalanguage cannot be avoided due to the cultural specificity of each language's world-view (Apresjan 2004a, 2005).

A major distinction between NSM and MSS lies in their different understandings of the status of a primitive and its role in semantic explications. NSM relies on the following assumption as a cornerstone of its theory:

> The elements which can be used to define the meaning of words (or any other meanings) cannot be defined themselves; rather, they must be accepted as 'indefinibilia', that is, as semantic primes, in terms of which all complex meanings can be coherently represented. (Wierzbicka 1996: 10)[4]

In-depth empirical research has allowed NSM scholars to distinguish about sixty-five indefinable concepts ("primitives") and confirm their existence in a large number of unrelated languages (Goddard & Wierzbicka 1994, 2002). These sixty-five primitives are used as constructive blocks in NSM semantic explications. The Moscow School of Semantics does not completely agree with the idea that any word can be treated as a "final atom of sense" and relies on the assumption that "semantic primitives are not in fact necessarily so extremely simple in their meaning and that, generally speaking, they do not possess the property of universality"

---

2. For a detailed discussion of the NSM theory see Goddard and Wierzbicka (1994, 2002); Wierzbicka (1996); Goddard (1998). More references are presented on the NSM homepage http://www.une.edu.au/lcl/nsm/index.php.

3. For a detailed discussion of the MSS theoretical assumptions see Apresjan (2000, 2005).

4. Within the NSM theory the terms "prime" and "primitive" are used interchangeably. This convention will be followed in this chapter.

(Apresjan 2000: 226). According to authors of this school, a "quasi-primitive" can comprise components that can be verbalized along with components that cannot be verbalized, which they call "quarks" (Apresjan 2000; Uryson 2002). Hence, semantic explications written within the MSS approach include semantic primitives along with meanings which are simpler than semantic primitives as well as lexical items which are more complex in meaning than semantic primitives (Apresjan 2004a, 2005).

The approaches of the two schools also differ in the treatment of the issue of the syntactic properties of semantic primitives. NSM presents its metalanguage as a natural language in miniature, which lies at the core of each language (Wierzbicka In press). It explores possible valency options of the established semantic primitives and tests their applicability in different languages. Thus, in NSM a concept is recognized as a semantic primitive if it meets the criterion of indefinability and has certain syntactic properties. MSS does not explore the factor of the possible valency options of semantic primitives – its metalanguage is "standardized" (Apresjan 2004a: 5), that is, it uses words in natural combinations which are close to those used in logical constructs.

This comparison has shown that, in spite of the similarities which unite these two approaches in opposition to other contemporary formal semantic theories, there exists a number of significant differences between them. However, both schools recognize that in doing semantic analysis one should rely on words from a natural language which are elementary in their meanings. If one can show that a concept cannot be defined further via other simpler concepts, it should be accepted as a semantic primitive. At the same time, if one can prove that a concept can be defined via other simpler concepts it should not be regarded as a semantic primitive.

In distinguishing primitives of mental predicates, both schools agree on the universality of KNOW/ZNAT', WANT/XOTET' and FEEL/ČUVSTVOVAT', but the controversy arises over the prime THINK and its possible equivalents in Russian – *dumat'* (which is translated into English as 'think') and *sčitat'* (which is usually translated into English as 'strongly believe'/'think').[5] The claim of the NSM theory is that THINK, within the boundaries of certain syntactic properties, is a universal semantic primitive. The MSS theory uses the propositional *sčitat'* within the frame *sčitat', čto* ('believe that') as a semantic primitive. However, *dumat'* is also used in semantic explications, because there are certain contexts in which *sčitat'* cannot be

---

5. Small capital letters are used for primitives in NSM in order to distinguish them from other usages of the word.

used (such as *dumat' o čem-to/kom-to* 'think about something/someone').[6] According to Apresjan, *sčitat'* and *dumat'* are close synonyms which can be distinguished only by means which are not verbalized in "natural" Russian and which are semantically simpler than semantic primitives (Apresjan 2001, 2005). Presumably, this hypothesis allows MSS followers to use both these words as semantic primitives.

The positing of *znat'* and *sčitat'* as semantic primitives by the MSS is grounded in the philosophical assumption of the universality of the opposition between *znanie* 'knowledge' and *mnenie* 'opinion' (cf. Zaliznjak 1991). This opposition may be rendered as 'knowledge' and 'belief' in English, but 'belief' is not the same as either the English 'opinion' or the Russian *mnenie*. *Mnenie* is a word which combines the notions of 'opinion', 'view' and 'position'. This difference in the representation of concepts, which are considered basic in the humanities, speaks volumes about their language-specificity. This is a perfect example of how the naturalization in linguistics of categories accepted in logic and philosophy can obscure and disguise linguistic analysis.

It might be objected that if the Russian *mnenie* does not mean the same as the English 'belief', then the translation of one by the other is erroneous, and that is all there is to it. Such an objection is based on two assumptions: First, that it is possible to find a better translation for each of these words, and second, that even if words like 'belief' and *mnenie* do not match in meaning, cognitive scientists and philosophers can continue using the word 'belief' anyway. However, by talking about human cognition in terms of untranslatable English words one is necessarily introducing an Anglo bias into the description. According to NSM, such a bias can be avoided even when one writes in English if one relies in one's analysis on English words which do match with semantic equivalents across language boundaries, such as KNOW and THINK.

This chapter will provide a semantic study of the words *dumat'* and *sčitat'*. This investigation is important for a number of reasons. Firstly, it will answer the question of which word should be used as a primitive in semantic explications in Russian. Secondly, it will give an insight into cross-linguistic variation in the categorization of the domain of mental states. Thirdly, it is important in terms of the description of cultural peculiarities of speech practices in different languages. In answering the question of whether a particular word can be regarded as a semantic primitive, this chapter will rely on the NSM assumption that for a positive answer two criteria for this word should be met: indefinability and the universality of its syntactic properties. For this purpose *sčitat'* and *dumat'* will be tested in the

---

6. For examples of the use of *sčitat'* and *dumat'* in semantic explications see Melčuk and Žolkovskij (1984), Apresjan (2004a, 2004b) and Padučeva (2004).

NSM canonical contexts proposed for the primitive THINK, and their semantic character – elementary or otherwise – will be assessed.[7]

3 *Dumat'* and *sčitat'* in the canonical contexts of the primitive THINK

To date, the following universal syntactic frames have been proposed for the semantic primitive THINK in the NSM theory (Goddard & Karlsson 2004; Goddard & Wierzbicka 2002):

[1] X thinks about someone/something

[2] X thinks something (good/bad) about someone/something

[3] X thinks: "– –"

[4] X thinks like this:

[5] X thinks in the same way

[6] X thinks that

In the following section the syntactic properties of *dumat'* and *sčitat'* will be tested in these contexts.

3.1 *Dumat'* as an exponent of the NSM prime THINK in Russian

Dumat' can be used in all the syntactic frames that have been proposed for THINK:

[1] X thinks about someone/something

[1a] *X dumaet o kom-to/čem-to*

[2] X thinks something (good/bad) about someone/something

[2a] *X dumaet čto-to (xorošee/ploxoe) o kom-to/čem-to*

Dumat' can also be used in "quasi-quotational" frames:

[3] X thinks: "– –"

[3a] *X dumaet: "– –"*

[4] X thinks like this:

---

7. This research is based on the data from *Nacional'nyj korpus russkogo jazyka* [National Corpus of the Russian Language]. Some ungrammatical examples were constructed by me and are marked with an asterix (*).

[4a]   *X dumaet tak:*

In frame [4a] the adverb *tak* is a portmanteau for the combination LIKE THIS. In this frame *dumat'* can introduce a flow of thought as in the following example from the *National Corpus of the Russian Language*:

(1) *On slušal pečal'nuju muzyku i dumal tak: neset ego, kak ščepku v more, a vot Puškin i Čajkovskij i ves' ėtot samyj Bol'šoj Teatr – oni vsegda na beregu.*
'He was listening to the sad music and thought (*dumat'*.3SG.PAST) like this: He was being carried away like a chip of wood out to sea, and Pushkin and Tchaikovsky and this Bolshoi Theatre – they were always on the shore.'

The construction capturing a similar way of thinking is also possible with *dumat'*:

[5]   X thinks in the same way

[5a]   *X dumaet takže*

In this frame the adverb *takže* is a portmanteau for the combination IN THE SAME WAY.

The compatibility of *dumat'* with propositional clauses introduced by *čto* 'that' fits well the restriction on the universality of the combination THINK THAT which was recently described by Goddard and Karlsson (2004). Goddard (2003a: 229) notes:

> that-complements are universally possible if they are anchored in a concrete temporal frame such that they depict an 'occurent thought'; for example, in contexts like I NOW THINK THAT – –

This conclusion is based on evidence from Swedish and other Scandinavian languages, which have several basic-level "verbs of thinking". Unlike other propositional verbs in Russian, *dumat'* is compatible with time markers indicating a momentary thought like *inogda* 'sometimes'/'now and then', *v ėtot moment* 'at that moment', *togda* 'at that moment', for example:

(2) *Inogda ja dumaju, čto mne stoilo stat' medikom.*
'At times I think (*dumat'*.1SG.PRES) that I should have become a doctor.'

(3) *Inogda ja dumaju, čto kulinary poxoži na alximikov.*
'At times I think (*dumat'*.1SG.PRES) that cooks are like alchemists.'

(4) *O sebe Astra v ėtot moment dumala v prevosxodnoj stepeni.*
'At that moment Astra thought (*dumat'*.3SG.PAST) about herself in the superlative degree.'

Thus, the Russian verb *dumat'* fits all the possible NSM canonical contexts associated with THINK. I will now discuss the possibility of using *sčitat'* in these frames.

3.2 *Sčitat'* as a possible exponent of the NSM prime THINK in Russian

In terms of its valency options, *sčitat'* is less diverse than *dumat'*. I will begin by commenting on context [6], that is, the frame involving the sentential *that*-complement, which is the most common and natural environment for *sčitat'*:

[6] X thinks that

[6b] X sčitaet čto

The following examples are taken from the *National Corpus of the Russian Language*:

(5) *Ja sčitaju, čto tak byt' ne dolžno.*
'I think (*sčitat'*.1SG.PRES) that it should not be like this.'

(6) *Aleksandr Benua sčital, čto pervopričina vsex nesčastij, svalivšixsja na gorod v dvadcatom veke, – otkaz ot imeni.*
'Alexander Benois believed (*sčitat'*.3SG.PAST) that the root of all misfortunes that befell the city [St. Petersburg] in the twentieth century was the denial of its name.'

This syntactic construction has some peculiarities of use in terms of its combinability with time markers. Since *sčitat'* introduces an opinion which has taken time to develop, it is not possible to combine it with time markers of momentary thought like *inogda* 'sometimes', *v ètot moment* 'at that moment' as in the following sentence:

(7) **Inogda ja sčitaju, čto on čestnyj čelovek.*
'Sometimes I think (*sčitat'*.3SG.PRES) that he is an honest person.'

It is possible, though, in sentences expressing a belief that a person or people held at a particular period of time in the past, as in the following example:

(8) *Togda sledovateli sčitali, čto Berezovskij zamešan v maxinacijax s den'gami "Aèroflota".*
'Then investigators believed (*sčitat'*.3PL.PAST) that Berezovsky was involved in machinations with the "Aeroflot" money.'

This context is not a true canonical context for THINK THAT because this kind of use of *sčitat'* in the past tense with a time marker implies the presence of the semantic component 'at that time for some time X thought that'. However according to Goddard and Karlsson (2004), only the expression of an "occurent thought" can be regarded as a canonical context for THINK within the frame THINK THAT. *Sčitat'* would be inappropriate in the following context, which requires a mental verb of a "momentary thought" and which is a true canonical context for THINK THAT:

(9) *Kogda v dver' postučali, ja *sčital, čto ėto ty.*
    'When someone knocked on my door, I thought it was you.'

Thus, the use of *sčitat'* with the *čto-* (that-) complement does not meet the restrictions of compatibility with time markers expressing an "occurent thought" which are characteristic of the canonical context for THINK THAT.

Sčitat' has some limitations of use in the quasi-quotational frame:

[4] X thinks like this:

[4b] *X sčitaet tak:*

The data from the Corpus suggest that combination [4] is possible for *sčitat'* as in the following example:

(10) *Čestno govorja, sčitaju tak: den' prošel, ničego neprijatnogo ne proizošlo – vot i xorošo.*
    'Frankly speaking, I think (*sčitat'*.1SG.PRES) like this: it is good if a day has passed and nothing unpleasant happened.'

However, it would be grammatically incorrect to use *sčitat'* in a context which introduces a "flow" of thought and implies 'thinking all the time for some time' as in Example (1) (recast here as (1a)):

(1a) *On slušal pečal'nuju muzyku i *sčital tak: neset ego, kak ščepku v more, a vot Puškin i Čajkovskij i ves' ėtot samyj Bol'šoj Teatr – oni vsegda na beregu.*
    'He was listening to the sad music and thought (**sčitat'*) like this: he was being carried away like a chip of wood out to sea, and Pushkin and Tchaikovsky and this Bolshoi Theatre – they were always on the shore.'

This example illustrates the fact that while *dumat'* can be used to record a mental process which lasts for some period of time, *sčitat'* cannot be used in such a way because it only introduces a result of thinking.

The contexts in which *sčitat'* is fully satisfactory from an NSM point of view are the expression of an analogous opinion and a quote:

[5] X thinks in the same way

[5b] *X sčitaet takže*

[3] X thinks: "– –"

[3b]   X sčitaet: "– –"

Examples from the Corpus illustrate this point:

(11)   *I bol'šinstvo moix sosluživcev sčitajut takže.*
'And the majority of my colleagues think (*sčitat'*.3PL.PRES) in the same way.'

(12)   *Peterburg – očen' privlekatel'nyj gorod dlja terroristov, – sčitajut čekisty.*
'St. Petersburg is a very attractive city for terrorists, – security officers think (*sčitat'*.3PL.PRES).'

(13)   *Ravnodušnym nečego delat' v ėtoj professii, – sčitaet veteran, č'ja tvorčeskaja žizn' načalas' v stalinskoe vremja s kritičeskoj publikacii.*
'Indifferent people have nothing to do in this profession, – thinks (*sčitat'*.3SG.PRES) a veteran, whose creative life began with a critical publication during Stalin's time.'

The major blow against *sčitat'* as a possible semantic prime is the existence of the following two canonical combinations in which the use of *sčitat'* is impossible:

[1]   X thinks about someone/something

[1b]   *X sčitaet o kom-to/čem-to

[2]   X thinks something (good/bad) about someone/something

[2b]   *X sčitaet čto-to (xorošee/ploxoe) o kom-to/čem-to

In summary, the analysis has shown that *dumat'*, due to its syntactic properties, can be regarded as a better candidate for a universal semantic prime than *sčitat'*. I will now turn to the semantic analysis of *sčitat'*.

4   The semantics of *sčitat'*

In this section I will argue that *sčitat'* is semantically more complex than *dumat'* and can be explicated via *dumat'*. My hypothesis, consistent with the NSM theory, is that *dumat'* cannot be explained via *sčitat'*, whereas *sčitat'* can be explained via *dumat'* because it has a more complex meaning.

The first semantic difference between the two verbs is that *sčitat'*, unlike *dumat'*, introduces an opinion which requires time to arrive at. It would be unnatural to use this verb in contexts presenting involuntary and casual ideas which do not need time and effort to elaborate. To illustrate this point I am referring in a slightly paraphrased form to an example quoted by Jurij Apresjan. This sentence can be used in a situation when someone is asked to feel the water in a bathtub and say how warm it is. In this context one can reply using the verb *dumat'* (Apresjan 2004b: 1129):

(14) *Ja dumaju, čto gradusov tridcat' pjat'.*
?*Ja sčitaju, čto gradusov tridcat' pjat'.*
'I think that it is thirty five degrees.'

It would be unnatural to use *sčitat'* in such a context because one needs some time to develop an opinion introduced by *sčitat'*.

Secondly, the time factor goes hand in hand with the issue of complexity of thought: *Sčitat'* introduces a 'considered opinion' which is based on a person's world view (that is, things that a person has thought about before). *Sčitat'* is appropriate when a person spends some time reflecting upon a particular matter and matching it against his/her system of beliefs. In a situation such as reporting the temperature of water in a bathtub one does not need to perform a complex mental action to give an opinion, that is why *dumat'* is more suitable then. *Sčitat'* can be used to speak about things that a person has invested a certain amount of time and effort to think about, relying on his/her system of beliefs. As the previously quoted examples (6, 8 & 10–13) show, *sčitat'* is used with complements expressing a complex thought.

Another important difference between the two verbs is that *sčitat'* introduces an opinion which is developed due to the person's will (cf. Apresjan 2004b; Melčuk & Žolkovskij 1984). When *sčitat'* is used, it means that the person decided to think in this way. An involuntary idea would not be introduced by *sčitat*, but only by *dumat'*. Linguistic evidence supporting this point can be found in the possibility of the compatibility of *dumat'* with the reflexive form of the verb *xotet' – xotet'sja –* in a dative construction and the impossibility of this structure for *sčitat'*:

(15) *Mne vsegda xotelos' dumat', čto delo, kotorym ja zanimajus', nazyvaetsja žurnalistikoj i trebuet ot professionala umenija videt' i pisat' ob uvidennom.*
'I (me.DAT) have always wanted (want.REF.PAST) to think (*dumat'*.INF) that my occupation is called journalism and it requires from a professional the ability to see and write about what one has seen.'

Sčitat' cannot be used in such a context:

(16) *Mne vsegda xotelos' *sčitat', čto delo, kotorym ja zanimajus', nazyvaetsja žurnalistikoj …*

According to Wierzbicka, this kind of dative construction is revealing of the Russian culture: It presents a desire for something as involuntary and inexplicable, denies responsibility and emphasizes spontaneity (Wierzbicka 1992). *Dumat'* is suitable for this context as well as other verbs like *spat'* 'sleep', *est'* 'eat', *pet'* 'sing', etc. This fact suggests that a thought expressed by *dumat'* can be involuntary and spontaneous. The same does not apply to the kind of thought expressed by *sčitat'*, that is why it does not occur in the dative construction. It means that *sčitat'* is devoid of the component of involuntary action and presents a conscious effort to develop an opinion.

Another example showing that *sčitat'* is used to introduce an opinion which depends on a person's willingness to think in a certain way, can be found in a contextual use of *sčitat'*. In a passage from the novel by Leo Tolstoy, *Anna Karenina*, Anna is requesting her friend for an opinion about her complex family situation in which she might appear in a negative light (Tolstoy 1953: 666–667):

(17) – *Čto že ty sčitaeš' o moem položenii, čto ty dumaeš', čto? - sprosila ona.*
 – *Ja polagaju … načala Dar'ja Aleksandrovna […]*
 – *Ja ničego ne sčitaju, - skazala ona, - a vsegda ljubila tebja, a esli ljubiš', to ljubiš' vsego čeloveka, kakoj on est', a ne kakim ja xoču, čtob on byl.*
 – 'So what do you think (*sčitat'*) about my situation, what do you think (*dumat'*) – she asked.'
 – 'I suppose … – Dar'ja Aleksandrovna started […]'
 – 'I don't think (*sčitat'*) anything – she said, - but I have always loved you; and if one loves anyone, one loves the whole person the way he is and not as one would like him to be.'

When asking for an opinion, Anna uses the word *sčitat'*. Her friend does not really want to speak about this situation and tells her that she thinks (*sčitat'*) nothing, explaining it by the fact that she loves her the way she is and finds it inappropriate to develop a judgmental opinion about her. The avoidance of use of the word *sčitat'* in this situation – *Ja ničego ne sčitaju* ('I don't think anything') – signals that in order to *sčitat'* one needs to want to do so. When the will is not there, *sčitat'* cannot be regarded as the right word to introduce an opinion.

The next difference to consider in the comparison of the two verbs is that *sčitat'* expresses a person's very assured, confident and grounded position because it is a result of a careful consideration of the situation. It does not collocate with phrases such as *ja ne uveren* 'I am not sure' or *ja mogu ošibat'sja* 'I may be wrong': **Ja sčitaju …, no ja ne uveren* 'I believe, but I am not sure', while *dumat'* is compatible with both of these phrases.

(18) **Ja sčitaju, čto on podlec, no ja ne uveren.*
 'I believe [*sčitat'*] that he is a rascal, but I am not sure.'

(19) **Ja sčitaju, čto ona krasiva, no ja mogu ošibat'sja.*
 'I believe [*sčitat'*] that she is beautiful, but I could be mistaken.'

Sčitat' expresses a very firm and assured point of view which a person decided to stick to at a certain moment and does not want to change. I agree with Anna Zaliznjak, who characterizes the opinion expressed by *sčitat'* as very stable because it is "characteristic of a personality" (Zaliznjak 1991: 191). It would be unnatural to use *sčitat'* in situations when a person is unsure or might change his or her mind. To support this point the incompatibility of *sčitat'* with momentary time markers signaling a transient idea can be quoted again. In Example (2), rephrased here as (2a), a person says that at times he thinks he should have become a doctor. This idea comes and goes, it is not a permanent belief of the person. Thus, *sčitat'* is not appropriate in this context:

(2a) **Inogda ja sčitaju, čto mne stoilo stat' medikom.*
 'At times I think that I should have become a doctor.'

Another illustration of this point in which *sčitat'* differs from *dumat'*, can be found in the fact that *dumat'* can express supposition as in the following examples:

(20) *Ja dumaju, čto menja segodnja ub'jut.*
 'I think (*dumat'*) that I will be killed today.'

(21) *Ja dumaju, čto on doma.*
 'I think (*dumat'*) that he is at home.'

Sčitat' would be impossible in such contexts because one cannot suppose and be firm about one's position at the same time.

As I have already shown, to introduce an opinion by *sčitat'* one needs willingly to spend some time and effort thinking about something and arrive at a certain way of thinking about it. The opinion introduced by *sčitat'* is a kind of thought that a person regards as a good one and might base his/her actions on. Certain contexts with *sčitat'* are evidence of this. When used in the past tense it can introduce a point of view that proved to be mistaken, but which a person used as a basis for action, believing at the moment of the action, that it was right. The following example from the Corpus illustrates such a case:

(22) *Èto byl tajnyj brak. Ja sčital, čto moe togdašnee otnošenie k podruge – èto i est' istinnaja ljubov', a poskol'ku temperamenta u menja bylo xot' otbavljaj, to rešil, čto nam nado nepremenno ženit'sja.*
 It was a secret marriage. I thought (*sčitat'*.3SG.PAST) that my feeling for my girlfriend then was real love, and since I had more than enough of temperament, I decided that we had to get married.

In this example the character realizes that the belief he had at a certain time in the past (that his feeling was real love) was wrong, though he based some actions on it (secretly got married).

Another usage specific to *sčitat'* occurs in constructions such as *budem sčitat', čto* ... and *davajte sčitat', čto* ... ('let's *sčitat'* that'), which relate to an idea that becomes a foundation for action (and is thus considered a good idea). These kinds of constructions indicate an agreement about a certain condition that people accept in order to continue further action. The following example can be quoted:

(23) *Esli govorit' ob ètom ne xočetsja, budem sčitat', čto voprosa ne bylo.*
If you don't want to talk about it, let's think (*sčitat'*) that there was no question.

In this example the people involved decide to agree in thinking that something did not happen between them (the question was not asked). They accept a certain proposition as a true or good one, knowing that it is not true. It justifies the inclusion of the semantic component 'I think it is good to think like this' in the meaning of *sčitat'* (see explication A below).

To summarize the essence of the semantics of *sčitat'* I will quote Jurij Apresjan on the character of thinking involved in *sčitat'*.

> ... serious conditions are required to develop an opinion (that which we *sčitaem* 'consider'). An opinion is usually the result of a fairly long and thorough process of consideration of all observable facts (note the original idea of *sčet* 'counting' which is present in *sčitat'*), weighing up other possible interpretations of them and selecting [by an act of will] the interpretation which best accords with the accumulated personal experience of the subject and which he is prepared to uphold as correct.[8]
> ... Generally speaking, the more complex a situation is, the greater the number of possible interpretations, and the harder it is to establish the truth, the more justification there is for the use of *sčitat'*. And the simpler, the more obvious and trivial it is, the greater the justification for using *dumat'*. (Apresjan 2000: 149)

Thus, *sčitat'* introduces the result of a thinking process which was voluntary, and involves the consideration of facts and weighing them against the world view or system of beliefs of a person.

It is interesting to consider the semantics of *sčitat'* in the light of its etymology. It derives from the homonymous word *sčitat'*, which means 'count' as in 'count money'.[9] When counting some things we see them clearly, we are in control and can provide an unambiguous answer. This link gives at least two insights into the

---

8. In the square brackets a more accurate variant of translation is given.
9. The etymological link between words of 'thinking' and 'counting' can be found in some other languages as well (Fortescue 2001: 29).

semantic character of *sčitat'* as a mental state verb. On the one hand, it explains that *sčitat'* is a word presenting a considered opinion, which is the result of a relatively long and careful assessment of the available facts. On the other hand, it shows that *sčitat'* also introduces a decided opinion on something, free of doubt. The unambiguity of counting is embedded in *sčitat'* as a verb of "propositional attitude": It presents a single way of interpreting the matter and does not ask for, or make reference to, other options or opinions.

Thus, *sčitat'* introduces the result of a thinking process which was voluntary, and involved the consideration of facts and weighing them against a person's world view or system of beliefs. In the light of all these considerations I propose the following explication for the verb *sčitat'*:

[A] *Ja sčitaju, čto [ty postupil pravil'no]*
(I think/believe that [you did the right thing])
  a. when I think about it I think that [– –]
  b. I have thought about it for some time
  c. I have thought about things like this before
  d. I think that it is good to think like this
  e. I want to think like this
  f. I know why I want to think like this
  g. I don't want to think about it in any other way

This explication shows that *sčitat'* implies a certain way of thinking about the matter (component a), which relies on thinking about it for some period of time (component b) and the general world view of the person (component c); this allows the person to think that it is a good way of thinking (component d). Component (e) shows that it is a voluntary position and the person knows the reasons for thinking in this way (component f). It is the ultimate position of the person, which s/he does not want to change (component g).

This explication can be easily done in Russian as well, which shows that *sčitat'* can be explicated via *dumat'*:

[B] *Ja sčitaju, čto [ty postupil pravil'no]*
(I think/believe that [you did the right thing])
  a. *kogda ja ob ètom dumaju, ja dumaju, čto [---]*
  b. *ja dumal ob ètom nekotoroe vremja*
  c. *ja dumal o takix veščax ran'še*
  d. *ja dumaju, čto tak dumat' xorošo*
  e. *ja xoču tak dumat'*
  f. *ja znaju, počemu ja xoču tak dumat'*
  g. *ja ne xoču dumat' ob ètom po-drugomu*

The suggested analysis shows that *sčitat'* includes several semantic components (combinations of the primes THINK, WANT, KNOW, GOOD, SOME TIME, BEFORE and others), components that cannot be used to explicate the meaning of *dumat'*. It would be impossible to explicate *dumat'* via *sčitat'* since it is impossible to explicate a more simple term via a more complex one. The evidence presented here shows that *sčitat'* is semantically more complex than *dumat'* and thus cannot be regarded as a semantic primitive.

Bearing the complex semantic character of *sčitat'* in mind, let us consider an explication proposed by the Moscow School of Semantics which uses *sčitat'* as a semantic primitive. In the definition of the verb *stydit'sja* (close in meaning to 'be ashamed' in English) two verbs of mental states are used – *sčitat'* and *dumat'* (Apresjan 2004c: 1122, emphasis added):

> *stydit'sja* ('to be ashamed') =
> ispytyvat' čuvstvo, kakoe byvaet, kogda sub"ekt **sčitaet**, čto imeet otnošenie k čemu-to ploxomu ili otklonjajuščemusja ot normy, iz-za čego drugie ljudi budut xuže o nem **dumat'**
> 'to experience a feeling which happens when a person believes [*sčitat'*] that s/he is related to something bad or divergent from the norm, which can make other people think [*dumat'*] worse about him/her.'

I will argue that it is not really necessary to use both *sčitat'* and *dumat'* in this definition. *Stydit'sja* is indeed a feeling which is caused by a certain way of thinking, but does this way of thinking have to be introduced by *sčitat'*? As has been shown in the semantic analysis conducted in this study, *sčitat'* is a verb associated with a strongly-held and voluntarily developed opinion which took time to arrive at, usually refers to complex matters and which is expressed very explicitly. In this definition the use of *sčitat'* is at least pragmatically unjustified. When one *stydit'sja* 'is ashamed' one does not really *want* to think that his or her behaviour is bad or divergent from the norm (as *sčitat'* would imply). On the contrary, when someone *stydit'sja* one would rather want *not* to confess that s/he is related to something bad or divergent from the norm. Moreover, it is an idea one would not like to stick with, which *sčitat'* implies. Without discussing the rest of the definition, it can be said that the use of *sčitat'* can be avoided here and *dumat'* substituted without changing the representation of meaning of *stydit'sja* incorporated in the explication.

5 *Sčitat'* in a broader linguistic and cultural context

Along with the factors of semantic structure and syntactic properties, it is interesting to consider issues of the morphological productivity, place in the language system, frequency of occurrence and cultural specificity of the words *dumat'* and *sčitat'*.

Indeed, *dumat'* and *sčitat'* are the most commonly used epistemic verbs in Russian. The whole range of mental state verbs in Russian is much less diverse than in English (for example, cf. Wierzbicka 2006). Among the existing epistemic verbs *sčitat'* and *dumat'* significantly outstrip other verbs in frequency, which indicates their importance as words for expressing opinions in Russian (see Table 1).

Table 1. Frequencies of occurrences of propositional *sčitat'* 'believe', *dumat'* 'think', *predpolagat'* 'suppose', *polagat'* 'guess', *predstavljat'* 'imagine' and *naxodit'* 'find' from the National Corpus of the Russian Language (per 1 million words)

dumat', čto	'think that'	228
sčitat', čto	'believe that'	114
predpolagat', čto	'guess that'	57
polagat', čto	'suppose that'	28
predstavljat', čto	'imagine that'	28
naxodit', čto	'find that'	6

However, the relatively high frequency of *sčitat'* is a phenomenon of contemporary Russian and is significant of present day cultural beliefs and attitudes. *Sčitat'* as a verb of propositional attitude became common in Russian only in the second half of the 19th century when it replaced a number of other verbs of thinking (*počitat'* 'consider', *myslit'* 'think', *mnit'* 'think'/'imagine') (Apresjan 2004b). For example, not a single case of *sčitat'* with a *čto-* (that-) complement can be found in Pushkin's works: He used *sčitat'* only in Accusative-Instrumental constructions. By contrast, *dumat'* remained a "basic" verb of thinking in Russian throughout ten centuries of its history, as shown in historical studies by Makeeva (2003). The existence of *dumat'* in the language for such a long time may be a factor which has contributed to the salience of *dumat'* as a basic verb of mental states.

Another factor that makes it possible to regard *dumat'* as a more basic word of thinking is its morphological productivity. *Dumat'* is a versatile word and it outstrips *sčitat'* in terms of morphological productivity. It can reflect various kinds and stages of thought: *podumat'* 'think of briefly', *pridumat'* 'think out'/'invent', *zadumat'* 'conceive'/'plan', *obdumat'* 'think over', *vzdumat'* 'take something into one's head', *zadumat'sja* 'begin to think', *prizadumat'sja* 'become thoughtful'/'hesitate'. *Sčitat'* is not morphologically productive, which indicates that its meaning is not simple enough to be a part of other meanings.

It is an interesting fact that *sčitat'* – a word regarded by a number of scholars as most basic among mental state words – is unique to the Russian language and is revealing of a way of thought specific to the Russian culture. Actually, none of the English epistemic verbs expresses such a strong degree of assurance as *sčitat'* does. To help show the cultural specificity of *sčitat'*, it can be contrasted with *to believe* in English. I will compare the meaning of *sčitat'* with the meaning of *to believe*, relying on the explication by Anna Wierzbicka (2006). According to Wierzbicka, "the epistemic phrase *I believe* (without the complementizer *that*) has to be distinguished from the phrase *I believe that*" (2006: 213). I quote below her explications for both these English phrases, but I will compare *ja sčitaju, čto* with the meaning of *I believe that* (explication D) because they occur in the same syntactic structure and hence should be closer in meaning (Wierzbicka 2006: 215, 218).

[C] *I believe ... (e.g. I believe you can get it in a tin)*
  a. I say: I think now that it is like this: you can get it in a tin
  b. I don't say I know
  c. I can say why I think like this
  d. I know that someone else can think not like this

[D] *I believe that there is a real need ...*
  a. When I think about it, I think that there is a real need
  b. I know that someone else can think not like this
  c. I can say why I think like this
  d. I think that it is good if someone thinks like this

If *sčitat'* (explication A) is compared with 'to believe that' (explication D), the first difference that can strike one most is how egocentric *sčitat'* is. There is no consideration of the position of other people (component b in *I believe that*); the process of thinking associated with *sčitat'* arrives at a position which is good for the person involved and is not related to the position of others (component d in *sčitat'* vs. component d in *I believe that*). *I believe that* is more "open" in the sense that it has the component 'I can say why I think like this' as if a person is expecting to be asked to justify his/her belief. *Sčitat'* involves a stronger grounding of one's position – 'I know why' (component f), but contains no sign of sharing it with other people. *Sčitat'* also embodies a more 'innate' and well thought over position (components b and c which are absent in *I believe that*). It is intensified by the 'will' component (e), which is not present in *I believe that*. *Sčitat'* also expresses the ultimate position of a person, which s/he does not want to change (component g).

More evidence for *sčitat'* being a word expressing opinion in a more 'assured' and firm way than *I believe that*, can be found in differences between the combinatorial properties of the two words. One case is when *sčitat'* can be used in phrases such as *davajte sčitat'*, *budem sčitat'* (let's *sčitat'*) to express a suggestion to agree upon some condition which might not be true but which the interlocutors decide to accept as true and use as a foundation for further action (see Example 23). As was stated earlier in this work, this use means that *sčitat'* introduces an idea which can be considered a foundation for further action even if the interlocuters know that it is not a true idea. In other words, when *sčitat'* is used it has a claim for introducing an ultimate truth. In this respect *sčitat'* is different from *I believe that* which introduces an opinion in a tentative way and acknowledges the possibility of other ways of thinking. This difference in meaning supports component (d) in *sčitat'* – 'I think that it is good to think like this'. This semantic component shows that the opinion introduced by *sčitat'* can be regarded as "good" in order to rely on it in undertaking further action. The impossibility of combining *I believe that* with *let's* can be explained by the presence of the components (b) and (d) in the semantic structure of *I believe that*: 'I know that someone else can think not like this' and 'I think that it is good if someone thinks like this'. The "goodness" component in *I believe that* has no claim for universality and is stated in a very relativistic way. It extends the claim of the speaker that other people can think differently about the same matter.

Another semantic feature that makes *sčitat'* different from *I believe that* is the impossibility of its usage with intensifiers. While it is possible in English to say 'I strongly/firmly believe that …', *sčitat'* cannot be used with any of the words that can intensify opinions in Russian – *gluboko* 'deeply', *sil'no* 'strongly' or *tverdo* 'firmly':

(25) I strongly/firmly believe that …
 * *Ja gluboko sčitaju, čto …*
 * *Ja sil'no sčitaju, čto …*

This fact can be interpreted in the following way. The verb *sčitat'* expresses a level of "opinion" or "belief" which cannot be extended further. The presence of component (d) – 'I don't want to think about it in any other way' – reflects the impossibility of the compatibility of *sčitat'* with intensifiers. This component makes *sčitat'* a much more assured verb than *I believe that*. It again excludes any consideration for the position of other people, such as incorporated in *I believe that*.

The direct way of expressing one's opinion embedded in the verb *sčitat'* can be related to the general tendency of being "direct" and "forceful" in speaking one's mind which is characteristic of the Russian language. A direct way of telling what one thinks is a quite common conversational feature in Russian (Proxorov & Sternin 2005). A somewhat similar observation was made by Svetlana Boym that "Russia is a country, where nobody observes small-talk conventions" (Boym 1994: 215). This tendency can be explained by the importance of the concepts of *pravda* and *istina* in the Russian language and culture. Both of these words are translated into English as 'truth', yet this does not distinguish the difference in meaning between the two words. As Anna Wierzbicka has shown, *pravda* and *istina* are important cultural words in Russian related to the existence of a conversational routine valuing people's 'telling the truth' (*govorit' pravdu*) (Wierzbicka 2002). This means that in some situations when English speakers, for example, would be very cautious about the expression of their opinion and emotions in order not to hurt the feelings of another person, Russians might prefer to say openly what they think. The value of 'telling the truth' explains the "directness" of Russian speech as it might be evaluated by English norms. Speakers of Russian tend to make their speech direct and powerful because they need to persuade the listener of its 'truthfulness'. The verb *sčitat'*, as a major verb for expressing opinions in Russian, embodies this persuasive element.

Anna Zaliznjak suggests that the cultural specificity of the verb *sčitat'* lies in the fact that it serves as "a world-creating operator: it creates a world in which the proposition introduced by this word is truthful (*istinno*)" (Zaliznjak 2005: 286). I agree with Anna Zaliznjak in that the essence of the meaning of this verb is related to the importance of notions of *pravda* and *istina* in the Russian language and speech practices related to them. However, I do not agree with her approach which explains the importance of *sčitat'* via complex abstract concepts taken from philosophy and logic. To explain the high frequency and importance of this word we need to relate it to central speech practices and a naïve picture of the world, and describe it in simple words found in natural language and used by all speakers.

6 Conclusion

There is a wide-spread illusion among cognitive scientists that one can discuss human cognition while bracketing, as it were, the question of language, as if the medium of description did not matter. Against this, NSM semanticists argue that the language of description (such as English) brings with it its own biases: Relying on one's analysis of the English word *belief* one ignores the fact that "belief" is a culture-specific conceptual category which is an artifact of the English language. At the same time, NSM semanticists do not accept the equally wide-spread idea that no medium of description is neutral, and that a bias, while real enough, is inevitable: Since there are empirically established universal human concepts (such as KNOW and THINK), using such concepts as a medium of analysis we can overcome the ethnocentric bias involved in relying on English (or any other natural language).

As linguistic research shows, certain similarities in the way the domain of mental states is categorized in many languages can be found (D'Andrade 1987; Fortescue 2001; Goddard 2003b), though "the exact division of the territory by the words of a specific language will vary, being largely conventional" and "in the fineness of grain of the specific lexical distinctions would one expect much variation" (Fortescue 2001: 38). This study confirms the assumption that only the words *think* and *know* among words expressing mental states have exact equivalents in natural languages and can be considered reliable tools in the description of universal tendencies. The expression of the result of a thinking process varies across languages and cultures. Still further research in cross-linguistic and cross-cultural semantics is needed to obtain the full picture of this variation. The main outcome of this study is that the verbs *sčitat'* as well as *to believe* are culture- and language-specific. Thus it would be preferable to avoid them in research conducted for cross-cultural and linguistic comparison as well as in research that claims to uncover universal tendencies in human thinking.

Acknowledgements

I am grateful to Anna Wierzbicka and Cliff Goddard for their helpful comments on an earlier version of this chapter.

References

Apresjan, Jurij. 2000. *Systematic lexicography*. Translated by Kevin Windle. Oxford: OUP.
Apresjan, Jurij. 2001. Sistemoobrazujuščie smysly 'znat' i 'sčitat' v russkom jazyke (The system-forming meanings of 'znat" and 'sčitat" in Russian). *Russkij jazyk v naučnom osveščenii* 1. 5–26.
Apresjan, Jurij. 2004a. O Moskovskoj semantičeskoj škole (About the Moscow School of Semantics). *Dialogue: Computational Linguistics and Intellectual Technologies*. Verxnevolžskij (Moscow) June 2–7, 2004. http://www.dialog-21.ru/Archive/2004/Apresyan.pdf.
Apresjan, Jurij. 2004b. Sčitat', dumat', polagat', naxodit', rassmatrivat', smotret', usmatrivat', videt'. In Apresjan (ed.), 1128–1137.
Apresjan, Jurij. 2004c. Stydit'sja, stesnjat'sja, smuščat'sja, konfuzit'sja. In Apresjan (ed.), 1122–1128.
Apresjan, Jurij. 2005. O Moskovskoj semantičeskoj škole (About the Moscow Semantic School). *Voprosy jazykoznanija* 1. 3–30.
Apresjan, Jurij (ed.). 2004. *Novyj ob"jasnitel'nyj slovar' sinonimov russkogo jazyka*, 2nd edn. Moskva: Jazyki Slavjanskoj Kul'tury.
Boym, Svetlana. 1994. *Common places: Mythologies of everyday life in Russia*. Cambridge, MA: Harvard University Press.
D'Andrade, Roy. 1987. A folk model of the mind. In Dorothy Holland & Naomi Quinn (eds.), *Cultural models in language and thought*, 112–148. Cambridge: CUP.
Dessaix, Robert. 2004. *Twilight of love. Travels with Turgenev*. Brisbane: Picador.
Fortescue, Michael. 2001. Thoughts about thought. *Cognitive Linguistics* 12(1). 15–45.

Goddard, Cliff. 1998. *Semantic analysis: A practical introduction*. Oxford: OUP.
Goddard, Cliff. 2003a. Natural semantic metalanguage: Latest perspectives. *Theoretical Linguistics* 29. 227–236.
Goddard, Cliff. 2003b. Thinking across languages and cultures: Six dimensions of variation. *Cognitive Linguistics* 14(2/3). 109–140.
Goddard, Cliff & Susanna Karlsson. 2004. Re-thinking 'think': Contrastive semantics of Swedish and English. In Christo Moskovsky (ed.), *Proceedings of the 2003 Conference of the Australian Linguistic Society*. http://www.als.asn.au.
Goddard, Cliff & Anna Wierzbicka. 2002. Semantic primes and universal grammar. In Goddard & Wierzbicka (eds.), Vol. 1, 41–86.
Goddard, Cliff & Anna Wierzbicka (eds.). 1994. *Semantic and lexical universals: Theory and empirical findings*. Amsterdam: John Benjamins.
Goddard, Cliff & Anna Wierzbicka (eds.). 2002. *Meaning and universal grammar: Theory and empirical findings*, Vols. 1 & 2. Amsterdam: John Benjamins.
Makeeva, Irina. 2003. Istoričeskie izmenenija v semantike nekotoryx russkix mental'nyx glagolov (Historical changes in the semantics of several Russian mental verbs). In Nina Arutjunova & Nina Spiridonova (eds.), *Logičeskij analiz jazyka. Izbrannoe* (Logical analysis of a language. Selected papers), 461–467. Moskva: Indrik.
Melčuk, Igor & Alexander Žolkovskij. 1984. *Tolkovo-kombinatornyj slovar' sovremennogo russkogo jazyka* (Explanatory-combinatory dictionary of the contemporary Russian language). Vienna: Wiener Slawistischer Almanach.
Nacional'nyj korpus russkogo jazyka (National Corpus of the Russian Language). URL: http://www.ruscorpora.ru.
Padučeva, Elena. 2004. *Dinamičeskie modeli v semantike leksiki* (Dynamic models in lexical semantics]. Moskva: Jazyki russkoj kul'tury.
Proxorov, Urij & Iosif Sternin. 2005. *Russkoe kommunikativnoe povedenie* (Russian communicative behavior). Moskva: Flinta/Nauka.
Solomon, Robert. 2003. Emotions, thoughts and feelings: What is a 'Cognitive Theory' of the emotions and does it neglect affectivity? In Anthony Hatzimoysis (ed.), *Philosophy and emotions*, 1–18. Cambridge: CUP.
The Natural Semantic Metalanguage homepage. URL: http://www.une.edu.au/lcl/nsm/index.php.
Tolstoy, Leo. 1953. *Anna Karenina*. Moskva: Xudožestvennaja literatura.
Uryson, Elena. 2002. Sojuz xotja skvoz' prizmu semantičeskix primitivov (The conjunction *xotja* through the prism of semantic primitives). *Voprosy jazykoznanija* 6. 35–54.
Wierzbicka, Anna. 1992. *Semantics, culture, and cognition*. Oxford: OUP.
Wierzbicka, Anna. 1996. *Semantics: Primes and universals*. Oxford: OUP.
Wierzbicka, Anna. 2002. Russian cultural scripts: The theory of cultural scripts and its applications. *Ethos* 30(4). 401–432.
Wierzbicka, Anna. 2006. *English: Meaning and culture*. Oxford: OUP.
Wierzbicka, Anna. In Press. The theory of the mental lexicon. In Tilman Berger, Karl Gutschmidt, Sebastian Kempgen & Peter Kosta (eds.), *Die slavischen Sprachen* (Handbücher zur Sprach- und Kommunikationswissenschaft (HSK)) [The Slavic languages (Handbook of Linguistics and Communication Science)]. Berlin: Mouton de Gruyter.
Zaliznjak, Anna. 1991. Sčitat' i dumat': Dva vida mnenija [Sčitat' and dumat': Two types of opinion]. In Nina Arutjunova, Vasilij Petrov, Nadezhda Rjabtseva & Vladimir Smirnov (eds.),

Logičeskij analiz jazyka. Kul'turnye koncepty (Logical analysis of language. Cultural concepts), 187–194. Moskva: Nauka.

Zaliznjak, Anna. 2005. Glagol sčitat': k tipologii semantičeskoj derivacii (The verb sčitat': Towards typology of semantic derivation). In Nina Arutjunova (ed.), *Logičeskij analiz jazyka. Kvantifikativnyj aspect jazyka* [Logical analysis of the language. Quantitative aspect], 280–294. Moskva: Indrik.

CHAPTER 5

Mental states reflected in cognitive lexemes related to memory
A case in Korean

Kyung-Joo Yoon

This study explores the issue of cross-linguistic variability in conceptual systems by investigating the semantics of various morphosyntactic realisations in Korean. Among a number of lexical items related to the mental experience of remembering, the present study focuses on three words, *kiekha-* 'remember', *kiekna-* 'memory comes, remember', and *chwuekha-* 'reminisce' in order to describe their semantic contents. The analytical tool adopted in this study is the Natural Semantic Metalanguage theory. Thus the three concepts are analysed by using the conceptual primitives proposed in the theory on the basis of linguistic evidence. The findings of the lexical semantics of the Korean language-specific concepts throw a good amount of light on the issue of universality and variation of conceptual systems across languages and cultures.

1   Introduction

It is widely accepted that languages differ enormously in the way they structure their conceptualisations. One of the current interests of cognitive linguistics seems to be related to the mental processes of humans in general. Although the questions of to what extent the cognitive experience of humans is universal and to what extent culture specific is of critical importance and intriguing, the answers to those have yet to be found in detail. While the issue of how mental states are characterised in different languages is gigantic, a fraction of this issue may be explored by cross-linguistic comparison of cognitive lexemes. The inextricable link between the life of a society and the lexicon of the language spoken by that society has been validated by a number of linguists and anthropologists (e.g. Sapir 1951; Wierzbicka 1997). Language is a window through which the way of thinking of the speakers can be shown.

Considering that the semantic domain of cognition is tightly associated with the area of mental experience, I will examine the relationship between language and cognition with reference to several Korean concepts that are comparable with the English concept of *remember* in the present study. By a lexical semantic analysis of the selected Korean cognitive verbs, I aim to illustrate the indigenous view of cognitive activities reflected in the Korean language. Korean has more than one expression that can be used as translational counterparts of the English concepts of *memory* and *remember*. Among a number of lexical items related to the mental experience of remembering, I have chosen *kiekha-* 'remember', *kiekna-* 'memory comes, remember', and *chwuekha-* 'reminisce'. These are verbs derived from two nouns, *kiek-* 'memory' and *chwuek-* 'memory'. These words are related to each other in terms of morphosyntactic characteristics.

An exhaustive analysis of the selected Korean concepts can throw a good amount of light on Korean ways of conceptualisation. What is not helpful in exploring culturally-situated forms of mental experience is the ethnocentric view that some English concepts are free from any language specificity. For instance, the concepts of *memory* and *mind* often appear to be treated as scientific and objective, taken-for-granted, universal categories in cognitive science. However, both concepts of *memory* and *mind* are Anglo-specific categories that do not have counterparts in many languages including Korean (Yoon 2003b). Therefore, in order to be clearly understood by everyone including outsiders, semantic analysis should not rely on English categorisation. The methodological difficulty of representing the meaning of language-specific concepts has not been an uncommon issue in the past. Now it is widely agreed that the analytical tool for this kind of semantic analysis is of profound importance since, without an appropriate and systematic tool, the meaning of language-specific concepts cannot be adequately represented. The analytical tool I adopt for the purpose of the present study is Natural Semantic Metalanguage theory (hence NSM), which has been proposed and developed by Wierzbicka and her colleagues for more than three decades (Goddard & Wierzbicka 1994, 2002; Wierzbicka 1972, 1996), because this framework enables the analysis attempted here to escape from ethnocentrism by providing a language-independent metalanguage. What I mean by "language-independent" is that this metalanguage is based on universal human concepts attested by a great deal of cross-linguistic research (see Goddard & Wierzbicka 1994, 2002, for details). The NSM approach has been found to be a practical tool, particularly for language-specific concepts, since it is not associated with any specific language and/or culture (cf. e.g. Goddard 1996a, 1996b, 1997a, 2001; Harkins & Wierzbicka 2001; Wierzbicka 1999).

The NSM approach is interested in capturing the necessary semantic components of the defined concept and paraphrasing them into a simple language that is self-explanatory. The current inventory of NSM theory consists of around 60 lexical items which are proposed by "a great deal of trial-and error experimentation in diverse areas of semantic analysis" (Goddard 1997b: 3). The members of the inventory are presented both in English and Korean in the Appendix in order to show that explications can readily be transposed into Korean without any change of meaning.[1] Although the explications are presented only in English in this study due to the compression of space, they can be transposed into Korean and, in principle, into any natural language.

In order to analyse the meanings of the given concepts, the collected data were examined firstly in naturally-occurring contexts to establish preliminary explications based on the linguistic use of native speakers. Formulating a hypothesis on the basis of linguistic evidence is essential for semantic analysis using the NSM approach. As a second step, the explications were tested and refined by being substituted for the defined expressions in their natural contexts. All the explications in this study are proposed following this process. Nonetheless, these explications are open to further discussion or modification, as it is possible that counterexamples may stand out. The aim is for explications to be open to improvement and be compatible with all usages.

The data collected for my investigation was mainly taken from a Korean corpus (KAIST). Only a small part of the examined data is cited here considering the length limitations of the present study. Nevertheless, all examples used were originally written in Korean and reflect contemporary usage of the analysed concepts among speakers of the Korean language in South Korea.[2]

---

1. The Korean Natural Semantic Metalanguage is constructed on the basis of testing the lexicon and syntax of the proposed NSM theory (see Yoon 2003a for details). The results of the tests generally support the NSM hypotheses. All the proposed semantic primitives are lexicalised in Korean, and their combinatorics are along the same lines as the proposed universal grammar. There is one primitive, SOME, that is found not to have one generic form in Korean. It is not clear at this stage whether the two different realisations of the concept of SOME are allolexes or not. While further studies are required to clarify this problem, the two different Korean words identified can be used for the meaning analysis of the Korean concepts in this study without causing a major problem.

2. Korean is spoken also in overseas Korean communities distributed world wide including China, Japan, the former Soviet Union, United States, Canada, Australia and New Zealand. Korean ranks twelfth in the world in terms of the number of speakers and it has also become widely taught as a second language (Lee & Ramsey 2000).

2   Mental verbs in Korean

The Korean cognitive verbs related to English *remember* consist of numerous morphosyntactic realisations derived from several nouns, *sayngkak* 'thought', *kiek-* 'memory' and *chwuek-* 'memory'. These words are used productively in the domain of cognition by agglutinating various verbal suffixes. As a result, there are various expressions which encode remember-like concepts. These cognitive verbs are shown by the noun stems as follows:

(i)   *sayngkak-*:   *sayngkakna-* 'come to think, be reminded of'
      sayngkaktoy- 'come to think'

(ii) *kiek-*:   *kiekha-* 'remember, recall'
      kiektoy- 'come to remember'
      kiekna- 'memory comes, remember'

(iii) *chwuek-*:   *chwuekha-* 'reminisce'
      chwuektoy- 'come to reminisce'

Apart from those above, there are a large number of other expressions that are composed of the three noun stems and predicatives, expressing meanings related to 'remember'. Some of the productive predicatives are: *-ey nam-* 'remain in memory/thought'; *-i iss-* 'have memory/thought'; *-i (toy) salana-* 'memory/thought comes to life again'; *-i tteolu-* 'memory/thought rises; come to remember/think'; and *-haynay-* 'manage to remember/think'. Among a number of cognitive verbs and expressions, the present research focuses on the meanings of *kiekna-* 'memory comes, remember', *kiekha-* 'remember', and *chwuekha-* 'reminisce', since compared to others they are considered basic in terms of frequency of use, complexity of meaning, and morphological structure.

The selected verbs are closely related to each other in terms of morphological, syntactic and semantic properties. The following are the morphological structures of the selected words, consisting of two parts, noun and verbal suffix. There is a parallel between the given words that belong to the two different stems: the first set is derived from *kiek-* 'memory', and the second set from *chwuek-* 'memory'.

(i)   *kiekha-*: *kiek-* ('memory') + *ha* ('do'): lit. 'do memory'
      kiekna-: *kiek-* ('memory') + *na* ('happen'): lit. 'memory comes/happens/rises'

(ii) *chwuekha-*: *chwuek-* ('memory') + *ha* ('do'): lit. 'do memory'

Although the meanings of the given words seem to be determined by various verbal suffixes, they cannot be explicated at the morphemic level. The meanings of these suffixes are polysemic depending on the semantic and syntactic properties of different stems (either noun or verb). Therefore, semantic analysis has to be done at the word level.

In terms of syntax, the two sets behave somewhat differently. Korean verbs formed by this morphological structure, noun stem suffixed by *-ha* 'do', are identified as single words in the mind of the speakers, but at the same time they can also be separated freely into two different parts, especially when attributives and the short formula of negation are used. The verbs *kiekha-* 'remember' and *kiekna-* 'memory comes, remember' can well be used in this way. They can be separated by case markers inserted between the noun stems and verbal suffixes, e.g. *kiek-* ('memory') + *-ul* (accusative marker) + *-ha*, and *kiek-* ('memory') + *-i* (nominative) + *-na*, as shown in (1a) and (1b), and (2a) and (2b). However, this rule is not applicable to the verb *chwuekha-* 'reminisce'. Moreover, the noun stem *chwuek-* 'memory' can never be combined with *-na*, unlike the other noun stem *kiek-* 'memory'. Although these differences may give a clue as to the semantic difference between *kiek-* and *chwuek-*, I will not pursue the issue of syntactic difference here leaving it for investigation in further study. The following shows that the selected cognitive verbs can be used with case markers inserted between the noun and its verbal suffixes:

(1) a. *na-nun ku   ttay   il-ul   kiekha-n-ta.*
       I-TOC that time event-ACC remember-IN-DEC
       'I remember those.'

   b. *na-nun ku   ttay   il-ul   kiek-ul   ha-n-ta.*
       I-TOC that time event-ACC memory-ACC do-IN-DEC
       'I remember those.'

(2) a. *na-nun ku   ttay   il-i   kiekna-n-ta.*
       I-TOC that time event-NOM remember-IN-DEC
       'I come to remember those.'

   b. *na-nun ku   ttay   il-i   kiek-i   na-n-ta.*
       I-TOC that time event-NOM memory-NOM rise-IN-DEC
       'I come to remember those.'

Regardless of the difference of syntactic construction (whether they are split or not) there is no difference of meaning (at least, in terms of compositional meaning) between *kiekha-* and *kiekna-*, and *kiek-ul ha-* and *kiek-i na-*, respectively, in the above contexts. However, the difference of the case markers indicates that *-ha* ending verbs are transitive whereas *-na* ending verbs are intransitive. In addition, *-ha* ending verbs can be used with an imperative mood suffix while *-na* ending verbs cannot, as shown in (3) and (4).

(3) eti-inci   kiekhay-pwa-la.
    where   remember-try-IMP
    'Try to think/remember where it is.'

(4) *eti-inci   kiekna-pwa-la.
    where   remember-try-IMP
    'Try to come to think/remember where it is.'

Moreover, -na ending verbs are not compatible with the word *mos* 'cannot', although *mos* can occur naturally with -ha ending verbs as shown in the examples below:

(5) a. amwu   kes-to   kiek   an   na-n-ta.
       any   thing-too memory   not   happen-IN-DEC
       'I don't remember anything.' (lit. Any memory does not happen)

    b. *amwu kes-to   kiek   mos   na-n-ta.
       any   thing-too memory   cannot   happen-IN-DEC
       'I cannot remember anything.' (lit. Any memory cannot happen)

The syntactic differences suggest that -ha ending verbs differ in meaning from -na ending verbs. Given these syntactic differences as providing evidence for semantic differences, I will explore more examples for semantic analysis. On the basis of the given examples selected from among other similar ones, differences of meaning between *kiekha-*, *kiekna-*, and *chwuekha-* will be explicated.

3   *kiekha-* 'remember'[3]

While there are many cases where *kiekha-* 'remember' and *kiekna-* 'memory comes, remember' can be used interchangeably, there are also cases where one cannot replace the other. In such contexts as (6) and (7), *kiekha-* can be used but not *kiekna-*. Examples (6) and (7) reflect the idea that the concept of *kiekha-* involves the speaker's volition to retrieve something.

(6) 그래서 우리는 푸네스처럼 모든 것을 기억하는 게 아니라 기억하고 싶은 것만을, 그리고 지우고 싶어도 잊혀지지 않는 상처 같은 것만을 기억하는 거지요.
    '... so we don't remember [*kiekha-*] all things like Punes, we remember [*kiekha-*] only what we want to remember [*kiekha-*] and a kind of scar that is not forgotten despite wanting to erase it.' (MT: K→ E, KAIST)

---

3. Translations of the examples in this section are mine. Some of them may sound clumsy and unnatural in English for I tried to capture the Korean way of speaking in the translations. At the same time, I had to transfer the meanings into English in such a way that they can be understood.

(7) 정말 기억하고 싶지 않은 사건이라 ...
'Since it is an event that I really don't want to remember [*kiekha-*] ...'
(MT: K→E, KAIST)

Example (8) indicates that the concept of *kiekha-* engages the speaker's capability of retrieving the memory.

(8) 내가 꼭 한 번 강의에 안 들어갔었는데, 그것을 기억하시다니 놀랍다. 나는 교수님이 그것을 기억하 시리라고 생각해 본 적이 없었다.
'It's amazing that he remembers [*kiekha-*] that I didn't go to his lecture. It happened only once. I didn't expect him to remember [*kiekha-*] that.'
(MT: K→E, KAIST)

The retrieving [*kiekha-*] depends on one's ability to do so. Therefore, one can ask or order other people to remember [*kiekha-*] on the assumption that they may have the capability to do so. Examples (9) and (10) below show that the imperative and propositive mood suffixes can naturally be combined with the verb *kiekha-*, as in the cases of other transitive verbs.

(9) 좋건 나쁘건간에, 우리는 해마다 돈을 받고 있다는 사실을 기억해라.
'Remember [*kiekha-*] the fact that we have been receiving money (from him) every year, whether you like or not.' (MT: K→E, KAIST)

(10) 모두 돈에 욕심을 낸 것으로 당국에 의해 고발되었음을 기억하자.
'Let us all remember [*kiekha-*] that we were accused by the government due to our greed for money.' (MT: K→E, KAIST)

On the basis of my examination of examples, I propose the following as the explication of the meaning of *kiekha-* 'remember':

[A] *na-nun Y-lul kiekha-n-ta.* ('I remember Y')
   a. I am thinking about Y now, because I want to
   b. I can think about it (Y) now
   c. because I know some things about it (Y)
   d. I knew these things some time before
   e. because I thought about these things at that time
   f. after this, I could think about it (Y) if I wanted to

Component (a) shows that the speaker's cognitive state of retrieving something (Y) is motivated by his/her volition as mentioned above. The use of the progressive form of the verb think, i.e. 'thinking' in this component is supported by the fact that the verb *kiekha-* is often used with the progressive aspect suffix *-ko iss-* (*kiekha-koiss* 'lit. be remembering about something/someone'), as shown in Example (11).

In Korean *kiekha-* 'remember' and *al-* 'know' are non-stative verbs that can be freely combined with progressive aspect suffixes.

(11) 나는 취했으나 나의 사명을 기억하고 있다.
'Despite being drunk I still remember [*kiekha* + progressive aspect] my mission.' (MT: K→E, KAIST)

Components (b) and (c) indicate that the speaker has the capacity to retrieve something based on his/her knowledge about the complement (Y) of the verb *kiekha-* 'remember'. One cannot say that one remembers [*kiekha-*] something about which one does not have any knowledge as shown in (12).

(12) *na-nun nay-ka molu-nun kes-ul kiekha-ko iss-ta.
I-TOC I-NOM not know-PM thing-ACC remember-PRG-DEC
'I am retrieving something that I don't know.'

When one remembers something, it does not necessarily mean that one can do so in a perfect way as it was or as it happened, though sometimes this is the case. It is indefinite how accurate the speaker's retrieving is. It could be perfect but it could also be partial. However, this knowledge ('I know some things about it') can be the basis of the retrieving. It is true that not everything learnt in the past can always be retrieved. There are things which one once knew about, and then forgot. Therefore, there must be other factors involved in retrieving [*kiekha-*] something (Y). For example, it could be one's strong desire to retrieve the thing or the nature and strength of the original event that impacted on one's life. However, in the concept of *kiekha-* 'remember', it is vague as to what other factors are involved. The logic of the components (b) to (e) is that one can retrieve something based on the knowledge that was established in the past by one's cognitive activity. Other factors that may contribute to retrieval [*kiekha-*] are not specified in the explication, leaving this aspect as vague as the concept itself is. Examples (13) and (14) exemplify what is reflected in components (d) and (e) about this aspect of the concept:

(13) 한 마디 의사교환 없이도 우리가 서로를 이해한 그 순간을 나는 지금도 아름다운 추억으로 기억하고 있다.
'I still remember [*kiekha-*] that beautiful moment when we understood each other without even a word or any exchange of opinion.' (MT: K→E, KAIST)

(14) 내 기억이 정확하다면 Wild Chrysanthemum 이란 긴 스펠링 영어 이름을 지녔다. 내가 왜 긴이름의 영어 스펠링을 지금까지 기억하고 있는지 그이유를 나는 알지 못한다. 물론 내가 이꽃들을 사랑하게된 약간의 이유는 있다.

'If my memory is accurate, it has a long name, Wild chrysanthemum. I don't know the reason why I still remember [*kiekha-*] that long spelling even now. Of course, there are reasons why I started to love this flower.' (MT: K→E, KAIST)

Component (f) suggests that the speaker thinks that s/he could retrieve the same thing after the time of learning about Y in accordance with her/his volition. If the speaker can retrieve something at the time of speaking, one can assume that s/he could have done the same previously as well. Examples (15) and (16) suggest that the use of *kiekha-* 'remember' implies the speaker's potential for retrieving between the time of cognitive action and the time of speaking.

(15) 1910~1920년대의 격동기 중국을 경험한 이들은 어렸을 적 부모님께 매를 맞아가며 외웠던 당나라 때의 시들을 지금도 기억하고 있다.
'Those who experienced the upheaval of China from 1910–1920 still remember [*kiekha-*] poems of the Tang dynasty that they had learnt by heart with a smack from their parents.' (MT: K→E, KAIST)

(16) 인간은 음운적 신호로 어휘를 배우고 기억하고 또 사용하도록 되어 있는 것처럼 보인다.
'It seems that the human learns, remembers [*kiekha-*], and uses vocabulary of a language by the phonetic symbols.' (MT: K→E, KAIST)

The complement (Y) of the verb *kiekha-* 'remember' in Korean can either be a noun phrase that refers to a person, a place, a period, an event or word, or a clause. The explication is supposed to cover all these complements. This is why such components as 'this thing (Y) happened to me before', which can carry the meaning of the speaker's past experience about Y, is not inserted after the first component of the explication. The explication has to have a wider predictive power for not only the past event but also for a person or a place that can frequently be used as the complement of *kiekha-* 'remember'.

Having proposed the meaning of *kiekha-* 'remember' in the given contexts, I present some other examples which are not compatible with this explication:

(17) 시집 식구들의 생일을 기억해라. 칭찬받는 며느리의 지름길이다.
'Try to remember [*kiekha-*] the birthdays of your in-laws. This is the best way for any daughter-in-law to get approval from her in-laws.' (MT: K→E, KAIST)

(18) Shakespeare에 나오는 글들을 기억해야 이번 영문학 시험을 잘볼수가 있어.
'I can do well in this exam on English literature if I memorise [*kiekha-*] passages from Shakespeare.' (MT: K→E, KAIST)

(19) 어떻게 국사공부를 잘할 수 있을까. 해답은 잘 기억하는 것이다.
 'How to get a good result in Korean history? The answer is to memorise [*kiekha-*] well.' (MT: K→E, KAIST)

Therefore, it seems reasonable to posit the second meaning of *kiekha-* 'remember' (*kiekha-*₍₂₎). It seems to be that the word *kiekha-* can mean either 'retrieving something that happened in the past' or 'storing something that is happening now for the future'. The closest translational equivalent of *kiekha-*₍₂₎ in English may be 'memorise' or 'learn by heart', although these English words cannot replace *kiekha-*₍₂₎ in all contexts, such as in (17). The word *kiekha-*₍₂₎ in Examples (17), (18), and (19) is translated into English as 'try to remember' or 'memorise', since there is no one word that corresponds to this concept in English. Using the word 'memorise' in such contexts as (17) is not as natural as in Korean. The Korean word *kiekha-*₍₂₎ contains the meaning of prospective retrieving: 'remember to remember' in the words of Sellen et al. (1997: 484). There is no semantic component of 'retrieving something based on past knowledge' in Examples (17) to (20). It is very natural for this use of *kiekha-*₍₂₎ to take the imperative mood suffix, as shown in (20).

(20) 이 사람의 비참한 신세를 꼭 기억하시오. 그리고 항상 조심하시오.
 'Try to remember [*kiekha-*] my awful situation and always be careful.' (MT: K→E, KAIST)

I propose the following explication for the second meaning of *kiekha-*₍₂₎, which expresses an active cognition in the currently occurring situation for the future retrieval.

[B] *na-nun Y-lul kiekha-ko sip-ta.* ('I want to memorise Y')
  a. I am thinking about Y now
  b. because I want to think about it (Y) after
  c. I want to think about it (Y), not other things now
  d. I have to think about it (Y) for some time
  e. I can know some things about it (Y) because of this
  f. because of this, if I want to think about these things after this
  g. I will be able to think at that time

Component (a) indicates the speaker's current state of cognition. Component (b) shows that the motivation of the cognition is prospective retrieving, and component (c) reflects the speaker's desire of concentrating on the current issue. Component (d) indicates that the speaker acknowledges the significance of the deliberate cognitive activities, going on for an uncertain period of time, in order to retrieve the same thing in the future. As a result, the speaker thinks that s/he will gain some knowledge about the topic as suggested in component (e). Components (f) and (g) demonstrate that the speaker expects that s/he will have the capacity to retrieve the thing in the future in accordance with her/his will.

Although sentences with the word *kiekha-* can be ambiguous in some contexts, the two meanings, i.e. *kiekha-*₍₁₎ and *kiekha-*₍₂₎, can often be distinguished using such clues as the temporal location of the complement: When the complement is something in the range of the past, this word is likely to express the retrieval of some information gained in the past, otherwise it is related to the second meaning.

4   *kiekna-* 'memory comes, remember'

The word *kiekna-* 'memory comes, remember' occurs more frequently than *kiekha-* 'remember' (cf. http://csfive.kaist.ac.kr/kcp/). The meaning implies involuntary retrieving. It is vague as to what triggers the retrieving. The trigger is not required for the use of the word *kiekna-*, unlike the English counterpart 'be reminded of (by)' which has an elliptical slot for the trigger. The motivation of remembering may vary from person to person, and the perceptual experiences leading to cognitive action can also be diverse, presumably hearing, seeing, and feeling (including touching and smelling). People sometimes comment on what triggered their involuntary memories when they want to or when they think it's important.

The study of involuntary memories has a relatively short history in the domain of cognitive psychology (cf. Kvavilashvili & Mandler 2004). In fact, the English concept *remember* does not distinguish involuntary from voluntary recalling. It is ambiguous as to whether the concept of remember in such contexts as 'Do you remember where you put the key?' expresses either voluntary or involuntary retrieving. *Remember* in 'I have to read this passage again to remember it' or 'I want to remember his address' seems to imply intention to retrieve, though with the contextual cues. In Korean, however, one is forced to make the distinction between intended and mind-popping retrieving. The Korean concept of *kiekna-* 'memory comes, remember' carries the meaning of non-deliberate retrieving, which is also called "involuntary remembering" (Winograd 1993), "remindings" (Schank 1982), "mind popping" (Mandler 1994), "passive memories" (Spence 1988), and "thoughts that come unbidden" (Linton 1986). This study focuses on the semantics of the linguistic expressions rather than psychological mechanisms of this phenomenon. On the basis of the examination of a large number of examples, I posit the following explication for *kiekna-* 'memory comes, remember'.

[C] *na-nun Y-ka/i kiekna-n-ta.* ('I remember Y': lit. 'memory of Y comes to me')
   a. I am thinking about Y now, not because I want to
   b. it can happen because I know some things about it (Y)
   c. I knew these things some time before
   d. because I thought about these things at that time
   e. after this, I didn't think about it all the time
   f. I cannot not think about it now

Component (a) indicates that the speaker is retrieving something (Y) involuntarily. The examples below show the contrast in meaning between *kiekha-* and *kiekna-*.

(21) a. *amwuli   kiekha-ci·anh-ulyeko-hayto   kiek-i   na-n-ta.*
        hard   remember-not-try-despite   memory-NOM   happen-IN-DEC
        'Despite trying hard not to remember it, I still [*kiekna-*] remember.'

   b. *eti-inci amwuli   kiekha-lyeko-hay-to   kiek-i*
        Where   hard   remember-try-despite   memory-NOM
        an   na-n-ta.
        not   happen-IN-DEC
        'Despite trying hard to remember where it was, I couldn't remember.'

It is very natural for the word *kiekna-* 'memory comes, remember' to be combined with such adverbs as *kapcaki* 'suddenly' and *kitayhacianh-* 'unexpectedly'. Component (b) expresses the speaker's treatment of the retrieving as a happening and of the previous knowledge as the cause of it. In Examples (22) and (23) there is no trigger or cause indicated for the involuntary retrieving.

(22) '이제 본과는 일본으로 간다'고 쓰셨던 기억이 납니다.
     'The memory of what you wrote comes to mind [*kiekna-*], "Now this department will move to Japan".' (MT: K→E, KAIST)

(23) 그때 그시절이 기억나서 울때도 있어.
     'Sometimes I cry, because memories of that time come to my mind [*kiekna-*].' (MT: K→E, KAIST)

Components (c) and (d) reflect the fact that the speaker's knowledge is based on a cognitive process that happened in the past. Example (24) shows that the speaker retrieves the fact that she wrote a letter to her interactant in the past. One can assume that the speaker must have used her/his brain to think when s/he wrote a letter. One cannot possibly use *kiekna-* for a situation about which one had not thought at all. It is vague as to how much information the speaker had in mind and occurred to him/her. If one is asked, one can stretch the information by adding such adverbs as *cokumbakkey* 'only a little bit' or *wancenhi* 'entirely' depending on one's preference, as shown in (25). The range of the amount of the restored information is not specified in the meaning of the word.

(24) 영화를 끝냈다는 소식을 알리기 위해 당신에게 편지를 썼던 것이 기억나네요.
'I remember [*kiekna-*] that I wrote a letter to you to let you know the news about the movie that I had finished then.' (MT: K→E, KAIST)

(25) 가장 기억에 남는 사랑의 상처'가 무엇이냐고 물었더니 '특별히 기억나지 않는다. 이 나이엔 그런 기억은 이제 남아있지 않다.'라고 말한다.
'When I asked (him/her) about the most memorable broken-heart, she/he said "Not much memory comes [*kiekna-*] to mind, at this age no such memory remains". (MT: K→E, KAIST)

Component (e) suggests the discontinuity of retrieving the same thing for an uncertain period of time. The deliberate effort to retain the acquired knowledge is lacking in the concept of *kiekna-*. It suggests that the retrieved knowledge has not been always kept in the mind of the speaker as shown in Example (26).

(26) A: "그건 술을 끊으라는 거였는데, 저는 약속했답니다."
B: "이제야 그 일이 기억나는군."
C: "물론 그 약속은 지키고 있겠죠?"
A: "That was his request to give up alcohol, as I had promised."
B: "Only now it comes to my mind [*kiekna-*]."
C: "I assume you are keeping that promise?" (MT: K→E, KAIST)

Component (f) indicates that the nature of *kiekna-* is something beyond the control of the speaker. This aspect of lack of control is evident, for example particularly among those who have had traumatic experiences, including wars, loss of parents at an early age, and various appalling hardships. This is consistent with the reports from a number of cognitive psychologists:

> "The so called flashbacks (i.e. the painful images of traumatic events) that characterise the Post Traumatic Stress Disorder, on the other hand, are preceded by attempts not to remember a certain stressful episode (Bekerian & Dritschel 1992). Similarly, unwanted or intrusive memories and thoughts may keep coming to mind despite attempts to suppress them (see Brewin 1998; Brewin, Christodoulides & Hutchinson 1996; Wegner 1994)" (Kvavilashvili & Mandler 2004: 48).

However, the Korean concept of *kiekna-* 'memory comes, remember' is used widely in ordinary conversations not only to refer to some traumatic memories but also for ordinary and pleasant memories. This concept represents the most common way of talking about retrieving something in Korean.

5   *chwuekha-* 'reminisce'

Similar to other predicates that are suffixed by *ha-* 'do', *chwuekha-* is a transitive verb that takes a direct object used with an accusative case marker. Compared to *kiekha-*, *chwuekha-* tends to be used nominally rather than predicatively in both written and spoken languages. While in the case of *kiekha-* 'remember' both noun and verb forms, *kiek-* 'memory' and *kiekha-* 'remember', are equally commonly used, in the case of *chwuekha-* 'reminisce' the noun form overrides the verb form in terms of frequency. The noun form is used in combination with various predicates in order to express a similar meaning to that of 'reminiscing':

chwuek- i	*iss-ta*
reminisce-NOM	there is-DEC
chwuek-ul	*toysali-ta*
reminisce-ACC	restore-DEC
chwuek-ul	*kkenay-ta*
reminisce-ACC	pull out-DEC
chwuek-ul	*toysaykita*
reminisce-ACC	ponder-DEC

Bilingual dictionaries of Korean and English suggest that the translational counterparts of *chwuek-* and *kiek-* are the same, that is, 'memory'. The exact semantic difference between *kiek-* and *chwuek-* is not identified in the literature. However, it is important to know the meaning of *chwuekha-* because this word is very commonly used in popular songs and novels to refer to various memories of day-to-day life. Sometimes, even native speakers appeared to be puzzled about the exact semantic differences between the two concepts, notwithstanding that they can choose one over the other depending on what they want to express. In fact, inquiries about the meaning difference between *kiek-* and *chwuek-* can be found on a website where people openly ask various questions.[4] On the same discussion forum a number of tentative definitions can be found. They were suggested by ordinary native speakers. The fact that people dispute the difference in meaning between the two words indicates that this is not obvious, even to the native speakers who would not otherwise be involved with linguistic debates. Most definitions that appear on the discussion forum, to which a number of people contributed, conclude that *chwuek-* is included in the meaning of *kiek-*. This is expressed using metaphors: "*kiek-* is an encyclopaedia and *chwuek-* is an anthology" and "*chwuek-* that is pulled out of the box of *kiek-*". In addition to this, some people tend to add

---

4. http://search.naver.com/search.naver?where=nexearch&query=%B1%E2%BE%EF%B0%F A+%C3%DF%BE%EF%C0%C7%C2%F7%C0%CC&frm=t1, accessed April 1, 2005.

the speaker's desire to choose information for retrieving as a part of the meaning of *chwuekha-*. According to the suggested definitions, *kiek-* is all that a person has in mind while *chwuek-* is only what one wants to retrieve among *kiek-*. As to what extent this kind of explanation is valid will be explored later in this section.

In what follows I will focus on the meaning of the verb *chwuekha-* in order to compare its semantic components with other verbs investigated previously, assuming that the meaning of the noun form, *chwuek-*, can be gleaned from it. My hypothesis is that the meaning of *chwuekha-* has both semantic similarities and differences with that of *kiekha-* (or other variants with the word *kiek-*). I rely on linguistic evidence taken from various examples in order to find out what aspects of meaning are shared by both concepts and what aspects distinguish the two concepts. The following are some examples in which the two concepts are used with slightly different meanings in the same sentence:

(27) 살아오면서 가장 즐겁고 행복했던 추억과 기억을 되살려 그 중 10가지만 적어보자. 즐거웠던 기억과 추억은 적는 것만으로도 우리를 행복하게 만들어준다. 이는 평생을 곱씹어도 좋을 만큼 귀한 재산이다.
'Let's recollect our memories [*kiek-* and *chwuek-*] and write down the 10 most happy ones. Writing down those memories [*kiek-* and *chwuek-*] make us happy. This is a priceless asset that lasts for one's life time.' (MT: K→E, Lee 2005)

(28) 그 시절 왜 그리 술이 마시고 싶었던지....... 지금 생각해 보면 아마도 지금의 추억으로 남기위해 그랬던 거 같습니다. 누구나 수학여행의 추억과 기억이 남아 있겠지만, 그때의 술맛은 환상적이었죠.
'Why did I have such strong desire to drink alcohol at that time? Looking back now, I wanted to drink, perhaps because, so that I could have a memory [*chwuek-*] of that time. Everyone may have memories [*chwuek-* and *kiek-*] about the school excursion (in the last year of high school). Any alcohol tasted fantastic at that time.' (MT: K→E, Iloveschool 2002)[5]

Korean speakers use the two concepts *kiek-* and *chwuek-* to refer to various kinds of memories, as seen in the above examples. One can also say that one reminisces [*chwuekha-*] about what one has retrieved [*kiekha-*] as shown in (29) below.

(29) 이러한 사소한 일들을, 왜 그런지 나는 낱낱이 기억하고 또 그것을 추억하고 있다.
'I don't know why but I remember [*kiekha-*] all those small things in detail and I am reminiscing [*chwuekha-*] about them.' (MT: K→E, KAIST)

---

5. Iloveschool [netizen]. 2002. Seoul: Mwunhakseykyeysa.

More examples suggest that this concept expresses retrieving something voluntarily, which is similar to the concept of *kiekha-*:

(30) 스냅 사진 스냅 사진들을 많이 찍어 두어라.훗날에 종종 그것들을 다시 펴보면서 지난 날을 추억하고 앞날을 꿈꾸는 것이 얼마나 흥미있는 일이겠는가
'Take as many snaps as possible. It will be a great fun to reminisce [*chwuekha-*] about past days and dream about future days.' (MT: K→E, KAIST)

(31) 그를 억지로 잊고자 하기는 싫다. 살아 있는 내내 그만을 추억하겠다는 고집도 아니다. 다만 지금은 잊혀지지 않을 뿐이고 ...
'I don't want to remove my memory of him by force. It doesn't mean that I am so stubborn that I will remember [*chwuekha-*] him my whole life. It's just I can't forget him now ...' (MT: K→E, KAIST)

In fact, the concept of *chwuekha-* 'reminisce' shares a number of semantic components with the concept of *kiekha-*$_{(1)}$. Retrieving something about which the speaker has learnt in the past is common to the two concepts. In this respect, the native speakers' intuition reflected in the tentative definitions at the web-discussion forum seems to be indicative. People correctly pointed out the close link between the two concepts by saying that *chwuek-* is a *kiek-* that the speaker wants to choose to remember. However, people appeared to be confused or misguided in saying that 'desire to retrieve' is what distinguishes *chwuek-* from *kiek-*. This is because one can always choose to retrieve information but that does not guarantee that it is always *chwuek-*. For instance, one can be eager to remember the telephone number of an old friend. One cannot use *chwuek-* in that case. It is absolutely inaccurate. There has to be something more than just wanting to retrieve.

There are some more examples below where the use of *chwuekha-* instead of *kiekha-* makes a difference in meaning. Although one can use *kiekha-* in the contexts of (31) above and (32) below, the meaning of the sentence would not be the same, which suggests that the two meanings are clearly distinguishable.

(32) 중국역사의 페이지마다 담배진처럼 짙게 배어 있는 유교문화의 잔존 향내를 여전히 추억하고 있는 노년세대들은 이제 대부분 70~80의 황혼이다.
'Old people who are in their seventies and eighties still reminisce [*chwuekha-*] about the extent of the scent of Confucianism that has remained in each page of the Chinese history book.' (MT: K→E, KAIST)

It seems to me that all the examples that contain the concept of *chwuekha-* involve the speaker's emotion associated with something that happened in the past.

Moreover, the speaker implies that s/he is going through an emotional state as a consequence of retrieving something at the time of speaking. In all examples, the person who is reminiscing [*chwuekha-*] implies that s/he feels something while s/he is reminiscing [*chwuekha-*] about something. This would explain why the concept of *chwuekha-* cannot be used in the case of remembering the telephone number of an old friend. It is highly unlikely that one is going through an emotional state at the time of speaking when one is thinking about a telephone number. At the same time, one would not have gone through an emotional state when one thought about the telephone number in the past either. A purely intellectual cognitive activity such as this would not be referred to by the concept of *chwuekha-*.

Regarding the nature of feelings that a speaker might have felt in the past, these appear to be positive in most cases based on the collected data and naturalistic observation, notwithstanding the fact that a mixture of negative and positive emotions can also be referred to. For example, although the speaker in (33) seems to imply that a pleasant feeling was being felt at the time of meeting someone s/he had known in the past, it is unclear whether the speaker in (34) felt only a positive feeling. From the context, the speaker could have felt both good and bad feelings in the past. When one remembers someone with whom one spent some time, it is likely that one has experienced both good and bad feelings associated with the person remembered.

(33) 지난날 두 사람이 만났던 일을 추억하며 감격에 젖어 있던 영정은 등승의 대답에 다소 기분이.
'Youngjong, who was undergoing strong touching feelings due to reminiscing [*chwuekha-*] about past days spent together, felt offended a bit by Tungsung's reply.' (MT: K→E, KAIST)

(34) 사람들은 묘비명을 읽으며 생전에 사랑했던 사람을 추억하면서.
'People reminisce [*chwuekha-*] about those whom they loved while they read tombstones.' (MT: K→E, KAIST)

It is implied that the speaker in (34) does not feel bad any more about the person who is remembered at the time of speaking, regardless of the type of emotion felt in the past. At the time of speaking, therefore, even though the speaker seems to go through an unspecified emotional state, it is not, at least, purely negative. In fact, if the emotional state of the speaker is not an entirely positive one, it can be a vague and unspecified one, presumably because it is a mixture of pleasant and unpleasant emotions. This is the case in all my examples. Keeping that in mind, note Example (35) below, which sounds awkward and unnatural.

(35) 투쟁하여 꾸준히 노력해야만 달성한다. 일본 통치하에서 살던 고뇌의 시일을추억하라!
'One has to continuously put in an effort in order to achieve that. Reminisce [*chwuekha-*] about those days of gnawing under the regime of the Japanese!' (MT: K→E, KAIST)

Some people may argue that the use of *chwuekha-* in a context like (35) is incorrect or a mistake. There are two possible explanations for the problematic nature of (35). Firstly, the concept of *chwuekha-* is mainly used to refer to positive emotions that can bring pleasant feelings back to the speaker at the time of speaking. People do not tend to remember something that can negatively impact on them, presumably due to the tendency of human nature to avoid unpleasantness. Secondly, and more importantly, (35) sounds awkward because the speaker implies that s/he does not feel bad any more about what s/he is thinking about at the time of speaking. In other words, the speaker in (35) implies that s/he has overcome the negative emotion in relation to those days under the regime of Japanese, which is awkward because in general Korean people still feel very bad about that issue.

For the same reason, it is awkward to say that one reminisces [*chwuekha-*] about the death of one's mother or father, presumably because one can never overcome the strong negative emotion associated with the death of one's parents. Therefore, when one uses the concept of *chwuekha-* one implies not only that one feels something as a consequence of retrieving, but at the same time that one does not, at least, feel entirely bad about it.

Another aspect associated with *chwuekha-* seems to be the duration of retrieving. The concept of *chwuekha-* implies that the speaker is going through a period of time that can vary but has a certain duration depending on individual situations. Hence, the expression *swunkancekulo-* 'instantaneously' is very unnatural when used in combination with the concept of *chwuekha-* 'reminisce', while it can be used with *kiekha-*.

(36) *밤늦게까지 술잔을 기울이며 담소를 나누었다. 지난 시절을 순간적으로 추억하며 즐겁게 이야기하던 이사가 정색을 하면서…
'We were having a chat over drinks until late. The director was in a good mood while he was instantaneously reminiscing [*chwuekha-*] about past days. Then he changed his face and …'

The complement of the verb *chwuekha-* 'reminisce' can either be a person or an event, as in the case also of *kiekha-*. On the basis of the preceding discussion, I posit the meaning of *chwuekha-* 'reminisce' as follows:

[D] *na-nun Y-lul chwuekha-n-ta.* ('I reminisce about Y')
   a. I am thinking about Y now, because I want to

b. I feel something because of this
c. I can't say: I feel bad
d. I can think about Y
e. because I know some things about it (Y)
f. I knew these things some time before
g. because I thought about it (Y) at that time
h. when I thought about it (Y) I felt something because of this
i. after this, I could think about it if I wanted to
j. when I think about these things, I feel something for sometime

The explication above suggests that the meaning of *chwuekha-* can be distinguished from that of *kiekha-*₍₁₎ by several components, namely (b), (c), (h) and (j). Components (b) and (c) indicate that, although the speaker's emotion at the time of speaking is not specified, it is not a purely negative one. Component (g) captures the fact that one must have gone through an emotional state at the time of a cognitive process in the past. The last component shows the involvement of the speaker's emotion for an unspecified period of time.

6 Conclusion

This study examines the meanings of several Korean cognitive verbs comparable to the English concept of *remember*, in order to address the question *How are mental states characterised in Korean*? The result of this study can be used as a partial answer to another interesting question: *How much cross-linguistic variability is there in the linguistic encoding of mental states*? This is not a speculative but an empirical attempt to offer a firm ground for cross-linguistic comparison of the semantic domain of human cognition. Some people seem to assume that the mental experience of remembering is a universal cognitive phenomenon, claiming that all languages must have a word for it (Eco 2000: 87–88 quoted in Wierzbicka In press) The predominant use of English as an international lingua franca in academic discourse seems to be responsible for this assumption to a large extent. However, considering that Korean does not have a general term corresponding to the English concepts of *memory* and *remember*, the claim that these concepts are universal cognitive phenomena is not validated. This suggests that the conceptualisation of mental processes related to *remember* can be as culture-specific as that of other aspects of human life.

The three Korean mental verbs that are suggested as translational counterparts of the English concept of *remember* have been examined in order to describe their semantic contents. This study relied on linguistic evidence taken from various examples in order to find out what aspects of meaning exist in common between those concepts and what aspects distinguish them. I have adopted the Natural Semantic Metalanguage theory as the analytical tool for the selected concepts because this method enables language-specific concepts to be paraphrased in simple and universal semantic primes. Unless the concepts are presented in universal terms, their meanings will not be readily apparent to outsiders.

As a result of the lexical semantic analysis outlined above, the meanings of the Korean cognitive verbs are described in such a way that everyone, including linguistic outsiders, can clearly understand them. It was found that Korean distinguishes voluntary retrieving from involuntary retrieving ('I am thinking about something because I want to' vs. 'I am thinking about something not because I want to'). With respect to the subtle meaning difference between *kiekha-* and *chwuekha-*, it was found that they share a number of the same semantic components but at the same time are distinct concepts. The meaning of *chwuekha-* 'reminisce' is found to have some other components that are lacking in the concept of *kiekha-*. The use of *chwuekha-* seems to imply the involvement of an unspecified emotion of the speaker at the time of speaking, though not solely a negative emotion. Moreover, it entails the speaker's experience in the past of going through an emotional state (either good or bad) caused by cognitive activities. These aspects are captured in the explication, along with the vague temporal duration involved with the meaning of *chwuekha-*.

The above explications reveal the Korean way of conceptualising mental processes related to remembering. The explications of mental verbs are formulated using a number of different semantic primitives. Some of those that recur in all explications are: the mental predicates – THINK, KNOW, FEEL; temporal concepts – WHEN BEFORE, AFTER, NOW, FOR SOME TIME; logical concepts – CAN, BECAUSE, NOT, IF; and others – SOMETHING, THIS, SOME, among others. The role of mental predicates and temporal concepts seems to be particularly critical in explicating the selected cognitive verbs. The Korean language-specific meanings are unpacked using these primitives that are arranged in different ways in accordance with the universal grammar proposed in the theory of NSM. The analyses show that one does not have to rely on complex and often obscure English-specific concepts, such as *mental* or *cognitive state*, *retrieve*, and *store* in explicating complex concepts. The meanings of the selected concepts reflect the Korean way of thinking about mental processes from a language-internal perspective. Accordingly, NSM allows Korean language-specific meanings to be known and understood by non-native speakers.

In terms of theoretical implications, the above analysis shows that mental verbs play an important role in expressing various cognitive experiences of speakers, and that cross-linguistic variability of mental states can readily be explored if concepts from the same semantic domain across languages are accurately chosen and analysed with an adequate analytical tool. The Natural Semantic Metalanguage theory offers the possibility of describing concepts from a language-internal viewpoint by using attested universal semantic primes and their inherited grammar. On the practical side, this kind of analysis can be applied in the areas of second language acquisition and translation studies. The misuse of concepts or words is often caused by wrong information or lack of proper information on the target languages.

Romanisation and abbreviations in interlinear glosses

Romanisation used in this study follows the Yale System without phonetic details.

ACC	accusative case marker	NOM	nominative case marker
DEC	declarative sentence end	PM	pre-nominal modifier
IMP	imperative sentence end	PRG	progressive aspect suffix
IN	indicative mood suffix	TOC	topic contrast particle

Typographical conventions

All translations of the Korean examples are mine. This is indicated by MT: K→E, which means "My translation from Korean to English". The square brackets (i.e. [ ]) that are used in translated texts from Korean to English indicate the original Korean word or expression.

Corpus used for Korean examples

KAIST. Retrieved October 2nd, 2004, from the World Wide Web: http://kibs.kaist.ac.kr

References

Bekerian, Debra A. & Barbara H. Dritschel. 1992. Autobiographical remembering: An integrative approach. In Martin A. Conway, David C. Rubbin, Hans Spinnler & Willem A. Wagenaar (eds.), *Theoretical perspectives on autobiographical memory*, 135–150. Dordrecht: Kluwer.
Brewin, Chris R. 1998. Intrusive autobiographical memories in depression and post-traumatic stress disorder. *Applied Cognitive Psychology* 12. 359–370.
Brewin, Chris R., James Christodoulides & Gary Hutchinson. 1996. Intrusive thoughts and intrusive memories in a nonclinical sample. *Cognition and Emotion* 10. 107–112.
Eco, Umberto. 2000. Ethics are born in the presence of the other. In Umberto Eco & Cardinal Martini (eds.), *Belief and nonbelief: A confrontation*, 85–98. London: Continuum.

Goddard, Cliff. 1996a. The 'social emotions' of Malay (Bahasa Melayu). *Ethos* 24(3). 426–464.
Goddard, Cliff. 1996b. Cross-linguistic research on metaphor. *Language and Communication* 16(2). 145–151.
Goddard, Cliff. 1997a. Contrastive semantics and cultural psychology: 'Surprise' in Malay and English. *Culture and Psychology* 3(2). 153–181.
Goddard, Cliff. 1997b. Semantic primes and grammatical catergories. *Australian Journal of Linguistics* 17. 1–41.
Goddard, Cliff. 2001. *Hati*: A key word in the Malay vocabulary of emotion. In Jean Harkins & Anna Wierzbicka (eds.), *Emotions in crosslinguistic perspective* [Cognitive Linguistics Research 17], 171–200. Berlin: Mouton de Gruyter.
Goddard, Cliff & Anna Wierzbicka (eds.). 1994. *Semantics and lexical universals: Theory and empirical findings*. Amsterdam: John Benjamins.
Goddard, Cliff & Anna Wierzbicka (eds.). 2002. *Meaning and universal grammar: Theory and empirical findings*, Vols. 1 & 2. Amsterdam: John Benjamins.
Harkins, Jean & Anna Wierzbicka (eds.). 2001. *Cross-cultural semantics of emotions*. Oxford: OUP.
Kvavilashvili, Lia & George Mandler. 2004. Out of mind: A study of involuntary semantic memories. *Cognitive Psychology* 48. 47–94.
Lee, Iksop & Robert S. Ramsey. 2000. *The Korean language*. Albany, NY: State University of New York Press.
Lee, Yosep. 2005. *Insayngul pakkwunun wusum cenlyak* [Strategies for changing one's life]. Seoul: Ttuintol.
Linton, Marigold. 1986. Ways of searching and the contents of memory. In David C. Rubin (ed.), *Autobiographical memory*, 50–67. Cambridge: CUP.
Mandler, George. 1994. Hyperamnesia, incubation, and mind popping: On remembering without really trying. In Carlo Umilta & Morris Moscovitch (eds.), *Attention and performance XV*, 3–33. Cambridge, MA: The MIT Press.
Sapir, Edward. 1951. *Selected writings of Edward Sapir in language, culture, and personality*. Berkeley, CA: University of California Press.
Schank, Roger C. 1982. *Dynamic memory*. New York, NY: CUP.
Sellen, Abigail J., Gifford Louie, J. E. Harris & A. J. Wilkins. 1997. What brings intentions to mind? An *in situ* study of prospective memory. *Memory* 5(4). 483–507.
Spence, Donald P. 1988. Passive remembering. In Ulric Neisser & Eugene Winograd (eds.), *Remembering reconsidered*, 311–325. Cambridge: CUP.
Wegner, Daniel M. 1994. *White bears and other unwanted thoughts*, 2nd edn. New York, NY: Guilford Press.
Wierzbicka, Anna. 1972. *Semantic primitives*. Frankfurt: Athenäum.
Wierzbicka, Anna. 1980. *Lingua mentalis: The semantics of natural language*. Sydney: Academic Press.
Wierzbicka, Anna. 1996. *Semantics: Primes and universals*. Oxford: OUP.
Wierzbicka, Anna. 1997. *Understanding cultures through their key words: English, Russian, Polish, German, Japanese*. New York, NY: OUP.
Wierzbicka, Anna. 1999. *Emotions across languages and cultures*. Cambridge: CUP.
Wierzbicka, Anna. In press. Is 'remember' a universal human concept? Memory and culture. In Mengistu Amberber (ed.), *The language of memory from a cross-linguistic perspective*. Amsterdam: John Benjamins.

Winograd, Eugene. 1993. Memory in the laboratory and everyday memory: The case for both. In James M. Pucket & Hayne W. Reese (eds.), *Mechanisms of everyday cognition*, 55–70. Hillsdale, NJ: Lawrence Erlbaum.

Yoon, Kyung Joo. 2003a. Constructing a Korean Natural Semantic Metalanguage. Canberra: Australian National University PhD thesis.

Yoon, Kyung Joo. 2003b. Korean *maum* vs. English *heart* and *mind*: Contrastive semantics of cultural concepts. In Christo Moskovsky (ed.), *Proceedings of the 2003 Conference of the Australian Linguistic Society*. http://www.als.asn.au.

Yoon, Kyung Joo. In press. The Natural Semantic Metalanguage of Korean. In Cliff Goddard (ed.), *Cross-linguistic semantics*. Amsterdam: John Benjamins.

Appendix

Table 1. The proposed Korean exponents of universal semantic primes (Yoon In press)*

Substantives:	NA *I*, NE *you*, NWUKWU *someone*, SALAMTUL *people*, MWUES *something/thing*, MOM *body*
Relational substantives:	CONGLYU(-UY) *kind*, PWUPUWN(-UY) *part*
Determiners:	I *this*, TTOKKATH- *the same*, TALU- *other*
Quantifiers:	HAN *one*, TWU *two*, MYECH/ETTEN -TUL *some*, MOTUN *all*, MANH- *much/many*
Attributes:	COH- *good*, NAPPU- *bad*
Descriptors:	KHU- *big*, CAK- *small*
Mental predicates:	SAYNGKAKHA- *think*, AL- *know*, WENHA-(V + KO·SIPH-) *want*, NUKKI- *feel*, PO- *see*, TUT- *hear*
Speech:	MALHA- *say*, MAL *words*, SASIL *true*
Actions, events movement, contact:	HA- *do*, ILENA-(SAYNGKI-) *happen*, WUMCIKI- *move*, TAH-(A·ISS) *touch*
Location, existence, possession, specification:	ISS- *be (somewhere)*, ISS- *there is*, KAC- *have*, -I- *be (someone/something)*
Life and death:	SAL- *live*, CWUK- *die*
Time:	TTAY (ENCEY) *when/time*, CIKUM *now*, CEN *before*, HWU *after*, OLAY(-TONGAN) *a long time*, CAMKKAN(-TONGAN) *a short time*, ELMA TONGAN *for some time*, SWUNKAN *moment/in one moment*
Space:	KOS (ETI) *where/place*, YEKI *here*, WI *above*, ALAY *below*, MEL- *far*, KAKKAP- *near*, CCOK *side*, AN *inside*
Logical concepts:	AN (V+CI·ANH) *not*, AMA (U)L KES I- *maybe*, (U)L·SWU·(KA)·ISS- *can*, TTAYMWUN(EY) *because*, (U)MYEN *if*
Intensifier, augmentor:	ACWU *very*, TE *more*
Similarity:	KATH- *LIKE*

* The NSM model has changed a lot since it was first advanced in the early 1970s. In Anna Wierzbicka's 1972 book *Semantic Primitives*, only 14 semantic primitives were proposed and in her 1980 book *Lingua Mentalis*, the inventory was not much bigger. Over the 1980s and 1990s, however, the number of proposed primes was expanded greatly, reaching a current total of 60 or so. The same period also saw the development of some important new ideas about the syntax of the semantic metalanguage. Each member of the inventory has been selected using various theoretical bases and following cross-linguistic investigations. The current inventory, therefore, has been established on the basis of empirical findings (cf. http://www.une.edu.au/lcl/nsm/).

CHAPTER 6

Taste as a gateway to Chinese cognition

Zhengdao Ye

> People from different cultures not only speak different languages but, what is possibly more important, inhabit different sensory worlds. (Hall 1966: 2)

> His eye then finds greater enjoyment in the five colours, his ear in the five sounds, his mouth in the five tastes, and his mind benefits from processing all that is in the world. (*Xunzi*, 1.14, 340–245 B.C.)

In the Western philosophical tradition, taste is regarded as a lower-level sense. This may explain why few linguistic studies have explored its role in human cognition. Yet, to fully understand the Chinese conceptual world, one has to understand the meanings of its rich 'taste'-based vocabulary. This study seeks to bring this important aspect of Chinese sensory and cognitive experience to the attention of researchers of human cognition. It proposes a Chinese model of cognitive states in relation to taste, and discusses the cultural bases for the peculiarly Chinese "embodied" way of experiencing. It also discusses the physiological basis that seems to underpin the general principles of the cognitive system observed in Chinese and in some Indo-European languages.

1 Introduction

Linguistic research into the relationships between physical experience and the conceptual system has so far paid scant attention to the role that taste plays in human cognition. This is related to the general view that taste is a lower-level sense in the Western philosophical tradition. That is, the sense of taste is viewed as being inferior to some other senses, such as that of sight and hearing (see e.g. Vinge 1975; Synott 1991). As such, it is generally regarded as a poor source domain for the target domain of mental states and mental activity (e.g. Danesi 1990; Sweetser 1990). Yet, to fully understand the Chinese conceptual world and the Chinese way of thinking, knowing and feeling (including literary thought), one has to understand the meanings of 'taste'-based vocabulary, a rich and salient domain in the Chinese language.[1] The purpose of this study is to bring this important aspect of the Chinese sensory and cognitive experience to the attention of researchers of human cognition. To this end, I will investigate some Chinese expressions based around the generic nominal term *wèi* 'taste', and explicate and represent their meanings using the framework of the Natural Semantic Metalanguage (NSM). From this we can see how Chinese 'taste' experiences are mapped onto various cognitive domains. By highlighting and illustrating the important role that taste plays in the formation of the Chinese conceptual system, this study raises and addresses a much neglected, yet important question – in what way can we study the bodily and conceptual experience of a cultural tradition where there has not been a divide between the body and the "mind"?

In Section 2, the important role that taste plays in Chinese language and thought will be illustrated with some examples. Section 3 introduces the methodology that this study uses for semantic analysis. In particular, it will explain why the theory of conceptual metaphor – which has been a dominant framework for analysing the link between bodily experience and conceptual systems – has not been chosen for the purpose of this study, taking into consideration aspects of Chinese philosophical tradition. In Section 4, a detailed semantic analysis of a set of Chinese 'taste'-related terms will be undertaken, and their semantic content and structure will be discussed. Section 5 will discuss the theoretical and methodological implications of this study. It proposes a Chinese model of cognitive states in relation to the Chinese sensory experience of taste based on our previous analysis. The physiological basis that seems to underpin the general principles of the cognitive system observed in Chinese and in some Indo-European languages will be discussed, as well as the cultural bases for the peculiarly Chinese "embodied" way of thinking, knowing and feeling. Outstanding issues for future research will be outlined.

2 A taste of Chinese 'taste'-related words

Wèi 味 'taste' plays an important role in Chinese language and thought.[2] Taste-related vocabulary is rich and abundant in Chinese, describing experiences that are far

---

1. Chinese in this chapter refers to Modern Standard Chinese (Mandarin).
2. The modern Chinese correlate of the English noun *taste* is the monosyllabic *wèi* 味 and the diasyllabic *wèidào* 味道 or *zīwèi* 滋味. *Wèi* and *wèidào* are polysemous, meaning both 'taste' and 'smell'. In classical Chinese, however, *wèi* means 'taste' only (e.g. GHC 1999), and *wèidào*, a verb-object phrase, means 'to taste/know the meaning of principle or truth'. It is of interest to note that Viberg's (1984) typological study of lexicalisation patterns of perception verbs has shown that "there is an obvious link between taste and smell" (Viberg 1984: 146). It should also be noted

beyond the purely gustatory. As a simple example, to say in Chinese that a woman or a man is 'womanly/feminine' or 'manly/masculine', one would evoke the notion of *wèi*: *yǒu nǚrén wèi* 有女人味 'have woman *wèi*' or *yǒu nánrén wèi* 有男人味 'have man *wèi*'. When something does not go the way that one anticipates, one can say *biànwèi le* 变味了 'the *wèi* has changed', *pǎowèi le* 跑味了 'the *wèi* has escaped', or *zǒuwèi le* 走味了 'the *wèi* has left'. As another example, right after the 2005 Chinese New Year's Eve gala on TV, the most widely watched program across Mainland China, there were various newspaper commentary articles about the 'taste' (i.e. quality) of the show. We can get a glimpse from the following title of an article:[3]

(1) 记者点评银屏年夜饭味道如何？
Jìzhě   diǎnpíng   yínpíng 'niányèfàn'   wèidào rúhé?
journalist commenting.on screen New Year's Eve.meal taste how
'A journalist's appraisal of the New Year's Eve gala.'

The following list of some of the *wèi*-related words found in a popular Chinese-English bilingual dictionary (DeFrancis 1997, with some of the translations modified) shows clearly that *wèi* plays a salient role in Chinese people's mental life.[4] For convenience, these words have been grouped under the headings of 'feeling', 'thinking', and 'knowing'. It is obvious that the mental states embodied in many of these words cut across these three categories, and some relate to all of them.

---

that the perception verb of 'taste' is *cháng* 尝, which also has the meaning of 'to try' and 'to experience'. However, unlike the English verb *taste*, *cháng* cannot take a copulative complement (e.g. 'X tastes delicious'). The meaning of *wèi* or *wèidào* includes both 'taste' and 'flavour'.

3. All the examples if unspecified are from http://yahoo.com.cn.

4. 4. According to Chao and Yang (1962: 32), *wèi* functions as a bound morpheme in modern Chinese. This, however, is not always the case. For example, *wèi* in the following line from a contemporary vernacular poem by He Qifang (cited in *The Great Dictionary of the Chinese Language*, HDC 1995, Vol. 3: 252) also functions as a free morpheme:

为什么海水有咸的味?
wèishěnme hǎishuǐ yǒu xián de wèi?
why   sea.water have salty LIG taste
'Why is the sea water salty?'

Also, in most of the *wèi*-related set phrases, it functions as a free morpheme, such as in the case of *wèitóngjiáolà* 味同嚼蜡 [taste-like-chew-wax] 'as tasteless as wax', 'insipid'. A Chinese frequency dictionary (XHZTB 1992) shows that there are 2743 occurrences of *wèi* from a computation of 11,873,029 randomly sampled characters (*zì*) in a corpus of Social and Natural Sciences, and that it ranks 774th among 7754 characters. Therefore, it occurs on a very frequent basis. It should be borne in mind that, in most cases, *zì* [character-word] in compounds of Modern Chinese can exist independently as a unit, and that they represent the folk notion of what constitutes a word for the Chinese people (see e.g. Ye In press).

a. feeling [5]
   zīwèi: 滋味 [grow-taste]: taste/feeling
   qùwèi: 趣味 [interest-taste]: interest; delight
   fáwèi: 乏味 [lack-taste]: dull; uninteresting
b. thinking
   huíwèi 回味 [return-taste]: to recall something and ponder on it; after taste
   wánwèi 玩味 [play with-taste]: to ponder; to ruminate
   rùwèi: 入味 [enter-taste]: to be absorbed in
   kǒuwèi: 口味 [mouth-taste]: personal taste
   yìwèi: 意味 [meaning-taste]: meaning, significance; interest; overtone
c. knowing
   tǐwèi 体味 [body-taste]: to understand; to appreciate
   pǐnwèi: 品味 [sample-taste]: to appreciate; taste (noun)

Wèi also occupies an important place in Chinese literary thought. Stephen Owen (1992) includes the term *wèi* in a glossary of basic terms that he believes are important in order to understand Chinese treatises on literature. He remarks that *wèi* is "an important master metaphor in describing the aesthetic experience of the text" and that "a complex set of gustatory terms was generated around *wèi*" (Owen 1992: 593).

For Chinese literary theorists (as well as for the Chinese reader), *wèi* signifies an important quality of an essay or literary work. *Yáo Nǎi* (1731–1815), for example, considered the following eight elements as the basis for the analysis of a literary piece: *shén* 神 (presiding spirit), *lì* 利 (moral principle), *qì* 气 (generative energy), *wèi* 味 (taste), *gé* 格 (structure), *lǜ* 律 (measure), *shēng* 声 (sound) and *sè* 色 (colour) (cited in Pollard 2000: 13, translation Pollard's).

In Section 4, I will analyse some *wèi*-related words in everyday usage to illustrate the important role that 'taste' plays in shaping the Chinese conceptual system. Due to confines of space, I will only be able to focus on a selected few from each of the three groups mentioned earlier. But before proceeding to the analysis of the meanings of the terms, it is necessary and important to first explain the methodological tool that will be employed to describe and represent the meanings of the terms under consideration.

---

5. Alongside the regular English translation, a character-by-character gloss is given. Like most Chinese compounds, composite characters in each of these compounds can exist as a self-sufficient unit with its independent meaning. In this chapter, I specifically deal with the meanings of the compounds that contain the *wèi* element.

3. Research methodology

In cognitive linguistics the most common theoretical framework for investigating how bodily experience contributes to the conceptual system is the "conceptual metaphor" theory typically associated with Lakoff and Johnson's seminal book *Metaphors We Live By* (1980), and their more recent book *Philosophy in the Flesh* (1999). The key tenets of this theory are that human thought is embodied largely in human sensory-motor experience, and that conceptual metaphor is the key mechanism in extending bodily experience to the shaping of abstract concepts. The conceptual metaphor theory has been widely adopted in studying the cognitive systems of other languages and cultures including Chinese (see, e.g. Yu 1998, 2003).

However, this study will not adopt this popular approach. The reasons for this are twofold. Firstly, although the idea of the "embodiment" of thought has been a welcome challenge to some of the deepest assumptions in Western philosophy – in particular those traditions where the mind is considered independent of the body – it would seem superfluous to apply metaphor theory to explain the relationship between the Chinese sensory and conceptual systems. This is because the body/mind dichotomy has never occurred in Chinese philosophical tradition and in Chinese folk beliefs. In the view of the Chinese people, the "mind" is always "embodied", as reflected most tellingly in the word *xīn*, often translated as *heart* or *mind*, which designates the seat of thinking, knowing, and feeling for the Chinese people. In the following quote, Hall and Ames (1987) argue convincingly that applying the dualistic mode of thinking of the Western tradition to the study of the Chinese way of thinking can conceal a true picture of the Chinese experience. They write:

> The dualistic relationship between *psyche* and *soma* that has so plagued the Western tradition has given rise to problems of a most troublesome sort. In the polar metaphysics of the classical Chinese tradition, the correlative relationship between the psychical and the somatic militated against the emergence of a mind/body problem. It is not that the Chinese thinkers were able to reconcile this dichotomy; rather, it never emerged as a problem. Because body and mind were not regarded as essentially different kinds of existence, they did not generate different sets of terminologies necessary to describe them. For this reason, the qualitative modifiers we usually associated with matter do double duty in Chinese, characterizing both the physical and the psychical. (Hall & Ames 1987: 20)

The second reason for not using the conceptual metaphor theory for the purpose of this chapter lies in its lack of commitment to provide an adequate interpretive and descriptive framework for detailed, fine analysis of the meanings of the concepts under cross-linguistic investigation. It may well be that the meanings of these concepts differ significantly from the categories of metaphors postulated on the basis of the English language and cultural experience. Furthermore, it seems that much work in studying the relationship between the body and the conceptual system in Chinese that is readily available to Western scholars has mainly sought to prove the universal applicability of the conceptual metaphor (often relying on uncritical and misleading translations) rather than paying attention to the exact meanings and structure of the concepts under discussion. As an example, in his discussion of anger metaphors in Chinese, Ning Yu (1998), glosses *qi* 'essence of life force/vital energy/breath', a key Chinese cultural concept, as 'gas' to support his claim that in Chinese, anger is conceptualised as GAS IN A CONTAINER. Regrettably, this lack of a culture-internal perspective often gives a distorted picture of Chinese bodily experience and its relationship to the Chinese conceptual system (cf. Ye 2002).

To use conceptual metaphor would still leave the following two questions, which are fundamental to understanding the Chinese experience and the Chinese conceptual structure, unaddressed and unresolved. The first question is how to provide a *unified* account of studying bodily experience in relation to concept formation in a non-Cartesian cultural and philosophical tradition. The second is how the semantic content and structure of a local meaning system such as that embodied in the Chinese language can be made accessible and intelligible to non-Chinese people with little, if any, loss in meaning.

The Natural Semantic Metalanguage (NSM) framework, a well-established and rigorous linguistic semantic theory developed by Anna Wierzbicka and colleagues over the last three decades, provides a possible solution to these questions. The basic idea underpinning NSM is that there is a set of semantic primitives that are shared by all languages, and that this set of semantic primitives can be the basis of a universally applicable metalanguage. Therefore, explications of terms and expressions based on this metalanguage should have an exact translation equivalent in any language. So far, sixty primitives, such as I, KNOW, THINK, FEEL, GOOD, HAPPEN, SEE and BECAUSE, along with a "universal grammar" that governs certain aspects of the combinatorial behaviour of these primitives, are argued to be universal from cross-linguistic investigations of typologically different and unrelated languages.[6]

In the next section, I will use the Natural Semantic Metalanguage to represent the meanings of the concepts under discussion. My primary goal is to provide an account of bodily experience and conceptual experience as they are understood and perceived by Chinese people. My second goal is to interpret the pathways that link sensory experience to the conceptual domain.

---

6. For detailed information on the inventory of the semantic primitives and how they are identified cross-linguistically, see Wierzbicka (1996); Goddard and Wierzbicka (1994, 2002). For the Chinese exponents of the metalanguage, see Chappell (2002). This chapter will use the English exponents of NSM. Due to space constraints, the Chinese versions of the explications will not be presented. For examples of Chinese translations of English explications, see Ye (2001, 2004).

4 Semantic analysis of Chinese 'taste' terms

4.1 *Zīwèi* 'taste/feeling'

Zīwèi is perhaps one of the most widely used *wèi*-related terms in Chinese. It has two distinct meanings – 'taste' (*zīwèi₁*) and 'feeling' (*zīwèi₂*). Using the NSM framework, its 'sui generis' taste meaning can be explained as follows:

[A]   *zīwèi₁* ('taste')
   a.   something is touching some places inside someone's *zuǐ* 'mouth' [M] [7]
   b.   because of this, this someone can feel something for some time
   c.   because of this, this someone can know something about this thing

Zīwèi also refers to feelings and emotions, as shown in the following extremely colloquial expression:

(2)   心里不是滋味
       xīnli   búshì   zīwèi
       heart.inside NEG.be   ziwei
       'feel something bad'

As another example:

(3)   真是诸多滋味在心头
       zhēnshì   zhùduō   zīwèi   zài   xīntóu
       true.BE   many   ziwei   LOC   heart.head
       '[When I thought that in all these years of managing the company, we had weathered the same wind and rain together, progressed and retreated, trusted and supported each other, and the company grew because of our painstaking effort,] many feelings were aroused in my heart.' (Hoogewerf & Chen 2003: 105)

In its 'feeling' sense, *zīwèi* typically occurs with *xīnli* [heart-inside] or *xīntóu* [heart-head], which can be seen as a criterion for distinguishing the two senses of *zīwèi*. Another criterion is that only when *zīwèi* refers to 'feeling and emotion' can it be modified by *yīfān*, a classifier, as reflected in the following line from a pop song (which is adapted from an ancient poem).

(4)   别有一番滋味在心头
       bié   yǒu   yī-fān   zīwèi   zài   xīntóu
       other have   one-CL   ziwei   LOC   heart.head
       'have rather unusual feelings'

---

7.   [M] stands for semantic molecule. A semantic molecule is a packet of meaning functioning as a unit in a larger explication or cultural script (see Wierzbicka 1996: 221, In press).

The explication for *zīwèi₂* is as follows:

[B]   *zīwèi₂* ('feeling')
   a. someone felt something, because this someone thought something
   b. this someone felt like someone feels when this someone *cháng* 'tastes' [M] something

Apart from the generic term *zīwèi*, specific taste describing terms in Chinese, such as *suān* 'sour', *tián* 'sweet', *kǔ* 'bitter', *là* 'hot/spicy', are used extensively to describe specific feelings (see Ye 2007, for a detailed semantic analysis of some of these terms). As a matter of fact, *suāntiánkǔlà* [sour-sweet-bitter-spicy], as a set phrase, means 'all kinds of emotions and feelings'.

4.2   *Huíwèi* 回味 [return to-taste] 'to enjoy in retrospect'

Huíwèi, which is often glossed as 'recall something and ponder it' (e.g. DeFrancis 1997: 258), is a commonly used expression.[8] It frequently appears in essay and song titles, such as in *wǎngshì zhǐnéng huíwèi* 往事只能回味 [past-event-only-can-*huíwèi*] 'The past can only be enjoyed in retrospect'; 'We cannot bring back the past', which has almost become a cliché. This 'something' that the experiencer wants to 'return to' mentally is always a fond and long-lasting memory. Perhaps 'to recollect the pleasant flavour of' or 'to enjoy in retrospect' may be a better translation of *huíwèi*. It seems that, intuitively, *huíwèi* is polysemous. *Huíwèi* is directly related to a gastronomic experience, with its focus on some special quality of the food that has "impressed" and brought pleasure to the experiencer and has subsequently left him or her with a fond memory. This is reflected in Example (5).

(5)   谁都喜欢回味, 吃过饺子, 人们会回味肉葱味儿; 吃过馒头, 回味那松软。
Shuí dōu xǐhuān huíwèi, chī-guò jiǎozǐ, rénmen huì huíwèi
who all like *huíwèi* eat-EXP dumpling people will *huíwèi*
ròucōngwèir; chī-guò mántou, huíwèi nà sōngruǎn
meat.shallot.flavour eat-EXP steamed.bun *huíwèi* that loose.soft
'Everyone likes *huíwèi*. After eating dumplings, people will *huíwèi* the flavour of the meat and shallots; after eating a steamed bun, people will *huíwèi* its softness.'

---

8.   *Huíwèi* is analysed here in its verbal form. It can also function as a noun, meaning something like 'aftertaste', whose range of use is however beyond the aftertaste that food brings, but extends to many other things, in particular a good article or a piece of music. A set phrase such as *huíwèi wúqióng* 回味无穷 [*huíwèi*-infinite] means 'long-lasting aftertaste'.

The meaning of *huíwèi₁* can be explicated as follows:

[C] *huíwèi₁* ('to recollect the pleasant flavour of')
   a. someone is thinking something like this now:
   b. "a short time before now, I *cháng-le* 'tasted' [M] something
   c. when I was *cháng* 'tasting' [M] it
   d. I could think many good things about it
   e. when I was thinking about these good things,
         I felt something good at that time
   f. I now want to think about these things for some time"
   g. because of this, this someone is thinking about these good things for some time
   h. when this someone is thinking about these good things
         this someone feels something very good

Huíwèi₁, which is deeply grounded in the gastronomic experience, serves as a prototype for modelling the meaning of *huíwèi₂*, which extends to other pleasant experiences that are non-gastronomic in nature, as exemplified by (6)–(7).

(6) 回味童年[的美好时光]
   huíwèi tóngnián [de méihǎo shíguāng]
   huíwèi childhood LIG good   time
   'recall and ponder [the happy moments of] one's childhood'

(7) 能取得这个成绩已经够我回味很长时间了。
   Néng qǔdé   zhè-gè   chéngjì yǐjīng gòu   wǒ huíwèi
   can   achieve this-CL result   already enough 1SG *huíwèi*
   hěncháng shíjiān-le.
   very.long time-PFV
   '[I am now still in a state of excitement.] To be able to achieve this result has already given me a long time to *huíwèi*.'

It seems that *huíwèi₁* usually takes place immediately after the gastronomic experience, whereas *huíwèi₂* can refer back to an experience a long time ago as in Example (6), which also shows a typical subject for *huíwèi* – a wonderful memory of the past. Example (7) was said by Liu Xiang, the men's 100 metre hurdle champion at the 2004 Olympic Games, in response to journalists' questions after the event. Both examples suggest strongly that the experiencers actively participated in the past experience. That is, the experiencers were actively 'doing something', not merely that 'something was happening to the experiencer'. Indeed, to say **huíwèi mǔqīn de aì* 回味母亲的爱 'to *huíwèi* mother's love' would be unacceptable because the experiencer is a passive receiver of another person's action, not the creator of his or her own 'enjoyment'.

If the focus of *huíwèi₁* is on the certain quality of the food that had given the experiencer a pleasant experience, it is the highlighted aspects of the non-gustatory experience in the meaning of *huíwèi₂* that made the experiencer wish to revisit it. The meaning of *huíwèi₂* can be explicated as follows:

[D] *huíwèi₂* ('to enjoy in retrospect')
    a. someone is thinking something like this now:
    b. "some time before now, I was doing something
    c. when I was doing this thing, I felt something very good at that time
    d. I could think many good things about it afterwards because of this
    e. when I thought about these good things afterwards, I felt something very good
    f. I want to think about these good things for some time"
    g. because of this, this someone is thinking these good for some time
    h. like people can think about good things for some time AFTER they *cháng* 'taste' [M] something good

To some extent, the 'enjoyment' aspect of the experience reflected in *huíwèi₁* (components c–e) and *huíwèi₂* (components c–d) brings to mind the English word *savour*. However, the meaning of *savour* differs from both senses of *huíwèi* in a number of important ways. Firstly, *savour* refers mainly to a concurrent experience. Although one can *savour* a moment from the past, such usage is relatively marginal, and marked (e.g. *savour the memorable episodes*). The expression *savour the moment* is usually understood as referring to current experience. On the contrary, the 'enjoyment' aspect of the past experience in *huíwèi* would be seen as the very 'trigger' for the experiencer to want to 'return to' the experience afterwards. The thought in *huíwèi* is decisively retrospective, not directed to the current activity.

Secondly, *savour* suggests that while the experiencer wants to 'indulge' themselves in an experience while it lasts, they seem to be aware that they cannot enjoy it again in such a way – 'I don't want to think about other things now; because if I do not feel what I feel now, I can't feel like this afterwards.'

'Many good things' in component (d) characterises the detailed and fine nature of the thought process that goes with *huíwèi*, which highlights certain aspects of the past experience.

When something is described as *hényǒu huíwèi* 很有回味 'full of aftertaste', it implicitly refers to food. This supports our position that *huíwèi₁* serves as a prototypical meaning for the meaning of *huíwèi₂*. Of course, many things can be described as 'full of aftertaste' or 'memorable', such as a piece of writing, a concert, or a show.

Surely, a person who ponders (*huíwèi₂*) his or her memorable childhood does not necessarily think of it in terms of gustatory experience. However, from a semantic point of view, especially that of the "bridging context" between two distinguishable but related senses – that is the recurrent context in which the new meaning arises as the result of pragmatic enrichment through context-specific inference (e.g. Evans 1992; Evans & Wilkins 2000; Wilkins 1996; cf. Traugott & Dasher 2002), component (h) (referring to tasting) provides a key link. Note that it is not included in the thought of the experiencer, but formulated in such a way that they reflect the intrinsic and parallel link between how a person thinks after an enjoyable gastronomic experience and how a person thinks after a memorable experience. Since this chapter is a first attempt to investigate the link between the Chinese sensory and conceptual experience, it is still at the stage of experimenting and exploring the ways in which the link between the two can be best and most accurately reflected.

The 'AFTER' element in component (h) also tries to reflect the lingering 'aftertaste' implied by both senses of *huíwèi*. To have 'aftertaste' is an important quality that Chinese people not only attach to food, but also to a good piece of writing, music, or a show. To quote Owen again:

> There were several sources of *wèi*'s appeal to theorists: it admitted broad shared categories that are held in common (e.g., "salty" or "sour"), while permitting both the cultivation and absolute particularity of individual taste. Another attraction of *wèi* is that it lingers after eating, as the *wèi* of texts endures, changes, and attenuates after reading. Chinese theorists tended not to speak of disjunctive acts of reflection on the "meaning" of a text, but rather of the "continuation" of the text in the mind after reading it over, a time in which the significance of the text gradually unfolds. (Owen 1992: 593–594)

The semantic structure and content of *huíwèi₁* and *huíwèi₂* have shown how Chinese people single out certain aspects of the gustatory experience (such as the 'enjoyable' aspect of the experience, which one can 'revisit' mentally afterwards) that are psychologically salient to them and extend them to fine mental processes, in particular how they are linked with feelings and thoughts. It is not an exaggeration to say that Chinese memory experience is very much embodied.

4.3   *rùwèi* 入味 [enter-flavour] 'full of flavour'; 'be absorbed in doing something'

Rùwèi can function as an attributive predicate or a verb complement. In its attributive use, *rùwèi* refers to food only, meaning that the food (such as soup or a dish) is tasty. This meaning of *rùwèi* can be explicated as follows:

[E] $X_{something}$ *rùwèi₁* ('X is flavourful')
    a.   sometimes someone can think like this about something:
    b.   "when I *cháng* 'taste' [M] this thing, I feel something very good
    c.   I think some very good things about it
    d.   I want to *cháng* 'taste' [M] it for a long time
    e.   I don't want to *cháng* 'taste' [M] anything else"

f.   this someone can think like this about all parts of this thing

Something is *rùwei* when all of its parts are saturated in flavour (component f). In this regard, the way that Chinese food is prepared and cooked is a relevant factor. Chinese food is usually finely chopped, allowing easy passage for flavour to 'penetrate' each part of the food. Also, small pieces can be easily retained in the mouth for a period of time, and only in this way can people chew each piece and 'play with' (*wánwèi*) it to get a deep and fine flavour out of the food. This characteristic of the Chinese culinary method has a bearing on the Chinese gustatory experience, and apparently gives rise to various thought-related experiences, which are finely tuned (e.g. *huíwèi* discussed earlier in Section 4.2).

A tasty thing naturally brings pleasant feelings to the 'taster', who can be indulgent in the eating experience. This is apparently the link between the attributive *rùwèi$_1$* and the complement *rùwèi$_2$*, when it is used to describe the 'self-indulgent' manner in which the experiencer is enjoying doing something. Consider the following example:

(8)   X 听得很 入味。
      X *tīng-de   hěn   rùwèi*.
      X listen-EXT very *rùwèi*
      'X is absorbed in listening to something.'

The meaning of *rùwèi$_2$* when it functions as a verb complement can be formulated as follows:

[F] X_{person} $V_{complement}$ *rùwèi$_2$* ('X is absorbed in doing something')
  a.   when someone is doing some things
          this someone can feel something very good because of this
  b.   this someone can think like this about it:
  c.   "I want to feel like this for a long time
  d.   because of this, I want to do this for a long time
  e.   I don't want to do anything else now
  f.   like I don't want to *cháng* 'taste' [M] anything else when I *cháng* 'taste' [M] something very good"

Component (a) shows that *rùwèi$_2$* is always about a present activity in which the experiencer actively participates, and that the person is 'enjoying' what he or she is doing.

Components (b)–(e) describe the mental state of the experience where a person is absorbed in what they are doing, i.e. they 'feel so good' that they do not want to do anything else at that moment.

Component (f) alludes to the strong connection between *rùwèi$_1$* and *rùwèi$_2$*. For native speakers, there is a strong evocation of the sense of taste in the meaning of *rùwèi₂*. This is why (f) is built into the thoughts of the experiencer in the explication (cf. the explication for *huíwèi₂* in Section 4.2). The experiencers of the two forms of *rùwèi* seem to have similar facial expressions – closing one's eyes, and 'wagging' one's head, which shows complete gratification and absorption. With *rùwèi₁*, the conjectured image of the facial expression of the experiencer may also include his or her chewing slowly and 'tasting' or 'playing with' the food in the mouth.

4.4 *tǐwèi* 体味 [body-taste] 'to understand through thinking about experience'

Tǐwèi not only means to know something through experience, but also to come to appreciate the exact quality and meaning of this something through thinking deeply about the experience. *Tǐwèi* usually takes as object an abstract concept, which stands for the quality that an experience embodies or brings, as reflected in the following example:

(9) 我家一直很穷苦, 我在穷苦中<u>体味</u>到家庭的艰辛。
    Wǒjiā   yīzhí   hěnqióngkǔ   wǒ-zài   qióngkǔzhōng
    1SG.family always very.poor.hardship 1SG-LOC poor.hardship.in
    <u>*tǐwèi*</u>-*dào   jiātíng de jiānxīn*
    tǐwèi-arrive family LIG hardship
    'My family has always been poor: from very young, I came to understand/appreciate what family hardship means.'

In Example (9), *tǐwèi* takes the resultative verb complement *dào* [arrive], which codes the aspectual meaning of 'achievement'. This example showcases the scenario of the experiencer arriving at the stage of having 'figured out' what family hardship is.

In the following example, *tǐwèi* takes the durative aspectual marker *-zhe* 着, showcasing a scenario where the experiencer is 'figuring out' what is embodied in an experience.

(10) <u>体味</u>着家/亲情的温暖
    <u>*tǐwèi*</u>-*zhe   jiā/qīnqíng   de   wēnnuǎn*
    tǐwèi-DUR   family/kin.bond   LIG   warmth
    'to experience the warmth of a family/family bond'

'Thinking' here plays an important role, because a person can come from a warm family without understanding what this 'warmth' means. Such an understanding can only be obtained by applying deep thinking about the experience.

For a better understanding of the meaning of *tǐwèi₁*, it is instructive to compare it with its related concepts of *tǐyàn* 'to experience firsthand' and *tǐhuì* 'to understand through something beyond the intellect', 'to comprehend intuitively', all of which suggest some degree of personal experience. *Tǐyàn* 'to experience firsthand' however does not imply 'thinking about' the experience. It only means to know something through firsthand experience (like 'been there and done it'). Thus, *tǐyàn àozhōu shēnghuó* [*tǐyàn*-Australian-life] simply means to experience Australian-style life by, for example, living in Australia. As a result, the experiencer knows what Australian life is like. But once a person has 'experienced' Australian life, or is in the process of 'experiencing' it, they can be said to *tǐhuì* 'understand intuitively' or *tǐwèi* 'to understand by thinking about the experience' certain aspects of Australian life, such as its hardship or comforts. In other words, *tǐyàn* is to know how or what it is like; *tǐhuì* and *tǐwèi* to know what it means.

The element of 'understanding' allows both *tǐhuì* and *tǐwèi* (but not *tǐyàn* 'to experience firsthand') to take 'objects' that are abstract concepts such as someone's words or the meaning of a piece of writing. For example:

(11) 体味/ 体会 /*体验老师的话
tǐwèi/ *tǐhuì*/**tǐyàn* lǎoshī de huà
tǐwèi/ *tǐhuì*/**tǐyàn* teacher LIG word
'to understand the meaning of the teacher's words'

Although both *tǐhuì* and *tǐwèi* are acceptable in the above example, they convey slightly different meanings. *Tǐwèi* implies a deep, fine and detailed thinking process, which is absent in the meaning of *tǐhuì*. It implies that the experiencer thinks about every aspect of the teacher's words in order to reach a comprehensive understanding of the teacher's message. Thus, using *tǐwèi* in the above example implies that the person will ponder the teacher's words in order to understand their deep meaning (which also implies that the teacher's words are full of meaning, subtle, and not so easy to understand). Whereas, the use of *tǐhuì* would suggest to get at the meaning of something simply by 'feeling' it. This difference between the two terms renders *tǐhuì* 'to understand intuitively' completely out of place in the following example:

(12) 痛苦是一本书, 研究它, 体味/?体会它, 咀嚼它, 会有诸多独特的感觉。
tòngkǔ shì yī-běn shū, yánjiū tā, tǐwèi/?tǐhuì tā,
pain be one-CL book study 3SG tǐwèi/?tǐhuì 3SG
jǔjué tā, huìyǒu zhùduō dútè de gǎnjué.
chew 3SG will.have many unique LIG feeling
'Pain is like a book. By studying it, thinking about it, and digesting it, one will come to have many special feelings about it.'

This is because the absence of the element of reflective thinking in the meaning of *tǐhuì* 'to understand intuitively' makes it incongruous with words like 'study it' and 'chew it', which suggest a fine, detailed, concentrated thinking process.

Chapter 6. Taste as a gateway to Chinese cognition   123

The same can be said with respect to the following example:

(13) 在贾志林家里，记者再一次体味了生离死别的人世悲情。
Zài   Jiǎng Zhìlín jiāli,   jìzhe   zài   yí-cí
LOC   name   home.inside reporter again one-time.CL
tǐwèi-le   shēnglísībié   de   rénshì   bēiqíng
tǐwèi-PFV live.apart.death.apart LIG human.world tragic/sad.feeling
'At the home of Jiang Zhiling, I, as the reporter, once again experienced the sorrow of life and death in this human world.'

The context in which the reporter uttered this sentence in (13) was following a mining explosion in Inner Mongolia. *Tǐhuì* 'to understand intuitively' would sound shallow and unsympathetic on the part of the reporter since the sorrow and grief experienced by the victims' family can only be appreciated and understood via deep thinking about the experience of the family (of course the reporter needs to be with the family to experience their sorrow in the first place).

It is not surprising then that *tǐhuì* 'to understand intuitively' cannot take the durative aspectual marker *-zhe* (*tǐhuì-zhe*), whereas *tǐwèi* can (cf. example 10). This is exactly because *tǐwèi* denotes a thinking process, which is not part of the meaning of *tǐhuì*. The adverbial phrases that are commonly used to describe the manner of *tǐwèi* include *xìxì de* [fine.RDP-ADV] 'finely, in detail'; *zǐxì de* [careful-ADV] 'carefully', and *yòngxīn* [use-heart] 'with heart', as exemplified by (14):

(14) 细细地体味自己对你的思恋
xìxì-de   tǐwèi zìjǐ   duìnǐ   de   sīliàn
fine.RDP-ADV tǐwèi self toward.2SG LIG missing/attachment
'[Only when you are not in front of me am I immersed in the feelings towards you], and to experience my longing for you in every fine detail.'

It is interesting to note that *tǐwèi* is widely used in Chinese travel advertisements, as reflected in the following examples:

(15) 体味神秘古老的异族文化历史变迁
tǐwèi shénmì   gǔlǎo   de   yìzú   wénhuà lìshǐ   biànqiān
tǐwèi mysterious ancient LIG yi.ethnic   culture history change
'Understanding the historical changes of the ancient Yi ethnic culture.'

(16) 体味旅游/ 垂钓的乐趣
tǐwèi lǚyóu/chuídiào   de   lèqù
tǐwèi travel/fishing   LIG enjoyment/fun
'to experience and appreciate the fun of travel/fishing'

(17) 体味江南人情风俗的细腻
      <u>tǐwèi</u> jiāngnán   rénqíng   fēngsú de   xìnì
      <u>tǐwèi</u> river.south people.atmosphere custom LIG fine/subtle
      'to experience and appreciate the subtleties of the life and customs of the water region to the south of Yangtze'

The use of *tǐwèi* incidentally reflects the emphasis that the Chinese people place on their travelling experience – reflecting more on the "meaning" of the experience than on experiencing as such.

The meaning of *tǐwèi* can be formulated as follows:[9]

[G] *tǐwèi* ('to understand through thinking about experience')
   a. when something (X) is happening to someone
      this someone can feel something because of this
      this someone can know something about it (X) because of this
   b. this someone can think something like this:
      "I want to know what this something is
      I can't know what it is if I don't think many things about it for some time
      I want to think many things about it for some time"
   c. because of this, this someone thinks many things about it for some time
   d. afterwards, this someone can think like this about it (X) because of this:
      "now I know what this something is"

Component (a) shows that *tǐwèi* is related to personal experience. Component (b) suggests that the experiencer is consciously aware that they can come to know that the meaning of the experience is something that can be reflected on, and something that the experiencer wants to do. 'Think many things' and 'for some time' in (c) describe the fine and detailed thought process. 'Because of this' in (d) indicates that 'realisation' and 'understanding' – 'now I know what this something is' – result from thinking about the experience. In general, this explication tries to capture the 'thinking' as a mental process in the meaning of *tǐwèi*.

In modern Chinese, the evocation of and the association with the gustatory experience in the meaning of *tǐwèi* may not be as strong as those present in *huíwèi* (Section 4.2) and *rùwèi* (Section 4.3), the two other *wèi*-related concepts analysed earlier. For this reason, the prototype of the gustatory experience is not built into the meaning of *tǐwèi* (unlike the other two explications discussed earlier). However, it is not difficult to appreciate the close link between the kind of mental states

---

9. It is obvious that the verb *taste* is closer in its meaning to *tǐyàn* 'to experience firsthand', which does not contain the thinking element. It seems that cross-linguistically the extension of the meaning of the perception verb 'to taste' to mean 'to experience' is quite common, and worth further investigation.

embodied in *tǐwèi* and those found in the Chinese gustatory experience, where the emphasis is placed on the reflection on the true essence of the food.

It should be pointed out that in classical Chinese, where monosyllabic words prevail, the use of *wèi* 'taste/flavour' as a verb to mean *tǐwèi* is common. Citing examples from *Lü˘ Shì Chūnqiū* dating back to ca. 239 B.C., *Gǔdài Hànyǔ Cídiǎn* (*A Dictionary of Ancient Chinese*), for example, explains that one of the meanings of *wèi* as a verb is *tǐwèi*. In fact, the *wèi* in *tǐwèi* can be thought of as retaining this verbal use.

Another point is that, as a noun, the meaning of *wèi* 'taste/flavour' can be extended to mean 'the meaning, essence, quality, or the significance' of something. This usage is prevalent in both classical and modern Chinese. If for the Chinese people, the taste of something means and signifies something, then it is not difficult to see how *wèi* can stand for 'the meaning or quality or essence' of something. The hallmark of the Chinese gustatory experience is to 'savour' the deeply entrenched *wèi*. Thus, to *tǐwèi* something is essentially to understand its meaning.

As we have seen from a number of explications, Chinese people attach particular importance to the 'thought' element of their gustatory-related experience, and to the active interaction of the thoughts of the experiencer and the experience itself. Once again, the Chinese culinary style (discussed in relation to the meaning of *rùwèi* in Section 4.3) is not irrelevant in the context of understanding how gustatory experience gives rise to culturally salient mental activities and mental processes such as 'thinking' for Chinese people.

4.5 *pǐnwèi* 品味 v. 'to taste in order to appreciate'; n. 'taste'

Used as a verb, *pǐnwèi* can refer to food-related objects, such as *hǎochá* 'good-tea' and *jiāyáo* 'good dish', and abstract concepts such as *rénshēng* 'life/life course', *gūdú* 'solitude', *shēngmìng de zhēndì* 'the true meaning of life', and *làngmàn* 'romance'. Therefore, two senses of *pǐnwèi* are posited, with *pǐnwèi₁* directly referring to gustatory experience, and *pǐnwèi₂* to non-gustatory experience. The explications of these two senses of *pǐnwèi* are as follows:

[H] *pǐnwèi₁* ('to taste in order to appreciate')
    a. sometimes, someone can think like this about something when this someone is *cháng* 'tasting' [M] something
    b. "it is something good
    c. I want to know many more good things about it
    d. if I don't think about it for some time when I am *cháng* 'tasting' [M] it, I cannot know more good things about it
    e. I want to think about it for some time when I am *cháng* 'tasting' [M] it"
    f. when this someone is *cháng* 'tasting' [M] it, this someone thinks about it for some time
    g. if this someone thinks like this, this someone can know many more good things about it

[1] *pǐnwèi*₂ ('to appreciate')
    a.   sometimes, someone can think like this about something:
    b.   "it is something good
    c.   I want to know many more good things about it
    d.   if I don't think about it for some time, I cannot know many more good things about it
    e.   because of this I want to think about it for some time"
    f.   because of this, this someone thinks about it for some time
    g.   if this someone thinks like this, this someone can know many more good things about it
    h.   like someone can know many more good things when this someone *cháng* 'tastes' [M] something

The gustatory prototype is built into the explication of *pǐnwèi*₂, which shows the strong presence of the prototypical reference in the non-gustatory experience.

It is worth noting that *pǐn* means 'to appraise' and 'to rate'. In the context of taste-related experience, *pǐnjiǔ* or *pǐnchá* 'to drink tea with critical appreciation of its taste and quality', i.e. 'tea tasting' or 'wine tasting', and *pǐncháng* 'to taste food in order to appraise, rate or grade its worth' are commonly used expressions.[10]

To a degree, *pǐnwèi* and *tǐwèi* (cf. Section 4.3) share some commonalities in that both have the meaning of 'to know the meaning of something' and both emphasise the element of 'thinking'. (Obviously, in the case of *pǐnwèi* when it refers to a food object, it means 'to appreciate the taste' of something, since *tǐwèi* does not usually take food objects.)

However, the differences between the two are also clear. Firstly, the objects of *pǐnwèi*, whether referring to food or abstract concepts, are always considered positive and desirable in the view of the experiencer. This aesthetic dimension, which is absent in the meaning of *tǐwèi*, is characteristic to *pǐnwèi*. Secondly, the experiencer of *tǐwèi* may not know the meaning of something that is embodied in the experience until he or she actually experiences and reflects on it; whereas the experiencer of *pǐnwèi* could have experienced it and known what it meant, but tried to apply fine and detailed thinking in order to extract more subtle meaning out of it.

As a noun, *pǐwèi* is close to 'taste' as in the evaluative sense of 'good taste' or 'bad taste' in English. This is one of the few areas where the Chinese taste-related vocabulary intersects the English one.

A person who has *pǐnwèi* knows what is good and what is bad, just as one can distinguish what is good from what is bad from tasting. Note that an important meaning of *wèi* as a verb in classical Chinese is to *biànbié* 'distinguish' and *pǐnwèi*

---

10. It is quite possible that the trade of wine-tasting would produce a rich set of taste-related professional vocabulary in English. However, it is expected that it will be restricted to the professionals of such a trade.

(e.g. GHC 1999: 1627). The meaning of *X yóu pǐnwèi* 'X has good taste' can be explained as follows:

[J] *X yóu pǐnwèi*. ('X has good taste')
   a.   sometimes someone can think like this about another someone:
   b.   "if something is good, this someone can know that it is something good like someone can know something is good when this someone *cháng* 'tastes' [M] this thing
   c.   if something is bad, this someone can know that it is something bad like someone can know something is bad when this someone *cháng* 'tastes' [M] this thing
   d.   I can think something good about this someone because of this"

5   Theoretical and methodological implications

A detailed semantic analysis of several *wèi*-related terms in the Chinese language has not only revealed a culture-internal understanding of the bodily and conceptual experiences of the Chinese people, but also demonstrated that the sense of taste plays an active and important role in their mental life. As we have seen from the foregoing analysis and discussion, gustatory experience forms a rich source of vocabulary for describing cognitive processes and activities in Chinese. In light of this case study of the Chinese language, it seems that the following model of mental states, processes and activities can be proposed in relation to the Chinese sensory experience of taste:

   [Chinese model of mental states in relation to the experience of *wèi*:]
   when someone *cháng* 'tastes' [M] something,
   this someone can feel something for some time because of this
   [this someone can feel something good; this someone can feel something bad]
   this someone can know something because of this
   [this someone can know that it is something good;
   this someone can know that it is something bad]
   this someone can think something about it for some time because of this

Comparing this model with observations on Indo-European languages, we can see striking differences and similarities in terms of the link between the sense of taste and mental states.

According to Sweetser (1990), the sense of taste (in contrast to the sense of vision) rarely takes on intellectual meanings. This is apparently not the case when we consider the meaning of words like *tǐwèi* 'to understand the meaning of something by thinking about it' in Chinese. Neither does Sweetser consider taste as a source for mental feelings. She considers the sense of touch as the main sensory source. Yet, in Chinese, *wèi* and emotions are closely related as exemplified by words like *zīwèi*.

Sweetser, however, does point out that taste is linked with personal likes and dislikes, which she considers to be a universal between the sense of taste and the mental world (Sweetser 1990: 37). Indeed, the meaning of words like *pǐnwèi* 'good taste' does seem to support Sweetser's universal claim on this score.[11]

Although the differences between the Chinese and Indo-European traditions seem to be quite striking, they are not surprising if we take into consideration the biological bases, and the cultural and philosophical orientations of each tradition. In doing so, it also helps us to pinpoint those aspects that are shared.

From a biological point of view, 'taste' experience is inevitably linked to food. It is the most *intimate* manner and one of the earliest and most *direct* ways of experiencing the external world (vision and hearing are indirect ways of perceiving things). During the gustatory experience, the very substance of the perceived objects must come into close contact and interact with other sense organs. Taste is the only sensory experience that takes places inside a part of the body, thus it is intrinsically internal and subjective. As expected, this intimate contact can give rise to good or bad feelings, as feelings and emotions are internal states (in both a physical and psychological sense) that are knowable only to the experiencer. In the Chinese tradition, the sense of taste seems to contain 'touch' implicitly (thus the semantic primitive TOUCH is used in the first explication).

It is not surprising either that we can know something about the perceived objects through the close contact experience. In fact, Sweetser mentions that the Latin *sapere* means both 'be wise, know' and 'taste', and that the French verb *savoir* means 'know', and its noun form *saveur* means 'savour, taste'. But she considers them to be "interesting cases". From there, she remarks that: "In general, the target domains of smell and taste are not the intellectual domain of *savoir*" (Sweetser 1990: 36). But it seems that, in most European languages, personal likes and dislikes are also intrinsically linked with the notion of 'know', and with the notion of 'want' ('I know that it is something good; I want it because of this'; 'I know that it is something bad; I don't want it because of this'). When Classen characterises taste as "aesthetic discrimination" (1993: 57), it is undoubtedly built upon the notions of 'knowing', 'feeling', and 'good' and 'bad'.

As to the 'thinking' element of the gustatory experience, it seems to be characteristic to the Chinese conceptualisation of their experience. Several cultural factors appear to have a bearing on this. Firstly, it is undeniable that Chinese people attach great importance to their gastronomic experience, and draw meaning and significance from it. As put by West (1997: 68), for the Chinese people, food "was elevated at an

---

11. Also the word *kǒuwèi* 'personal taste', which is not discussed in this chapter.

early period from necessity to art, from sustenance to elegance; the subsequent high cultural status assured that food would remain a key ingredient in the language and structure of literature and art". Secondly, the Chinese culinary style permits 'thinking' to take place in a fine and detailed way (cf. *rùwèi*). Thirdly, the sense of taste has always been treated as one of the major modes of perceiving and experiencing the outside world for the Chinese people. The quote from early Chinese philosophical writings presented at the beginning of this chapter is an example.

This study has demonstrated the value of investigating, from a culture-internal perspective, the relationship between the physical experience and conceptual system of a culture. Moreover, it has shown how local meaning systems and understanding can be made accessible to cultural outsiders whilst retaining their cultural traditions. In the context of studying the relationships between bodily and conceptual experience, the issue of the body-mind dichotomy has to be faced. Ots makes the following important comment:

> Dualistic thought restrains and circumscribes bodily perceptions and bodily awareness, it alienates 'us' from our body: it is the mind thinking of the body rather than the body perceiving itself. Thus the difficulty of cross-cultural translation of concepts between dualistic and monistic modes of thought is but another facet of the difficulty of translating between the mind and the body. If we want to know more of the 'body sui generis' we must relearn to perceive without these restrains, i.e., perceive in a 'pre-objective' way. (Ots 1990: 22)

The NSM approach employed in this study can be viewed as a solution to what Ots calls the "pre-objective" approach. It allows researchers to position themselves within the cultural system under investigation, with meanings framed through the first person – 'I'. This 'I' breaks off the subject-object distinction and allows researchers to be situated in the "lived-body" (Merleau-Ponty 1962), treating it as "body-subject" rather than "body-object". This is consistent with the holistic approach to the body-mind in Chinese culture, and the introspective Chinese philosophical tradition.

This study is only a first attempt to "enter" the Chinese taste experience, and only touches upon a small selection of taste terms. It also suggests areas for further investigation. Firstly, as mentioned in this chapter, *wèi* plays an important role in Chinese literary thought, and is very closely related with the aesthetic experience of the Chinese people. This line of research will lead to a deep understanding of the Chinese aesthetics. Secondly, an understanding of the relative value of the sense of 'taste' in relation to the other senses will reveal Chinese sensory organisation.[12] It can be expected that this will not only expand our knowledge of the Chinese experience, but also contribute to the search for the universal and culture-specific aspects of human experience and conceptualisation.

---

12. See Ye In press, for the role that 'sound' plays in Chinese knowledge inception.

Abbreviations

ADV	adverbial	LOC	locative
CL	classifier	NEG	negative marker
DUR	durative aspect maker	PFV	perfective aspect marker
EXP	experiential	PL	plural
EXT	marker of a postverbal extent complement	RDP	reduplication
LIG	marker of ligature in dependency relations (i.e. *de*)	SG	singular

Acknowledgements

This study owes a great deal to Evans and Wilkins' (1998, 2000) papers. I wish to thank Cliff Goddard, Bevan Barrett, and two anonymous reviewers for their helpful comments on earlier versions of this chapter.

References:

Chappell, Hilary. 2002. The universal syntax of semantic primes in Mandarin Chinese. In Goddard & Wierzbicka (eds.), Vol. 1. 243–322.

Chao, Yuan-Jen & Lien-Sheng Yang. 1962. *Concise dictionary of spoken Chinese* (Guo Yu Zi Dian). Cambridge, MA: Harvard-Yenching Institute, Harvard University Press.

Classen, Constance. 1993. *Worlds of sense: Exploring the senses in history and across cultures*. London: Routledge.

Danesi, Marcel. 1990. Thinking is seeing: Vision metaphors and the nature of abstract thought. *Semiotica* 80(3/4). 221–237.

DeFrancis, John (ed.). 1997. *Alphabetically-based computerized Chinese-English dictionary*. NSW: Allen & Unwin.

Evans, Nicholas. 1992. Multiple semiotic systems, hyperpolysemy and the reconstruction of semantic change in Australian languages. In Günter Kellermann & Michael D. Morrissey (eds.), *Diachrony within synchrony: Language, history and cognition*, 475–508. Bern: Peter Lang.

Evans, Nicholas & David Wilkins. 1998. *The knowing ear: An Australian test of universal claims about the semantic structure of sensory verbs and their extension into the domain of cognition* [Arbeitspapier 32]. Cologne: Institut für Sprachwissenschaft.

Evans, Nicholas & David Wilkins. 2000. In the mind's ear: The semantic extensions of perception verbs in Australian languages. *Language* 76(3). 546–592.

GHC. 1999. *Gǔdài Hànyǔ Cídiǎn* (A Dictionary of Ancient Chinese). Běijīng: Shāngwù Chūbǎnshè.

Goddard, Cliff & Anna Wierzbicka (eds.). 1994. *Semantic and lexical universals: Theory and empirical findings*. Amsterdam: John Benjamins.

Goddard, Cliff & Anna Wierzbicka (eds.). 2002. *Meaning and universal grammar: Theory and empirical findings*, Vols. 1 & 2. Amsterdam: John Benjamins.

Hall, David L. & Roger T. Ames. 1987. *Thinking through Confucius*. New York, NY: State University of New York Press.

Hall, Edward. 1966. *The hidden dimension.* New York, NY: Doubleday.
HDC. 1995. *Hànyǔ Dà Cídiǎn* (The Great Dictionary of the Chinese Language) (10 vols). Shanghai: Hànyǔ Dà Cídiǎn Chǎnshè.
Hoogewerf, Rupert & Tong Chen (eds.). 2003. *Cáifù Qínggǎn* (The Emotional Make-up of China's Entrepreneurs). Hainan: Hǎinán Chūbǎnshè.
Lakoff, George & Mark Johnson. 1980. *Metaphors we live by.* Chicago, IL: The University of Chicago Press.
Lakoff, George & Mark Johnson. 1999. *Philosophy in the flesh: The embodied mind and its challenge to western thought.* New York, NY: Basic Books.
Merleau-Ponty, Maurice. 1962. *Phenomenology of perception.* London: Routledge and Kegan Paul.
Ots, Thomas. 1990. The angry liver, the anxious heart and the melancholy spleen: The phenomenology of perceptions in Chinese culture. *Culture, Medicine and Psychiatry* 14(1). 21–58.
Owen, Stephen. 1992. *Readings in Chinese literary thought.* Cambridge, MA: Harvard University Press.
Pollard, David. 2000. *The Chinese essay.* Translated, edited and with an introduction by David Pollard. New York, NY: Columbia University Press.
Sweetser, Eve. 1990. *From etymology to pragmatics: Metaphorical and cultural aspects of semantic structure.* Cambridge: CUP.
Synott, Anthony. 1991. Puzzling over the senses: From Plato to Marx. In David Howes (ed.), *The variety of sensory experience,* 61–75. Toronto: University of Toronto Press.
Traugott, Elizabeth C. & Richard B. Dasher. 2002. *Regularity in semantic change.* Cambridge: CUP.
Viberg, Åke. 1984. The verbs of perception: A typological study. In Brian Butterworth, Bernard Comrie & Östen Dahl (eds.), *Explanations for language universals,* 123–162. Berlin: Mouton de Gruyter.
Vinge, Louise. 1975. *The five senses: Studies in a literary tradition.* Lund: Kraftstorg.
West, Stephen H. 1997. Playing with food: Performance, food, and the aesthetics of artificiality in the Sung and Yuan. *Harvard Journal of Asiatic Studies* 57(1). 67–106.
Wierzbicka, Anna. 1996. *Semantics: Primes and universals.* Oxford: OUP.
Wierzbicka, Anna. In press. The theory of the mental lexicon. In Tilman Berger, Karl Gutschmidt, Sebastian Kempgen & Peter Kosta (eds.), *Die slavischen Sprachen* (Handbücher zur Sprach- und Kommunikationswissenschaft (HSK)) [The Slavic Languages (Handbook of Linguistics and Communication Science)]. Berlin: Mouton de Gruyter.
Wilkins, David P. 1996. Natural tendencies of semantic change and the search for cognates. In Mark Durie & Malcolm Ross (eds.), *The comparative method reviewed,* 264–304. New York, NY: OUP.
XHZTB. 1992. *Xiàndài Hànyǔ Zìpíng Tōngjìbiǎo* (Frequency charts of Modern Chinese character-words). Běijīng: Guójiā Yǔwěi (National Language Committee).
Xunzi. 340–245 B.C. *Xunzi: A translation and study of the complete works by J. Knoblock.* California, CA: Stanford University Press.
Ye, Zhengdao. 2001. An inquiry into 'sadness' in Chinese. In Jean Harkins & Anna Wierzbicka (eds.), *Emotions from crosslinguistic perspective,* 359–404. Berlin: Mouton de Gruyter.
Ye, Zhengdao. 2002. Different modes of describing emotions in Chinese: Bodily changes, sensations, and bodily images. *Pragmatics and Cognition* 10(1/2). 307–340.

Ye, Zhengdao. 2004. Chinese categorization of interpersonal relationships and the cultural logic of Chinese social interaction: An indigenous perspective. *Intercultural Pragmatics* 1(2). 211–230.

Ye, Zhengdao. 2007. 'I feel *kǔ* in my heart': 'Sadness', taste, and Chinese attitudes toward emotion. Paper presented at the *XVth Conference of International Society of Researchers on Emotion*. Coolum, Australia.

Ye, Zhengdao. In press. Memorization, learning and cultural cognition: The notion of *bèi* [auditory memory] in the Chinese written tradition. In Mengistu Amberber (ed.), *The language of memory: A crosslinguistic perspective*. Amsterdam: John Benjamins.

Yu, Ning. 1998. *The contemporary theory of metaphor: A perspective from Chinese*. Amsterdam: John Benjamins.

Yu, Ning. 2003. Chinese metaphors of thinking. *Cognitive Linguistics* 14(2/3). 141–165.

CHAPTER 7

"Then I'll huff and I'll puff or I'll go on the roff!" thinks the wolf

Spontaneous written narratives by a child with autism

Lesley Stirling and Graham Barrington

We present a qualitative analysis of narratives written spontaneously by a 7-year-old child with autism,[1] using insights and analytical tools from discourse analysis to examine the episodic macrostructure and perspective marking of the stories. The results indicate sophisticated planning and structuring at the global level and highly expressive framing of the narratives. However, they also suggest problems in mental state representation at complex levels of nesting, and difficulties with inhibitory control and attentional flexibility relevant to negotiating the shifts between local and global story-telling goals. We discuss the implications of the findings in relation to theories of autism, and conclude that discourse evidence of this kind can complement experimental evidence in addressing hypotheses about autism, language and cognition.

1   Introduction

The material presented in this study stems from the application of tools of discourse analysis to data produced spontaneously by a child with an interesting mix of ability and disability in language use. It is motivated by a desire to utilise insights

---

1.   Lincoln's family prefer that we use his real first name to identify him. We are very grateful to Lincoln, his family, and his speech therapist for their generosity in allowing us to study Lincoln's written narratives and to record his oral narratives and for the useful supplementary discussions we have had with them. Versions of this study have been presented at a seminar at the University of Melbourne and at the International Language and Cognition Conference at Coff's Harbour in September 2004. We thank members of the audiences at these presentations, and two anonymous reviewers, for helpful comments and suggestions.

from the fields of narrative theory, discourse analysis and theories of autism to elucidate the cognitive framing of the story-telling task, the nature of that task and the representational forms that that task demands. The data collected is unique in being naturalistic and rich in complexity and offers an exciting opportunity to apply and sharpen tools of analysis with respect to the organisation and interaction of higher level linguistic units, with consequent insights for language and cognition. The research is equally motivated by a desire to better understand the experience of the child with autism in tackling the story-telling task.

Narrative capacity has been a focus of research efforts aimed at better understanding human cognition and language use for some decades. Of particular interest has been the study of variations in performance in the setting of language disorders. Autism, as an early-onset, pervasive developmental disorder involving impairments in cognition, social interaction and communication, has been considered to offer potentially significant insights into the understanding of human cognition more generally. In the study of this disorder there has been a significant body of work on language and communication focusing on narrative.

In this chapter we report on a case study of a then 7-year-old child who had been diagnosed with autism and we present a qualitative analysis of uncommonly rich narrative data written spontaneously by him in the course of self-directed play. An in-depth qualitative analysis provides the opportunity to better appreciate and delineate salient discourse features of autism and hypothesise cognitive correlates. It thereby provides the ground for analytical tool development and hypothesis generation that may inform future research in a relevant population.

Despite the recent focus on narrative in understanding communication in autism, little work has been done on spontaneous or written narratives, in part because of the desire to collect data under experimentally controlled conditions, and in part because of the difficulty of coming by such data from children with autism (an exception is Volkmar & Cohen 1985 who discuss a spontaneous written narrative, though not in terms of its linguistic characteristics; Solomon 2004 investigates spontaneous oral narratives as discussed below). Most linguistic data pertaining to children with autism derives from oral conversational elicitations. Such data runs the risk of social interactive impairment confounding linguistic performance and may not accurately represent narrative ability. The predomination of severe language disability in autism and frequent co-existing intellectual impairment makes the chancing upon rich narrative data even more infrequent.

The stories made available to us by Lincoln and his family therefore represent a unique resource. They include a one page personal narrative written during a school-based speech therapy session as a spontaneous response to events in the environment, and two retellings of familiar children's stories, "The Three Little Pigs", and "The Three Billy Goats Gruff", set out over 9 and 13 pages respectively, and written spontaneously by Lincoln on his home computer for his own amusement. We supplemented this data with elicited oral retellings of the same stories and discussions with Lincoln about the stories.

It has been suggested that there are important insights to be gained from more naturalistic methodologies compared with experimental studies of children, and that experimental studies may underestimate children's abilities (Dunn 1991; Ochs & Solomon 2004). The unprompted and self-designed nature of the texts we consider here might lead one to suppose that they are conducive to showing up the child's capabilities rather than his deficits, and indeed our attention was first drawn to them because they seemed to represent surprisingly sophisticated aspects of language use when compared with Lincoln's significant language impairments as evidenced in social interaction. Our orientation thus reflects Happé's (1999) statement that in understanding disability "success is more interesting than failure". While the narratives are in some respects unusually sophisticated for any child of this age, they do also evidence a pattern of errors and problems, and it is the pattern of abilities vis-à-vis disabilities in this data which is instructive when exposed to the techniques and concepts of discourse analysis.

Our analysis of Lincoln's stories focuses on two macro-linguistic features: episodic macrostructure and perspective marking. Both these features are revealing of the cognitive processes involved in story-telling, and are highly relevant to the major current explanatory theories of autism. They are also features of Lincoln's stories which immediately strike a reader as indicative of the range of his story-telling competencies.

The structure of the ensuing chapter is as follows: After briefly describing autism and reviewing previous work which has been done on autism and narrative, we move to the presentation of our own analysis, which is structured according to the results of analysing three sets of data of increasing complexity: the personal narrative, and the retellings of the two children's stories, "The Three Little Pigs" and "The Three Billy Goats Gruff". We show how this data calls for increasingly complex versions of a simple model of knowledge state management which we propose in order to capture one aspect of the narrative task. We then discuss the implications of the analysis of data presented and relate this to existing theories of autism, hypothesising that at least part of a characteristic oddness of autistic narrative may be due to difficulties with the management of relative knowledge states as related to the models we present.

2 Autism

Autism is a pervasive developmental disorder, defined by the DSM-IV (*Diagnostic and Statistical Manual of Mental Disorders*, Fourth Edition – American Psychiatric Association 1994) as involving the three grouped areas of: (1) *Qualitative impairment in social interaction*; (2) *Qualitative impairments in communication* and (3) *Restricted repetitive and stereotyped patterns of behaviour, interests and activities*, plus a developmental aspect, with onset prior to 3 years of age. The impairments in communication must include at least one of: delay in or total lack of the development of spoken language; marked impairment in the ability to initiate or sustain a conversation with others; stereotyped and repetitive use of language or idiosyncratic language, and lack of varied spontaneous make-believe play or social imitative play appropriate to developmental level.

Approximately three quarters of children with autism have an IQ of less than 70 (beyond two standard deviations from the mean and accepted as indicating intellectual disability). Furthermore, while by definition all autistic children have language delay and deficit, roughly half of all autistic individuals never acquire functional language (Tager-Flusberg 1999; Tager-Flusberg, Joseph & Folstein 2001). The child we are interested in here belongs to the subpopulation termed "higher-functioning" who are of normal intelligence and have functional language.

Dominant hypotheses about the underlying cognitive problems of autism have focused on three proposals. The "Theory of mind" account (Baron-Cohen, Leslie & Frith 1985; Baron-Cohen 1995) postulates a fundamental deficit in the ability to ascribe mental states to others ("mind-blindness"), i.e. that autistic children lack a "theory of mind" and therefore have difficulties comprehending another's perspective. The "Executive control" hypothesis (Ozonoff, Pennington & Rogers 1991; Russell 1997) postulates that autistic children have problems with executive control functions, i.e. planning, flexibility in attention and the inhibition of immediate objectives to serve larger level goals. The "Weak central coherence" theory (Frith 1989) is based on the concept of central coherence as the ability to draw together diverse information to construct a higher level meaning in context, and hypothesises that in autism there is a loss of this preference for higher-level meaning (distilling the gist), a focus on local processing of information, and a difficulty in shifting between the local and the global.

3 Autism and narrative

As we have seen, language deficit is recognised as one of the key diagnostic indicators of autism and there has been considerable work done on language and communication in autism (reviewed in Tager-Flusberg 2000). Over the past two decades, there has been an increasing interest in the study of higher level discourse units, in particular narratives, in this field. A narrative is an encapsulated form of discourse which requires sophisticated skills of planning and information encoding and which thereby offers a unique testing ground for an individual's linguistic, cognitive and socio-cultural abilities. Bruner and Feldman (1993) have even claimed that narrative capacity is in some sense primary and gives rise to the range of other deficits that have been argued to underlie the disorder of autism. Narrative data are ideally suited to examining "Theory of mind", "Executive control" and "Weak central coherence" hypotheses, since telling a story involves taking account of the perspective of both the characters and the audience, and requires planning and shifting between local and global objectives.

With the exception of a recent ethnographic study by Elinor Ochs and others (Ochs & Solomon 2004), virtually all the work on autism and narrative has been done using experimental paradigms, with stories elicited via various experimental strategies and the data then coded quantitatively for a range of specific features. These typically include length in clauses, syntactic complexity, and story structure as represented by the presence of major story elements such as defined beginnings, setting and orientation, major episodic developments, and resolutions. Stories have also been coded for "evaluative" elements, where the notion of an "evaluation" dimension of narratives comes from Labov and Waletzky (1967), and this coding has generally been based on the scheme developed by Reilly, Klima & Bellugi (1990), which codes for: causality; references to and description of characters' internal affective and cognitive states and behaviours; whether causal explanations are provided for these; negatives; hedges; character direct speech, onomatopoeia and sound effects; intensifiers and attention-getters (including emphatic markers and repetition).

The general perception has been that individuals with autism have difficulty producing narratives and indeed given the wide variation in intelligence and functional language ability profiled above, clearly a sizeable proportion of the group are not capable of producing narratives at all. Earlier studies of autism and narrative suggested that children with autism produced narratives less frequently in conversational interaction (Capps, Kehres & Sigman 1998); produced narratives which were relatively impoverished in various pervasive respects (Bruner & Feldman 1993; Loveland et al. 1990; Loveland & Tunali 1993); produced fewer of certain kinds of "evaluative" devices such as character speech, sound effects, emphasis and repetition (Tager-Flusberg 1995; Capps, Losh & Thurber 2000) and in particular fewer descriptions of mental states (Baron-Cohen, Leslie & Frith 1986; Tager-Flusberg 1992). However research in this area has given rise to seemingly contradictory results. For example Tager-Flusberg (1995), Tager-Flusberg and Sullivan

(1995) and Capps, Losh and Thurber (2000), looking at autistic children's production of stories in response to wordless picture books such as *Frog, Where Are You?* (Mayer 1969), found no variation from the norm in the number of mental state references they produced.

One problem has been that until very recently no separation was made in studying autistic children's narratives between lower-functioning and higher-functioning children: The few studies which have been focused specifically on higher-functioning children (in particular, Losh & Capps 2003; also Solomon 2004) have surprised the researchers in that, at least for story-book type narratives, few significant differences were identified in the performance of these autistic children as compared with a population of typically developing children. In gross terms, length, structure, complexity and use of affective-evaluative devices were within normal ranges (although Losh & Capps 2003 found that fewer story components were included in the "Frog stories" of children with autism). The major area reported in these studies as reflecting difference was in the encoding of causal-explanatory links within the narratives. This is supported by other work suggesting more general difficulties in inference-making in autism (Norbury & Bishop 2002 report that higher-functioning autistic children in their study of story comprehension and recall had difficulties in making inferences). Even here, however, there have been differences between reported studies, with some reporting no differences in the amount of marking of causality (Tager-Flusberg & Sullivan 1995), or fewer identifications of causes of internal states but similar or greater mention of causes of actions (Capps, Losh & Thurber 2000). With respect to other genres of narrative, Losh and Capps (2003) did find some significant differences in narratives of personal experience in complexity of syntax and frequency and diversity of evaluative comment.

Furthermore, in her study of narrative introductions in the everyday conversation of higher-functioning children with autism, Solomon (2004) found that contrary to previous belief, the children in the study did participate in spontaneous, interactive narrative activity. Their actual narratives were less competent than their narrative introductions; they were often long, circular, and repetitious, with unusual details and micro-segmented progression of narrative events. The children could not give a "gist" (macrostructure) when introducing a story – rather they did so just using the character's name.

The differences between higher-functioning children with autism and typically developing children thus turn out to be more subtle than had at first been thought, and less readily accessible via research methodologies focused on general cross-group comparison; some of these researchers have found that the differences have been better tapped by more detailed post hoc study of the data or the use of probing questions post narrative (e.g. Losh & Capps 2003; Tager-Flusberg & Sullivan 1995). Thus there remains a clear need for developing methods and measures which are better able to meaningfully investigate these subtle differences.

While not denying the need and usefulness of experimentally constrained studies, the motivation for our study has been to explore whether and how in-depth qualitative analysis of some of these stories can complement the cross-population, quantitative surveys of a collection of linguistic features.

4 This case study

Lincoln, aged 6 years and 11 months at the time of producing the first of the texts discussed here, has been diagnosed with autism and has significant language impairment, readily apparent in any conversational setting, and characteristic social deficits and behavioural routines, but is otherwise in the "higher-functioning category": He is of above average or superior intelligence and does exceptionally well in areas such as maths, computers and music. He has had intensive professional intervention since the age of 2, and attends a mainstream school with a full-time aide.

Lincoln was originally diagnosed with "severe language disorder" at age 2 and was not diagnosed with autism until age 7 (mid 2003). The diagnosis ("pervasive development disorder – autism") was made by a paediatrician in consultation with a multidisciplinary team consisting of a clinical psychologist, speech therapist & occupational therapist. On the standardised Childhood Autism Rating Scale (CARS) assessing the presence of autistic features in current behaviour his disability was categorised as severe. The speech pathology assessment, referring to results of the Clinical Evaluation of Language Fundamentals (CELF) and the Test of Language Development – Primary, also identified severe difficulties in receptive and expressive language (2 or more Standard Deviations below the mean). On nonverbal IQ tests he scored above average or superior.

The texts we are chiefly interested in here were produced over a span of 15 months (May 2003 – August 2004) beginning when Lincoln was 6.11 years old and ending at age 8.2. They are listed below.

Texts
Spontaneous written personal narrative:
– *Put a brick on the sound machine!*   27 April 2004
Spontaneous written story retellings:
– *The Three Little Pigs*   ~ May 2003
– *The Three Billy Goats Gruff*   ~ November 2003

Elicited oral story retellings:

- *The Three Little Pigs (1)*   29 May 2004
- *The Three Billy Goats Gruff*   29 May 2004
- *The Three Little Pigs (2)*   1 August 2004
- *Frog, Where Are You?*   1 August 2004

We also had access to what on the basis of information from Lincoln's carers we assume to be the major source of his knowledge about the two stories he retold: books and accompanying "reader theatre" plays which he used at school (Smith 1997a, 1997b). Note, incidentally, that there was apparently up to a year between his exposure to these and his reconstruction of the stories.

In this study we will focus chiefly on Lincoln's written narratives, especially the story retellings, but we do refer in passing to some characteristics of the oral retellings for comparative purposes.

5 A simple two-part model of knowledge state management: Personal narrative

While the main focus of our study is on Lincoln's written story retellings, we will first briefly consider the original descriptive personal narrative, *Put a brick on the sound machine!* The main reason we want to include some discussion of this text is that it shows that Lincoln is capable of producing an original narrative account, given that the remaining texts are retellings of familiar children's stories. This text was produced by Lincoln in a speech therapy session at school. He could not concentrate because of the noise of builders next to the room, so instead he wrote an account of what was happening. There was no input from the speech therapist. The text is reproduced below.

> Text 1
> Name: Lincoln Date: 27-4-04
> Put a brick on the sound machine!
> Today I watched the builders build a new classroom. I hear a noise. It's the wood sound machine. The builder drant one cut of wood, and stuck it on the floor! And back to drant another cut of wood. So he stuck it on the floor! He got an extra drant cut. Put it on the floor. Hammer it in! Drant a cut of wood! Put it on the floor! The next builder used a wheel barrow to make noise. He takes wood and bricks in it. The first builder put a drant two cuts of wood! Put it on the floor! Drant a cut of wood! Hammer it in! Put it on the floor! Use a tape mesher! Drant a cut of wood! Put it on the

floor! Hammer it in! The noises I can hear is the hammer going BANG! BANG! And the sound machine going DREEEEWE1! I hear that BANG! THE END!

There is obviously a great deal that could be said about this text. We wish to note here chiefly the effective rhetorical structure and highly expressive nature of the text. It has a completely appropriate beginning and an apposite title and makes excellent use of repetition and punctuation in evoking a relevant response from the audience. The main point of the text is evidently to convey how the sound environment Lincoln is in has been affecting him. Note that "the sound machine" is the cross-cut saw and "drant" and "dreeeewe1" encode the sound the saw makes as it cuts, and seem to be inflectional forms of the same lexeme (this is supported by what Lincoln has told us in conversation about this text).

One reason for starting with this text is that it allows us to introduce a simple, two-part model of knowledge state management, which we take to be the minimal applicable to narratives of this kind. This is represented in Figure 1. At issue here is a body of knowledge of the content of the story which we assume the narrator has and which we assume the audience builds a representation of through their interpretation of the text. This figure is to be read as representing the knowledge states of the narrator and the audience through the time course of the telling of the story as represented from left to right. The idea is that the narrator has consistent complete knowledge of the content of the story (represented on the vertical axis for narrator and audience independently) from the beginning of the story telling (text writing), while the knowledge of the audience (reader) grows from zero to complete as they are exposed to the unfolding story. Note that there are "characters" in the piece, but there is no reported speech or other interaction between the characters, and the fact that this is a personal account written in the first person means that there is no obvious distinction between Lincoln as the writer and the narrator.[2] This model is of course an oversimplification of the cognitive processes involved in the tasks of narrative production and comprehension in many ways, however it captures an essential element of the task which we must assume able story-tellers to be aware of and orient themselves towards.

---

2. Narrative theory generally does argue that we should operate with a distinction between an "author" and a "narrator" even for first person accounts: On the grounds that in such cases the narrating "I" is a construction and not necessarily identical with the author. But given the nature of the texts at issue here and to keep things simple we will not make this distinction at this stage.

142   Lesley Stirling and Graham Barrington

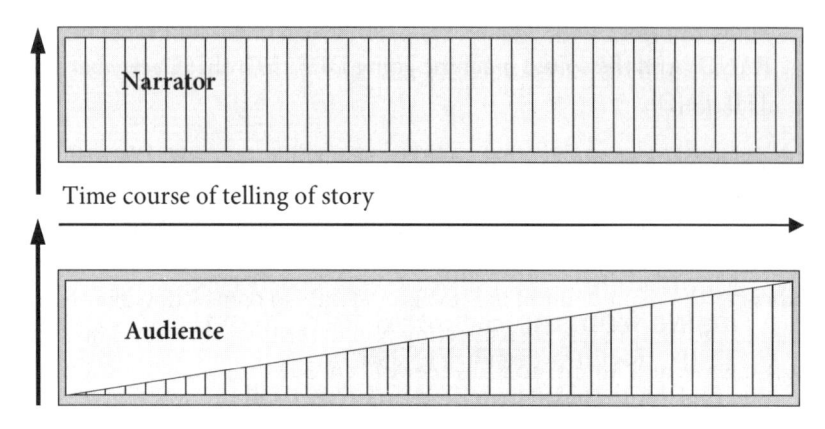

Figure 1. A simple two-part model of knowledge state management – personal narrative

6   Lincoln's spontaneous written story retelling

Lincoln produced the two written story retellings to be considered here using the "Kid Pix®" (Broderbund) computer program. Starting at the beginning of the story, he typed each page into the Kid Pix picture frame, printed it out, then deleted it so that he could write the next page (this method is a function of the particular constraints of the program and the way he interacted with it; while pictures (here pages) can be saved, in the version of Kid Pix he was using it was not possible to save a series of pictures (pages) as a unified sequence). An example of a page from the earlier story is given in Figure 2 and a page from the later story in Figure 3; the full text of the stories is given in the Appendix.

> WOLF PAGE 1
>
> **The wolf came to the house of straw.**
> **"LITTLE PIG LITTLE PIG LET ME IN!"**
> **"No No I'll not let you in!"**
> **"THEN I'LL HUFF & I'LL PUFF & I'LL BLOW YOU HOUSE IN!" Yelled the wolf.**

Figure 2. A page from "The Three Little Pigs"

Features to note here are the title of the page (in a distinct font type: this will be discussed later), the representation of direct speech, and the effective use of case and punctuation.

> Now what can we do?
>
> Meanwhile... BIG Billy Goat Gruff got inside from the Brager Bright Stoon.
> TRIP, TROP, TRIP, TROP!
> "OH NO! not again." said the troll.
> "I'M VERY HUNGREY I'M DEARSFDGDING YOU AND YOUR PREDARA FROM THE BRAGER BRIGHT STOON!" He yelled and HU HO HE HA!
>
> **WELL DONE! THE TROLL IS IN THE WATER!**

Figure 3. A page from "The Three Billy Goats Gruff"

In addition to the features noted for Figure 1, notice that on this page there is also a comment at the bottom of the page; again this will be discussed later. This example page includes an unusually great number of neologisms.

6.1 A simple three-part model of knowledge state management: Retold narratives

> *You must attend to the commencement of this story, for when we get to the end we shall know more than we do now ...* Hans Christian Andersen (1872) "The Snow Queen"

In moving to consideration of these narratives, we need to adopt a somewhat more complex model of knowledge state management, given in Figure 4 below, in that in addition to keeping track of the narrator's knowledge state and the audience's knowledge state, there are characters in the story who speak and interact and the story-teller needs to keep track of their knowledge states as well. Some characters will know more than others and/or characters may have access to different information. What we have here is again obviously an oversimplified model.[3] But the idea is that

---

3. Again, narrative theory, in considering the full range of narrative types, is concerned with the issue of how much the narrator knows and in distinguishing different types of narrator on

Time course of telling of story

Narrator

Characters

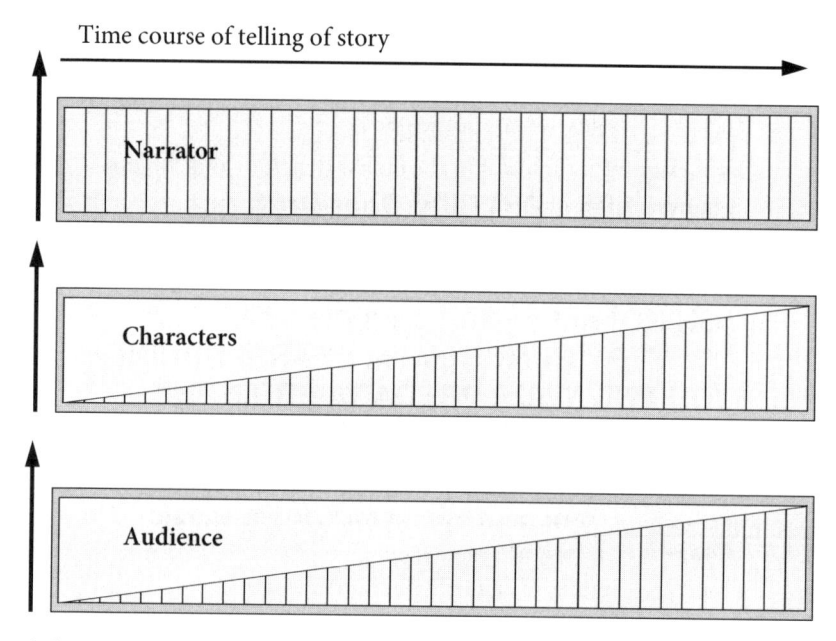

Audience

Knowledge of story

Figure 4. A simple three-part model of knowledge state management: Retold narratives

at the beginning of the story, the characters don't know what happens at the end: The storyteller needs to take account of this when he presents characters speaking and interacting. For the audience, there is no general rule; in terms of their actual knowledge of the content of the story, they may be in the same position as the characters (if the narrator keeps them in suspense) OR in the same position as the narrator (if the story is a culturally well-known one), or somewhere in between at the whim of the narrator (so that they may know more than individual characters but perhaps less than the whole); independently of their actual knowledge state, the narrator may act as if they are in one or the other position. Clearly if we are interested in the way assumptions made by the writer about the audience's knowledge affect the form of the text, then these are important considerations: For culturally familiar stories like this one, a writer would normally be operating under different assumptions than for other kinds of stories. These issues also underlie the understanding in work on narrative theory that a

---

this basis. In particular, the various versions of this representation considered in this study do not allow for a less than omniscient narrator.

rereading of a text is significantly different from a first reading. These issues need not concern us here however.

7. Episodic macrostructure of the retold stories

There has been a significant interest in the global structure and coherence of narrative across a number of disciplinary fields. Part of language users' competency for narrative production must include the ability to produce narratives with appropriate macrostructure. Narratives are by definition centred around sequences of clauses or sentences which are related in characteristic ways: In particular, some of them will describe temporally ordered events involving repeated reference to one or more participants. A key aspect of global coherence in narratives will also be the assumption or overt encoding of causal relations between these events, and the overall move from an initial complication to a final resolution of this, which represents the "point" of the story (see, for example, Labov & Waletzky 1967; Fabb 1997). However, numerous studies have shown that in addition to these characteristics of narrative discourse, narrative is hierarchically organised into intermediate level units of structure and processing which are often called "episodes" and which are linguistically and psychologically well-founded (for example, Grimes 1975; Hinds 1979; Longacre 1979; Chafe 1979; van Dijk 1982; Tomlin 1987; Berman & Slobin 1994; Stirling 2001; Ji 2002). The rich literature on the development of children's ability to produce and recall narratives has shown that typically developing children are sensitive to macrostructure at a very early age (e.g. Hickmann 2003: 125), but acquire the ability to produce well-formed narratives relatively late (Berman & Slobin 1994 report an increasing capacity for the hierarchical organisation of narratives, in which segments are marked off as episodes, between the ages of 5 and 9).

We can take an "episode" to be a semantic unit (a "conceptual paragraph") corresponding to a chunk of narrative, typically including a sequence of more than one sentence, governed by a cohesive theme, topic or event sequence and often characterised by maintenance of the same actors, place and time. Conversely, episode boundaries represent major breaks or attentional shifts in the flow of information in the discourse and often coincide with major changes in participants, temporal and/or spatial continuity, and/or other thematic breaks (for evidence, see for example Ji 2002). In children's stories episodes often correlate with single pages or double-page spreads (the page turn co-occurs with an episode shift).

One of the advantages of the data we are considering here is that Lincoln gives us his macrostructure very explicitly in his division of the story into titled pages. As we noted above, Lincoln produced the stories by typing each page in Kid Pix, printing it out and then deleting it before moving on to the next. His use of titles such as "Wolf page 1", anticipating further wolf pages, is therefore strongly suggestive of a prior overall plan of the structure of the story which he intends to follow. As we have also seen, he even uses different fonts in what at least sometimes appears to be a meaningful way, e.g. there is a special "wolf" font for the titles of the wolf pages. Table 1 lists the pages with their titles and corresponding story episode for "The Three Little Pigs", and Table 2 lists pages, titles, footer comments and story episodes for "The Three Billy Goats Gruff". (Page numbers are supplied here by us for convenience in referring to the text and were not included by Lincoln; while we have not been able to completely replicate the fonts used in the page titles we have tried to mimic the flavour of the changes in font and style used – see the Appendix for a facsimile of the original stories.)

Table 1. Macrostructure of "The Three Little Pigs"

Page number	Page title	Story episode
1	[no title]	Title page
2	THE THREE LITTLE PIGS	Mother pig sends them off to build houses
3	NEXT PAGE:	Pig 1 builds straw house
4	THE HARD PAGE	Pig 2 builds stick house
5	Very Hard Hard Page:	Pig 3 builds brick house
6	wolf page 1	Wolf threatens pig 1
7	**Straw blow:**	Wolf blows down straw house
8	wolf page 2	Wolf threatens pig 2
9	STICK HOUSE BLOW PAGE:	Wolf blows down stick house
10	wolf page 3	Wolf threatens pig 3 & makes plan to go on roof
11	Sorry the brick house won't blow?	Wolf can't blow down brick house; goes on roof
12	ROOF ON A PAGE:	Pig 3 builds fire
13	[no title]	End page: wolf gets burnt & goes home

There is a clear structural parallel between the two stories of "The Three Little Pigs" and "The Three Billy Goats Gruff": In each case there are three trials of increasing difficulty, and part of the general story schema is reflected in Lincoln's use of titles such as "The Hard Page" and "Very Hard Hard Page". In discussion with Lincoln about why he chose these titles for "The Three Billy Goats Gruff" rewrite, he commented that he chose "The Hard Page": "because it was very hard" (which suggests to us an indication of degree of difficulty for characters in story); the "Very Hard Hard Page", "because the brager bright stoon is going to get in the way" ("it's like a bridge") so it was hard for the Billy Goat Gruff to get across the bridge; and the "Very Hard Hard Page" because the troll was waving his gold sticker.

Chapter 7. "Then I'll huff and I'll puff or I'll go on the roff!" thinks the wolf 147

Table 2. Macrostructure of "The Three Billy Goats Gruff"

Page number	Page title	Story episode	Commentary
1	[no title]	Title page	
2	The three billy goats gruff	Setting the scene	
3	The next page	Appearance of troll	
4	The Hard Page	Little BGG – challenge	
5	The Hard Page	Little BGG – resolution	Well done you did it to grass!
6	Very Hard Hard Page	Middle BGG – challenge	Remember, call him
7	Very Hard Hard Page	Middle BGG – resolution	Well done you did it to grass!
8	Now what can we do?	Big BGG	Well done! The troll is in the water!
9	[no title]	End page: resolution	You help the 3 billy goats gruff get it on!

We analysed Lincoln's stories for typical indicators of episodic structure as mentioned above, such as continuation or shift in spatial location, time interval, and involvement of characters. Table 3 represents the episodic structure of Lincoln's "Three Little Pigs" story, comparing his pagination with our analysis of these indicators. The first row (SPACE) indicates the spatial location of the events taking place on each page (L1 to L4) and cites any explicit statements of shift in location. The second row (TIME) indicates the temporal anchoring relative to the pages and cites any explicit references to temporal location. The third row (ACTORS) indicates which participants in the story are involved in the events reported on each page. Finally, row 4 of the table provides a thematic summary of the events reported on the page in question. Overall, as can be seen from this table, the pages correlate beautifully with what we would on the basis of these indicators identify as episodes in the narrative structure. Each page represents at most one location and usually a single temporal interval. The rhetorical structure of the story corresponds neatly with the pagination. On the occasions where the events over two pages have the same spatial location, there is a rhetorical development in the story which justifies this shift: For example between pages 5 and 6, 7 and 8, and 9 and 10 where in each case there is the making of the threat on the first page and the fulfilment of it on the second. There is also an association of page breaks with shifts in focal character. This story lends itself to a neat structure of this kind, as there are clearly distinguished episodes relating to each little pig, building a different house in a different place.

Table 3. An episodic analysis of the retold "Three Little Pigs"

Page	1	2	3	4	5	6	7	8	9	10	11	12
SPACE	L1 Mother pig's house *Off went ... Pigs*	L2 Straw house *the*	L3 Stick house	L4 Brick house	L2 *The wolf came to the house ... Straw house*	L2 Straw house	L3 *The wolf came to the house ... Stick house*	L3 Stick house	L4 *The wolf came to the house ... Brick house*	L4 Brick house – on roof *the wolf got on the roof ...*	L4 Brick house – inside	L4 Brick house *the big bad wolf got all the way home*
TIME	T1 *One day ...*	T2 *today*	T3	T4 *this time*	T5	T6	T7	T8	T9	T10	T10/11	T12/13
ACTORS	mother pig; 3 Little Pigs	1st Little Pig; straw; straw house	2nd Little Pig; sticks; stick house	3rd Little Pig; bricks; brick house	wolf; straw house; 1st Little Pig	wolf; straw house; 1st Little Pig	wolf; stick house; 1st 2nd Little Pigs	wolf; stick house; 1st 2nd Little Pigs	wolf; brick house; Little Pig	wolf; brick house; roof	3 Little Pigs; fire	wolf, wolf's feet
THEME	Mother sends 3 LPs off to build own houses	Pig 1 builds house	Pig 2 builds house	Pig 3 builds house	Threat by wolf	Fulfill threat	Threat by wolf	Fulfill threat	Threat by wolf	Try to fulfill threat	Follow plan to get rid of wolf	End of the wolf

As can be seen from this table, the beginnings of pages sometimes coincide with explicit mention of spatial shift (*The wolf came to the house of sticks*), as do the ends (*Off went the three Little Pigs*; *but the wolf got on the roof...*; and indeed the final *and the big bad wolf got all the way home*). In addition, many of Lincoln's story pages are introduced by explicit, preposed markers of temporal shift (in particular in "The Three Billy Goat's Gruff": *Once upon a time; After a little uile; Soon; Next; Meanwhile*). Causal markers of meso-level rhetorical structure such as *but* (unexpectedness) and *so* (causality) are also used in both stories, and *so* in particular often occurs at the beginnings of pages (*So he huffed and he puffed*) or at the ends of pages (*So that when he build the house of bricks!*).

We mentioned in Section 4 that Lincoln's parents and teachers identify "reader theatre" books and plays used at school (Smith 1997a, 1997b) as the major source of Lincoln's knowledge about these stories, which are nevertheless clearly readily accessible in the culture. Since we can take these texts to be (a) representative of the familiar childhood stories and (b) specifically representing Lincoln's exposure to these stories, we felt that they would represent a reasonable choice of comparator with Lincoln's stories. We did a detailed comparison of Lincoln's stories with these texts. Lincoln's retellings are shorter overall and with fewer episodes (distinct episodes are collapsed into one) and they exclude some details (non-central elements are omitted), both of which are general features of story retellings no matter who produces them (Bartlett 1932; Mandler & Johnson 1977). However the episode boundaries are in similar or equally justifiable places, again reflecting the finding that in general, the episode level is the most likely to be remembered in story retelling (Mandler 1978; Rumelhart 1977).

It is evident then that Lincoln's story retellings exhibit a clear idea of what it is to tell a story (story schema) and sophisticated episodic macrostructure. What can this tell us? We have seen that some theorists have characterised autism in terms of a focus on the local, on detail, and an inability to take account of the global, of context (the "Weak central coherence" hypothesis). On the face of it the evidence presented in this section might seem incompatible with such claims. We need to be cautious, however, since global narrative coherence is also about an understanding of the "point" of the story and the causal and explanatory threads which underpin the episodic structure, and there is some evidence that these aspects of global coherence are weaker here.

In comparison with the source materials, in Lincoln's retellings there is a lack of explicit mention of transitions between locations (e.g. no description of the pigs actually transitting from the blown down house to the brother's house as each house is blown down, or of the pigs moving on down the road as each finds materials to build their house – although in the later oral retellings of the stories he does put in at least some of these transitions). There is also a lack of elaboration of more important parts of the story such as the building of the brick house (as stronger but harder work etc.), and the denouément (e.g. there is no description of the wolf actually going down the chimney, and no explanation of how the wolf gets burned). There is no explicit mention of the "point" of the story. Notice however that implicit in the titular distinctions between "hard" and "very hard" pages, there is some evaluation of the relative difficulty of the tasks faced by the characters, as indicated above.

These features of the narratives may nevertheless seem suggestive of a lack of engagement with causal structure, even though as we mention above there is some use of the causal marker *so*, and in his oral retellings there are also some explicit causal connections between events of the form "he did X to achieve Y". Such a finding would be consistent with previous work on autism and narrative which as we reported above indicated the major area of difference between children with autism and a typically developing population to be in the area of indication of explicit causal links. However, without explicit comparison with the kind of output a population of typically developing children of similar chronological and/or mental age would produce on a task such as the one Lincoln set himself, we cannot say that these features are specifically related to Lincoln's autism. Note that Berman and Slobin (1994) report that causal (and mental state) representations start to appear in children's "Frog stories" between ages 5 and 9, and Boscolo and Cisotto (1999) note that causal relations are only occasionally represented in the narratives of even typically developing children of the same age range. Goldman, O'Banion Varma & Sharp (1999) note that children's representations of causal connections among major story events tend to be underrepresented in story retellings as compared to the children's understanding of the story as elicited through questioning.

8 Perspective

By "perspective" we mean all those discourse phenomena in which the point of view or attitude of the speaker is made explicit or in which the existence and nature of different points of view is reflected. Taking someone's perspective is a cognitive ability which may be explicitly manifested in discourse through a range of linguistic practices: Representation of speech, thought and perception, use of deictic expressions, choice of referring expression, voice alternations, and use of other subjective, expressive and evaluative elements including modals, exclamations, and intensifiers. Within the field of discourse analysis, there has recently been a large amount of work on perspective-taking in discourse, a significant subset of which focuses on the production of narrative or on narrative retelling (e.g. Wiebe

1994; Duchan, Bruder & Hewitt 1995; Sanders & Spooren 1997; Mushin 2001; Graumann & Kallmeyer 2002).

Children typically go through a developmental process in coming to understand and being capable of expressing the points of view of others (Selman 1980; Berman & Slobin 1994; Reilly, Zamora & McGivern 2005). Children with autism are often said to have difficulty with perspective-taking, emotion recognition, the pragmatics of language use generally, and specific aspects of deictic language including temporal reference, and use of pronouns, especially the distinction between 1st and 2nd person pronouns. Indeed, the "Theory of mind" account of autism raises the question of whether individuals with autism can effectively utilise linguistic markers of perspective and whether an analysis of their discourse might readily identify deficits in this area.

As we saw in Section 3, in studies of narrative in autism, researchers have commonly looked for cues to "Theory of mind" difficulties by coding and quantifying children's use of a range of what are described as "affective-evaluative" elements, including representation of mental and emotional states and causality, direct speech, onomatopoeia and sound effects, and intensifiers and attention-getters. In this section we review some aspects of perspective marking in Lincoln's narratives, and in so doing try to situate the consideration of some of these same markers within broader more recent theories of perspectivisation.

8.1 Broad overview

While there is no space here to review in Lincoln's texts the use of all aspects of language discussed under the heading of "perspective" (for example we do not consider the complex matters of tense and spatio-temporal deixis more generally), we first make some broad descriptive observations about aspects of perspective marking in Lincoln's narratives which show that Lincoln seems to be managing some aspects of perspectivisation well.

8.1.1 *Expressive framing of the text*

Expressive framing of the text is a global aspect of perspective marking which is normally considered to indicate a perspective centred on the story character(s), in contrast to reportive framing, where story events are presented from the external perspective of the narrator (Li & Zubin 1995; Mushin 2001; Quasthoff 2002). Expressive framing involves animation of the story and is thus prototypically marked by the use of direct speech (Banfield 1982) as well as prosodic differentiation between characters' voices, onomatopoeia and sound mimicry, and use of other features such as repetition, and definite reference to represent the knowledge state of the story characters rather than that of the narrator and audience.

Lincoln's narratives are certainly expressively framed rather than reportive. They reflect a preference for reporting characters' speech using the standard conventions of direct speech representation: sometimes with and sometimes without the use of reported speech introducing verbs. The variety of verbs used is also striking: *said*, *yelled* and in the oral retellings also *screamed* and *cried*. In his written texts he makes use of contrasts between upper and lower case, punctuation and onomatopoeia to indicate distinct character voices and effectively dramatise the narrative. In the oral retellings similarly he manipulates the pitch, volume and tempo of his speech to represent multiple voices of characters and to indicate focal moments of the action; onomatopoeia and sound effects are also used in the oral retellings. By all accounts Lincoln is here demonstrating quite sophisticated ability to perspectivise.

8.1.2 *Shifts in perspective between characters*

Some representation of characters' mental states is given in Lincoln's story retellings. The mental state predicates *think* and *worry* are used. For example, Lincoln makes explicit mention of the three little pigs thinking about the wolf and the roof (something not in the original reader theatre story he had read at school). In one of the oral retellings of this story he says: *The three little pigs are so worried about the wolf coming down the chimney. So, "I know, I will light the fire" said the third little pig.* In the other oral retelling of the story he says *The wolf has an idea* and subsequently reports the wolf's evaluation of this idea as *"That's a good idea" said the wolf*. In the written version he dramatises the wolf being burnt from the wolf's perspective: *"OUCH OUCH OUCH!" up went his feet like fire ... "OUCH OUCH OUCH!"*

It is not entirely clear how the presence of features such as these in Lincoln's texts should be interpreted. In the literature on perspective and narratology, use of direct speech is usually taken to indicate that the narrator is taking the perspective of the character whose speech is being reported (e.g. Banfield 1982). Yet what does it mean to use direct speech if there is little evidence of ability to use less direct methods of reporting? Berman and Slobin (1994: 15) report that younger children in their "Frog story" studies use fewer expressive options, and Nordqvist (2001) claims that there is generally little use of reported speech in children's narratives, especially written narratives, and that there are correlations between the development of reported speech forms and the development of Theory of mind and perspective-taking ability. However Nordqvist also shows that when children do use reported speech, it is direct speech which occurs first. There may of course be significant differences between the retelling of familiar children's stories, as here, and the production of narratives on the basis of picture books, as in these other studies. Mushin (1998) has also pointed out that direct speech has a dual status: Although the content of the reported speech is deictically centred in the reported speaker, the direct speech is *itself* an "objective" feature in that it represents a report of observable, public domain phenomena. More generally, we can ask whether Lincoln's apparently effective use of (some) perspective markers and expressive and dramatic presentation of the narrative is an area of particular competence, or an epiphenomenon associated with a coping strategy. These issues require further investigation.

8.2 Managing knowledge states

We have been presenting increasingly complex descriptions of the knowledge state modelling part of the task of narrative telling as we consider the different kinds of narratives which Lincoln has produced. We view such knowledge state modelling as a perspective managing task, in that it concerns the requirement on the narrator to keep track of the relative knowledge states of the characters in the story and of themselves as narrator as compared with the audience (cf. Mushin 2001: 14). Although young typically developing speakers and writers can take account of the needs of their audience to some extent, this is a relatively late development (Boscolo & Cisotto 1999; Berman & Slobin 1994: 15).[4] In this final section we wish to review some elements of Lincoln's narratives which seem to us to be unusual, independent of specific problems with inflectional morphology or use of neologisms, and which we believe can be described in terms of difficulties with the task of knowledge state management.

We first present and discuss three examples of language use which we believe can be accounted for as indicating difficulties managing the knowledge states of characters and audience vis-à-vis narrator, as modelled in Figure 4 above.

8.2.1 *Example 1: Advance notice to the characters of parts of the plot*
In Lincoln's written retelling of "The Three Little Pigs", the story begins with the following sentence:

(1) One day a mother pig said to her 3 Little Pigs: "It's time to make homes of your houses the big bad wolf went to blow 2 houses down."

As indicated above, we later asked Lincoln to tell this story orally, and he did so on two occasions (29 May 2004 and 1 August 2004). Both of the oral retellings of this

---

4. Berman and Slobin (1994: 15) discuss the "deer" episode in the "Frog Story" as representing a particular challenge to narrators in this regard, as it requires them to contrast a narrator's omniscient perspective with a character's temporary lack of knowledge, a lack also shared by the audience: demanding at the levels of cognition, communication and linguistic encoding. The youngest children in their study (4–5 years old) could not do this, and only some of the school age children (9+) could cope successfully with this task.

story include similar reported utterances by the mother pig near the beginning of the story:

(2) "now,
you three little pigs go and build your very own homes,
but <u>don't</u> worry!
the big bad wolf will be after ya!" [29/5/04]

(3) "OK,
it's time to make homes of your houses,
but don't worry,
the big bad wolf will be after ya." [1/8/04]

In all these cases, the mother pig in effect gives "advance notice" to the little pigs of the threat of the wolf. It is of course an anomaly for other reasons for the mother to instruct the little pigs not to worry and follow this immediately by the statement that the big bad wolf will be after them: This contradiction suggests that there is perhaps a problem here with understanding or representing characteristic emotional states of others and the causal relations between them. Independently of this, it could be argued that our normal assumption about the story would be that none of the pigs knows in advance that the wolf will be after them, so that this perhaps represents some "leakage" between what is appropriate knowledge for the writer, the narrator and perhaps even the audience, and what is appropriate for the characters. One could construct a more elaborate motivation for the inclusion of this element in the story, around the assumption that mothers have a propensity to warn their children about the dangers of the world (especially if they are about to set off into it by themselves for the first time) and that this mother might well warn her children about a wolf – it might be instructive to test such a hypothesis more explicitly in a constructed situation. But in any case this element is one which does not occur in traditional tellings of the story, including the reader theatre versions which Lincoln was exposed to.

8.2.2 Example 2: Whose mind is changing?

In the written retelling of "The Three Billy Goats Gruff", each time the first two Billy Goats Gruff cross the bridge, the troll is reported as talking to them about the changing of minds.

(4) "Please don't ear [sic] me up!" said Little Billy Goat Gruff. "My sister's bigger! So I'm gotta do my hands!" The troll said, "OK. You can pass quick before I changed your mind." and off went Little Billy Goat Gruff.

(5) "Please don't eat me up! My brother is the biggest. "Very well." said the troll wathing his gold sticker. "Goodbye. you've got to be good. Off you go utill I changed your mind. OK." Off she went.

These examples represent mention of mental states, with complexity added by the apparent reversal of first and second person pronouns (i.e. what we might normally expect to see is rather "O.K. You can pass quick before I change my mind"). Note also the anomalous use of "utill" ("until") in Example (5) rather than a more appropriate temporal connective such as "before". Children with autism are often reported as having difficulties keeping straight first and second person pronouns, and while Lincoln's parents report that this has been an area of difficulty for him, we note that it is not a problem evident anywhere else in his texts; it may be that it surfaces as a difficulty here precisely because of the complex mental states involved.

Talk about "changing one's mind" involves significant complexity in terms of mental state representation, and here is additionally complex because the action with respect to which the mind is changed, is under the control of the Billy Goat Gruff rather than the troll: "I" am the agent of "change my mind", but "you" are the agent of the action at issue (crossing the bridge). It may be that Lincoln simply doesn't understand this rather complex expression, and that he encodes it rather as a causal link whereby new knowledge of one character's mental state requires an update in another character's mental state (what *I* say changes *your* intended actions), so that in this understanding of the expression, it would be harder to find a meaning for "before I change my (own) mind". However we speculate on how this is encoded, it does seem clear that this is a complex mental state representational task, and it is not surprising that it is a place where difficulties arise.

8.2.3   *Example 3: Segueing between reported speech and reported thought*
In both the written and oral retellings of "The Three Little Pigs", at the denouément of the story Lincoln reports the thought of the wolf in the following terms:

(6) Written retelling:
"No No I'll not let you in!"
"THEN I'LL HUFF & I'LL PUFF OR I'LL GO
ON THE ROFF!" thinks the wolf.

(7) Oral version 1 [29/5/04]:
"no no no.
not by the hair of –
of our chinny chin chin.
we will not let you in!"

> "then I'll huff and I'll puff,
> and I'll blow your house down,
> or I'll go on the ch-
> go and climb down on the roof,
> on the roof,
> and go down the chimney"
> thinks the wolf.

Here despite Lincoln's apparent facility with the conventions of representing direct speech, there is no separation between the wolf's speech to the pigs and the wolf's reported internal plan to go on the roof: Rather there is a seamless segue from reported speech to reported thought. In the second oral retelling of the story (in 8), these elements of the story are in fact kept separate, as they are interspersed with other material.

> (8) Oral version 2 [1/8/04]:
> "well I'll huff,
> and I'll puff,
> and blow your house in."
> said the wolf.
> "We'll see about this."
> "phu – phu – phu" ((blowing noises))
> "nya nya nya nya nya"
> "eugh!"
> The wolf is wockily bockily destroyed.
> "Ee,
> I'll XX,
> I'll give em pavement.
> I'll climb down,
> the chimney,
> hee hee."

Access to the wolf's thoughts is information from the narrator. Information from reported speech can update other characters' knowledge states, but information from the narrator about reported thought should only be able to update the audience's knowledge state, not that of the characters. Once again, as one would predict, this is not evident in the original texts. So again there seems to be a difficulty here with managing relative knowledge states as modelled in Figure 4.

Assuming once again that the usages exemplified in these three examples should be taken as anomalous for a child of Lincoln's developmental stage (something which we have not been able to verify for this study),[5] there are various ways in which they could be described and explained. They could be seen as evidence of difficulty with inhibitory control and attentional flexibility: That is, Lincoln as narrator can't stop himself from revealing information which should by rights come later in the story. They could be seen as representing a difficulty in switching from the global perspective of the story narrator to the local perspective of the characters. Finally, they could be seen as reflecting problems in mental state representation, particularly at complex levels of nesting.

A fourth example prompts us to construct a yet more complex model of the narrative task which Lincoln has set himself.

8.2.4   Example 4: Meta-narrative commentary in "The Three Billy Goats Gruff"

With this final example, we return to the written retelling of "The Three Billy Goats Gruff". Recall that in this narrative, in addition to page titles appearing at the top of the picture frame, Lincoln included what we described as "commentary", appearing at the bottom of the frame. What are we to make of this commentary? Table 4, extracted from Table 2 above, shows the macrostructure of the last two thirds of the story, the pages which have commentary: The previous 3 pages do not.

Table 4. Commentary in Lincoln's "The Three Billy Goats Gruff"

Page title	Story episode	Commentary
The Hard Page	Little BGG – resolution	Well done you did it to grass!
Very Hard Hard Page	Middle BGG – challenge	Remember, call him
Very Hard Hard Page	Middle BGG – resolution	Well done you did it to grass!
Now what can we do?	Big BGG	Well done! The troll is in the water!
[no title]	End page: resolution	You help the 3 billy goats gruff get it on!

It seems to us, in part on the basis of discussion with Lincoln, that these comments are to be taken as coming from Lincoln rather than the story narrator, and as being directed to the characters, and in the last case, perhaps to the narrator. It is unclear what the second comment is intended to mean (does *call him* mean "call the big brother"?), but the message conveyed by the others is clear. In comments 1, 3, and 4 the addressee is the major protagonist in the story episode (one of the three Billy

---

5.   Lucariello (1990: 141) reports that younger, non-autistic children ("Kindergarten children" – age not specified) sometimes "scrambled" story information in answering questions about stories, e.g. events presented as occurring later in story time were inappropriately used to address issues arising earlier in story time.

Goats Gruff in each case) who is being congratulated on his/her performance in that episode, while in the final comment, although the message is again one of congratulation, the addressee cannot be any of the three Billy Goats Gruff because the addressee is being either exhorted to or (more likely) commended for helping them; hence our suggestion that it may be the narrator or Lincoln himself who is being addressed here. (Note that there is a clear difference between these comments and the titles of pages; while some of the latter may also reflect Lincoln's thinking about the story (as discussed above) they are clearly framed by Lincoln as "titles".) One way we can view these comments is as instances of what Labov and Waletzky (1967) and Labov (1972) have called "evaluation", albeit included as somewhat peripheral to the story rather than embedded within its linear sequence.

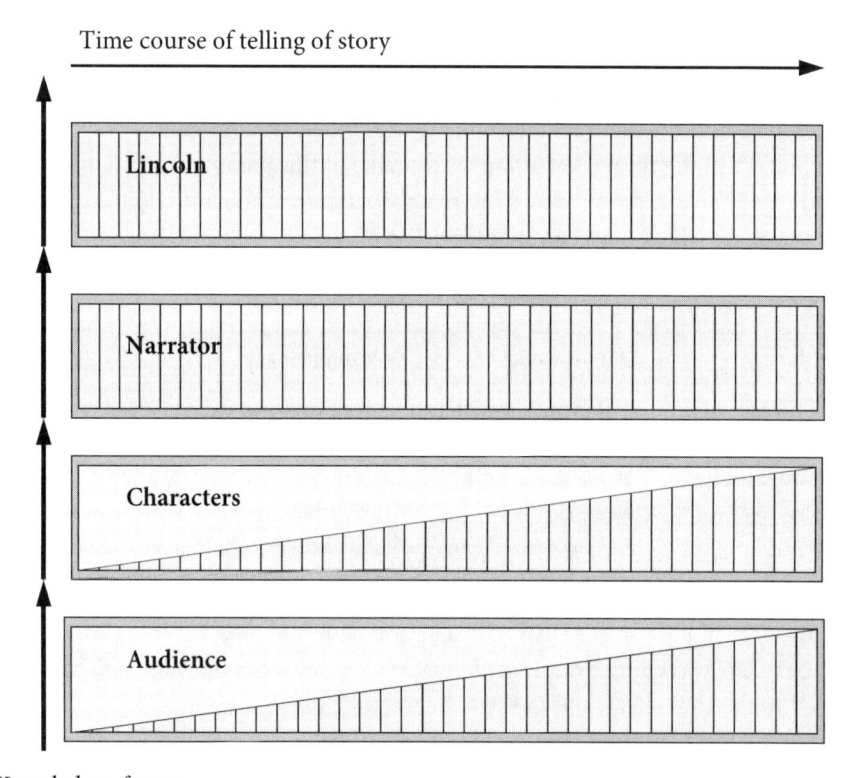

Figure 5. A more complex four part model of knowledge state management

It may be that a better model for understanding Lincoln's retelling of the story than the classical fairy tale arises from interactive digital media, with which Lincoln is very familiar, and which differ from traditional narratives in numerous interesting ways (Ryan 2001). For example, computer games have a highly interactive nature. The player may be involved IN a story, playing a character and/or managing the characters. The computer usually provides feedback on the player's performance.

We could speculate therefore that in fact a better model for this story is one where the narrator tells the story and "controls" the characters, thereby getting the story action to happen. Lincoln then would be "playing" the narrator, dramatising the roles of the characters, and speaking to both the characters and the narrator. Such an understanding would require a more complex model still of knowledge states, with 4 parts, as represented in Figure 5. This model is, as indicated in Note 2, in fact more in tune with current narrative theory, which standardly makes the assumption that we need to distinguish between at least a "narrator" and an "author".[6]

9   Conclusions

We have suggested that in the context of a case study of this kind, it is most instructive to focus on evidence of ability, and in this vein we have identified a number of striking features of Lincoln's narrative performance. He is clearly able to use a range of devices for managing perspective, and he demonstrates the ability to construct a planned episodic macrostructure which captures a global narrative schema, while also illustrating understanding and use of some local causal links.

If we seek insights from these findings into the theories which have been proposed to account for autism in the psychological literature, then there are at least some programmatic observations which we can make. The "Theory of mind" account would suggest, in keeping with the "mind-blindedness" deficit proposed, that a child with autism tackling the narrative task would demonstrate an evident difficulty in managing perspective. There are methodological issues in knowing how to test such a hypothesis, some of which we have discussed. However, for whatever errors or idiosyncrasies of performance Lincoln's narratives might be seen to manifest, performance in this area is not strikingly aberrant. Lincoln expressively frames and dramatises his story retellings, using direct speech, onomatopoeia, multiple voices and some representation of characters' mental states. Nevertheless it is important to note that the idiosyncrasies of performance we identify do appear to arise at places involving complex nested mental state representations.

---

6.   And indeed, often a distinction is made between the actual author and an "implied" author, in recognition of the need to distinguish between the presence with a particular standpoint and characteristics which is inferred by the reader as lying behind the work, and the actual author of the text; this distinction need not concern us here.

Our observations concerning episodic macrostructure can be seen to speak to the two other theories we have mentioned here, which share some predictions regarding gross features of narrative performance. The "Weak central coherence" account of autism would predict a lack of ability to comprehend or present a "gist" of a story and a tendency to focus on story details to the detriment of relating and evaluating these in support of a more global "point". We have no evidence that Lincoln can give a "gist" for his stories. However, Lincoln's page titles and meta-narrative commentaries do appear to indicate that he understands that the parts of the story serve a global purpose. He appears to understand that characters have goals, and that the cumulative attainment or frustration of these goals is played out across a series of episodes. To this degree, there is evidence that Lincoln is aware of and tackling the task of orienting his story around an underlying causal-explanatory structure.

The "Executive control" account would predict that the child with autism writing a story should demonstrate deficits in: Planning the global episodic structure; flexibly shifting attention between the competing demands of local and higher level storytelling goals; and appropriately suppressing or revealing information at different stages of the story. Reflecting on Lincoln's narrative performance from this perspective we note that he demonstrates significant abilities in planning and in negotiating on the one hand the local and on the other hand the global demands of the storytelling task. Nevertheless, we also note a "stickiness" in Lincoln's shifts between local and global perspectives of the narrative planning task for instance evident in examples demonstrating a failure to suppress the revealing of information by characters in inappropriate circumstances.

In the context of the observations we have made here the question which remains is: Where Lincoln's narrative performance *is* recognisably more profoundly unusual (beyond morphosyntactic and lexical irregularities), to what should we attribute this? It is evident that Lincoln clearly can manage some local narrative tasks such as some causal-explanatory links, and the presenting of the perspective of individual characters. He also has a global conception of narrative and can negotiate, plan for and adhere to a global schema. What remains in question is his ability to articulate between local and global dimensions of the overall narrative task.

Most previous investigations of autism and narrative have involved quantitative analysis of experimentally constrained, grouped autistic data, where the method of relating the data to the theories may take the form of frequency counts of linguistic features such as mental state predicates or proposed causal link markers. In contrast, an in-depth qualitative analysis of the spontaneous narratives that we present here offers an insight into the way a child with autism perceives and structures the narrative task. We have proposed a simple model of one aspect of the narrative task in terms of managing relative knowledge states and used this to capture the different task requirements of three different types of story. It seems to us that the shifts required of the storyteller in the management of relative knowledge states as illustrated here are a potentially fruitful entry to investigating the cognitive processes involved in the storytelling task. We suggest that at least part of the characteristic oddness of autistic narrative may be due to a mismatch between what the task demands by its nature and the way a child with autism may perceive and structure this task, and have shown in particular that problematic areas of Lincoln's narratives can usefully be explored in terms of difficulties in the management of relative knowledge states. By understanding the cognitive processes involved in the narrative task as framed from this perspective, it may then become possible to relate these observed deficits in a more concrete fashion to the various theories which have been proposed to account for autism in the psychological literature.

References

American Psychiatric Association. 1994. *Diagnostic and statistical manual of mental disorders: DSM-IV*. Washington, DC: American Psychiatric Association.
Banfield, Ann. 1982. *Unspeakable sentences: Narration and representation in the language of fiction*. Boston, MA: Routledge and Kegan Paul.
Baron-Cohen, Simon. 1995. *Mindblindness: An essay on autism and theory of mind*. Cambridge, MA: The MIT Press.
Baron-Cohen, Simon, Alan M. Leslie & Uta Frith. 1985. Does the autistic child have a "Theory of mind"? *Cognition* 21. 37–46.
Baron-Cohen, Simon, Alan M. Leslie & Uta Frith. 1986. Mechanical, behavioural and intentional understanding of picture stories in autistic children. *British Journal of Developmental Psychology* 4. 113–125.
Baron-Cohen, Simon, Helen Tager-Flusberg & Donald Cohen (eds.). 1993. *Understanding other minds: Perspectives from autism*. Oxford: OUP.
Bartlett, Frederic C. 1932. *Remembering*. Cambridge: CUP.
Berman, Ruth & Dan Slobin. 1994. *Relating events in narrative: A crosslinguistic developmental study*. Hillsdale, NJ: Lawrence Erlbaum.
Boscolo, Pietro & Lerida Cisotto. 1999. On narrative reading-writing relationships: How young writers construe the reader's need for inferences. In Goldman, Graesser & van den Broek (eds.), 161–178.
Bruner, Jerome & Carol Feldman. 1993. Theories of mind and the problem of autism. In Baron-Cohen, Tager-Flusberg & Cohen (eds.), 267–291.
Capps, Lisa, Jennifer Kehres & Marian Sigman. 1998. Conversational abilities among children with autism and developmental delay. *Autism* 2. 325–344.
Capps, Lisa, Molly Losh & Christopher Thurber. 2000. "The frog ate the bug and made his mouth sad": Narrative competence in children with autism. *Journal of Abnormal Child Psychology* 28(2). 193–204.
Chafe, Wallace. 1979. The flow of thought and the flow of language. In Givón (ed.), 159–181.

Dijk, Teun van. 1982. Episodes as units of discourse analysis. In Deborah Tannen (ed.), *Analyzing discourse: Text and talk*, 177–195. Washington, DC: Georgetown University Press.

Duchan, Judith F., Gail Bruder & Lynne Hewitt (eds.). 1995. *Deixis in narrative*. Hillsdale, NJ: Lawrence Erlbaum.

Dunn, Judith. 1991. Understanding others: Evidence from naturalistic studies of children. In Andrew Whiten (ed.), *Natural theories of mind: Evolution, development, and simulation of everyday mindreading*, 51–61. Oxford: Blackwell.

Fabb, Nigel. 1997. *Linguistics and literature: Language in the verbal arts of the world*. Oxford: Blackwell.

Frith, Uta. 1989. *Autism: Explaining the enigma*. Oxford: Blackwell.

Givón, Talmy (ed.). 1979. *Discourse and syntax* [Syntax and Semantics 12]. New York, MA: Academic Press.

Goldman, Susan, Arthur C. Graesser & Paul van den Broek (eds.). 1999. *Narrative comprehension, causality and coherence*. Mahwah, NJ: Lawrence Erlbaum.

Goldman, Susan, Keisha O'Banion Varma & Diana Sharp. 1999. Children's understanding of complex stories: Issues of representation and assessment. In Goldman, Graesser & van den Broek (eds.), 135–159.

Graumann, Carl F. & Werner Kallmeyer (eds.). 2002. *Perspective and perspectivation in discourse*. Amsterdam: John Benjamins.

Grimes, Joseph E. 1975. *The thread of discourse* [Janua Linguarum, Series Minor 207]. The Hague: Mouton.

Happé, Francesca. 1999. Why success is more interesting than failure: Understanding assets and deficits in autism. *The Psychologist* 12(11). 540–546.

Hickmann, Maya. 2003. *Children's discourse: Person, space and time across languages*. Cambridge: CUP.

Hinds, John. 1979. Organizational patterns in discourse. In Givón (ed.), 135–156.

Ji, Shaojun. 2002. Identifying episode transitions. *Journal of Pragmatics* 34. 1257–1271.

Labov, William. 1972. The transformation of experience in narrative syntax. In *Language in the inner city: Studies in the black English vernacular*, 354–396. Philadelphia, PA: University of Pennsylvania Press.

Labov, William & Joshua Waletzky. 1967. Narrative analysis: Oral versions of personal experience. In June Helm (ed.), *Essays on the verbal and visual arts*, 14–22. Seattle, WA: University of Washington Press.

Li, Naicong & David A. Zubin. 1995. Discourse continuity and perspective taking. In Duchan, Bruder & Hewitt (eds.), 287–307.

Longacre, Robert E. 1979. The paragraph as a grammatical unit. In Givón (ed.), 311–335.

Losh, Molly & Lisa Capps. 2003. Narrative ability in high-functioning children with autism or Asperger's syndrome. *Journal of Autism and Developmental Disorders* 33(3). 239–251.

Loveland, Katherine, Robin McEvoy, Belgin Tunali & Michelle L. Kelley. 1990. Narrative storytelling in autism and Down syndrome. *British Journal of Developmental Psychology* 8. 9–23.

Loveland, Katherine & Belgin Tunali. 1993. Narrative language in autism and the Theory of Mind hypothesis: A wider perspective. In Baron-Cohen, Tager-Flusberg & Cohen (eds.), 247–266.

Lucariello, Joan. 1990. Canonicality and consciousness in child narrative. In Bruce K. Britton & Anthony D. Pellegrini (eds.), *Narrative thought and narrative language*, 131–149. Hillsdale, NJ: Lawrence Erlbaum.

Mandler, Jean M. 1978. A code in the node: The use of a story schema in retrieval. *Discourse Processes* 1. 14–35.

Mandler, Jean M. & Nancy S. Johnson. 1977. Remembrance of things parsed: Story structure and recall. *Cognitive Psychology* 9. 111–151.

Mayer, Mercer. 1969. *Frog, where are you?* New York, NY: Puffin.

Mushin, Ilana. 1998. Viewpoint shifts in narrative. In Jean-Pierre Koenig (ed.), *Discourse and cognition: Bridging the gap*, 323–336. Stanford, CA: CSLI.

Mushin, Ilana. 2001. *Evidentiality and epistemological stance: Narrative retelling*. Amsterdam: John Benjamins.

Norbury, Courtenay F. & Dorothy V. M. Bishop. 2002. Inferential processing and story recall in children with communication problems: A comparison of specific language impairment, pragmatic language impairment and high-functioning autism. *International Journal of Language and Communication Disorders* 37(3). 227–251.

Nordqvist, Åsa. 2001. *Speech about speech: A developmental study on form and function of direct and indirect speech* [Gothenburg Monographs in Linguistics 19]. Göteborg: Göteborg University (PhD thesis, Göteborg University Department of Linguistics).

Ochs, Elinor & Olga Solomon (eds.). 2004. *Discourse studies 6.2. Special Issue: Discourse and autism*. London: Sage.

Ozonoff, Sally, Bruce F. Pennington & Sally J. Rogers. 1991. Executive function deficits in high-functioning autistic children: Relationship to Theory of Mind. *Journal of Child Psychology and Psychiatry* 32. 1081–1105.

Quasthoff, Uta. 2002. Global and local aspects of perspectivity. In Graumann & Kallmeyer (eds.), 323–345.

Reilly, Judy S., Edward S. Klima & Ursula Bellugi. 1990. Once more with feeling: Affect and language in atypical populations. *Development and Psychopathology* 2. 367–391.

Reilly, Judy S., Anita Zamora & Robert McGivern. 2005. Acquiring perspective in English: The development of stance. *Journal of Pragmatics* 37. 185–208.

Rumelhart, David E. 1977. Understanding and summarizing brief stories. In David Laberge & S. Jay Samuels (eds.), *Basic processes in reading: Perception and comprehension*, 265–303. Hillsdale, NJ: Lawrence Erlbaum.

Russell, James (ed.). 1997. *Autism as an executive disorder*. Oxford: OUP.

Ryan, Marie-Laure. 2001. Beyond myth and metaphor: The case of narrative in digital media. *Game Studies* 1(1). http://www.gamestudies.org/0101/ryan/.

Sanders, Jose & Wilbert Spooren. 1997. Perspective, subjectivity, and modality from a cognitive linguistic point of view. In Wolf-Andreas Liebert, Gisela Redeker & Linda Waugh (eds.), *Discourse and perspective in cognitive linguistics*, 85–112. Amsterdam: John Benjamins.

Selman, Robert L. 1980. *The growth of interpersonal understanding: Developmental and clinical analysis*. New York, NY: Academic Press.

Smith, Annette. 1997a. *The three little pigs*. (Retold by Annette Smith, Illustrated by Isabel Lowe). Petone, NZ: Nelson Price Milburn.

Smith, Annette. 1997b. *The three billy goats gruff*. (Retold by Annette Smith, Illustrated by Pat Reynolds). Petone, NZ: Nelson Price Milburn.

Solomon, Olga. 2004. Narrative introductions: Discourse competence of children with ASD. *Discourse Studies* 6(2). 253–276.

Stirling, Lesley. 2001. The multifunctionality of anaphoric expressions. *Australian Journal of Linguistics* 21(1). 7–23.

Tager-Flusberg, Helen. 1992. Autistic children's talk about psychological states: Deficits in early acquisition of theory of mind. *Child Development* 63. 161–172.

Tager-Flusberg, Helen. 1995. 'Once upon a ribbit': Stories narrated by autistic children. *British Journal of Developmental Psychology* 13. 45–59.

Tager-Flusberg, Helen. 1999. The challenge of studying language development in children with autism. In Lisa Menn & Nan Bernstein Ratner (eds.), *Methods for studying language production*, 313–332. Mahwah, NJ: Lawrence Erlbaum.

Tager-Flusberg, Helen. 2000. Understanding the language and communicative impairments in autism. In Laraine M. Glidden (ed.), *International review of research on mental retardation 20. Special Issue on autism*, 185–205. New York, NY: Academic Press.

Tager-Flusberg, Helen & Kate Sullivan. 1995. Attributing mental states to story characters: A comparison of narratives produced by autistic and mentally retarded individuals. *Applied Psycholinguistics* 16. 241–256.

Tager-Flusberg, Helen, Robert Joseph & Susan Folstein. 2001. Current directions in research on autism. *Mental Retardation and Developmental Disabilities Research Reviews* 7. 21–29.

Tomlin, Russell. 1987. Linguistic reflections of cognitive events. In Russell Tomlin (ed.), *Coherence and grounding in discourse*, 455–479. Amsterdam: John Benjamins.

Volkmar, Fred R. & Donald J. Cohen. 1985. The experience of infantile autism: A first-person account by Tony W. *Journal of Autism and Developmental Disorders* 15. 47–54.

Wiebe, Janet. 1994. Tracking point of view in narrative. *Computational Linguistics* 20(2). 233–287.

Chapter 7. "Then I'll huff and I'll puff or I'll go on the roff!" thinks the wolf   165

Appendix

Text 2. "The Three Little Pigs"[7]

> THE THREE LITTLE PIGS
>
> **One day a mother pig said to her 3 Little Pigs:**
> **"It's time to make homes of your houses the big bad wolf went to blow 2 houses down."**
> **Off went the three Little Pigs.**

> NEXT PAGE:
>
> **The 1st Little Pig found the straw.**
> **"This house can be build today."**
> **So he build the straw house.**

> THE HARD PAGE
>
> **The 2nd Little Pig found the sticks.**
> **"This house can be very good."**
> **So he build the stick house.**

---

7. The title pages of each text have been excluded from these facsimile reproductions as they include Lincoln's full name.

> VERY HARD HARD PAGE:
>
> The 3rd Little Pig found the bricks.
> "Hmm... a hard one This Time."
> So that when he build the house of bricks!

> WOLF PAGE 1
>
> The wolf came to the house of straw.
> "LiTTLE PIG LITTLE PIG LET ME IN!"
> "No No I'll not let you in!"
> "THEN I'LL HUFF & I'LL PUFF & I'LL BLOW YOU HOUSE IN!" Yelled the wolf.

> **Straw blow:**
>
> So he huffed and he puffed,
> He blow down the straw house.
> "HELP!" yelled the LIttle Pig all in time.

Chapter 7. "Then I'll huff and I'll puff or I'll go on the roff!" thinks the wolf

wolf page 2

The wolf came to the house of sticks.
"LITTLE PIG LITTLE PIG LET ME IN!"
"No No I'll not let you in!"
"THEN I'LL HUFF & I'LL PUFF & I'LL BLOW YOU HOUSE IN!" Yelled the wolf.

STICK HOUSE BLOW PAGE:

So he huffed and he puffed
He blow down the stick house.
"HELP!" yelled the two Little Pigs to times.

wolf page 3

The wolf came to the house of bricks
"LITTLE PIG LITTLE PIG LET ME IN!"
"No No I'll not let you in!"
"THEN I'LL HUFF & I'LL PUFF OR I'LL GO ON THE ROFF!" thinks the wolf.

Sorry the brick house won't blow?
The wolf huffed and he puffed
He can't blow the brick house.
but the wolf got on the roof.....

ROOF ON A PAGE:
The Three Little Pigs thinks that the wolf
got on the roof at all...
The 3rd Little Pig build the fire.

"OUCH OUCH OUCH!"
up went his feet like fire...
"OUCH OUCH OUCH!"
and the big bad wolf got all the way home.

The End

Text 3. "The Three Billy Goats Gruff"

THE THREE BILLY GOATS GRUFF

Once upon a time the 3 Billy Goats Gruff had even eated the grass. Soon they have to cross the brager bright stoon. They said how to get onto the brager bright stoon. "We can cross it!" they said. "Wait until the troll comes," snaped Little Billy Goat Gruff.
and comes to life.

THE NEXT PAGE

After a little uile, the big TROLL! came onto the ground. He was in the bush. He went out of the bush and came out yelling, "THIS BRAGER BRIGHT STOON IS MINE!" He yelled and desied that the three Billy Goats Gruff have to cross the Brager Bright Stoon.

THE HARD PAGE

Soon, Little Billy Goat Gruff came on the Brager Bright Stoon.
Trip, Trop, Trip, Trop!
"Who is crossing on my Brager Bright Stoon?" said the troll.
"IT'S ME!!!! Little Billy Goat Gruff."
The Troll said, "I gotta ear YOU up!"

> THE HARD PAGE
>
> "Please don't ear me up!" said Little Billy Goat Gruff. "My sister's bigger! So I'm gotta do my hands!" The troll said, "OK. You can pass quick before I changed your mind." and off went Little Billy Goat Gruff.
>
> **WELL DONE YOU DID IT TO GRASS!**

> VERY HARD HARD PAGE
>
> Next, Middle Billy Goat Gruff crossed the Brager Bright Stoon as well.
> Trip, Trop, Trip, Trop!
> The troll said, "Who is THAT on my Brager Bright Stoon?" the troll cried.
> "IT ME! MIDDLE BILLY GOAT GRUFF."
> "That's IT! I gotta eat YOU UP! HA HA HA HA HA!" said the troll.
>
> **REMEMBER, CALL HIM.**

> VERY HARD HARD PAGE
>
> "Please don't eat me up! My brother is the biggest. "Very well." said the troll wathing his gold sticker. "Goodbye. you've got to be good. Off you go utill I changed your mind. OK." Off she went.
>
> **WELL DONE YOU DID IT TO GRASS!**

Chapter 7. "Then I'll huff and I'll puff or I'll go on the roff!" thinks the wolf

Now what can we do?

Meanwhile... BIG Billy Goat Gruff got inside from the Brager Bright Stoon.
TRIP, TROP, TRIP, TROP!
"OH NO! not again." said the troll.
"I'M VERY HUNGREY I'M DEARSFDGDING YOU AND YOUR PREDARA FROM THE BRAGER BRIGHT STOON!" He yelled and HU HO HE HA!

WELL DONE! THE TROLL IS IN THE WATER!

The 3 Billy Goats Gruff is saved and it happens when it goes too far, the troll ran back into the castle very quick. and never seen again!

THE END

YOU HELP THE 3 BILLY GOATS GRUFF GET IT ON!

CHAPTER 8

Interaction between language and cognition in language development

Heather Winskel

In the temporal domain two distinct language typologies have been identified based on whether languages have grammatical marking of the imperfective-perfective aspectual system or not (Berman and Slobin 1994). In Spanish, Turkish and English which have distinct grammatical or obligatory marking of this aspectual contrast, narrators tend to encode the overlapping events depicted. In contrast, in German and Hebrew, which lack this aspectual contrast, narrators tend not to distinguish the overlapping temporal contours depicted. Thai makes an interesting comparison as it does have these aspectual contrasts but they are not obligatory. There appears to be a third language typology represented by languages such as Thai which have an imperfective-perfective aspectual contrast, but one which is not obligatory in usage.

1   Introduction

First, I will give a background context to the current debate on the relative contribution of cognition and language-specific factors to the development of language in children. Second, I will examine recent research that has reopened the linguistic relativity debate and in particular focus on a less deterministic conceptualisation, termed "thinking-for-speaking" (Slobin 1996, 2003, 2004). In relation to thinking-for-speaking, research has predominantly investigated the spatial domain with much less attention paid to the temporal domain. The current chapter will examine language acquisition in the temporal domain in Thai, which is of particular interest as it has distinctive features with regards to the temporal domain and languages previously studied. Narratives are elicited by the same *Frog, Where Are You* story used by Berman and Slobin (1994), so that comparisons can be made with previously studied languages.

2 Background context

There has been much debate about the relationship between language and cognition, in particular the influence that language has on cognition, and if language can influence the way that we think of the world. According to the Whorfian hypothesis, speakers of different languages have different ways of thinking, viewing or perceiving the world (Whorf 1956). Attempts to test the effects of language on non-linguistic cognition were not sufficiently convincing in the 1960s and 70s, and consequently interest in linguistic relativity waned and was superceded by a more cognitive-dominated perspective influenced by Piagetian thought (Bowerman 1996). In relation to language acquisition, cognition was considered to be the driving force behind language acquisition. Support for this perspective came from cross-linguistic research and the striking commonalities found in the order of acquisition of linguistic terms across different languages. For example, locative terms were found to emerge in a remarkably consistent order both within and across languages, e.g. Johnston and Slobin (1979), and it was assumed that as spatial terms such as *in, on, under, up, down, in front* and *behind* emerge they are directly mapped onto spatial concepts that children have already formed on the basis of their nonlinguistic development (Slobin 1973, 1985). According to this view, all children initially adhere to a universal and uniform starting organisation of semantic space and only later, after more linguistic experience, diverge in the direction of the semantic system of the input language (Slobin 1985).

There are basic, biological arguments for universality in categories in the spatial domain, but recent research has indicated that languages vary considerably in how they semantically partition the world in the spatial domain (e.g. Bowerman 1996; Bowerman & Levinson 2001). An example is locative placement, which is defined as the caused movement of an object from or to a location. In English there is a major semantic division between "containment" and "contact" with an external surface, i.e. whether an object is *in* or *on* another whether an object is *taken off* or *out* in relation to another, whereas in Korean, there is a major semantic division or distinction between actions that result in *tight fit* and actions that result in various other types of contact (Bowerman 1996). These differences have been utilised to examine developmental processes and how early language-specific semantic divisions are acquired. Melissa Bowerman and colleagues have found that both English and Korean learners are sensitive to and start to produce language-specific spatial categories or divisions from an early age, as early as 18 months and even earlier when they are beginning to produce their first words (Bowerman & Choi 1994; Choi & Bowerman 1991; Choi et al. 1999). This line of research shows that in relation to spatial semantic development, there is not only an influence of non-linguistic spatial conceptualisation but also an impact of the language-specific semantic categories of the input language. This shows that children are very sensitive to language-specific semantic categories and how forms map onto different functions in a language from very early on. We can conclude from this that it is not just a one-way mapping from pre-existing concepts in linguistic expression as was previously thought, but rather there is an interaction between nonlinguistic cognition and semantic categories of the input language on language development.

3   Resurgence of interest in linguistic relativity

Recently, there has been a resurgence of interest in linguistic relativity (e.g. Bowerman & Levinson 2001; Gentner & Goldin-Meadow 2003; Gumperz & Levinson 1996; Levinson 2003). One of the strongest arguments for the view that a speaker's language can have an influence on cognition comes from relative versus absolute orientation for describing the location of objects (Levinson 1996; Levinson et al. 2002). Relative systems, for example used by English or other European speakers, tend to locate objects by reference to the position and orientation of the speaker e.g. *to the left of the house, in front of the tree*. In absolute systems, reference is made to a fixed, external bearing, such as compass points or landscape features, e.g. *west of the house, north of the tree*, and about a third of languages in the world use this type of reference, e.g. Arrernte in central Australia or Guugu-Yimidhirr of northern Queensland (Levinson 1997; Masjid et al. 2004). This means that in general, for example, English speakers do not know which direction their friend approached from yesterday, i.e. south or east, whereas speakers of absolute systems which encode this distinction do. Pederson et al. (1998: 586) suggest that use of such linguistic systems "actually forces the speaker to make computations he or she might otherwise not make". Furthermore, Levinson and colleagues have demonstrated convincingly, using a number of spatial tasks, that this difference between the two language types has additional cognitive consequences (Levinson 1996; Levinson et al. 2002; Masjid et al. 2004).

4   Thinking-for-speaking

A more subtle, less deterministic version of linguistic relativity has been formulated by Slobin, which he has termed "thinking-for-speaking". This is a type of thinking "that is carried out on-line in the process of speaking" as the linguistic categories of the language that one speaks shapes or filters the way that aspects of the world are expressed (Slobin 1996: 75). Children learn from an early age to attend to and encode aspects of the world using grammatical or obligatory language-specific categories available in their language. According to Slobin (2003: 5), "obligatory" means "that the dimension in question cannot be regularly referred to without the expression in question". Children acquiring a language tune into the obligatory or habitually-used categories of their language and represent events in the style of their particular language from an early age and in a typical way that their language encodes experience. Hence, the child learns "language-specific patterns of thinking for speaking" from early in language development (Slobin 1996: 77). So it is reasoned that speakers from languages that *do* have these obligatory categories and speakers from languages that *do not* have these categories have different mental space for the particular semantic domain being encoded. Some languages encode a domain on a regular basis whereas other languages do not. Distinctions which have to be accessed more frequently or habitually become automated and hence more accessible to speakers of languages that make this distinction. According to Slobin (2003), terms which are more accessible and codable are characterised as being short, frequently occurring and typically part of a small set of options. For example, a concept expressed by a single verb is more codable than a phrase or clause, e.g. in Satellite- versus Verb-framed languages *run* is more codable than *while running*. In conclusion, children appear to hone in or show "selective attention" from an early age to the obligatory or habitually-used language-specific categories of their native language.

5. The temporal domain

In relation to thinking-for-speaking, research has focused on the spatial domain, in particular Satellite- and Verb- framed languages (e.g. Slobin 1996, 2003, 2004), however, much less attention has focused on the temporal domain. In the temporal domain two distinct language typologies have been identified, based on whether languages have grammatical marking of both poles of the imperfective-perfective aspectual contrast or not (Berman & Slobin 1994). Imperfective aspect views an event from within and without beginning and end points, whereas perfective aspect views a situation as a single whole with initial and terminal points (Li & Shirai 2000). Imperfective aspect is of particular significance as it plays an important function in backgrounding events and gives an unbounded or durative meaning to the event; in English, for example, it is realised by the morpheme *-ing* (Hopper 1979). It also plays an important role in the expression of simultaneity or the overlap of events or actions.

Berman and Slobin (1994) used a wordless picture book consisting of 24 pictures, entitled *Frog, Where Are You?* by Mercer Mayer (1967) to elicit narratives from Spanish, Turkish, English, German and Hebrew children and adults. Narratives were elicited from 10 participants from each of the following age groups: 3-year-olds, 6-year-olds, 9-year-olds and adults. The linguistic means of encoding the temporal relations depicted in Pictures 2 and 12 of the *frog story* were focused on, as both pictures depict overlapping temporal relations (Figure 1). Picture 2 shows "the boy and dog sleeping while the frog is escaping" and Picture 12 depicts a punctual event of "the boy falling" coinciding with the ongoing situation of "the bees chasing the dog". These picture frames provide "more controlled windows" into how narrators express overlapping temporal relations (Strömqvist & Verhoeven 2004: 8).

If we place the languages studied by Berman and Slobin (1994) on a grammatical aspectual continuum, then we can see that Spanish has the richest aspectual system with grammatical marking of both poles of the durative-nondurative distinction (Slobin 1996). English has the progressive, which provides explicit marking of the durative pole only, and in Turkish the progressive is more restricted to the past tense. German and Hebrew lack distinctive marking of either pole of the aspectual contrast, although they do both have past tense, which can give a bounded or perfective reading to an event or action (Slobin 1996).

Spanish – perfect, progressive, imperfective/perfective
English – perfect, progressive
Turkish – progressive in past tense
German – perfect
Hebrew – none

It has been found that in Spanish, Turkish and English which have distinct grammatical or obligatory marking of the imperfective-perfective aspectual contrast, narrators tend to make use of these options to encode overlapping events depicted in Pictures 2 and 12 of the *frog story* picture book. In contrast, in German and Hebrew, which lack this aspectual contrast, but instead have the option to mark this aspectual distinction through other more indirect linguistic means, narrators tend not to distinguish the temporal contours of the overlapping temporal events depicted, as in Example (1). It is reported that only two out of the fifty German narrators used an alternative lexical strategy, e.g. replication of the verb to give a durative meaning to the action 'run' as illustrated in Example (2) (Slobin 1996). These characteristic linguistic patterns were also evident in the youngest 3-year-old age group studied.

Picture 2

Picture 12

Figure 1. Pictures 2 and 12 from *Frog, Where Are You?* (Mayer 1967)

(1) Da   fällt der Junge hin.   Und der läuft da   weg.
    there fall the boy down and he run there away
    'There the boy falls down. And he runs away there.'

(2) Der Hund rennt rennt rennt.
    the dog runs runs runs
    'The dog is running.'

In addition, German and Hebrew do not tend to "compensate" using other devices, such as temporal connectives or adverbials, e.g. *when, while* or *meanwhile*. Hence, there appear to be differences in what temporal experiences are encoded by speakers from these two language typologies.

Temporal connectives also emerge earlier in the three aspectual languages – Spanish, English and Turkish – than in German and Hebrew. The first overt temporal marker relevant to simultaneity, *when*, is acquired by the youngest 3-year-old age group in the Spanish, English and Turkish children, but not in German and Hebrew children, and even at 5-years of age Spanish, English and Turkish children use the connective more frequently than the German and Hebrew children. Hence, depending on the relative complexity of these morphological distinctions within a given language, children display a greater focus on the temporal contour of events in the aspectual languages, i.e. Spanish, English and Turkish than in Hebrew and German. The obligatory, grammaticalised or habitually-used categories within a language appear to be particularly salient to the young language learner and furthermore, have a channeling effect on the attention of the learner towards closely related temporal functions (Strömqvist & Verhoeven 2004).

In another cross-linguistic study, Maya Hickmann found in Mandarin Chinese, which has non-obligatory aspectual morphemes, that narrators tend to "compensate" for the optional nature of aspectual markers by utilising temporal connectives (temporal conjunctions and adverbials) to mark situational overlaps in discourse to a greater extent than in the other languages studied – French, English and German (Hickmann 2003). She used a similar elicitation procedure as used in the *frog story*, but the series of pictures were shorter and consisted of two different sequences of pictures; one about a cat (6 pictures) and the other about a horse (5 pictures). There was also precocious acquisition of temporal connectives in Mandarin Chinese children in comparison with the European languages. In addition, usage of temporal connectives increased with age, particularly after seven years of age.

6 The Thai aspectual system

Thai offers an interesting comparison as, like Mandarin Chinese, it has a rich aspectual system including the imperfective-perfective contrast, but aspectual marking is not grammatically marked on the verb and not obligatory (Koenig & Muansuwan 2005). A summary of the Thai aspectual system is included in Table 1; however, it is important to note that the actual number of aspect markers in Thai is somewhat contentious, ranging from 8 to at least 17 aspect markers (Kanchanawan 1978; Koenig & Muansuwan 2005; Schmidt 1992; Thepkanjana 1986). Thai has two separate imperfective aspect markers, *kam0laŋ0* and *ju:1*1 as illustrated in Examples (3) and (4). The preverbal imperfective marker *kam0laŋ0* signifies 'the process of doing something', and postverbal *ju:1* signifies 'the continuation of an event' and translates as 'stay/be alive' (Burusphat 1991). While *kam0laŋ0* is more limited to the progressive meaning and restricts its usage to dynamic verbs, *ju:1* has evolved into a more general imperfective aspect marker which includes stative meaning (Meepoe 1998), hence the two imperfective markers have distinctive though overlapping aspectual meanings.

(3) *ma:4 **kam0laŋ0** ɛ:p1 du:0 kop1*
     dog   IMPFV   sneak look frog
     'The dog is peeping at the frog.'

(4) *dek1 nɔ:n0 **ju:1***
     child sleep IMPFV
     'The child is sleeping.'

The optional and infrequent use of aspect morphemes in Thai (and Mandarin Chinese) means that situation aspect, the intrinsic aspect of the verb and its predicate, plays an important role in the temporal interpretation of clauses and sentences (Smith & Erbaugh 2005). The aspectual situation type provides the essential information in clauses without explicit aspectual morphemes. Verbs and their predicates that are intrinsically unbounded will be perceived as having duration, whereas telic verbs, intrinsically bounded with end points, will be perceived as punctual. So, for example in (5) the two unbounded clauses without explicit aspectual marking were used to refer to the two overlapping actions depicted in the *frog story* – 'the child sitting in the water while the dog is on his/her neck'.

---

1.   Tones are marked in the Thai examples cited in this chapter as follows; 0=mid, 1=low, 2=falling, 3=high, 4=rising. This system is based on the system that was developed at the Linguistics Research Unit (LRU) of Chulalongkorn University (Luksaneeyanawin 1993). IPA transcription is used for the transcription of all other Thai text.

Table 1. The aspectual system of Thai*

Preverbal aspect markers		Postverbal aspect markers	
kam0laŋ0	PROG	ju:1	IMPERFV
		tɔ:1	continue
*daj2	PAST, PERFV	set1	PERFV finish
tça1	be about to	tçob1	PERFV end
khɤ:j0	experience	sia4	PERFV (lose, waste)
phəŋ2	about to	*lɛ:w3	PERFV already
		paj0	IMPERFV (go)
		paj0	PERFV (go)
		ma: 0	PERFV (come)
		khun2	SEMI-PERFV (ascend)
		loŋ0	SEMI-PERFV (descend)
		ʔɔ:k1	SEMI-PERFV (exit)

*   Adapted from Koenig and Muansuwan (2005). Koenig and Muansuwan (2005) do not consider these aspectual particles but other linguists do e.g. Burusphat (1991) and Kanchanawan (1978).

(5) dek1 kɔ:2 naŋ2 naj0 na:m3 su1nak3 kɔ:2 khi:1 khɔ:0 dek1
    child AUX   sit   in   water   dog   AUX   ride   neck   child
    'The child sits in the water, the dog rides on the child's neck.'

In addition, Thai utilises verb serialisation (see Example 6), which affects the aspectual interpretation of the clause, to serve various functions typically expressed using prepositions, inflections, adverbials and connectives in non-serial languages, e.g. Indo-European languages. The selection and choice of verbs is important in Thai, in particular in clauses without explicit aspectual marking, as it influences the aspectual interpretation of the clause and is also implicated in signaling the co-occurrence and sequencing of temporal events in narrative.

(6) kop1 kɔ:2 phlo:1 khun2 ma:0   tça:k1 khuat1
    frog   AUX   emerge up   come   from   bottle
    'The frog emerges/ed out of the bottle.'

7   The Thai *frog story* data

Thai *frog story* narratives available through CHILDES (MacWhinney 2000; Zlatev & Yangklang 2003) were examined for temporal expressions used in the *frog story* narratives. Pictures 2 and 12 of the *frog story* were specifically focused on, as both pictures depict overlapping events or actions and, furthermore, comparisons can be made with previously studied languages (Berman & Slobin 1994).

Based on the premise that "obligatoriness" or habitual usage is of primary importance for linguistic expression within the temporal domain we can conjecture that, as the aspectual system of Thai is *not* obligatory, Thai narrators will display similar patterns to German and Hebrew narrators and have a tendency to *not* distinguish the overlapping temporal events depicted (Berman & Slobin 1994). The results for Thai in Table 2, which shows the percentage of narrators using a different tense/aspect form for Picture 12, tend to support this prediction as Thai narrators use aspectual markers to encode the overlapping temporal relation depicted in a similar proportion to Hebrew and German rather than to English, Spanish and Turkish. So, even though Thai has aspectual markers, they are not used frequently by Thai narrators to encode the temporal distinctions depicted in the *frog story*. If we examine the overall usage of imperfective aspect markers in the Thai *frog story* illustrated in Figure 3, it can be seen that there is greatest reliance on aspectual markers by the youngest children, as they do not yet have other temporal devices available to them to serve a comparable function.

Table 2. The percentage of child narrators using a different tense/aspect form for Pictures 2 and 12

	Picture 2	Picture 12
Spanish	82	80
English	56	76
Turkish	53	61
Hebrew	29	15
German	8	33
Thai	20	15

In relation to the use of "compensatory" temporal connectives, German and Hebrew narrators (without obligatory aspectual marking) tend not to use "compensatory" connectives, whereas Mandarin Chinese narrators (with optional aspectual marking) do (Berman & Slobin 1994; Hickmann 2003). If we examine Table 3, which shows the percentage of temporal connectives used in Picture 2, it can be seen that Thai narrators do use more "compensatory" temporal connectives than German or Hebrew but not as many as English or Turkish narrators. Spanish does not use temporal connectives as frequently as English and Turkish, as it has a rich aspectual system, and hence use of temporal connectives are thought to be somewhat redundant (Slobin 1996). Furthermore, if we examine usage of temporal connectives by the different age groups in Thai, it can be seen that the 6-year-olds use temporal connectives the most with a gradual decline in usage with age as other linguistic options become available (as illustrated by Figures 3 and 4). So there

Chapter 8. Interaction between language and cognition in language development 183

appears to be a "compensatory" reliance on usage of temporal connectives in Thai, particularly in the 6-year-old age group who do not yet have the full range of linguistic options available to older narrators. So the pattern exhibited by Thai narrators for encoding the temporal contours depicted diverges from the characteristic pattern exhibited by German and Hebrew narrators, and there appears to be a greater "compensatory" reliance on connectives to express temporal relations, as occurs in Mandarin Chinese.

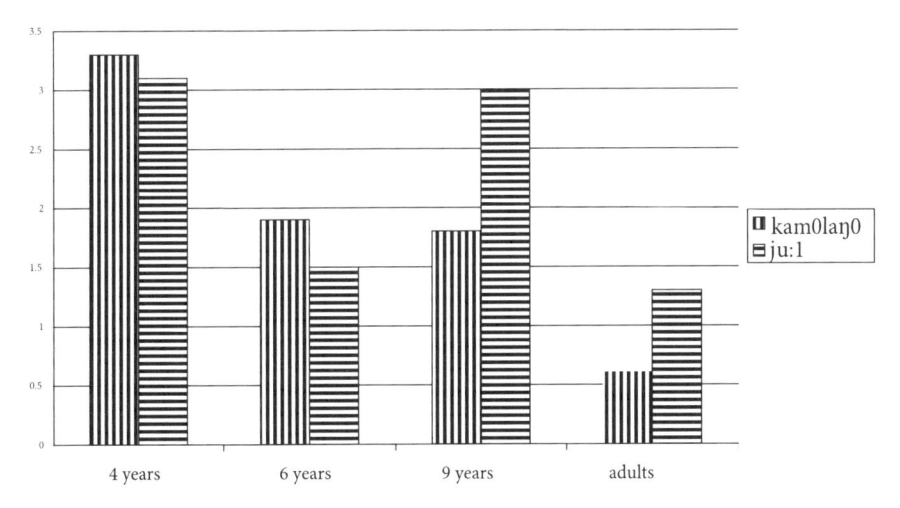

Figure 2. Use of imperfective aspect markers, *kam0laŋ0* and *ju:1* across age groups in the Thai *frog story*. (The percentages that the form occurs per total number of clauses per age group are given)

Table 3. The percentage of child narrators using temporal connectives for Picture 2

	Picture 2
Spanish	24
English	66
Turkish	47
Hebrew	24
German	13
Thai	37

Based on results from Mandarin Chinese, it can also be predicted that there would be precocious acquisition of temporal connectives in Thai (Hickmann 2003). If we examine Figure 4, which shows the linguistic devices used in the Thai *frog story* to express overlapping temporal relations, it can be seen that there is contradictory evidence for the early or precocious acquisition of temporal connectives as *phɔ:0 di:0* 'just at that time' and *phɔ:0* 'when' emerge relatively early in the 4-year-olds, whereas *muua2* 'when' and *kha1na1 thi:2* 'while' emerge relatively late in the older 9-year-old narratives.

Further, if we examine the usage of temporal connectives by the different age groups in Thai in Figure 4, it can be seen that the 6-year-olds do show a reliance on the temporal connective *phɔ:0* 'when' to express temporal relations, whereas in the 9-year-olds a range of additional temporal connectives (*phɔ:0* 'when', *muua2* 'when', *kha1na1 thi:2* 'while', *kha1na1diaw0kan0* 'meanwhile', *ra1wa:ŋ0* 'during', *phɔ:0 di:0* 'just at that time') are used for this function. However, the use of temporal connectives declines in the adults as other options become available, including relative clauses and causal connectives. This pattern of usage of temporal connectives across age in Thai diverges from the results found by Hickmann (2003) for Mandarin Chinese, as use was found to increase with age. So it appears that somewhat different linguistic strategies are being employed by adults from the two languages.

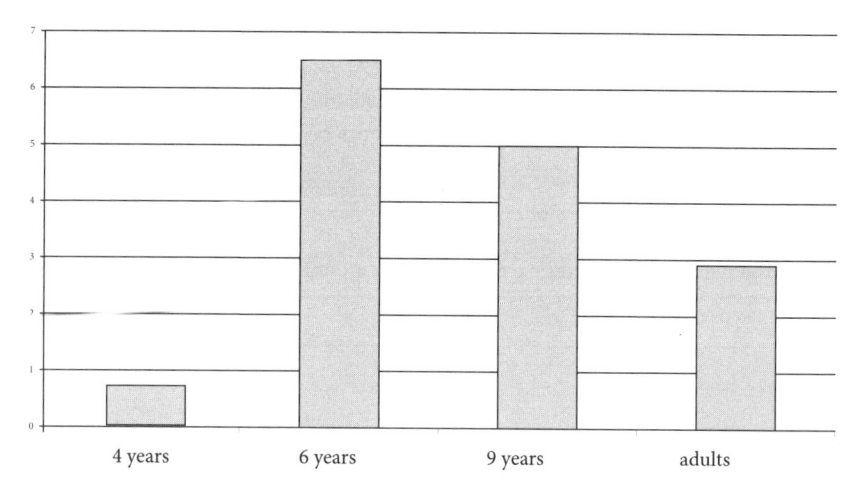

Figure 3. The temporal connectives (temporal conjunctions and adverbials) used across age groups in the Thai *frog story*. The Thai temporal conjunctions and adverbials includes *phɔ:0* and *muua2* both with a 'when' type function, *kha1na1 thi:2* 'while', *kha1na1diaw0kan0* 'meanwhile', *ra1wa:ŋ0* 'during', *phɔ:0 di:0* 'just at that time' based on Hickmann (2003). (The percentages that the form occurs per total number of clauses per age group are given)

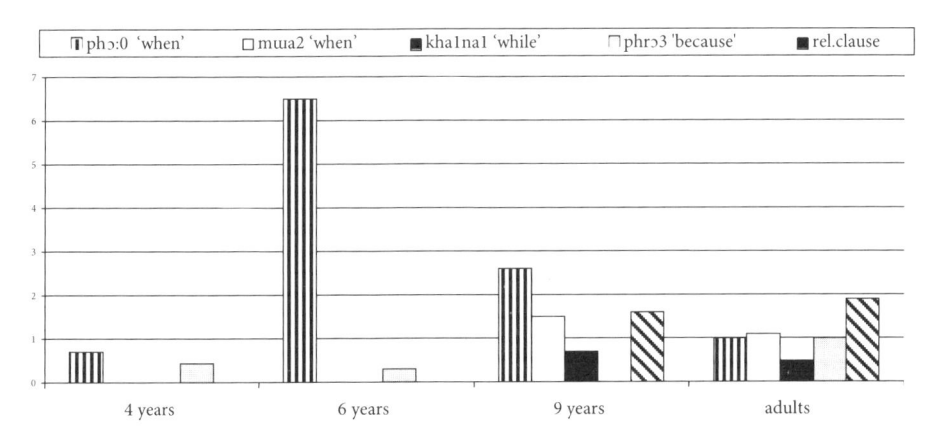

Chapter 8. Interaction between language and cognition in language development 185

Figure 4. The main linguistic devices used to encode temporal relations across age groups in the Thai *frog story*. (The percentages that the form occurs per total number of clauses per age group are given)

8 Typological and language-specific patterns

In relation to thinking-for-speaking, distinctive patterns emerged in the way that speakers refer to the temporal distinctions depicted in the *frog story* dependent on the "obligatoriness" of aspectual marking in the two language typologies identified by Berman and Slobin (1994). In relation to languages such as Thai with optional aspectual usage a more complex picture is emerging, and it appears from these preliminary findings that narrators do tend to encode these temporal distinctions using a range of linguistic devices.

This highlights the importance of considering not only shared typological linguistic characteristics, but also language-specific factors and what particular rhetorical options are available within a language. Consequently, the range of linguistic strategies used to express temporal relations in Thai was examined for the overall *frog story* and for Pictures 2 and 12. The youngest age group used imperfective aspect markers the most (Figure 3). In Pictures 2 and 12 (Table 4), imperfective morphemes were also used the most by the youngest children, in particular for Picture 2. In contrast, the 9-year-olds did not use aspect markers for either Picture 2 or 12, but used "compensatory" temporal connectives the most. The strategy of using verb serialisation, e.g. *bin0 ta:m0* 'fly follow', which presupposes two events or actions to represent the actions depicted in Picture 12 of 'the bees chasing the dog', increases with age. In relation to the overall *frog story* data in Figure 4, it can be seen that the older narrators, 9-year-olds and adults, use additional linguistic strategies such as relative clauses and causal connectives that imply the occurrence of two overlapping actions. Hence, it can be seen that Thai narrators use a range of rhetorical options, both explicit and implicit for expressing overlapping temporal relations which varies with age.

Table 4. Linguistic devices used in Thai to encode the temporal distinctions depicted (percentage of narrators per age group)

Linguistic strategies	4 years Picture 2	4 years Picture 12	6 years Picture 2	6 years Picture 12	9 years Picture 2	9 years Picture 12	Adults Picture 2	Adults Picture 12
Imperfective aspect marker	40	10	20	10	0	0	20	10
Temporal Connective	10	20	40	20	60	40	50	20
*Causal connective	0	10	0	10	0	0	10	30
**Verb serialisation	0	0	0	50	0	80	0	60
†Relative clause	0	0	0	0	0	10	0	0

Below are some examples of linguistic strategies used in Table 4.

*Causal connective:
(i) ma:4 kɔ:2 lɤ:j0 wiŋ2 **phrɔ3wa:2** phuŋ2 laj2 ta:m0 ma:4
    dog   AUX   pass run   **because**   bee   chase follow dog
    'The dog runs **because** the bees chase the dog.'

**Verb serialisation:
(ii) phuŋ2 kɔ:2 **bin0** **ta:m0** su1nak3
     bee   AUX   **fly**   **follow** dog
     'The bees **fly** (and) **follow** the dog'.

†Relative clause:
(iii) ma:4 kɔ:2 **thi:2** phuŋ2 tça1   laj2   toj1   nan3 kɔ:2
      dog   AUX   **which** bee   irrealis chase sting that AUX
      wiŋ2 pha:n1 na:2   dek1   tçhaj0 bop1 ma:0
      run   pass   front child boy   Bob   come
      'The dog **which** the bees chase to sting, runs past in front of the boy Bob.'

There appears to be a third language typology emerging, represented by languages such as Thai and Mandarin Chinese which have an imperfective-perfective aspectual contrast, but one which is optional, as illustrated in Table 5. Furthermore, there appears to be a "compensatory" use of temporal connectives and a greater reliance on situation aspect for the expression of temporal relations within the temporal domain. Thai narrators have a tendency to express the overlapping temporal relations depicted using a combination of both explicit and more implicit linguistic devices. In the other two language typologies previously identified by Berman and Slobin (1994), it can be seen that German and Hebrew narrators tend not to express the temporal relations depicted, whereas English, Spanish and Turkish tend to express this distinction.

Table 5. Contrastive analysis of the three language typologies

	German and Hebrew	English, Spanish and Turkish	Thai and Mandarin Chinese
Has explicit durative-non-durative aspectual marking	No	Yes	Yes
Obligatory vs non-obligatory usage	Not obligatory	Obligatory	Optional
Temporal connectives utilised	Tendency not to	Tendency to utilise temporal connectives particularly in English and Turkish	"Compensatory" usage occurs
Early acquisition of temporal connectives	No	Yes	Contradictory results
Overlapping temporal relations expressed	Tendency not to	Tendency to	Appears to be a tendency to

The extent to which languages within typological groups adhere to and diverge from these core or shared linguistic attributes and strategies adopted, needs to be investigated further. For example, to what extent do narrators from languages such as Thai and Mandarin Chinese use "compensatory" temporal connectives and additional linguistic devices to encode temporal relations. It is important to understand to what extent the shared typological characteristics of a group of languages (in a particular semantic domain) determines or influences the linguistic strategies adopted by speakers of particular languages, and also how much they diverge and are influenced by language-specific factors. Even when languages offer the same set of options for encoding an event, speakers may differ in the patterns or frequency of use of these options. Clearly, further research is needed to investigate or tease apart shared typological patterns and intra-typological differences or language-specific patterns.

It can be seen that early caretaker-child interactions, and the input that the child is exposed to, is critical in the formation of language-specific semantic categories and the rhetorical style unique to the particular language. Child-directed utterances provide clues about the typological characteristics of the specific input language to the young language learner, for example through the use of variation sets (a series of utterances produced with a constant communicative intention, but with changing form) in early interactions with the child. The use of these variation sets changes and adapts to the age of the child (Kuntay & Slobin 1995) and gives clues to the language learner about the characteristics or properties of the language being learnt (Bowerman et al. 2002). This is an additional fruitful line of research to examine the relationship between the characteristics of the input language that the child is exposed to and the subsequent usage patterns exhibited by the child.

In conclusion, there is growing evidence that language does influence cognition to some extent. It may be effective only during the actual process of thinking-for-speaking (Slobin 1996), or it could have longer-term effects on non-linguistic cognition as demonstrated by Levinson and colleagues in the spatial domain. Cross-linguistic research indicates that the salience and ease of access of the linguistic devices available to encode the relevant semantic distinctions influence acquisition, with obligatory or habitually-used linguistic categories more readily accessible and salient to the young language learner (Hickmann 2003; Slobin 1996, 2003). If obligatory aspectual marking is available then children tend to use these forms extensively from an early age (Weist, Kaczmarek & Wysocka 1993). Even though aspectual marking is not obligatory but optional in Thai, the expressions are relatively codable or transparent and accessible to the child, as separate invariant morphemes are used; consequently, aspectual morphemes are used by the youngest children to express temporal relations. Furthermore, due to the optional nature of aspect in Thai, it appears that other "compensatory" mechanisms come into play, including temporal connectives and situation aspect.

In relation to language development, recent research indicates that the child, from an early age, tunes in and acquires the characteristic style or pattern of usage specific to the language they are exposed to. Hence, we need a more balanced perspective in future research, which considers language development in terms of an interaction between both language-specific factors and cognition.

References

Berman, Ruth A. & Dan I. Slobin (eds.). 1994. *Different ways of relating events in narrative: A crosslinguistic developmental study*. Hillsdale, NJ: Lawrence Erlbaum.
Bowerman, Melissa. 1996. The origins of children's spatial semantic categories: Cognitive versus linguistic determinants. In Gumperz & Levinson (eds.), 145–176.
Bowerman, Melissa & Soonja Choi. 1994. Linguistic and nonlinguistic determinants of spatial semantic development: A cross-linguistic study of English, Korean and Dutch. *Boston University Conference on Language Development*. Boston, MA.

Bowerman, Melissa & Stephen C. Levinson. 2001. *Language acquisition and conceptual development*. Cambridge: CUP.
Bowerman, Melissa, Penelope Brown, Sonja Eisenbeiß, Bhuvana Narasimhan & Dan I. Slobin. 2002. Putting things in places: Developmental consequences of linguistic typology. Input and language. In Eve V. Clark (ed.), *Stanford Child Language Research Forum* 31. Stanford CA: CSLI. http://cslipublications.stanford.edu/hand/miscpubsonline.html.
Burusphat, Somsonge. 1991. *The structure of Thai narrative*. Dallas, TX: The Summer Institute of Linguistics.
Choi, Soonja & Melissa Bowerman. 1991. Learning to express motion events in English and Korean. The influence of language-specific lexicalisation patterns. *Cognition* 41. 83–121.
Choi, Soonja, Laraine McDonough, Melissa Bowerman & Jean M. Mandler. 1999. Early sensitivity to language-specific spatial categories in English and Korean. *Cognitive Development* 14. 241–268.
Gentner, Dedre & Susan Goldin-Meadow (eds.). 2003. *Language in mind: Advances in the investigation of language and thought*. Cambridge, MA: The MIT Press.
Gumperz, John J. & Stephen C. Levinson (eds.). 1996. *Rethinking linguistic relativity*. Cambridge: CUP.
Hickmann, Maya. 2003. *Children's discourse: Person, space and time across languages*. Cambridge: CUP.
Hopper, Paul J. 1979. Aspect and foregrounding in discourse. In Talmy Givón (ed.), *Discourse and Syntax* [Syntax and Semantics 12], 213–241. New York, NY: Academic Press.
Johnston, Judith R. & Dan I. Slobin. 1979. The development of locative expressions in English, Italian, Serbo-Croatian and Turkish. *Journal of Child Language* 6. 529–554.
Kanchanawan, Nitaya. 1978. Expression for time in the Thai verb and its application to Thai-English machine translation. University of Texas PhD dissertation.
Koenig, Jean-Pierre & Nuttanart Muansuwan. 2005. The syntax of aspect in Thai. *Natural Language and Linguistic Theory* 23. 335–380.
Kuntay, Aylin C. & Dan I. Slobin. 1995. Putting interaction back into child language: Examples from Turkish. *Psychology of Language and Communication* 6. 5–14.
Levinson, Stephen C. 1996. Relativity in spatial conception and description. In Gumperz & Levinson (eds.), 177–202.
Levinson, Stephen C. 1997. Language and cognition: The cognitive consequences of spatial description in *Guugu Yimithirr*. *Journal of Linguistic Anthropology* 7(1). 99–131.
Levinson, Stephen C. 2003. *Space in language and cognition: Explorations in cognitive diversity*. Cambridge: CUP.
Levinson, Stephen C., Sotaro Kita, Daniel B. M. Haun & Björn H. Rasch. 2002. Returning the tables: Language affects spatial reasoning. *Cognition* 84. 155–188.
Li, Ping & Yasuhiro Shirai. 2000. *The acquisition of lexical and grammatical aspect*. Berlin: Mouton de Gruyter.
Luksaneeyanawin, Sudaporn. 1993. Speech computing and speech technology in Thailand. *Symposium on Natural Language Processing in Thailand*. Chulalongkorn University, 17–21 March 1993, 276–321.
MacWhinney, Brian. 2000. *The CHILDES project: 3rd edn. Vol. 2: Tools for analyzing talk, The Database*. Mahwah, NJ: Lawrence Erlbaum.
Masjid, Asifa, Melissa Bowerman, Sotaro Kita, Daniel B. M. Haun & Stephen C. Levinson. 2004. Can language restructure cognition? The case for space. *Trends in Cognitive Sciences* 8(3). 108–115.

Mayer, Mercer. 1967. *Frog, where are you?* New York, NY: Dial Press.
Meepoe, T. Amy. 1998. The interaction between lexical aspect and progressive imperfective in Thai: A discourse analysis of *kamlaŋ* and *yùu*. *Journal of Language and Linguistics* 16(2). 56–66.
Pederson, Eric, Eve Danziger, Stephen Levinson, Sotaro Kita, Gunter Senft & David Wilkins. 1998. Semantic typology and spatial conceptualization. *Language* 74. 557–589.
Schmidt, Todd P. 1992. A non-linear analysis of aspect in Thai narrative discourse. In Karen L. Adams & Thomas J. Hudak (eds.), *Annual Meeting of the South-East Asian Linguistics Society* 2, 327–342. Tempe, AZ: Arizona State University.
Slobin, Dan I. 1973. Cognitive prerequisites for the development of grammar. In Charles A. Ferguson & Dan I. Slobin (eds.), *Studies of child language development*. 175–208. New York, NY: Holt, Rinehart and Winston.
Slobin, Dan I. 1985. Crosslinguistic evidence for the Language-Making Capacity. In Dan I. Slobin (ed.), *The crosslinguistic study of language acquisition, Vol. II: The data*, 157–256. Hillsdale, NJ: Lawrence Erlbaum.
Slobin, Dan I. 1996. From "thought and language" to "thinking for speaking". In Gumperz & Levinson (eds.), 70–96.
Slobin, Dan I. 2003. Language and thought online: Cognitive consequences of linguistic relativity. In Gentner & Goldin-Meadow (eds.), 157–191.
Slobin, Dan I. 2004. The many ways to search for a frog: Linguistic typology and the expression of motion events. In Strömqvist & Verhoeven (eds.), 219–257.
Smith, Carlotta S. & Mary Erbaugh. 2005. Temporal interpretation in Mandarin Chinese. *Linguistics* 43(4). 713–756.
Strömqvist, Sven & Ludo Verhoeven. 2004. Typological and contextual perspectives on narrative development. In Strömqvist & Verhoeven (eds.), 3–14.
Strömqvist, Sven & Ludo Verhoeven (eds.). 2004. *Relating events in narrative: Typological and contextual perspectives*. Mahwah, NJ: Lawrence Erlbaum.
Thepkanjana, Kingkarn. 1986. Serial verb constructions in Thai. University of Michigan PhD dissertation.
Weist, Richard M., Aleksandra Kaczmarek & Jolanta Wysocka. 1993. The function of aspectual configurations in the conversational and narrative discourse of Finnish, Polish and American children. *Papers and Studies in Contrastive Linguistics* XXVII. 79–106.
Whorf, Benjamin L. 1956. *Language, thought, and reality: Selected writings of Benjamin Lee Whorf*, Edited by John B. Caroll. Cambridge, MA: The MIT Press.
Zlatev, Jordan & Peerapat Yangklang. 2003. Frog stories in Thai: Transcription and analysis of 50 Thai narratives from 5 age groups. Ms.

CHAPTER 9

What figurative language development reveals about the mind

Herbert L. Colston

The study addresses what language reveals about cognition under an umbrella of figurative language and Theory of Mind (ToM) development. A brief review is provided of original work that led to the claim that figurative language is developed late. This is followed by a short overview of more recent findings that support an early development view. Next a recent study on the development of naturalistic hyperbole production is reviewed that also supports an at least rudimentary claim that figurative language cognition is in place early. A conclusion then explicates why, notwithstanding supporting empirical evidence, the early development of ToM, and accordingly figurative language cognition, should be an a priori assumption of a "Language as Sensation/Perception of Others' Minds (LASPOM)" view.

1   Introduction

A major motivation in the concomitant study of language and cognition is the desire to unearth operations, states and processes of the human mind based upon an analysis of the language used by a given speaker who owns that mind. To that end, a primary focus ought to be on how changes in the purported cognitive functioning of individuals are apparent in the language used by those individuals. If indeed one can infer something about cognition from something about language, then any changes going on in cognition should be paralleled by relevant changes in language. Developmental change in children thus provides an appealing platform upon which to conduct a study of language and cognition.

One area that should thus afford a unique insight into language and cognition is that of figurative language development. According to a substantial amount of empirical data, figurative language comprehension, and by some accounts production as well, seems to develop late relative to other linguistic accomplishments. Some explanations of this phenomenon have also pointed to a cognitive function,

Theory of Mind (ToM) thought, at least in part, to underlie figurative language comprehension that also seems to develop relatively late. There is thus already a claimed link between language and cognitive functioning in this area, in terms of the concurrent development of those linguistic and cognitive components.

What I hope to accomplish in the following study is, at end, a demonstration that remains supportive of the contention that cognition can be understood via analysis of language, both generally as well as in this specific realm of figurative language comprehension and cognitive development. However, I make this demonstration by in fact debunking the idea that figurative language is a late-developing phenomenon. Indeed, I end up arguing that figurative language cognition as well as the proposed underlying cognitive function ToM are in fact both early developing, and arguably, reasonably ever-present phenomena.

What follows is first a brief review of the original work that led to the claim that figurative language is developed late. This is followed by a short overview of some more recent findings that seem to support the early development view. Next I point to a recent study that also provides support for the claim that at least rudimentary figurative language cognition is in place early. I conclude with an explication of why, notwithstanding the supporting evidence, the early development of figurative language should be an a priori assumption if one holds the view that language functioning reveals cognitive functioning – especially given the particular cognitive functioning/language functioning link proposed for the development of figurative language.

2   The late development view

The dominant view of figurative language development is that children do not show full adult competency at comprehending or using metaphorical or ironic language until roughly age 7 or 8 years unless the testing procedure is very undemanding or if the metaphorical topic is very familiar to the child (Winner 1988, 1995). Indeed, development continues even after that age, in some instances in a linear fashion for a large number of years (e.g. idiom use and comprehension), (Ackerman 1982; Brasseur & Jimenez 1989; Douglas & Peel 1979; Gibbs 1987; Levorato & Cacciari 1992; Nippold & Taylor 1995, 1996).

A variety of phenomena might be involved in this relatively late-developing figurative language ability. In addition to the already mentioned full arrival of ToM, there is also the ability to entertain false beliefs (Olson & Astington 1987; Flavell, Flavell & Green 1983; Taylor & Flavell 1984; Wimmer & Perner 1983; Winner 1988), the ability to conduct complex metarepresentational thought (Colston & Gibbs 2002), the full development of complicated conceptual metaphorical structures, the full ability to process cross-domain conceptual mappings (Winner 1988), and others. All of these may be considered potential explanations for a relatively late-developing figurative language cognition in children.

A different approach, however, maintains that although there may not be full adult competency with figurative language in middle childhood, there is something very close to it, with perhaps just one or a few additional components missing (Winner 1988). This account I'll refer to as the early development view.

3 The early development view – recent work

Alternative arguments might be presented that the claim that children significantly younger than age 7 actually may demonstrate something akin to adult competency at producing and comprehending some aspects of figurative language, but either, 1) the methods used for studying this ability in middle childhood shroud those capacities (Colston 2005; Colston & Kuiper 2002), or, 2) the capabilities, although perhaps approaching full adult levels, are just incomplete in some limited ways.

To briefly consider the methodological limitations first, akin to research in other areas of human cognitive development, the age at which children are believed to begin comprehension or production of figurative language may appear artificially high due to the methodologies employed to study that capacity (Vosniadou & Ortony 1986). Only through the use of increasingly complex and clever techniques (dishabituation paradigms; Baillargeon 1993), have researchers determined that children can exhibit some cognitive functions much earlier than was once believed possible. The same may be needed for figurative language cognition.

As to the proximity to adult capacity, consider Winner's (1988) argument that metaphor comprehension is present in pre-school aged children, at least with respect to the ability to perceive similarities. What seems to be missing in early childhood, that develops later and releases more adult-like comprehension performance, is sensitivity to topic-vehicle structure (e.g. understanding that it is the slowness of turtles that maps onto a person's behavior when comprehending the metaphor, *Grampa is a turtle*).

Or, consider Gibbs' (1994: 433) general synopsis of the early development view:

> The evidence from developmental psychology does not support the traditional idea that the ability to use and understand figurative language develops late. Instead, young children possess significant ability to think in figurative terms as long as they possess the domain-specific knowledge needed to solve problems and understand linguistic expressions. Development of figurative language understanding may have more to do with the acquisition of various metacognitive and metalinguistic skills than with development of the ability to think figuratively per se.

So it remains unclear exactly what the status is regarding the development of figurative language capabilities in middle childhood. In part as a means of addressing this discrepancy, some recent work was conducted on the development of a relatively simple form of figurative language, hyperbole.

4 The development of hyperbole

As mentioned, it appears from some sources of evidence that many forms of figurative language show distinct developmental changes in terms of their comprehension. There are a number of issues however, that might be raised about this developmental progression; a) relatively little work has focused upon the wide variety of figurative forms (most work has been conducted on metaphor and verbal irony), b) the development of production has not been as frequently addressed, and c) little work has made use of authentic productions. The following study was conducted to address these issues.

In the first portion of the study, authentic productions of a lesser-studied figurative form, hyperbole, by adult and child speakers, were collected for comparison. Hyperbole, for purposes here is defined as a speaker over- or under-stating the magnitude of something (e.g. "we've been waiting a million years!"), may be considered a form of figurative, or at least non-literal, language given that a speaker does not intend for the veridical meaning to be taken by an addressee, but rather intends to express a more figurative interpretation (e.g. "we've been waiting a very, very long time!").

4.1 Study 1: Hyperbole production by adults

This study sought to evaluate the hyperbolic language used by adult speakers in naturalistic settings, to enable later comparison of similar language use by children. Two paradigms were utilized in this evaluation. One had participants textually record instances of hyperbolic language that they overheard, that they received as addressees, or that they witnessed or otherwise encountered in other real speakers (meaning that fictional speakers, e.g. literary or television characters, were not allowed), as the utterances occurred, over a period of time. The second paradigm had participants textually record hyperbolic language, as soon as possible after it occurred, that the participants themselves used over a period of time.

4.1.1 *Participants*
Forty-five undergraduate students at a midwestern American university took part in this study as part of Psychology course requirements. Of these, 15 participants

were in the "self" condition (recording their own uses of hyperbole), and 30 were in "other" condition (recording others' uses of hyperbole). Participants served in only one of the conditions. Demographics of the participants per se were not recorded, but instead demographics of the speakers were taken (which *were* the participants in instances where they were recording themselves). The mean age of the speakers was 22.99 years (SD = 7.81), the range was 14–59 years. Utterances from male speakers constituted 51% of the data.

4.1.2   Materials

A half-page questionnaire was prepared to enable recording of the utterances. The questionnaire provided space to write down one full verbatim hyperbolic utterance and a brief description of the situation in which the utterance was used. Questionnaires also presented a number of questions and scales about the utterance, the situation, the speaker, the addressee(s), etc. Variables recorded with the questionnaire included, 1) whether or not the speaker's expectations were being violated during the context in which the hyperbolic utterance was used (affirmative, negative or, "don't know"), 2) a rating of the degree of surprise expressed by the speaker (scale ranging from, "very unsurprised" [coded as 1], through "very surprised" [coded as 7]), 3) the gender of the speaker, 4) the age of the speaker, 5) whether the speaker was the participant or some other person, and 6) whether the addressee(s) was an individual or a group.

Booklets containing 14 of these questionnaires were prepared (assuming a minimum of one recorded utterance per day for the 2 week duration of the study). Instructions on the cover provided detailed instructions on how to complete each item in the questionnaire, along with a description and examples of hyperbole (the term "exaggeration" was provided to participants for simplicity). Included in the instructions was an emphasis that utterances were to be recorded verbatim, with no altering of the grammar, vocabulary, punctuation, etc.

4.1.3   Procedure

The participants in the study met with the experimenter at a prescribed time and location, individually or in small groups. The experimenter read the instructions aloud to the participants and answered any questions. Participants were then told to bring the completed or worked-on booklets back to the experimenter after a two week duration. Upon returning the booklets, participants were debriefed.

4.1.4   Screening

The resulting data were initially screened and adjusted to eliminate errors and ambiguities. The first step to this process was elimination of utterances that did not fit the operational definition of hyperbole – a speaker overstating or understating the magnitude of something. Of the original total of 436 recorded utterances, 20 (5%) were not instances of hyperbole according to this operational definition. Additionally, 17 (4%) hyperbole utterances were from child speakers (under age 11 years). The non-hyperbolic utterances were removed from subsequent analyses. The hyperbolic utterances from child speakers were used in Study 2 (see Section 4.2).

Next, the demographic data were adjusted to enable descriptive and inferential statistical analysis. Fourteen (4%) speakers' ages were somehow ambiguous (e.g. giving an age range, putting a question mark next to a number, indicating the decade instead of exact year [40s], etc.). These instances were adjusted according to common and/or reasonable procedures (e.g. using the midpoint of an age range, adopting the number next to a question mark, using the midpoint of the indicated decade, etc.). Two (< 1%) additional speakers' ages were left blank. The mean of the other speakers was entered for these two cases. Four (1%) speakers did not have gender indicated. Using age and gender from other speakers recorded by that participant enabled 3 of these to be inferred (2 male and 1 female), the remaining speaker was assigned female to keep this variable balanced. Four (1%) speakers did not have the addressee variable (individual or group) indicated. These were randomly assigned values (2 given "individual", 2 given "group"). Two (< 1%) speakers did not indicate whether an expectation was violated or not in the uttering of the hyperbolic utterance. The option "don't know" was assigned to these instances. Nine (2%) utterances were not given surprise ratings. The mean for the remaining utterances was entered for these cases. Finally, 1 (< 1%) utterance did not have the speaker variable (self versus other) indicated. This was inferred to be "other" according to other utterances and their demographics supplied by that participant.

Finally, recorded utterances that contained multiple instances of hyperbole were separated to enable precise coding. Of the now 399 utterances (after removing children speakers and non-hyperboles), 355 (89%) were single hyperboles, 40 (10%) were double hyperboles (e.g. "You're a baby. There's no snow out there" – spoken after a small snowfall), and 4 (1%) were triple hyperboles ("I bet we're going to be waiting in her driveway for like 5 hours. She's always late. I don't think she's ever been on time"). The separation produced a working total of 447 hyperbolic utterances.

4.1.5 *Coding*

The data were then coded according to 11 additional variables. This coding was conducted by two researchers independently, using precise operational definitions developed ahead of time by the researchers, as well as by a set of 8 norming participants who did not take part in the study.

For the 10 (deemed most difficult) coding tasks completed by the researchers, intercoder reliability was never less than 97%. Cases of disagreement were discussed, and consensus was reached for all such instances. These variables constituted; 1) was an extreme case formulation used in the hyperbole? 2) was a specific quantity used in the hyperbole? 3) was a numeral used in the hyperbole? 4) was an explicit comparison used in the hyperbole and if so, what type? 5) was the hyperbole an inverted form? 6) was a rhetorical question used with the hyperbole? 7) was the target content positive in nature, including cases that were ambiguous? 8) was the target content positive in nature including only cases that were unambiguous? 9) was the referent topic the speaker or something else? and 10) a measure of the complexity of the hyperbole. A relatively simple additional variable, 11) whether the hyperbole involved a deflation or an inflation of the actual target quantity in the given situation, was coded by the norming subjects.

4.1.6 *Norming*

The remaining analysis variable was coded by 8 norming participants who did not participate in the main study. These participants were provided with the verbatim hyperbolic utterances, screened and separated as described above, with a blank space next to each utterance, in a booklet with instructions on the cover. The instructions asked participants to read and then indicate next to each utterance whether the hyperbole was an inflation or a deflation of the target quantity. Participants were asked to mark the blank spaces with an "M" (more) for inflation, or an "L" (less) for a deflation. Universal agreement was obtained on the majority of the utterances (84%). In cases where there was not universal agreement among the 8 norming participants, the majority view was adopted for that utterance.

4.1.7 *Analysis*

First a brief note on the calculations of means. Statistical analyses that were targeted at characteristics of individual instances of hyperbole (e.g. whether or not an extreme case formulation was used in the hyperbole) were conducted on the set of 447 separated hyperbolic utterances. Analyses that were targeted at characteristics of the speaker or contextual situations (e.g. gender of speaker, polarity of content, etc.) were conducted on the set of 399 utterances from before the separation, to forestall double counting of some variable levels. Percentages presented are calculated accordingly.

The descriptive results of the adult data for affirmative/negative variables were as follows. The incidence of extreme case formulations being used to make hyperbolic utterances was evenly split. Half of the hyperboles used extreme case formulations (51%). Specific quantities were used in less than a quarter of the utterances (23%). These specific quantities were most often stated in the form of textual or digital numerals (19% of all utterances). Inverted hyperboles were almost nonexistent (1%). Rhetorical questions were rarely used (6%). In general, the content of hyperbolic commentary was negative in polarity. Potentially positive content was 9% of the total, unambiguously positive content was 6%. Expectations also were reported to have been violated around a third of the time (34%). Expectations were reported to not have been violated roughly an equivalent amount of the time (37%). For the remaining utterances (29%) participants did not know the status of expectation violation.

The results of the target exaggeration, addressee configuration and referent content analysis revealed that the target exaggeration direction was predominantly inflation (80%). The addressee(s) of the hyperbolic utterance were individuals approximately two thirds of the time (68%), the remaining addressees being groups. The content of the comments was predominantly a topic other than the speaker (61%).

The comparison type and complexity level results showed that few utterances involved comparisons (9% total). Of these, the most frequent type was "like/as" comparisons (5%) followed in equal frequency by direct and greater/less-than comparisons (2% each). The complexity analysis revealed a fairly uneven spread. Slightly over a third of the utterances were at the least-complex level by our coding. A quarter of the utterances were at the second-most-complex level. The remaining utterances were fairly evenly divided between the other levels. Beginning with the least complex and moving toward the most complex levels of hyperbole, the frequencies at each level were: 37%, 10%, 15%, 24%, and 14%.

4.1.8   *Conclusions on adult data*

A few brief conclusions might be warranted from these results. First, adults typically use hyperbole as a means of complaining – most content of adult hyperbolic talk is negative, ranging from 91% to 94% whether one distinguishes possibly positive content or definitely positive content, respectively.

Second, a degree of cynicism might be present in situations where hyperbole is used – despite the near universal use of hyperbole to point out negative things, only about a third of the time are the speakers reported to have found those negative things unexpected (34%). At least a third of the time the situations are reported to explicitly *not* have violated expectations (37%).

Third, the form hyperbole takes is typically rather simple – speakers more often use extreme case formulations (51%), or a specific quantity term (23%), the latter being primarily numerals (19%), instead of more intricate forms such as comparisons (9%), rhetorical questions (6%), or inversions (1%). Such simplicity is also apparent in the level of complexity observed in hyperbole – more than half the time (62%) hyperbolic commentary specifically states some magnitude that is reasonably impossible in one way or another, in the real world. Only 14% of the time is the stated magnitude at a possible and probable level.

Fourth, who is spoken to, and what is being spoken about, are predominantly individuals (68%) and something other than the speaker (61%), respectively. Whether these tendencies are characteristic of hyperbole or the same for other discourse, however, is unclear.

Lastly, most hyperbolic commentary involves an inflation of magnitudes that have turned out greater than the expected (80%) rather than a deflation of magnitudes that have turned out less than expected. This might be predicted both by the mere nature of magnitudes as well as the common ordinary experience of adults. There is less constraint for things to turn out more than expected (toward infinity) than there is for things to turn out less than expected (toward zero) (Colston & Keller 1998), and, despite the clear restrictions present in all people's behavior, most adults likely perceive themselves as being relatively free in their actions, or have at least become accustomed enough to the restrictions they're under, to not unduly attend to them. The same might not be said for children.

4.2 Study 2: Hyperbole production by children

The second study sought to evaluate the hyperbolic language used by child speakers in natural settings. One paradigm was utilized in this evaluation. Caregiver participants textually recorded instances of hyperbolic language that they overheard, received as addressees, witnessed or otherwise encountered in child speakers, as they occurred, over a period of time. As in the first experiment, fictional speakers, e.g. literary or television characters, were not allowed.

4.2.1 *Participants*

Twenty undergraduate students at a midwestern American university took part in this study as part of Psychology course requirements. Demographics of the participants were not recorded, with demographics of the speakers instead being taken. The mean age of the speakers was 7.39 years (SD = 2.55), the range was 2.5–10 years. Utterances from male speakers constituted 50% of the data.

4.2.2 *Materials*

The same questionnaire used in Experiment 1 was used in the present experiment. Booklets and instructions were also the same except the instructions directed participants to record hyperbolic utterances spoken only by children aged 10 years or less. As in the first experiment, the instructions emphasized that utterances were to be recorded verbatim, with no altering of the grammar, vocabulary, punctuation, etc.

4.2.3   Procedure
The procedure was the same as in Study 1.

4.2.4   Screening
The resulting data were screened and adjusted in the same manner as in Study 1. None of the original 112 recorded utterances were removed for not fitting the operational definition of hyperbole – a speaker overstating or understating the magnitude of something, nor were there any utterances from adult speakers (over age 10 years).

Next, the demographic data were adjusted to enable descriptive and inferential statistical analysis. One (< 1%) speaker did not have the addressee variable (individual or group) indicated. This datapoint was randomly assigned the value, "individual". All the other demographic variables were indicated according to instructions.

Finally, recorded utterances that contained multiple instances of hyperbole were separated to enable precise coding. Of the original 112 utterances, 94 (84%) were single hyperboles, 15 (13%) were double hyperboles, and 3 (3%) were triple hyperboles (see Study 1 for examples). The separation produced a working total of 133 hyperbolic utterances.

4.2.5   Coding and norming
The data were coded according to the same 11 variables used in Study 1. This coding was also conducted by two researchers independently for all of the variables except inflation/deflation, which was coded by the 8 norming participants who worked on the adult data. The same operational definitions from Study 1 were used.

For the coding tasks completed by the researchers, intercoder reliability was never less than 98%. Cases of disagreement were discussed, and consensus was reached for all such instances.

Universal agreement was obtained by the norming participants on nearly all of the utterances (90%). In cases where there was not universal agreement among the 8 norming participants, the majority view was adopted for that utterance.

4.2.6   Analysis
As in Study 1, statistical analyses were conducted on either the set of 133 separated hyperbolic utterances or the set of 112 utterances from before the separation as appropriate. Percentages presented are calculated accordingly.

The descriptive results of the child data for affirmative/negative variables were as follows. The incidence of extreme case formulations being used to make hyperbolic utterances was unevenly split. Nearly two thirds of the hyperboles used extreme case formulations (62%). Specific quantities were used in less than a quarter of the utterances (23%). These specific quantities were most often stated in the form of textual or digital numerals (18% of all utterances). Inverted hyperboles were almost nonexistent (1%). Rhetorical questions were rarely used (8%). In general, the content of hyperbolic commentary was negative in polarity. Potentially positive content was 4% of the total, unambiguously positive content was 2%. Expectations also were reported to have been violated around a third of the time (35%). Expectations were reported to not have been violated nearly half of the time (44%). For the remaining utterances (21%) participants did not know the status of expectation violation.

The results of the target exaggeration, addressee configuration and referent content analysis revealed that the target exaggeration direction was predominantly inflation (66%). The addressee(s) of the hyperbolic utterance were individuals three quarters of the time (75%), the remaining addressees being groups. The content of the comments was predominantly a topic other than the speaker (69%).

The comparison type and complexity level results demonstrated that few utterances involved comparisons (2% total). These were evenly split between "like/as" comparisons and direct comparisons (1% each). The complexity analysis revealed a fairly uneven spread. Slightly over half of the utterances were at the least-complex level by our coding. A small portion of the utterances were at the most-complex level. The remaining utterances were fairly evenly divided between the other levels. Beginning with the least complex and moving toward the most complex levels of hyperbole, the frequencies at each level were: 57%, 14%, 11%, 11%, and 7%.

4.3 Comparison of adult and child hyperbole

Next, the adult and child hyperbole production data were statistically compared. The results were fairly straightforward and are as follows. No differences were obtained between the hyperbolic utterances used by adults versus children across each of the following variables, 1) frequency of specific quantity terms, 2) frequency of numerals, 3) frequency and type of comparison statements, 4) frequency of inverted hyperbole, 5) frequency of rhetorical questions, 6) frequency of definitely positive content, 7) expectation violation, 8) speaker surprise ratings, 9) referent content, 10) the configuration of addressees, and 11) distribution of single, double and triple hyperboles.

Statistically significant differences were found on 1) the relative frequency of inflation versus deflation in the hyperbole, 2) a complexity measure, 3) frequency of extreme case formulations, and 4) frequency of possibly positive content. For inflation/deflation, X^2 (1, N = 580) = 11.61, p <.001. For the complexity measure, X^2 (1, N = 580) = 26.10, p <.001. For the frequency of extreme case formulations, X^2 (1, N = 580) = 4.87, p <.05. Finally, for the frequency of possibly positive content, X^2 (1, N = 511) = 3.93, p <.05.

Several conclusions are warranted from these comparison results. First, despite a few differences, adult's and children's production of hyperbole is remarkably similar. The topics are similar, the forms are similar, the details are similar, the rarities are similar, the omissions are similar, etc.

Second, where differences are found, with one exception, they probably have nothing to do with linguistic or cognitive differences between adults and children per se, but rather concern the greater experience involved in adults simply having talked longer and in a greater variety of contexts than children (e.g. the differences between adults and children in terms of hyperbole complexity and the frequency of extreme case formulations – these two measures are also related, greater use of extreme case formulations is the main reason for why the children's hyperboles are less complex).

The third conclusion is the exception just mentioned. Adults and children do differ on degree of magnitude deflation and frequency of possibly positive content, which could very likely reflect an essential, if not cognitive, then at least experiential difference. A common, ordinary aspect of a child's everyday experience in the world is one of restraint. Children are being socialized, they're learning boundaries on acceptable behavior, their emotional, physical & verbal responses and behaviors are being trained, etc. Moreover, children are predominantly energetic, emotional, active, curious, etc., people, and these tendencies are going to run counter to the above mentioned socialization and training. Thus, children often experience a restraint on their behavior, from caregivers, other adults, other children, communicated and known rules, etc., and an ordinary response to such restraint is frustration.

Children are thus probably more likely than adults to exhibit frustration due to constraint. Not to say that adults don't experience frustration. But at least they no longer experience frustration on the myriad of ordinary, even trivial, everyday experiences that children regularly encounter (e.g. how fast to walk, how far to walk ahead of companions, how loudly to talk, etc.), because the acceptable levels of such behaviors are more automatized in adults.

So, one difference in the use of hyperbole, the frequency of using it for deflation of magnitudes, is likely due to this experiential difference. Both adults and children use hyperbole to complain, but for children the complaint is more often directed at being constrained (e.g. "I never get to ..."), something they find to be a particularly negative experience.

4.4 Comparison of younger and older child hyperbole

Finally, the younger and older child hyperbole production data were statistically compared. The results were also straightforward. No differences were obtained between the hyperbolic utterances used by younger (defined as younger than 7 yrs [N = 47 utterances]) versus older children (defined as older than 6 yrs [N = 86 utterances]) across each of the following variables 1) frequency of extreme case formulations, 2) frequency of specific quantity terms, 3) frequency of numerals, 4) frequency and type of comparison statements, 5) the relative frequency of inflation versus deflation in the hyperbole, 6) frequency of inverted hyperbole, 7) frequency of possibly positive content, 8) expectation violation, 9) speaker surprise ratings, 10) the complexity measure and 11) distribution of single, double and triple hyperboles.

Statistically significant differences were found on 1) the frequency of rhetorical questions, 2) the frequency of definitely positive content, 3) referent content and 4) the configuration of addressees. For rhetorical questions, X^2 (1, N = 133) = 14.14, p <.001. For definitely positive content, X^2 (1, N = 133) = 5.62, p <.05. For the referent content, X^2 (1, N = 133) = 14.35, p <.001. Finally, for the configuration of addressees, X^2 (1, N = 133) = 18.24, p <.001.

Several conclusions are warranted from these comparison results. The foremost of these is that there is very little difference in the hyperbole used by younger versus older children. The great majority of our measures showed no differences in the topic, form, detail, rarity, omission, etc., of hyperbolic utterances.

Moreover, where slight differences are found they are either likely not of general relevance to cognitive development or their ramifications for development are ambiguous. For the frequency of definitely positive content, referent content and addressee configuration, for example, the differences observed are most likely due to simple experiential factors. Younger children talk more about themselves (47%) versus their environment relative to older children (16%), and younger children address individuals (96%) versus groups more often than do older children (62%). But these differences likely reflect just the greater experience in older children at talking about broad topics and to groups of addressees. The definitely positive content, found to be greater in younger children's hyperbole (6%) versus older children's (0%), could also reflect the slightly higher naiveté in the younger group in that they may express slightly more excitement about positive things. But, given the overwhelmingly negative content in both groups' hyperbole (94% and 100% in younger and older children, respectively), there is still a preponderance of hyperbole being used to complain about a constraint, as argued earlier. The last difference observed – a greater presence of rhetorical questions in younger children's hyperbole (19% vs. 1%), is ambiguous. On one hand, it might actually reflect a greater complexity in the younger children's hyperbole, to the extent that a rhetorical question is considered a pragmatic inference-generation tool. It could also, however, reveal just a lesser ability in the younger children at selecting relevant question topics. Our operational definition for rhetorical questions, "when a standard question-response adjacency pair organization is violated, such that a question is in fact, not seeking an answer or is seeking some response or inference in addition to the answer" does not allow determination of this question. We found no genuine inquiries in any of the children's utterances, or the adults for that matter (e.g. are you going to let that phone ring forever?, why is everything so expensive?). As such, all inquiry forms were counted as rhetorical.

We thus lastly take these findings as evidence that our children's data constitute a representative sample of hyperbolic language from a uniform group, rather than showing a change at the supposed onset of figurative language use/comprehension.

4.5 Study 3: Replication check

To corroborate these findings, a third study was conducted using a sample of the authentic items from the studies reported above. Representative samples of utterances were selected from the pool of adult and child hyperbolic utterances. The chosen utterances were very carefully selected to preserve the same distribution of descriptive statistics found in the pools as wholes. The sample utterances were then randomly combined and prepared into booklets with accompanying rating scales for presentation to adult participants for consideration.

In four rating tasks, adult participants rated a) the age of the speaker, b) the degree of complaint interpreted from the utterance, c) the amount of constraint likely being experienced by the speakers of the utterances, and d) the sophistication of the utterances.

Although a significant difference was found in the rated age, the results were very interesting. The average age ascribed to the adult speakers was 25 years, and that given for the child speakers was 20. So even though children were rated as being younger than the adults, they were still thought to be adults. Note also that the actual mean ages of the sampled speakers were 23 and 7 years respectively (as was also the case for the full set of speakers from which these samples were drawn). Moreover, the fact that the adults were rated as being older than the children is very likely due to several adult speakers being judged to be more senior citizens. Content of those utterances (e.g. retirement), was considered to reveal a relatively older speaker, thus drawing up the mean age of the adult group. So the found rated-age difference is very likely not attributable to a systematic difference in the general kind of hyperbole being used by adult and child speakers.

Statistically significant differences were also found in the complaint and constraint measures with child hyperboles being rated higher on both measures. No significant difference was found in the rated sophistication of the two samples of hyperboles.

These findings are taken as confirmatory evidence that adult and child productions of hyperbole are generally indistinguishable in terms of most aspects of their structure. It is also believed, however, that these utterances nonetheless reflect a distinct experiential difference between adults and children – that of complaining about being constrained.

4.6 Late versus early figurative cognition development: Consideration of hyperbole

We can now discuss the ramifications of the present findings for the early development and late development views of figurative language cognition. First, to be fair to the late development view, one must recognize that hyperbole is a relatively simple form of figurative language. It doesn't switch to different conceptual domains like metaphor, idioms, or proverbs (Gibbs 1987; Gibbs, Johnson & Colston 1996). It doesn't involve counterfactuality as in verbal irony. It doesn't have the wide variety of subtypes such as metonymy, which is itself a whole host of kinds of figure. Understatement can also be fairly simple, but understatement is borderline ironic (considered in some accounts as one of the subtypes of irony) and it produces many of the pragmatic effects of irony (Colston & O'Brien 2000a). Understatement can also be extremely subtle. But hyperbole is arguably simpler than all of these other figures because it typically involves a fairly straightforward, frequently nonsubtle, inflation of a discrepancy between expectations, desires or preferences, and reality (Colston & Keller 1998). The development of hyperbole production might then be able to begin earlier, or proceed more rapidly, than the development of some of these other figures, given this relative simplicity.

Hyperbole also provides a very close match with the common childhood characteristic of imaginativeness, without going quite as far as say, metaphor, which involves conceptualizing one thing in terms of something typically quite different. For instance, a hyperbolic comment typically states something as being bigger, greater, or more than it is (e.g. I don't want to ride with Grampa, he takes *forever*), but it stays within the referent domain (time). Metaphor, on the other hand, typically changes domains (e.g. I don't want to ride with Grampa, he's a *turtle*). Hyperbole might then develop sooner than other figures because of this ready alignment with imaginativeness – it's easier to imagine something as bigger than it is, for instance, than to imagine something being completely different from what it is.

The late development view might even accord with the current results if one doesn't agree with the simplicity or imaginativeness-match explanations. If one considers the rather poignant fit between the primary pragmatic function of hyperbole and one of the quintessential childhood experiences, this alone might account for the relatively early development of hyperbole. As discussed previously, a common childhood experience is that of constraint. Children commonly encounter discrepancies between expectations/desires/preferences and reality, with reality typically being somehow less than wanted. Such constraint also usually results in frustration. Hyperbole's central pragmatic function is to point out just these kinds of discrepancies, most frequently for the purpose of drawing attention to them. So it may be that hyperbole develops early because what it does and how it does it – make others notice a discrepancy by inflating it – provides an exceptional fit with what kids often wish to do – complain about a constraint.

On the other hand, the present findings clearly demonstrate a very similar to adult-like production of a figurative form, at and before the point at which the comprehension of other figurative forms appear. This might seem at odds with the late development view. Consider first the relationship between comprehension and production. Typically, at least in early childhood, comprehension outpaces production. One would then expect that if this pattern holds for figurative language, then production should appear at or after comprehension. Yet, the current results are showing production of a figurative form at or prior to comprehension of other figurative forms.

One possible explanation is again the comparative simplicity, link with imagination, and pragmatic-function-fit set of explanations. But another could be that, very simply, there is relatively little known about the production of many forms of figurative language. Again, most studies have addressed comprehension. So one important lesson from the present work is that we need more studies on the onset and progression of production of varieties of figurative language. Although there have been some studies on idiom (Levorato & Cacciari 1995), metaphor (Levorato & Cacciari 2002; Polanski 1989; see also Winner 1988 for a review), and simile production development (Broderick 1991), few involve *naturalistic* production development, nor do they address the wide array of figures. My suspicion is that the naturalistic production of forms of figurative language might happen much earlier than is generally believed, and thus be consistent with the present findings.

Another solution would be to abandon the notion that all language is either literal or figurative and instead adopt the view that language is instead best described as varying along a wide variety of veridicality dimensions (Colston & O'Brien 2000a, 2000b; Colston 2005; Gibbs 1994). Such a view acknowledges that all language is indirect to a degree if only because of its underdeterminedness. But some language may provide even greater nonveridicality by using the figurative mechanisms briefly discussed above for irony, metaphor, etc., as well as a variety of mechanisms not discussed here. On this view, hyperbole might be nearer the veridical end of the continuum than some other figures, and its early production would thus make sense accordingly.

Or, one might stand pat with the more extreme version of the early development view and argue that the current findings instead demonstrate that children are fully capable of using, and by extension comprehending, figurative language at near adult capacities, much earlier than is generally now thought. If so, one must then explain the discrepancy between the current findings with hyperbole, and other studies that have supported the late development view. There are a variety of arenas in which to conduct such a comparison, for brevity here we will consider only one of the more major theoretical underpinnings used to explain the late development view, ToM.

5. Why figurative language cognition should develop early: Theory of Mind

A major contender explanation proposed for the late-development of figurative language comprehension is that of the concurrently relatively late-developing, or at least so-thought, ToM. The general argument here is that without full-blown ToM, children cannot understand that a speaker can have something in mind other than what he or she says. Children are thus more or less trapped in being able to see only the so-called "literal meaning" of an utterance, and are then either confused about what a figurative speaker intends or takes them to be lying, rather than gleaning the fully intended meaning.

In the following section, exception will be taken to this view. An argument will be offered that, beyond the demonstration in the preceding sections that figurative language comprehension and production can develop much earlier than ToM, ToM still wouldn't work as a late figurative development account because first, some recent work suggests that ToM development actually occurs much earlier than has been generally suggested. Moreover, late-developing ToM cannot explain late-developing figurative language because successful normal language functioning of *any* kind it will be argued in fact *requires* something like a ToM.

5.1 Theory of Mind development research

Consider first a representative study that demonstrated a ToM influence in the language comprehension of 18 month olds. Repacholi and Gopnik (1997) first tested 14 and 18 month old toddlers for their preference between two food types. They then watched an adult taste the same two types of food and show a clear preference for one (and distaste for the other). The adult would then ask the child to give them "some", and hold their hand equidistant from the choices. Fourteen month old children would give the adult the food the children themselves preferred, irrespective of the adult's preference. But the older toddlers would hand over the adult's preferred food type, independent of their own preference. This study is thus showing the beginning operation of non-egocentric thinking right around the onset early stage 1 language functioning.

There is also much other work showing the operation at age 2 years of such an implicit ToM on the standard kinds of false-belief tasks that typically don't show ToM to be operational, at least when measured explicitly, until 4 years of age (Clements & Perner 1994). Other work on deception has also shown the presence of ToM at the beginning stages of language functioning (Chandler, Fritz & Hala 1989; Hala, Chandler & Fritz 1991; Hala & Chandler 1996; Sullivan & Winner 1993; Carlson, Moses & Hix 1998).

5.2 On the necessity of Theory of Mind for language

Notwithstanding this empirical evidence, I wish to propose an argument that ToM, or at least something very similar to it, is in fact a requirement of *all* normal language functioning and would thus have to be present at the very earliest stages of language functioning. To illustrate, consider an analogy between language and sensory/perceptual processes. On this view, language is considered a process that, rather than enabling the traditional "sensation/perception" of some physical environment, instead as an analog affords "sensation/perception" of the content of another person's mind. Viewed this way, several classical theoretical constructs of language functioning, discussed immediately below, fall readily in place. Moreover, if one adds only one additional component to this view of language-as-sensation/perception-of-others'-minds (LASPOM), then the notion of a ToM becomes a necessity for the system to function.

In terms of the classical theoretical constructs, consider first the long-standing distinction between, and interdependence of, standard sensation and perception processes. It is a well-established fact from work in sensation and perception, that in order for a person to see, hear, touch, etc., something in his or her environment, *and* arrive at what we subjectively experience as that seeing, hearing, etc., of that environmental thing, two distinct but related processes must intertwine. The person must first have sensory processes that act to absorb environmental energy of some sort (light, sound waves, etc.) and convert them to neural energy. But simultaneously, the person must enact constructive, active, experience- and schematic-driven neural processes *upon* that stimulus information in order to make sense of it. Indeed, even this description of the interdependence is an oversimplification because often, active, constructive, motivated, etc., processes will even *precede* the operation of sensory processes. Consider how a person will often exert planned, motor processes to enable initial or better reception of sensory information (e.g. squinting, turning one's head, cupping one's ear, etc.).

The point for the analog with language is that these processes act very much like the traditional "bottom-up" and "top-down" processes proposed early in the history of modern psycholinguistics to describe how comprehension functions. A person for instance does not merely passively absorb the spoken or written language heard or read around them. Rather, people actively create, activate, modify and use varieties of schematic structures upon hearing or reading that language to enable prediction, reference assignment, expectation assessment, inference generation and a variety of other processes of comprehension.

Despite all the similarities between sensation/perception and language, there is nevertheless one difference between standard sensation/perception of one's physical environment, and LASPOM view presented here. This difference, it might also be argued, in fact *necessitates* the presence of ToM in language functioning. The sensation/perception of one's environment is primarily a unidirectional process where a person senses/perceives an environment. LASPOM instead is a bi-directional system (and indeed, multi-directional system), where a person "senses/perceives" another's mind, but so also does that other person "sense/perceive" the first person's mind. In order for one person to gain access into another person's mind via language, that person must also allow access into their own mind. This reflexive cognitive property in my view, *is* Theory of Mind, and is in part what makes language cognition possible.

Viewing ToM this way also aligns with other theoretical psycholinguistic constructs. The unique shared experience of bi-directional "sensation/perception" of mind content motivates a kind of honor system where both parties must honestly and earnestly cooperate in the shared "sensation/perception". If they don't adhere to this honor system, then the successful "sensation/perception" of each others' minds, or comprehension, will not happen. Something very similar to this might be argued to also underlie the Gricean cooperative principle (Grice 1975), the Clarksian construct of common ground (Clark, Schreuder & Buttrick 1983), and other mechanisms like ingratiation, empathy, etc.

Of course it is not the case that people always follow this honor system, indeed much of human behavior can be traced directly to people's violation of it. But even here the mechanisms of manipulation of the "sensation/perception" of mind content rely upon an intimate knowledge of that "sensation/perception", and how it can be lead astray. Akin to wide varieties of genuine sensory/perceptual manipulation (e.g. illusions, "magic", appearance enhancement), language "sensation/perception" manipulations require at least implicit understanding of how the underlying sensory/perceptual systems work.

6 Conclusion

Why would young children ever bother to say anything if they didn't have some semblance of ToM? If a 24 month old child tells a caregiver that they're hungry, even with a simple one word utterance ("Milk?", "More?", etc.) they're a priori assuming that the adult doesn't know this. Why otherwise would they speak?

Or, if young children do not have knowledge that other people have minds, then why don't they try to engage inanimate objects in conversation? Why wouldn't a child tell a refrigerator that they're hungry (e.g. hold the empty cup up to the Frigidaire and say, "Milk?", etc.)? Granted, children will often engage in pretend talk with inanimate things, but this is very different from a genuine attempt to converse.

That young children will on occasion get exasperated with adults who don't know something also seems to demonstrates implicit ToM. Granted, what the adult is expected to know may be unrealistic and thus children may not have mastered the correct content or potential for content of that other mind, but they clearly implicitly know that it is there and that it knows/doesn't know something. Why else would they get frustrated that this other mind is so inexcusably empty!

Lastly, the very fact that children will often take a figuratively-speaking person to be lying seems at odds with a late ToM view. In fact, the mere belief that a speaker is *ever* lying seems to betray a keen understanding of deception, albeit possibly misplaced, that wouldn't be possible without implicit ToM.

It thus doesn't seem so much the case then that children do not know of the presence of other minds, and that those other minds may know or not know something. Rather, children have undeveloped knowledge about the capacities and content of those other minds, and/or children are not *consciously* aware of the presence, capacities and content of other minds. Their own minds have limited capacities and content. They thus would not likely know just how much others know or what others can do. But that those other minds are there and function, seems a necessary condition for language, especially given the LASPOM view of language presented here.

References

Ackerman, Brian P. 1982. Contextual integration and utterance interpretation: The ability of children and adults to interpret sarcastic utterances. *Child Development* 53. 1075–1083.
Baillargeon, Renee. 1993. The object concept revisited: New directions in the investigation of infants' physical knowledge. In Carl E. Granrud (ed.), *Visual perception and cognition in infancy*, 265–315. Hillsdale, NJ: Lawrence Erlbaum.
Brasseur, Judith & Beatrice C. Jimenez. 1989. Performance of university students on the Fullerton subtest of idioms. *Journal of Communication Disorders* 22(5). 351–359.

Broderick, Victor K. 1991. Production and judgment of plausible similes by young children. *Journal of Experimental Child Psychology* 51(3). 485–500.

Carlson, Stephanie M., Louis J. Moses & Hollie R. Hix. 1998. The role of inhibitory processes in young children's difficulties with deception and false belief. *Child Development* 69. 672–691.

Chandler, Michael, Anna S. Fritz & Suzanne Hala. 1989. Small-scale deceit: Deception as a marker of two-, three-, and four-year-olds' early theories of mind. *Child Development* 60. 1263–1277.

Clark, Herbert, H., Robert Schreuder & Samuel Buttrick. 1983. Common ground and the understanding of demonstrative reference. *Journal of Verbal Learning & Verbal Behavior* 22(2). 245–258.

Clements, Wendy A. & Josef Perner. 1994. Implicit understanding of belief. *Cognitive Development* 9. 377–395.

Colston, Herbert L. 2005. Social and cultural influences on figurative and indirect language. In Herbert Colston & Albert N. Katz (eds.), *Figurative language comprehension: Social and cultural influences*, 99–130. Hillsdale, NJ: Lawrence Erlbaum.

Colston, Herbert L. & Raymond W. Gibbs. 2002. Are irony and metaphor understood differently? *Metaphor and Symbol* 17(1). 57–80.

Colston, Herbert L. & Shauna B. Keller. 1998. You'll never believe this: Irony and hyperbole in expressing surprise. *Journal of Psycholinguistic Research* 27(4). 499–513.

Colston, Herbert L. & Melissa S. Kuiper. 2002. Figurative language development research and popular children's literature: Why we should know, 'Where the Wild Things Are'. *Metaphor and Symbol* 17(1). 21–43.

Colston, Herbert L. & Jennifer O'Brien. 2000a. Contrast and pragmatics in figurative language: Anything understatement can do, irony can do better. *Journal of Pragmatics* 32. 1557–1583.

Colston, Herbert L. & Jennifer O'Brien. 2000b. Contrast of kind vs. contrast of magnitude: The pragmatic accomplishments of irony and hyperbole. *Discourse Processes* 30(2). 179–199.

Douglas, Joan D. & Bettina Peel. 1979. The development of metaphor and proverb translation in children grades 1 through 7. *Journal of Educational Research* 73(2). 116–119.

Flavell, John H., Eleanor R. Flavell & Frances L. Green. 1983. Development of the appearance-reality distinction. *Cognitive Psychology* 15. 95–120.

Grice, Paul H. 1975. Logic and conversation. *Syntax and Semantics* 3. 41–58.

Gibbs, Raymond W. 1987. Linguistic factors in children's understanding of idioms. *Journal of Child Language* 14(3). 569–586.

Gibbs, Raymond W. 1994. *The poetics of mind: Figurative thought, language and understanding*. Cambridge: CUP.

Gibbs, Raymond W., Michael D. Johnson & Herbert L. Colston. 1996. How to study proverb understanding. *Metaphor and Symbolic Activity* 11. 233–239.

Hala, Suzanne & Michael Chandler. 1996. The role of strategic planning in accessing false-belief understanding. *Child Development* 67. 2948–2966.

Hala, Suzanne, Michael Chandler & Anna S. Fritz. 1991. Fledgling theories of mind: Deception as a marker of three-year-olds' understanding of false belief. *Child Development* 62. 83–97.

Levorato, Maria C. & Cristina Cacciari. 1992. Children's comprehension and production of idioms: The role of context and familiarity. *Journal of Child Language* 19(2). 415–433.

Levorato, Maria C. & Cristina Cacciari. 1995. The effects of different tasks on the comprehension and production of idioms in children. *Journal of Experimental Child Psychology* 60(2). 261–283.

Levorato, Maria C. & Cristina Cacciari. 2002. The creation of new figurative expressions: Psycholinguistic evidence in Italian children, adolescents and adults. *Journal of Child Language* 29(1). 127–150.

Nippold, Marilyn A. & Catherine L. Taylor. 1995. Idiom understanding in youth: Further examination of familiarity and transparency. *Journal of Speech & Hearing Research* 38(2). 426–434.

Nippold, Marilyn A. & Catherine L. Taylor. 1996. Idiom understanding in Australian youth: A cross-cultural comparison. *Journal of Speech & Hearing Research* 39(2). 442–448.

Olson, David R. & Janet W. Astington. 1987. Seeing and knowing: On the ascription of mental states to young children. *Canadian Journal of Psychology* 41(4). 399–411.

Polanski, Virginia G. 1989. Spontaneous production of figures in writing in students: Grades four, eight, twelve and third year in college. *Education Research Quarterly* 13(2). 47–55.

Repacholi, Betty M. & Alison Gopnik. 1997. Early reasoning about desires: Evidence from 14- and 18-month-olds. *Developmental Psychology* 33. 12–21.

Sullivan, Kate & Ellen Winner. 1993. Three-year-olds' understanding of mental states: The influence of trickery. *Journal of Experimental Child Psychology* 56. 135–148.

Taylor, Marjorie & John H. Flavell. 1984. Seeing and believing: Children's understanding of the distinction between appearance and reality. *Child Development* 55. 1710–1720.

Vosniadou, Stella & Andrew Ortony. 1986. Testing the metaphoric competence of the young child: Paraphrase vs. enactment. *Human Development* 29. 226–230.

Wimmer, Heinz & Josef Perner. 1983. Beliefs about beliefs: Representation and constraining function of wrong beliefs in young children's understanding of deception. *Cognition* 13. 103–128.

Winner, Ellen. 1988. *The point of words*. Cambridge, MA: Harvard University Press.

Winner, Ellen. 1995. Introduction: 10th anniversary special issue: Developmental perspectives on metaphor. *Metaphor and Symbolic Activity* 10. 247–253.

CHAPTER 10

Would you rather 'embert a cudsert' or 'cudsert an embert'?

How spelling patterns at the beginning of English disyllables can cue grammatical category

Joanne Arciuli and Linda Cupples

Disyllabic English nouns and verbs are distinguished phonologically according to their most common patterns of lexical stress: trochaic for nouns and iambic for verbs. We examined whether "orthography" might also provide potentially useful information concerning grammatical category. A dictionary analysis revealed clear probabilistic, orthographic (non-morphological) cues to grammatical category at the beginnings of disyllabic English words. Moreover, native speakers were sensitive to the presence of these cues in carefully constructed nonwords when asked to assign stress and construct sentences: Noun-like nonwords were used as nouns and assigned trochaic stress more often than verb-like nonwords, which were used more often as verbs and assigned iambic stress. We concluded that English orthography does contain cues for both grammatical category and lexical stress.

1   Introduction

The theoretical question of how children learn to assign words to syntactic or grammatical categories (e.g. noun, verb, determiner, etc.) has attracted considerable debate in the language acquisition literature over a number of years (e.g. Braine 1992; Pinker 1984, 1987). Its importance stems from the widely held assumption that the ability to categorise words is necessary if children are to learn about the grammatical rules that govern word combinations in their language, for example, the fact that in English Example (1) is permissible but (2) is not, because the verb *put* requires a location argument.

(1)   Joe put the book on the table.

(2) *Joe put the book.

Grammatical categorisation is not a process that is restricted to children, however. Skilled language comprehension also relies on the ability to identify (albeit implicitly) words' syntactic or grammatical categories. Thus, research has shown that comprehension is hindered when language users misidentify the grammatical category of an ambiguous word like *duck*, which can be used as either a noun (meaning 'swimming bird') or a verb (meaning 'bend down quickly') (e.g. Boland 1997). On the other hand, comprehension can be facilitated and effects of category ambiguity reduced when the likelihood of correctly identifying an ambiguous word's syntactic category is increased by the use of a preceding syntactically constrained context (e.g. 'Laurie took the *prune* out of the fruit bowl and ate it') (Folk & Morris 2003).

Traditionally, theoretical and empirical research investigating assignment of words to grammatical categories has focused on semantic and/or distributional cues; for example, the fact that nouns often refer to entities or things, whereas verbs tend to refer to relations (actions, processes, events and states). These semantic mappings are by no means perfect, however. Many nouns also refer to relations, for example, *removal, revolution*. A more recent focus in the literature has been the association between phonology and grammatical category. It has been reported that English nouns tend to contain a higher number of syllables than verbs, and that both children and adults are sensitive to this correlation (Cassidy & Kelly 1991, 2001). It has also been reported that monosyllabic nouns and verbs display a higher degree of phonological similarity (in respect to features such as place and manner of articulation) within grammatical categories than between categories. Importantly, those words whose phonological characteristics are typical of their grammatical class tend to elicit faster lexical decision and naming times than words with atypical phonology, even after controlling for variation in other potentially important variables, such as familiarity (Monaghan, Chater & Christiansen 2004). More relevant to the present research, however, it has also been shown that *disyllabic* English nouns and verbs differ with respect to their most frequently occurring patterns of "lexical stress".

Kelly and Bock (1988) examined 3,000 disyllabic English nouns and 1,000 disyllabic verbs. Most nouns (94%) exhibited trochaic (first-syllable) stress (e.g. 'ZEbra'), whereas most verbs (69%) exhibited iambic (second-syllable) stress (e.g. 'forGET'). This pattern of results is similar to an earlier analysis of nouns and verbs conducted by Sereno (1986). A discussion of the origins of these differences in stress across disyllabic nouns and verbs is provided by Kelly (1992) and centres on rhythmic biasing contexts created by word order and inflectional patterns in English.

Having found evidence for an association between lexical stress (trochaic vs. iambic) and grammatical category (noun vs. verb) in English disyllables, it remains to demonstrate that English language users are sensitive to this correlation. Davis and Kelly (1997) provided some data in support of this view using a speeded grammatical classification task. Native and non-native speakers of English were asked to judge whether individually presented spoken English disyllables were nouns or verbs. The results showed that non-native speakers were significantly faster and more accurate at classifying words whose stress patterns were typical of their grammatical category (trochaic nouns and iambic verbs) than words with atypical stress patterns (iambic nouns and trochaic verbs). While the findings for native speakers showed a similar pattern of results, the differences were not significant.

A more recent study provides stronger evidence that native speakers of English are also sensitive to the correlation between lexical stress and grammatical category in English disyllables. Arciuli and Cupples (2004) used an onset-gating paradigm, in which participants are asked to identify spoken words that are presented in increasing increments. Using this task, both native and non-native speakers were sensitive to differences in stress typicality, requiring shorter exposure durations to identify trochaic nouns and iambic verbs as compared to iambic nouns and trochaic verbs (after controlling for important lexical variables such as length, frequency, uniqueness points and neighbourhood characteristics).

In demonstrating that English language users are sensitive to the correlation between lexical stress and grammatical category in English disyllables, both Davis and Kelly (1997) and Arciuli and Cupples (2004) sought evidence for advantaged processing of spoken nouns and verbs with stress patterns that were typical of their grammatical category. An alternative approach is to investigate the way in which adult speakers of English choose to assign grammatical category when provided with information about lexical stress or vice versa. This approach was adopted by Kelly (1988) who demonstrated that when participants were presented with pairs of printed nouns or verbs (one trochaic and one iambic) and asked to use one of each pair as the alternative grammatical category, they chose iambic nouns to be used as verbs significantly more often than trochaic nouns and they chose trochaic verbs to be used as nouns significantly more often than iambic verbs. Similarly, Kelly and Bock (1988) showed that native English speakers were significantly more likely to assign trochaic (first-syllable) stress to a written disyllabic pseudoword when it was in a sentence context acting as a noun than when it was acting as a verb.

The empirical findings described above demonstrate that there is an association between lexical stress and grammatical category in English disyllables, and that skilled adult users of English are sensitive to the association. As such, the results are in line with recent theorising in regard to the representation and processing of grammatical category information in human language users, whereby categorical information (in particular the noun-verb distinction) is envisaged not as a purely syntactic dichotomy, but rather a classification that emerges at multiple levels of representation, including semantics and phonology (e.g. Black & Chiat 2003). An obvious question that arises is whether information about grammatical category might also be reflected in "orthography".

In regard to this possibility, it is noteworthy that both Kelly (1988) and Kelly and Bock (1988) used printed stimuli in their experiments. More recently, Arciuli and Cupples (2003) described the findings from a speeded grammatical classification task also using written input. In this study, both native and non-native speakers of English were faster to classify typically stressed nouns and verbs versus atypically stressed nouns and verbs (when stimuli were matched on other relevant variables including frequency). These results indicate that orthographic (spelling) patterns might be providing useful information regarding grammatical category, either directly or via their association with particular patterns of lexical stress (i.e. orthography cues stress which then cues category).

With regard to the processing of lexical stress in particular, there has been growing interest in the possibility that there might be non-morphological orthographic cues present in "word-endings" (as opposed to suffixes, which are bound morphemes) (e.g. Kelly, Morris & Verrekia 1998; Zevin & Joanisse 2000). Unfortunately, much of the research to date has been limited by the absence of an operational definition of what constitutes a "word-ending" and the use of small-scale analyses to investigate the presence of such cues in English words. In an effort to investigate this possibility more thoroughly Arciuli and Cupples (2006) provided an operational definition of "word-ending", conducted a large dictionary analysis to identify potential cues, and conducted extensive follow-up behavioural testing to gauge participants' sensitivity to these cues. In short, we found strong evidence that the "endings" of English disyllabic nouns and verbs contain probabilistic orthographic cues to both grammatical category and lexical stress.

In this research, we defined a word-ending as the letter string beginning at the second phonemic vowel of a disyllabic word (and including any following consonants); that is, the rime of the final syllable (e.g. 'ow' in *follow*, 'ark' in *embark*, and 'upt' in *erupt*). A dictionary analysis of English disyllables was conducted using the CELEX database (Baayen, Piepenbrock, & van Rijn 1993). A total of 340 word-endings (accounting for over 7,000 disyllabic words) were analysed in detail. Most words were nouns (61.7%) and verbs (26.6%). In line with previous research, most words exhibited trochaic stress (61.4%), and fewer words had iambic stress (33.2%) or stress on both syllables (5.4%). More importantly, the findings provided strong evidence to support the proposal that some word-endings are associated with noun status and trochaic stress, whereas other endings are associated with verb status and iambic stress. Thus, the analysis showed that endings that occur frequently in nouns also tend to occur frequently in words with trochaic stress

($r = .70$), whereas endings that occur frequently in verbs also tend to occur frequently in words with iambic stress ($r = .75$).

To determine whether readers are sensitive to these orthographic markers of grammatical category and stress, we constructed two sets of nonwords containing endings with clear biases. "Noun-like" endings ('an', 'age', 'ine', 'ern', 'el', 'ure', 'on') were simultaneously exhibited in nouns and words with trochaic stress in more than 50% of cases, and "verb-like" endings ('end', 'ect', 'ose' 'uct', 'oke') were simultaneously exhibited in verbs and words with iambic stress in more than 50% of cases. These nonwords were presented to a group of 29 native English-speaking participants in two tasks: stress assignment and sentence construction. For stress assignment, participants read silently through the list of written nonwords and underlined the part of each nonword (beginning or ending) they would emphasise more if reading aloud. For sentence construction, participants used each nonword in a written sentence, adding inflections where appropriate. The results showed that readers were sensitive to the correlation between orthography on the one hand and grammatical category and lexical stress on the other. Nonwords with "noun-like" endings were significantly more likely to be used as nouns and assigned trochaic (first-syllable) stress than nonwords with "verb-like" endings, which in turn were more likely to be used as verbs and assigned iambic (second-syllable) stress. Non-parametric correlations were also computed to examine directly the association between grammatical category assignment and stress assignment for each nonword. As expected, the results demonstrated that nonwords used more often as nouns also tended to be assigned trochaic stress ($r = .59, p < .001$) and nonwords used more often as verbs tended to be assigned iambic stress ($r = .66, p < .001$). We concluded that there are clear non-morphological cues[1] available to skilled adult readers of English, which might assist with grammatical classification and, in a closely related way, assignment of lexical stress.

An obvious and important extension of this research is to examine "word-beginnings" for the presence of probabilistic non-morphological orthographic cues to grammatical category and lexical stress. In some respects, it might seem more sensible if such cues were incorporated at the beginnings of words than at the ends, so that language users could make use of the information at an earlier point in processing. Recent research into the importance of word-beginnings in the assignment of lexical stress has been described by Rastle and Coltheart (2000) and Kelly (2004).

---

1. In the context of our previous research and this chapter, non-morphological cues are defined as orthographic sequences that do not generally correspond to bound morphemes, such as '-ment', '-ion', '-ness', etc. Hence, in our study of 340 word endings, only 14% were identified as affixes by Fudge (1984).

Rastle and Coltheart's (2000) aim was to account for stress assignment within the *non-lexical (rule-based) mechanism* of the Dual-Route Model of reading, where serial left-to-right processing is considered to be fundamental. However, their focus on "morphological" units (they emphasised the role of "prefixes", which are bound morphemes) distinguishes their approach from the one adopted here.

Kelly (2004), on the other hand, adopted a "non-morphological" approach in his examination of English stress assignment, focusing on the role of increasing numbers of consonants in "word-onsets" (i.e. initial consonants) as a cue to trochaic (first-syllable) stress. Although Kelly's approach was similar to ours, in that he conducted a dictionary analysis of a large corpus of disyllabic words (from the MRC Database), it focused primarily on phonological aspects of word beginnings rather than orthography (e.g. 'th' and 'sh' were classified [quite appropriately] as single phoneme beginnings even though they each contain two letters), and it was more limited in focusing only on stress assignment (not grammatical category). Moreover, close inspection of Kelly's findings appears to undermine his general conclusion that increasing numbers of consonants in word-initial position are associated with trochaic stress. In particular, although words beginning with /b/, /d/, /f/, /k/, and /s/ receive trochaic (first syllable) stress more often when they begin with a cluster (e.g. /bl/, /dr/, /st/) than a single consonant, the same pattern was not observed for words beginning with /p/ or /t/, and the difference was marginal for words beginning with /g/ (83% trochaic stress as a consonant-cluster vs. 77% as a consonant-singleton) (see Kelly 2004: 236).

In sum, findings reported by both Rastle and Coltheart (2000) and Kelly (2004) are largely consistent with the view that word-initial orthography might provide readers with valuable information regarding stress assignment in English disyllables. However, "grammatical category" was not a focus for either of these researchers. In regard to this omission, an unresolved issue from our previous research into word-endings (Arciuli & Cupples 2006) was whether orthography cues *both* lexical stress *and* grammatical category directly, or whether orthography cues only one aspect (stress or category), which is then used to infer the other (e.g. trochaic stress cues noun status or vice versa). We argued that orthography cued *both* category *and* stress directly, and that when those cues were consistent (orthography cued a combination of noun status and trochaic stress, or a combination of verb status and iambic stress) single word processing was advantaged. Assuming this argument is sound, it is clear that any research examining orthographic correlates of lexical stress should also take grammatical category into consideration. Similarly, any research that is designed to examine the role of orthography in grammatical classification ought to consider the influence of lexical stress. As such, our approach provides an important advance on previous studies by Rastle and Coltheart (2000) and Kelly (2004), in that we attempted to identify non-morphological probabilistic cues to *both* grammatical category *and* lexical stress simultaneously.

We first conducted a dictionary analysis of a large database of English words (the CELEX database). In doing so, we defined "word-beginning" as the letter string up to and including the first vowel or vowel cluster of a disyllabic word, for example, 'se' in *settle*, 'pe' in *pertain*, 'u' in *usher*, and 'a' in *adore*. We expected to find an association between orthography on the one hand and grammatical category and lexical stress on the other; that is, we predicted that some word-beginnings would occur more often in nouns and words with trochaic (first-syllable) stress, whereas other beginnings would occur more often in verbs and words with iambic (second-syllable) stress. Having found the predicted association, we conducted an experiment, which was designed to determine whether skilled native English readers are sensitive to this correlation in tasks requiring them to assign grammatical category and lexical stress to pronounceable nonwords.

2   Dictionary analysis

The aim of the dictionary analysis was to examine disyllabic English words in order to identify the relationship between orthographic patterns in word-beginnings on the one hand and grammatical category (noun vs. verb) and lexical stress (trochaic vs. iambic) on the other. Based on previous research we expected to find that some word-beginnings would occur more often in nouns than verbs whereas other beginnings would occur more often in verbs than nouns. Similarly, we predicted that some word-beginnings would occur more often in trochaically stressed words whereas other beginnings would occur more often in iambically stressed words. As part of a more in-depth analysis of word-beginnings, we were also interested in examining effects of length, vowel-identity and consonant-identity.

In regard to possible length effects, Kelly's (2004) findings relating to word onsets are relevant given the close (though imperfect) association in English between orthography (the focus of our analysis) and phonology (the focus of his analysis). Therefore, on the basis of Kelly's study we hypothesised that orthographic length would influence stress patterns. In particular, as length increases so too should the likelihood of trochaic stress. Notably, however, our primary measure of length was in terms of number of letters in entire word-beginnings (including vowels), not number of phonemes in word-onsets. Finally, we systematically examined the impact of length on assignment of grammatical category, an aspect that has not been addressed in any previous research.

In light of the considerable variability observed in Kelly's data for words with different initial consonants (i.e. the contrast mentioned above between words beginning with /g/, /p/ and /t/ vs. /b/, /d/, /k/, /f/, and /s/), our analysis also focused on possible effects of vowel-identity and consonant identity on category and stress. If Kelly's proposition regarding the fundamental importance of onsets (with his particular emphasis on the number rather than identity of consonants) is correct, then we might expect: (1) no significant effect of vowel-identity (either within CV structures or vowel-only beginnings) on the assignment of stress (or grammatical category), and (2) consistent effects across CV structures containing different consonants.

2.1 Method

Initially, all disyllabic words were extracted from the CELEX database. Words containing hyphens, those containing capitalised letters and those that occurred in more than one grammatical category (e.g. 'capture,' 'yellow') were removed. Further analysis focused on word-beginnings (i.e. word-initial syllables of the disyllabic words extracted from CELEX). All possible word-beginnings were extracted (approximately 700 word-beginnings), which included orthographic sequences such as 'bai', 'che', 'ci', 'co', 'du', 'fee', 'la', 'scrou' and 'u'. A computer program was then compiled to perform the following steps. First, for each word-beginning, information on lexical stress and grammatical category was extracted. It should be noted in this regard that the CELEX database does not include information on the grammatical status and stress of every word; thus, there were necessary omissions from our final list of beginnings. Then, for each beginning, the program produced summary statistics concerning the percentages (based on types not tokens) of disyllabic nouns and verbs as well as the percentages of disyllabic words with trochaic stress, iambic stress and stress on both syllables. Of the resulting usable information, 340 word-beginnings were randomly selected for more detailed analysis.

2.2 Results

Our list of 340 beginnings accounted for over 5,000 disyllabic words. The list includes many examples such as 'ai', 'cha', 'fle', 'ha', 'loo', 'tho' and 'yu' confirming that these beginnings were derived via non-morphological processes (see Note 1).

Correlational analysis of our beginnings data (using two-tailed tests) confirmed that certain beginnings (e.g. 'tu', 'sta', 'li') occur more frequently in nouns and in words with trochaic stress. We refer to these beginnings as "noun-beginnings". As expected, there was a significant positive correlation between beginnings ascribed noun status and beginnings ascribed trochaic stress ($r=.23, p<.001$). Other beginnings (e.g. 'i', 'de', 'be') were typically seen in verbs and in words with iambic stress. We termed these beginnings "verb-beginnings". The correlation between verb status and iambic stress was also significant ($r=.50, p<.001$).

Interestingly, although statistically significant, these correlations were not as high as those obtained in our previous analysis of word-endings (Arciuli & Cupples 2006), a point to which we shall return later.

2.2.1 Effects of length

We conducted two analyses to examine the association between length, on the one hand, and grammatical category and lexical stress on the other. First we used a measure of orthographic onset length (in line with Kelly's earlier study of phonemic onsets). Second, we looked at the length of entire word beginnings (onset plus vowel[s]) in terms of number of letters.

Effects of onset-length (0 to 4 consonants) were evaluated initially in a series of one-way ANOVAs. The dependent variables were percentage of disyllabic nouns, percentage of disyllabic verbs, percentage of disyllabic words with trochaic stress, and percentage of disyllabic words with iambic stress. Summary means are shown in Table 1.

Table 1. Mean percentage of nouns versus verbs and words with trochaic versus iambic stress as a function of onset length (dictionary analysis)

No. of consonants in onset	% Nouns	% Verbs	% Words with trochaic stress	% Words with iambic stress
0	48.04	28.61	62.15	26.12
1	72.98	5.50	93.08	5.67
2	76.37	3.44	97.35	1.84
3	69.52	4.86	100	0
4	100	0.00	100	0

There were significant effects of onset-length in each of the four analyses and the overall pattern confirmed our predictions. As onsets increased in length more words were nouns ($F(4,335) = 2.47$, $p = .044$) and more words exhibited trochaic stress ($F(4,335) = 23.14$, $p < .001$). The reverse pattern was observed for the other dependent variables. As the length of word-beginnings increased, there was a lower percentage of verbs ($F(4,335) = 10.89$, $p < .001$) and a lower percentage of words with iambic stress ($F(4,335) = 16.83$, $p < .001$). It is obvious, however, that these changes in category and stress were by no means linear across the four categories of onset length (from 0 to 4 consonants). When pairs of adjacent means were compared statistically, all dependent variables showed a significant change from 0 to 1 consonant ($t(151) = 2.56$, $p = .011$ for percent nouns; $t(151) = 5.00$, $p < .001$ for percent verbs; $t(151) = 6.14$, $p < .001$ for percent trochaic; $t(151) = 4.68$, $p < .001$ for percent iambic). In line with Kelly's proposals, there was also a significant change in stress pattern from 1 to 2 consonants ($t(303) = 3.29$, $p < .001$ for percent trochaic; $t(303) = 3.56$, $p < .001$ for percent iambic). None of the remaining contrasts were significant.[2]

Effects of length in terms of number of letters in the entire word beginning (1 to 5 letters) were evaluated in the same way, initially via a series of one-way ANOVAs. The same dependent variables were used. Summary means are shown in Table 2.

Table 2. Mean percentage of nouns versus verbs and words with trochaic versus iambic stress as a function of entire word beginning length (dictionary analysis)

No. of letters in entire word-beginning	% Nouns	% Verbs	% Words with trochaic stress	% Words with iambic stress
1	36.42	34.57	42.65	43.12
2	73.57	8.94	86.35	10.93
3	73.38	4.42	96.52	2.63
4	76.50	2.19	99.61	0
5	73.61	5.56	100	0

There were significant effects of length in three of the four analyses and a marginally significant effect in the fourth analysis. The overall pattern of results was in line with the analyses of onset-length described above. As number of letters increased, the percentage of nouns increased ($F(4,335) = 2.12$, $p = .078$) and, as one might expect, there was a lower percentage of verbs ($F(4,335) = 11.06$, $p < .001$). With regard to stress, as the number of letters in each word-beginning increased, more words exhibited trochaic stress ($F(4,335) = 45.54$, $p < .001$) and fewer words exhibited iambic stress ($F(4,335) = 40.35$, $p < .001$). Once again, these changes were not linear. They were strong and consistent in the contrasts between beginnings containing 1 letter (zero consonants) vs. 2 letters (either two vowels as in 'ai-' or a single consonant plus one vowel as in 'bi-') ($t(66) = 4.12$, $p < .001$ for percent nouns; $t(66) = 3.66$, $p < .001$ for percent verbs; $t(66) = 5.03$, $p < .001$ for percent trochaic; $t(66) = 4.31$, $p < .001$ for percent iambic). Significant differences in stress pattern also emerged in the contrasts between 2- and 3-letter beginnings and a non-significant trend was seen for percent verbs (percent nouns was the only variable to show no effect in this contrast) ($t < 1$ for percent nouns; $t(238) = 2.40$, $p = .017$ for percent verbs; $t(238) = 5.59$, $p < .001$ for percent trochaic; $t(238) = 5.57, p < .001$ for percent iambic). Finally, only stress pattern differed significantly in comparisons

---

2. A significance level of .0125 (.05 divided by 4) was adopted for all contrasts, because four individual contrasts were conducted on each main effect (i.e. for consonant length we compared 0 vs. 1 consonant, 1 vs. 2 consonants, 2 vs. 3 consonants, and 3 vs. 4 consonants; and for length of entire word beginnings we compared 1 vs. 2 letters, 2 vs. 3 letters, 3 vs. 4 letters and 4 vs. 5 letters).

of 3- vs. 4-letter beginnings ($t(264) = 3.13, p = .002$ for percent trochaic; $t(264) = 3.49$, $p < .001$ for percent iambic). All remaining comparisons of adjacent means were non-significant.

In comparing these results for entire word beginnings with those for onsets only, it is interesting to note that where differences in stress assignment are concerned, entire beginnings show more consistent effects; that is, three out of four comparisons of adjacent means were significant when examining length of the entire word beginning as compared with two out of four comparisons for onset length. This pattern of results is reinforced when we look at overall effect sizes obtained earlier in our one-way ANOVAs. Effects obtained using number of letters in entire word-beginnings as a measure of length are stronger than effects obtained using onset-length, but only with regard to stress assignment (effect sizes [partial eta-squared] were .352 vs. .216 respectively for the percentage of words with trochaic stress and .325 vs. .167 respectively for the percentage of words with iambic stress).

2.2.2   *Effects of vowel-identity*

In order to examine the possible effects of vowel-identity in CV structures we returned to the complete list of word-beginnings and investigated each CV structure in our list. There were 18 beginnings for the vowel 'a' (no 'xa', 'za', or 'qa'), 20 beginnings for 'e' (no 'qe'), 19 beginnings for each of 'i' and 'o' (no 'qi', 'xi', 'qo' or 'xo'), and 17 beginnings for 'u' (no 'zu', 'xu', 'wu' or 'qu').

A series of one-way ANOVAs was conducted using the same dependent variables listed in the investigations of length effects. Summary means are presented in Table 3.

Table 3. Mean percentage of nouns versus verbs and words with trochaic versus iambic stress as a function of vowel identity in CV structures (dictionary analysis)

Vowel in CV structure	% Nouns	% Verbs	% Words with trochaic stress	% Words with iambic stress
a	79.24	6.48	88.98	9.01
e	71.01	10.62	81.54	15.5
i	72.97	6.23	91.37	6.21
o	71.86	5.41	89.99	7.55
u	74.29	4.39	88.99	7.02

The results indicated no systematic effects of vowel-identity in CV structures. There was no effect of vowel on the percentage of nouns ($F < 1$) or the percentage of verbs ($F < 1$). Similarly, there was no effect of vowel on the percentage of words with trochaic stress ($F(4,88) = 1.00$, $p > .10$) or on the percentage of words with iambic stress ($F(4,88) = 1.51$, $p > .10$).

Having found no significant effects of vowel-identity in CV beginnings, we went on to look for possible effects of vowel-identity in word-beginnings that contained only vowels. These beginnings are listed in Table 4.

Table 4. Mean percentage of nouns versus verbs and words with trochaic versus iambic stress as a function of vowel identity in vowel-only word-beginnings (dictionary analysis)

Beginning	Nouns	Verbs	Trochaic	Iambic
a	37.66	32.28	41.14	57.59
ae	50	50	100	0
ai	87.1	0	100	0
au	54.55	9.09	63.64	36.36
e	35.03	50.25	37.56	61.42
ea	75.86	3.45	100	0
ei	100	0	100	0
eu	100	0	100	0
i	31.21	39.49	41.4	50.96
o	57.3	17.98	68.54	29.21
oa	71.43	0	100	0
oi	100	0	100	0
ou	30.77	50.77	44.62	9.23
u	20.9	32.84	24.63	16.42

While this set comprised only a small number of beginnings, a visual inspection of the means indicates that there are clear cues to grammatical category and stress. For example, the beginning 'ai' is associated with noun status and trochaic stress in disyllabic words (87.1% and 100% respectively) whereas the beginning 'e' is associated with verb status and iambic stress (50.25% and 61.42% respectively). A median split analysis was conducted on these data to provide "quantitative" evidence of significant variability in category and stress assignment as a function of vowel identity. "Biased" vowels ($N = 7$) occurred at the beginning of nouns on more than 56% of occasions (e.g. 'ai') whereas "unbiased" vowels ($N = 7$) occurred at the beginning of nouns on fewer than 56% of occasions (e.g. 'e'). As would be expected, a one-way ANOVA confirmed that biased vowels were significantly more likely than unbiased vowels to occur in nouns ($F(1,12) = 37.31$, $p < .001$). More interestingly, however, biased vowels were also significantly more likely than unbiased vowels to occur in words with trochaic stress ($F(1,12) = 18.91$, $p < .001$), and significantly less likely to occur in verbs ($F(1,12) = 31.29$, $p < .001$) and words with iambic stress ($F(1,12) = 8.00$, $p < .02$).

2.2.3 Effects of consonant-identity in CV word-beginnings

We investigated the effect of consonant-identity using the same list of CV structures created to investigate possible differences between vowels. Our motivation in undertaking this analysis was to follow-up on Kelly's proposal that it is the *number* of consonants rather than their identity that acts as a cue to stress (and possibly grammatical category). If Kelly's proposition is correct then we should see all CV structures behaving in a similar way, with little variation between them as a function of consonant identity. A close look at CV structures indicates, however, that this is not the case.

Table 5 provides an illustration of the effects of consonant variation in CV structures.

Table 5. Mean percentage of nouns versus verbs and words with trochaic versus iambic stress as a function of consonant identity in 'C + e' word-beginnings (dictionary analysis)

Beginning	Nouns	Verbs	Trochaic	Iambic
be	35.05	46.39	29.9	70.1
ce	92.31	0	100	0
de	26.72	62.6	23.66	61.07
fe	50	3.33	100	0
ge	78.57	0	78.57	21.43
he	63.89	2.78	86.11	2.78
je	62.5	0	87.5	12.5
ke	92.86	0	100	0
le	67.57	10.81	86.49	13.51
me	84.09	0	86.36	13.64
ne	78.38	2.7	97.3	2.7
pe	56.45	19.35	69.35	30.65
re	29.41	55.88	25.29	54.12
se	66.67	10	83.33	16.67
te	83.78	0	83.78	8.11
ve	72.41	0	93.1	3.45
we	84.62	0	100	0
xe	100	0	100	0
ye	100	0	100	0
ze	100	0	100	0

These CV structures contain only one consonant. Moreover, the vowel is the same in every case. However, a simple visual inspection of these beginnings reveals clear and variable cues to stress and grammatical category (e.g. 'de' strongly cues verb status and iambic stress whereas 'ke' appears to cue noun status and trochaic stress). To confirm this impression, we once again performed a median-split analysis. "Biased" beginnings (N = 10) occurred in nouns on more than 75% of occasions (e.g. 'ke', 'me') whereas "unbiased" beginnings (N = 10) occurred in nouns on fewer than 75% of occasions (e.g. 're', 'je'). Once again, as expected, a one-way ANOVA confirmed that biased beginnings were significantly more likely than unbiased beginnings to occur in nouns ($F(1,18) = 36.64, p < .001$). More importantly, however, biased beginnings were also significantly more likely to occur in words with trochaic stress ($F(1,18) = 7.30, p < .02$), and significantly less likely to occur in verbs ($F(1,18) = 6.98, p < .02$) and words with iambic stress ($F(1,18) = 6.50, p = .02$).

2.3 Discussion

Like the earlier analysis of word-endings described by Arciuli and Cupples (2006), this dictionary analysis of the beginnings of English disyllables reveals a rich source of non-morphological orthographic information that could be used by readers in a probabilistic way to assist them in assigning words to grammatical categories (nouns and verbs) and in assigning patterns of lexical stress.

Interestingly, the overall correlations between grammatical category and lexical stress are not as strong for beginnings as they were in our earlier analysis of word-endings, but are significant nonetheless and indicate an association between noun status and trochaic stress on the one hand and between verb status and iambic stress on the other. These results are in line with previous research by both Kelly and Bock (1988) and Sereno (1986).

Importantly, our dictionary analysis also provides detail on fine-grained aspects of these orthographic cues; for example, effects of length on assignment of grammatical category and stress in English disyllables. In this regard, Kelly (2004) had suggested that increasing onset-length (in terms of number of phonemic consonants) was associated with assignment of trochaic stress. Here we compared the effects of "orthographic" length (measured in number of letters) of word-onsets versus entire "word-beginnings" (i.e. onset plus vowel[s]). Importantly, we included examination of how these units might also cue grammatical category. Our results show that both measures of length are associated with grammatical category and stress pattern. As length increases, so too does the proportion of nouns and the proportion of words with trochaic stress. Interestingly, the association between length and stress assignment was somewhat stronger when using number of letters in the entire word-beginning as an operational unit (rather than onsets). This difference in strength was observed when comparing both overall effect sizes and the significance of individual contrasts between adjacent length categories. In fact, the results of our individual contrasts appear to undermine somewhat Kelly's argument that the length of consonant clusters is of critical importance in stress assignment, because the most marked changes were seen between word-onsets containing 0 consonants and 1 consonant (rather than between word-onsets containing varying numbers of consonants).

Additional analyses were carried out to provide further support for the notion that entire word-beginnings (as opposed to just the number of consonants contained within onsets) provide clear cues to category and stress. First we examined the effects of vowel-identity in CV structures and found no systematic differences. However, we also carried out an examination of all vowel-only beginnings. Qualitative and quantitative analysis revealed that vowel-only beginnings contain clear and varied cues to both category and stress, with some of these beginnings cuing noun status and trochaic stress, and others cuing verb status and iambic stress. Additionally, we undertook an analysis of the effect of consonant-identity in one particular CV structure 'C + e'. This analysis also revealed clear and variable cues to grammatical category and lexical stress.

Taken together these results suggest that there is a rich source of non-morphological orthographic cues to grammatical category and lexical stress in the beginnings of English disyllables. Moreover, the extent of these cues may be underestimated if one attends to onsets rather than entire word-beginnings (onset plus vowel[s]). Identification and detailed description of these statistical regularities does not, however, guarantee that readers are sensitive to them. In this regard, it is noteworthy that some of the correlations we observed in our dictionary analysis are rather small given the large number of cases involved. This fact makes it all the more important for us to seek behavioural evidence that readers actually do make use of the types of orthographic cues we are proposing during the course of stress assignment and grammatical categorisation.

3. Readers' sensitivity to orthographic cues

The aim of this experiment was to determine whether skilled native readers of English are sensitive to the association that was observed in our dictionary analysis between orthography on the one hand and grammatical category and lexical stress on the other. We used nonwords to investigate this association, because it allowed us to manipulate orthographic beginnings carefully while simultaneously controlling endings. In line with our previous research examining word-endings (Arciuli & Cupples 2006), we predicted that skilled language users would assign noun status and trochaic (first-syllable) stress more often to nonwords with "noun-like" beginnings than nonwords with "verb-like" beginnings, and that they would assign verb status and iambic (second-syllable) stress more often to nonwords with "verb-like" beginnings than nonwords with "noun-like" beginnings.

3.1 Method

Participants
A total of 29 undergraduate students took part in the experiment during their normal tutorial classes. All were native speakers of English.

3.1.2 Materials

Our dictionary analysis was used to identify two sets of orthographic word-beginnings, which differed in terms of the frequency with which they occur in disyllabic nouns versus verbs and in disyllabic words with trochaic versus iambic stress. Important characteristics of these word-beginnings are summarised in Table 6. "Noun-like beginnings" were associated significantly more often than "verb-like beginnings" with use as a noun (75.6% vs. 32.5%) ($t(15) = 9.17, p < .001$) and with trochaic stress (88.1% vs. 33.2%) ($t(15) = 12.04, p < .001$); whereas "verb-like beginnings" were associated significantly more often than "noun-like beginnings" with use as a verb (47.8% vs. 12.2%) ($t(15) = 6.97, p < .001$) and with iambic stress (59.2% vs. 9.3%) ($t(15) = 12.28, p < .001$).

Table 6. Orthographic beginnings used in experiment

	Noun-like beginnings			Verb-like beginnings	
Beginning	Percent Noun/ Trochaic	Percent Verb/ Iambic	Beginning	Percent Noun/ Trochaic	Percent Verb/ Iambic
cu	76.2 / 92.9	4.8 / 7.1	be	35.1 / 29.9	46.4 / 70.1
va	62.5 / 87.5	16.7 / 12.5	de	26.7 / 23.7	62.6 / 61.1
vi	69.0 / 90.5	7.1 / 7.1	e	35.0 / 37.6	50.3 / 61.4
pe	56.5 / 69.4	19.4 / 30.6	re	29.4 / 25.3	55.9 / 54.1
gro	83.3 / 100	16.7 / 0.0	a	37.7 / 41.1	32.3 / 57.6
shri	66.7 / 100	33.3 / 0.0	i	31.2 / 41.4	39.5 / 51.0
ca	80.8 / 85.0	5.8 / 15.0			
sa	92.6 / 92.6	2.9 / 7.4			
mi	74.4 / 74.4	18.9 / 2.2			
cha	85.3 / 85.3	5.9 / 11.8			
pla	83.8 / 91.9	2.7 / 8.1			
Mean	75.6 / 88.1	12.2 / 9.3	Mean	32.5 / 33.2	47.8 / 59.2

Two sets of nonwords containing the targeted beginnings were derived. There were 24 nonwords with "noun-like" beginnings and 24 with "verb-like" beginnings, all of which obeyed the phonotactic and orthographic constraints of English. Importantly, the two sets of nonwords contained orthographic endings that were not strongly biased overall with regards to grammatical category or stress placement according to our earlier dictionary analysis (Arciuli & Cupples 2006). The endings contained in nonwords with "noun-like" beginnings were seen in nouns on 45.8% of occasions and verbs on 35.6% of occasions ($t(12) = 1.24, p > .10$). These same endings were found in words with trochaic stress on 52.4% of occasions and words with iambic stress 43.1% of the time ($t < 1$). A similar pattern was seen in nonwords with "verb-like" beginnings, whose endings were found in nouns on 46.3% of occasions and verbs 41.9% of the time ($t < 1$), and in words with trochaic stress on 42.2% of occasions compared to 49.4% for words with iambic stress ($t < 1$). Some example nonwords are 'cudsert', 'pembain', 'sagrust', 'chandise' ("noun-like" beginnings) and 'ephate', 'bentide', 'agore', 'reteal' ("verb-like" beginnings). The complete set of nonwords is included in Appendix A.

Two lists were constructed, each of which contained the full set of 48 nonwords in a different pseudorandom order. One list was used for stress assignment and the other for sentence construction.

3.2 Design and procedure

All participants completed both tasks: Approximately half (16) of the participants completed stress assignment first followed by sentence construction, whereas presentation order was reversed for the remaining (13) participants. For stress assignment, participants were told to read silently through the list of written nonwords and underline which part of each nonword (beginning or ending) they would emphasise more if reading aloud. For sentence construction, they were instructed to use each nonword in a written sentence containing at least six words, adding inflections where appropriate.

3.3 Results

3.3.1 *Sentence construction*

The initial step in analysing the sentence construction data was to classify participants' responses according to their use of the nonwords as nouns, verbs, or other form classes. Some examples of nonword uses classified as nominal versus verbal are shown in Table 7. Although classification was straightforward in most cases, we conducted a reliability check on approximately 27% of the data. A trained linguist was asked to classify all sentence responses from 8 of the 29 participants. The mean level of agreement across the eight participants was high at 98.4% (range: 95.8% to 100%).

Table 7. Examples of participants' responses classified as noun versus verb uses (with stimulus nonword in parentheses)

Noun uses

The *asplain* was much larger than expected. (*asplain*)
It was with *chadrain* he left the stage. (*chadrain*)
Beware! Don't get caught by a *plabate*! (*plabate*)
She only had a few *grozels* to spend. (*grozel*)
There was *shripel* everywhere from the roof. (*shripel*)

Verb uses

He could not *shripel* that he had won. (*shripel*)
The cat began to *valate* in the garden. (*valate*)
"*Estense* them all," the soldier cried. (*estense*)
A deck of cards *caskeled* on to the floor. (*caskel*)
The boy was *plabating* the girl. (*plabate*)

Having classified participants' uses of the nonwords as nouns, verbs, or other form classes, we computed the percentage of times that nonwords with different beginnings (noun-like vs. verb-like) were used as nouns or verbs for each participant and for each item (nonword). The means are shown in Figure 1.

Statistical analysis of these data revealed a significant interaction between use as a noun or verb and type of orthographic beginning ($F_1(1,27) = 64.42$, $p < .001$; $F_2(1,46) = 20.00$, $p < .001$). Importantly, this interaction effect was equally strong regardless of whether the sentence construction task preceded or followed the stress assignment task (both $Fs < 1$). Simple contrasts revealed that, as expected, nonwords with "noun-like" beginnings were used as nouns more often than nonwords with "verb-like" beginnings (49.6% vs. 25.9%) ($F_1(1,27) = 55.78$, $p < .001$; $F_2(1,46) = 27.27$, $p < .001$) and nonwords with "verb-like" beginnings were used as verbs more often than nonwords with "noun-like" beginnings (59.6% vs. 40.5%) ($F_1(1,27) = 53.19$, $p < .001$; $F_2(1,46) = 12.33$, $p < .001$).

3.3.2 Stress assignment

The percentage of times nonwords with different types of orthographic beginnings were assigned trochaic versus iambic stress was computed for each participant and for each item (nonword). Since there were only two possible response choices (trochaic or iambic stress) these data provide redundant information (i.e. percent iambic

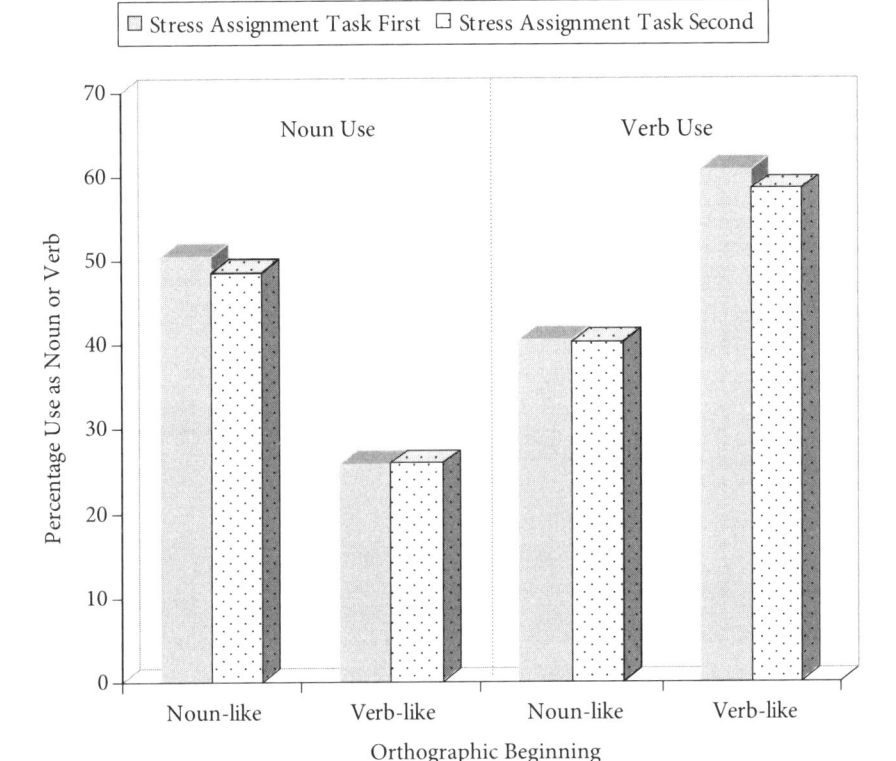

Figure 1. Percentage use as a noun or verb as a function of orthographic word-beginning and task presentation order

stress = 100 minus percent trochaic stress). Consequently, the means for trochaic stress only are shown in Figure 2.

As for the sentence construction task, there was a main effect of type of nonword beginning on stress assignment, such that nonwords with "noun-like" beginnings were assigned trochaic (first-syllable) stress significantly more often than nonwords with "verb-like" beginnings (55.5% vs. 29.6%) ($F_1(1,27) = 80.88, p < .001$; $F_2(1,46) = 31.29, p < .001$). In addition, it is interesting to note that this effect was somewhat stronger when the stress assignment task followed the sentence construction task than when it preceded it, resulting in a significant interaction ($F_1(1,27) = 4.11, p = .053$; $F_2(1,46) = 7.12, p < .05$).

3.3.3 *Stress assignment and grammatical category: Correlations*

Having demonstrated that skilled language users are sensitive to orthographic cues contained in the beginnings of English nonwords when asked to assign stress and grammatical category, it remains to examine directly the association between

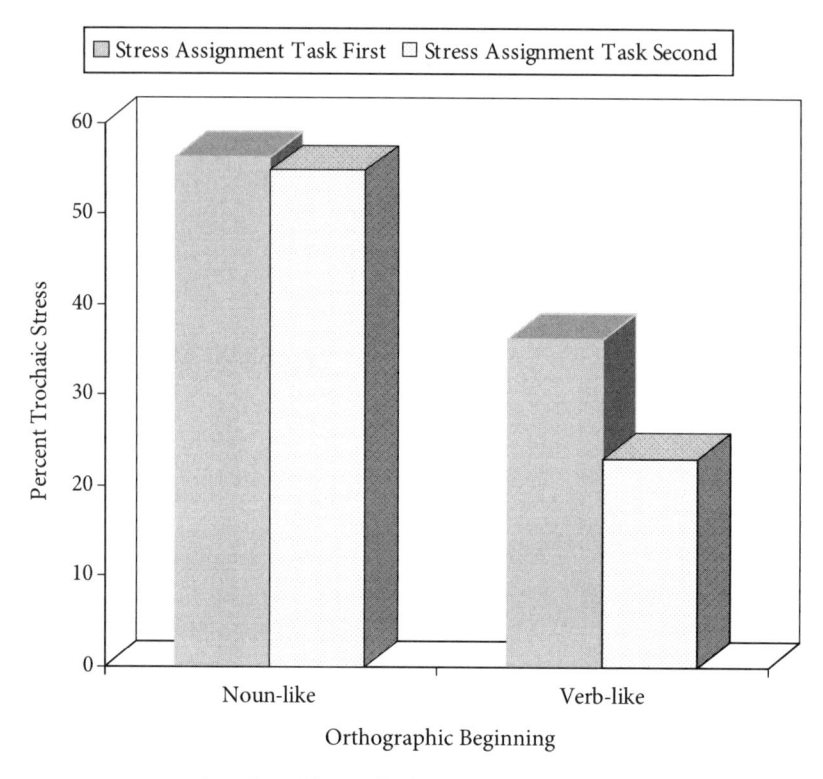

[Figure: bar chart showing Percent Trochaic Stress by Orthographic Beginning (Noun-like vs Verb-like) for Stress Assignment Task First and Stress Assignment Task Second]

Figure 2. Percentage of trochaic (first-syllable) stress as a function of orthographic word beginning and task presentation order

assignment of stress and assignment of grammatical category on a per item basis. As described above, we had previously computed the percentage of participants who used each nonword as a noun and the percentage who used it as a verb. Similarly, we had computed the percentage of participants who assigned trochaic (and iambic) stress to each nonword. These figures formed the basis for a correlational analysis, which revealed, as expected, a positive association across the entire set of nonwords between noun usage and trochaic stress assignment (Spearman's *rho* [N = 48] =.67, *p* <.001), and a positive association between verb usage and iambic stress assignment (Spearman's *rho* [N = 48] =.58, *p* <.001).

3.4 Discussion

The main finding from this experiment is that skilled native users of English were sensitive to orthographic cues to grammatical category and lexical stress present in the beginnings of disyllabic nonwords. Nonwords containing initial orthographic sequences that had been identified in our dictionary analysis as occurring more frequently in nouns and words with trochaic (first-syllable) stress were generally used as nouns during sentence construction and were ascribed trochaic stress during our stress assignment task. On the other hand, nonwords containing initial orthographic sequences that had been identified as occurring more frequently in verbs and words with iambic (second-syllable) stress were typically used as verbs and ascribed iambic stress. Our correlational analysis indicated that there was a direct association between grammatical category assignment and stress assignment for each nonword. As expected, nonwords used as nouns tended to be assigned trochaic stress and nonwords used as verbs tended to be assigned iambic stress.

Another interesting finding from this experiment is the interaction involving task presentation order in the analysis of stress assignment. Participants who completed stress assignment *after* sentence construction, showed a more marked difference between nonwords with noun-like versus verb-like beginnings, suggesting that participants' assignment of words to grammatical categories in the sentence construction task influenced their assignment of lexical stress. This finding is intriguing in light of the question we raised in the introduction regarding whether orthography cues *both* grammatical category and lexical stress, or whether it cues one of these aspects, which in turn cues the other. This result, along with the absence of any hint of an interaction with task presentation order in the sentence construction data (see Figure 1), seems to indicate that orthography might cue grammatical category which in turn cues stress. Although it would be premature to draw strong conclusions on the basis of a single experiment like the one reported here, with a marginally significant interaction effect, the issue is clearly worthy of further investigation.

4 Conclusion

The focus of this research was the question of how skilled native users of English assign words to grammatical categories. In particular, we asked whether there might be non-morphological cues in the orthographic beginnings of English words to assist readers in this process. The results of our dictionary analysis provide clear evidence that such cues do exist in English disyllables and could, potentially, be used in a probabilistic way to assign grammatical category (status as a noun or verb) and lexical stress (trochaic or iambic). Moreover, these cues overlap to a significant degree, with some word-beginnings cuing a combination of noun status and trochaic stress and other beginnings cuing a combination of verb status and iambic stress. The results of the dictionary analysis also provide insight into the nature of the non-morphological component that provides the most useful information to readers. Our results suggest that entire word-beginnings rather than word-onsets provide stronger cues.

Having identified these potential cues, we conducted an experiment aimed at demonstrating that skilled native readers of English are sensitive to them. In line with our predictions, we found that readers' assignment of category and stress to disyllabic nonwords varied significantly as a function of type of word-beginning. Participants assigned noun status and trochaic stress (more often than verb status and iambic stress) to nonwords with beginnings that were typical of real trochaic nouns, whereas they assigned verb status and iambic stress to nonwords with beginnings that were typical of real iambic verbs. These results extend our earlier findings in regard to non-morphological probabilistic cues contained in word-endings of English disyllables (Arciuli & Cupples 2006).

Although the question of whether orthography cues grammatical category directly or via its association with particular patterns of lexical stress remains unresolved, it is noteworthy that neither the results reported here nor the earlier findings in regard to word-endings (Arciuli & Cupples 2006) provide support for the view that orthography cues stress, which in turn cues category. On the contrary, we interpreted our earlier findings as indicating that orthography probably cues both category and stress simultaneously; and the effects of task presentation order reported in the current experiment (see Figure 2) suggest that, if anything, orthography cues grammatical category directly, which in turn can influence assignment of stress.

In sum, the current findings and those from our earlier research contribute to a growing body of evidence suggesting that English orthography contains a rich source of non-morphological probabilistic cues to both grammatical category and lexical stress, and that readers make use of these cues (e.g. Arciuli & Cupples 2006; Kelly 2004; Kelly, Morris & Verrekia 1998; Zevin & Joanisse 2000). An intriguing question, which we are continuing to investigate, is whether readers' sensitivity to the associations between orthography on the one hand and grammatical category and stress pattern on the other might also be observed in tasks that more clearly reflect standard processes operating during the course of lexical retrieval (i.e. "normal" reading). If they are, then we might expect to find that lexical processing is facilitated for words with orthographic characteristics that are typical of their grammatical category and stress pattern when compared with words whose orthography is atypical. Experiments 1 and 2 conducted by Arciuli and Cupples (2006) using lexical decision and word naming provide some intial evidence to suggest that such cues are likely to be utilised during normal reading. However, those experiments were not designed specifically to investigate this issue. Further research needs to be conducted before definitive conclusions can be drawn.

In addition, we do not as yet have fine-grained information regarding the contribution of beginnings vs. endings to the processing of grammatical category and stress. Certainly, given the advantages of multiple redundant cues in language processing, it would be beneficial to encode cues in *both* word-beginnings and word-endings. In line with this view, we have now demonstrated in two separate studies that both beginnings and endings provide salient usable cues for readers (using nonword stimuli and tasks requiring assignment of category and stress information). It may be, however, that these cues are not contributing equally. When compared with the results of our earlier research (Arciuli & Cupples 2006), the results of the dictionary analysis presented here suggest that cues in word-beginnings may not be as strong as those contained in word-endings. We are currently conducting additional research to investigate this question.

In closing, this study lends support to the theoretical proposal that grammatical categorisation is not a purely syntactic phenomenon (e.g. Black & Chiat 2003); rather, grammatical category is reflected on a variety of linguistic levels, including semantic, phonological and, as indicated here, orthographic. It is important that future research be conducted with real words, readers of varying ages and a variety of tasks to provide a comprehensive understanding of the processes underlying grammatical category assignment during visual word recognition, because, as far as we are aware, no current psycholinguistic models of reading adequately address the processing of grammatical category and lexical stress.

Acknowledgements

We are grateful to Matthew Johnson who assisted with the computer programming included in the dictionary analysis. We are also grateful to Verna Rieschild for her assistance with our reliability analysis in the Experiment. Preliminary results from this research were presented at the International Language and Cognition Conference, held in September 2004 at Coffs Harbour, New South Wales.

References

Arciuli, Joanne & Linda Cupples. 2003. Effects of stress typicality during speeded grammatical classification. *Language and Speech* 46(4). 353–374.
Arciuli, Joanne & Linda Cupples. 2004. Effects of stress typicality during spoken word recognition by native and non-native speakers of English: Evidence from onset-gating. *Memory & Cognition* 32(1). 21–30.
Arciuli, Joanne & Linda Cupples. 2006. The processing of lexical stress during visual word recognition: Typicality effects and orthographic correlates. *Quarterly Journal of Experimental Psychology* 59(5). 920–948.
Baayen, R. Harald, Richard Piepenbrock & Hedderik van Rijn. 1993. *The CELEX lexical database* (CD-ROM). Linguistic Data Consortium, University of Pennsylvania, Philadelphia, PA.
Black, Maria & Shula Chiat. 2003. Noun-verb dissociations: A multi-faceted phenomenon. *Journal of Neurolinguistics* 16(2–3). 231–250.

Boland, Julie E. 1997. Resolving syntactic category ambiguities in discourse context: Probabilistic and discourse constraints. *Journal of Memory and Language* 36(4). 588–615.

Braine, Martin D. 1992. What sort of innate structure is needed to "bootstrap" into syntax? *Cognition* 45(1). 77–100.

Cassidy, Kimberly W. & Michael H. Kelly. 1991. Phonological information for grammatical category assignments. *Journal of Memory and Language* 30(3). 348–369.

Cassidy, Kimberly W. & Michael H. Kelly. 2001. Children's use of phonology to infer grammatical class in vocabulary learning. *Psychonomic Bulletin & Review Journal* 8(3). 519–523.

Davis, Sally M. & Michael H. Kelly. 1997. Knowledge of the English noun-verb stress difference by native and nonnative speakers. *Journal of Memory and Language* 36(3). 445–460.

Folk, Jocelyn & Robin Morris. 2003. Effects of syntactic category assignment on lexical ambiguity resolution in reading: An eye movement analysis. *Memory & Cognition* 31(1). 87–99.

Fudge, Erik. 1984. *English word stress*. London: Allen & Unwin.

Kelly, Michael H. 1988. Phonological biases in grammatical category shifts. *Journal of Memory and Language* 27(4). 343–358.

Kelly, Michael H. 1992. Using sound to solve syntactic problems: The role of phonology in grammatical category assignments. *Psychological Review* 99(2). 349–364.

Kelly, Michael H. 2004. Word onset patterns and lexical stress in English. *Journal of Memory and Language* 50(3). 231–244.

Kelly, Michael H. & J. Kathryn Bock. 1988. Stress in time. *Journal of Experimental Psychology: Human Perception and Performance* 14(3). 389–403.

Kelly, Michael H., Joanna Morris & Laura Verrekia. 1998. Orthographic cues to lexical stress: Effects on naming and lexical decision. *Memory & Cognition* 26(4). 822–832.

Monaghan, Padraic, Nick Chater & Morten H. Christiansen. 2004. Inequality between the classes: Phonological and distributional typicality as predictors of lexical processing. In Richard Alterman & David Kirsh (eds.), *Annual Conference of the Cognitive Science Society* 25, 810–815. Mahwah, NJ: Lawrence Erlbaum.

Pinker, Steven. 1984. *Language learnability and language development*. Cambridge, MA: Harvard University Press.

Pinker, Steven. 1987. The bootstrapping problem in language acquisition. In Brian MacWhinney (ed.), *Mechanisms of language acquisition*, 399–441. Hillsdale, NJ: Lawrence Erlbaum.

Rastle, Kathleen & Max Coltheart. 2000. Lexical and nonlexical print-to-sound translation of disyllabic words and nonwords. *Journal of Memory and Language* 42(3). 342–364.

Sereno, Joan A. 1986. Stress pattern differentiation of form class in English. *Journal of the Acoustical Society of America* 79. S36.

Zevin, Jason & Marc F. Joanisse. 2000. Stress assignment in nonword reading. *Journal of Cognitive Neuroscience* 41B, Supplement 5.

Appendix A

Table 8. Nonwords used in experiment

"Noun-like" beginnings		"Verb-like" beginnings	
custew	sabbade	bemave	reteal
cudsert	sagrust	bentide	rezert
cussant	minteal	denade	arbove
valate	mingrace	delide	abrond
varise	milphust	elbate	ampralt
vittain	misfew	endire	asplain
pedruss	mirvile	embert	aldrove
pembain	miplant	ephate	agore
pensade	chandise	estense	alode
grozel	chamade	estire	impate
shripel	chadrain	eroke	imbade
caskel	plabate	rembile	imbure

CHAPTER 11

Ethnobiological classification and the environment in Northern Australia

Brett Baker

Among Indigenous Australian folk taxonomic systems, we find two general characteristics. Firstly, the great majority of botanical names refer to species, while genera remain unnamed. I argue that this fact follows from the unique structure of the Australian flora, which is dominated by species from just a few very large genera. The importance of this fact has hitherto not been recognised by ethnobiological systematics. Secondly, taxonomic names are simple, monomorphemic ("monomial") names. Moreover, the binomial names characteristic of folk generics elsewhere are not permitted in most Australian languages. Both these characteristics are difficult to reconcile with the universals of folk taxonomy proposed by Berlin and associates (Berlin, Breedlove & Raven 1973; Berlin 1992).

1   Introduction

In this chapter I discuss a portion of the folk taxonomies of two Australian languages of which I have personal experience – Ngalakgan and Wubuy, both spoken in Arnhem Land, in the "Top End" of the Northern Territory.[1] In these languages,

---

1. Ngalakgan is now effectively moribund, the last fluent speaker having passed away in 2004. The data reported on here was collected during the period 1993 (when there were 4 or more fluent speakers) until 2001. Since 2004, I have also carried out fieldwork on Wubuy, which is still spoken by around 100 people (almost all of them adults) in Numbulwar, NT. This language is known as "Nunggubuyu" in the literature (e.g. Heath 1982). More properly, the name Nunggubuyu refers, literally, to the 'people who speak Wubuy'. It cannot be claimed that these societies are untouched by contact with European settlement (see Merlan 1998, for discussion). Nevertheless, the body of knowledge that people in these speech communities appear to possess about indigenous plants is similar in its fundamental features to that of societies with demonstrably less contact, such as the Western Desert people reported on in Goddard & Kalotas (1985).

we find that the vast majority of terms for plant taxa refer to species, not to any more inclusive taxa. Indeed, terms for taxa more inclusive than species are rare. This characteristic appears to be true of the ethnobiological taxonomies of other Aboriginal societies for which we have detailed information (e.g. Anindhilyakwa: Waddy 1988; Lardil: McKnight 1999; Wagiman: Liddy et al. 2006). I argue in the conclusion that the preponderance of terms denoting species can be explained partly on the basis of the unique nature of the Australian flora itself. To my knowledge, the importance of the distinction between the nature of Australian flora, and the botanical environment in other parts of the world, for the structure of folk taxonomies has not been identified before. More generally, the relationship between the structure and diversity of a local plant community and the folk taxonomy that describes that community deserves further study than is possible here. I discuss these systems in Sections 3.1 and 3.2. Berlin and associates in various publications have proposed that there are universal principles to the structure of folk taxonomic systems of classification of the natural world (e.g. Berlin, Breedlove & Raven 1973; Berlin 1992, among others). In Section 3.3, I discuss the extent to which the systems typical of Indigenous Australian groups can be characterised in terms of Berlin's proposals.

In Section 4, we find that names for taxa in Indigenous Australian languages do not have the characteristics we expect of terms for species, since they are almost always monomorphemic (unable to be analysed into smaller meaningful units). Even if we analyse these names as "folk generics" (which typically have monomorphemic names), I demonstrate that Berlin's linguistic principles for the growth of species terms could never be applied to these same Indigenous Australian groups because of inherent constraints on the structure of nominal expressions. Rather, the linguistic behaviour of biological terminology in Indigenous Australian groups argues in favour of their analysis as "rigid designators", as suggested by Cruse (1986: 141). Hence, the fact that taxonomic names in Aboriginal languages are monomorphemic cannot be taken as evidence for their status as folk generics.

In Section 2 which follows, I outline the basic nature of Berlin's system and his claims about universals of folk taxonomy.

2 The Berlin folk taxonomic system

Table 1 sets out Berlin's general system of folk taxonomic levels, together with an example from the folk taxonomy of European plants in English. It will be useful to refer to this example when we come to consider the typical structure of the flora taxonomies of Indigenous Australian groups.

Table 1. Berlin's schema of folk taxonomic systems

Unique beginner	Plant	Level 0
Lifeform	Tree	Level 1
Genus	Oak	Level 2
Species	White oak	Level 3
Variety	Swamp white oak	Level 4

Berlin's chief proposal is that folk taxonomies are organised in terms of folk taxonomic "ranks" – levels in a hierarchy of inclusiveness and contrast. The building block of Berlin's systems of ethnobiological classification is the "folk generic", about which he has to say this:

> The most numerous taxa in folk biological taxonomies will be taxa of generic rank. In both ethnobotanical and ethnozoological systems of classification, the number of folk generics reaches an upper limit at about five hundred to six hundred taxa in systems typical of tropical horticulturalists. Roughly 80 percent of folk generic taxa in typical folk systems are monotypic and include no taxa of lesser rank. While most folk generics are taxonomically included in taxa of lifeform rank, a small number is conceptually unaffiliated due to morphological uniqueness or, in some cases, economic importance. Generic taxa are among the first taxa learned by children as they acquire their society's system of biological classification ... There is some evidence that foraging societies have poorly developed or lack entirely taxa of specific rank. No foraging society will exhibit taxa of varietal rank (Berlin 1992: 23–24).

Berlin claims that folk genera are recognisable on the basis of two characteristics, one linguistic, the other cognitive. The linguistic criterion is that the names are "monomial". This term refers to the idea that folk generic names are not semantically complex, they should consist of a single root morpheme (as in 'oak', above), or a single compound, but unproductive, name such as 'Poison Ivy', 'Dogwood', or 'Stringybark'. In semantic terms, folk genera are referentially simple. By contrast, binomial names such as 'Pin Oak', 'Bluegum', and 'Golden Wattle' are referentially complex. In these names, one part, called the "generic" (in this case *oak, gum, wattle*), names the class to which the referent belongs: These are species from the genera 'oak', 'gum' and 'wattle'. The other part, the specific, helps to differentiate this referent from other members of the same class, and hence, species from the same genus form "contrast sets". Often, the specific element names characteristic attributes of the referent: shape, colour, texture, and taste.

In terms of cognition, folk genera are supposed to correspond to "basic level categories" (e.g. Rosch 1978). The importance for cognition of Berlin's claim about folk generics is that they are a universal category, and that they are the starting point for systems of taxonomic classification. Essentially, Berlin's claim is that humans perceive the natural world in a fundamentally similar way. His claim amounts to a prediction that the "fundamental discontinuities in perception" are at the level of biological genera, at least for flora (Berlin 1992: 9, 68 *et passim*). The objective means by which an observer might determine which are the fundamental discontinuities in a local environment is not clear from Berlin. I discuss this idea in the conclusion, claiming that, in the Australian context at least, the fundamental discontinuities are at the species level in the case of large genera such as *Eucalyptus*.

As an example of how Berlin's system works, I consider here the folk taxonomy of plants for speakers of Australian English. Superficially at least, the Berlin system seems to apply straightforwardly to this taxonomy. The typical case in Australian English seems to be that monomial, basic level categories correspond in fact to biological genera.

(1) In Australian English *gum, wattle, bottlebrush, paperbark* and *tea-tree* are the folk generic labels for biological genera *Eucalyptus, Acacia, Callistemon, Melaleuca,* and *Leptospermum*.

These folk generics do not name particular species, they are labels that can be applied to any species which the observer decides is a member of the genus (whether or not this is in fact the case). (In the conclusion, I show that Berlin's system does not, in fact, make the correct predictions when we consider the system further.)

While, on the surface at least, Berlin's system appears to work for Australian English, when we come to consider the taxonomies of Indigenous Australians we find that the Berlin system produces odd results. It is to these systems that I now turn.

3 Indigenous Australian folk taxonomies

Several Indigenous Australian folk taxonomies have been studied in detail, including those of the Anindhilyakwa (Groote Eylandt: Waddy 1988), Nunggubuyu (Gulf: Heath 1978, 1982), Yankunytjatjara (Western Desert: Goddard & Kalotas 1985), Lardil (Gulf: McKnight 1999), Wagiman (western Top End: Liddy et al. 2006) and various languages of central Arnhem Land (Coleman 1994). They have many fundamental similarities. I will illustrate with material from my own fieldwork on several languages of the Roper River area of southern Arnhem Land.

3.1 The structure of the Ngalakgan plant taxonomy

In Ngalakgan, a traditional language of south central Arnhem Land, we find many features which are typical of the botanical classification systems of Indigenous

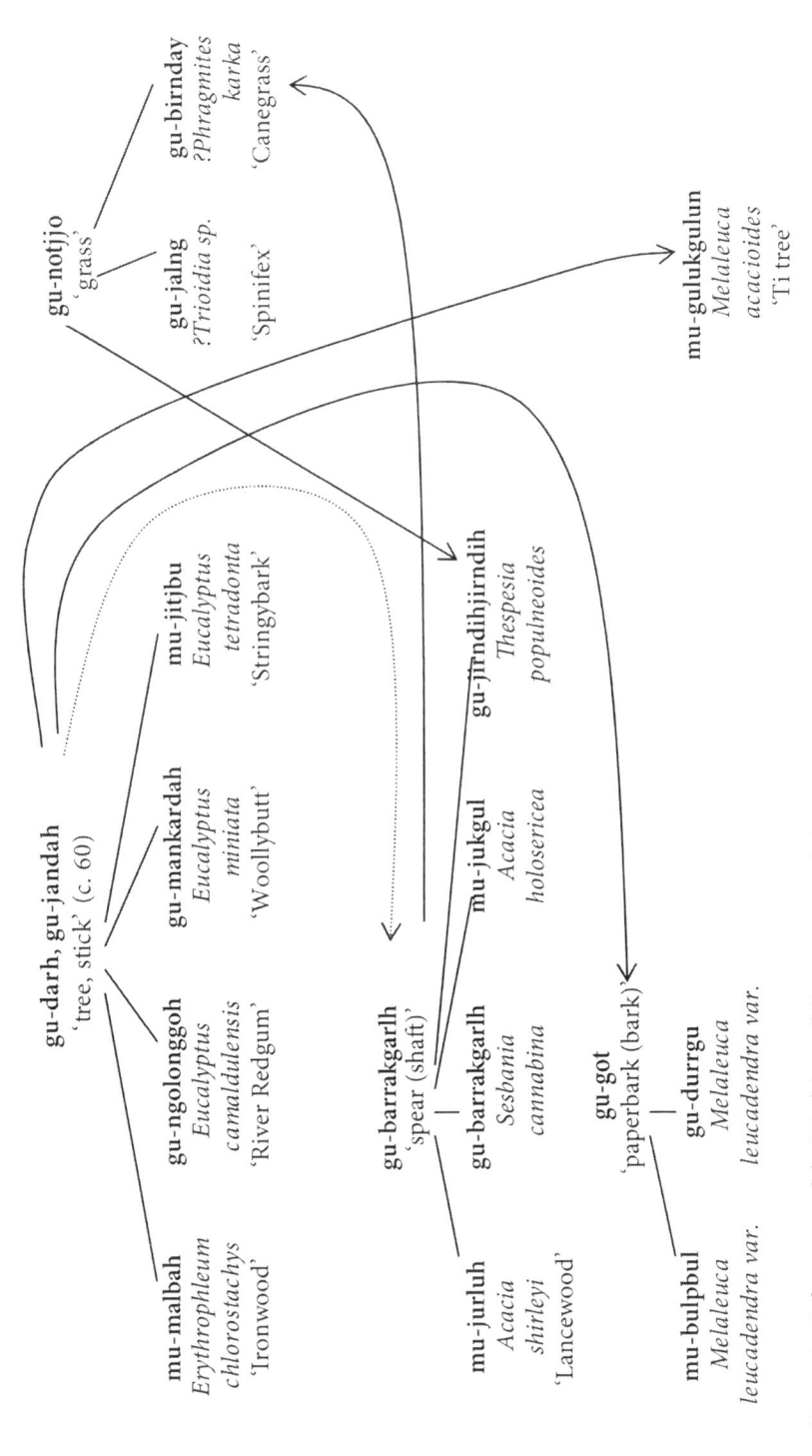

Chapter 11. Ethnobiological classification and the environment in Northern Australia 243

Figure 1. A fragment of the Ngalakgan folk taxonomy of plants

Australians as reported in the literature. Most notably, the taxonomy is relatively "flat": The vast majority of names refer to biological species. There are very few higher level names apart from "lifeform" terms, and often nothing recognisable as a genus name (except in the domain of animals, for which see the following section). The only set of terms which correspond naturally and consistently to biological taxa are the species terms.

Figure 1 sets out a portion of the folk taxonomy of flora in Ngalakgan. It is quite different to that of English and many other languages. The names that we find on this taxonomy do not look like the names we would find on an English folk taxonomy. Apart from the initial gender prefix (which all nouns in Ngalakgan and Wubuy take, optionally), they are all simple names, with no further analysis possible of their meaning.

When we look more closely at the structure, we find that there are no genuine terms for biological genera. All of the terminal names (the names which contain no further subordinate names) refer to species. And most of these terminal names can only be classified by superordinates at the level of 'lifeform' ('tree' or 'grass'), if at all. Even major genera like *Eucalyptus*, *Acacia*, *Melaleuca*, *Ficus*, and *Terminalia* go unnamed, in contrast to the Australian English system exemplified briefly above. Indeed, the entire system of higher-level classification is very sparse. Apart from major lifeform categories 'tree', 'grass', there is little else in the way of higher-level groupings. There is no generic word for 'vine', or 'herb' in Australian languages with which I am familiar (though we get a generic for 'vine' and not for 'grass' in other Australian languages such as Yidiny: Dixon 1977).[2]

At the higher taxonomic levels, the boundary between names for "genuine" biological taxa, and names for other kinds of functional classificatory groups is fuzzy. Apart from the lifeform terms, I argue that the superordinate terms that do exist, are almost always related to function or use rather than (biological) taxonomic classification *per se*. For example, terms such as *barrakgarlh* 'spear' do not name genera, they name a class of flora that can be used for a particular purpose: making spear shafts. In addition, *barrakgarlh* names one common species which is a source of shafts: *Sesbania cannabina*. That is, this species appears to behave like the prototype for the hypernym. Likewise, *gu-got* 'paperbark' is a name of the same kind: It names the useful barks of paperbark species (*Melaleuca spp.*), and can also

---

2. One set of flora does consistently receive a generic label in Top End languages: the waterlilies (*Nymphaea* and *Nymphoides* spp. and possibly other, unrelated spp.), which formed a staple traditionally and are still eaten. In Ngalakgan, the generic term for these is *mu-burpba*, which also refers in particular to the fruit of the mature plant, the most prized part for food. The structure of waterlily taxonomy is exceedingly complex, with all parts of the plant as well as various growth stages commonly distinguished in Top End languages. I have not discussed it in detail here, but see e.g. Heath (1982).

designate trees with this characteristic.[3] Paperbarks with this kind of bark were all used for a particular set of purposes (building shelters, wrapping food, cooking etc.). However, some species and varieties of *Melaleuca* do not have bark which is usable in the same way – the small leaved paperbarks such as *M. acacioides*, *gulukgulun* in Ngalakgan – and are not classified as *gu-got*, though *gulukgulun* does have other uses as a medicine. Other genera, such as *Eucalyptus*, do not have a well-defined set of functions and this is the reason, I would claim, that they lack a hypernymic term.

One notable exception to the generalisation that terminal taxonomic names correspond to species is the set of 'firestick' terms. For example the term *arara* in Wubuy refers to "certain species belonging to the family Verbenaceae. Applied focally to *Clerodendrum inerme* (but not other *Clerodendrum* spp.), and to *Premna acuminata*, but is also applicable to the other *Premna* sp. [which occurs locally] *Premna obtusifolia*" (Heath 1982: 214). A specimen I collected with this name was identified as *Premna acuminata*. I also collected *Clerodendrum floribundum* which has a different name: *alburrunggu-(ining)* (lit. 'belonging to turkeys'). But this species of *Clerodendrum* cannot be called *arara*, because plants called by this name are specifically used for making fire, and *C. floribundum* cannot be used in this way. The plants denoted by the term *arara* are noticeably distinct, even to the untrained eye, and hence this name must be considered to be a label applied to a group of species united in function, rather than a purely biological term.[4]

---

3. Names from Ngalakgan and Wubuy are sometimes cited with an initial gender prefix such as *gu-* or *mu-* in Ngalakgan. These mark categories of nouns similar to the gender categories of European languages such as German. On most nouns, these gender prefixes are optional, depending on context.

4. Since presenting this paper I have been given a copy of Liddy et al. (2006), a documentation of the ethnobiological classification of Wagiman, spoken traditionally in the Daly River area of the western Top End. This work was carried out in collaboration with a linguist and a botanist, and shows that some terms, notably some terms for *Eucalyptus*, *Acacia* and *Ficus* species, refer in fact to more than one botanical species. For instance, the Wagiman term *bolomin* refers to several "white-trunked ghost gums and other white gums: *C. bella*, *E. brevifolia*, *C. confertiflora*, *C. grandiflora*, *C. polysciada*, *E. umbrawarrensis*" (Liddy et al. 2006: 32). These species are very similar in appearance, and may indeed be indistinguishable to speakers (I am not clear on whether this is in fact the case). It is probable that more detailed botanical identification of the denotation of Ngalakgan and Wubuy flora terms would uncover terms with similar ranges of reference. Unfortunately, this must be left to future research. However, the fact that some names may refer to more than one species does not diminish the basic points made in this chapter: that genuine terms for genera do not exist in the ethnobotanical terminology of Ngalakgan or other Australian languages, and that this fact can be related to the nature of the biological system itself in Australia.

One may ask whether terms such as *gu-got* are significantly different in kind from other major classificatory terms such as *mu-may* 'vegetable food'. This term likewise names a class of taxa on the basis of function, rather than biological characteristics. If this is the case, it may be asked to what extent the system of flora classification in Ngalakgan and Wubuy can be considered a "taxonomy" in the classical sense. Cruse (1986: Chapter 6) discusses the formal criteria for taxonomic classification. He concludes that the most general criterion is whether two terms satisfy the relation "is a *kind/type* of". It appears that the relation between, say, *gu-durrgu* (*Melaleuca leucadendra var.*) and *gu-got* is a relation of this kind, but this has not been checked with native speakers. However, functional terms such as *barrakgarlh* 'spear shaft; *Sesbania cannabina*' also satisfy this criterion, even though these are not always used as biological taxonyms. For instance, one can ask 'What kind of spear did you get?' and receive in answer a name for a species which is a source of spear shafts, as in this actual example (Baker 2002a: 69):

(2) a. *Yanah-ba nu-gu-barrakgarlh ju-gu-mehme*?
what-INT MASC-REL-spear 2sS-NEUT-get.PP
Speaker A: 'What kind of/which spear did you get?'

b. *jukgul, mu-jukgul*
A. holosericea VEG-A. holosericea
Speaker B: 'Acacia, an acacia one.'

c. *mu-jukgul ju-gu-mehme*?
VEG-A. holosericea 2sS-NEUT-get.PP
Speaker A: '[Oh, it was] an <u>acacia</u> one that [spear] you got?' [11/9/97]

In this exchange, Speaker B responds to Speaker A's question asking 'What kind of spear did you get?' with a species term, referring to an *Acacia* species which is used (among other things) for spear shafts. On this basis, it seems reasonable to conclude that *jukgul* is a "kind of" *barrakgarlh*, and therefore, that *barrakgarlh* is a hypernym of *jukgul* (and other species names) in a taxonomic relationship.

However, for terms such as *barrakgarlh* and *gu-got* to truly constitute names for levels in a taxonomy, they must in turn be subsumable under higher-level biological terms such as *darh* 'tree'. In the case of *barrakgarlh* this would be difficult to test, since the term is ambiguous between the generic meaning '(any) spear shaft' and its specific application to *Sesbania cannabina*. However, in Wubuy there are also several generic terms for spears and spear shafts, none of which refer polysemously to tree species. These terms cannot be said to be "kinds" of *rangag* 'tree', and hence, it appears that this term at least is not truly part of the biological taxonomy. The situation with *gu-got* 'paperbark tree; paperbark bark' is a little more complicated. This term (as with the Wubuy term *liwa* 'paperbark tree; paperbark

bark') does seem to refer to trees as a biological class, not just the usable bark, and hence *gu-got* can be said to be a kind of *darh* 'tree'. It is therefore not entirely clear how one could restrict taxonomic relationships in Australian languages to just those that are biologically based, if this is even a desirable thing to attempt.

Given this fuzziness between "genuine" superordinate biological taxonomic terms, and superordinate terms of other classificatory bases, is it then problematic to assess such a system in terms of Berlin (1992)? I do not believe so. The existence of some classificatory terms in addition to the genuinely biological ones would not seem to prevent us from assessing those biological names in terms of the degree of "fit" with the Berlin system, and with ethnobiological taxonomies in general. We can regard the functional classificatory terms as names which are in some cases drawn from parallel systems of classification (e.g. *barrakgarlh*) and in other cases partially integrated into the biological system while also classifying taxa on other bases (*gu-got*).

It is worth noting that some (functional) classificatory terms which could potentially exist, do not in fact exist in Ngalakgan or nearby languages. For instance, the class of medicinal plants is relatively well-defined, and there exists a Kriol term *mirritjjin* referring to this class.[5] However, there is no indigenous term for this class in Ngalakgan, Wubuy or any other languages of this area of which I am aware (though we do find such a term in Arrernte: Wilkins 2000). In both languages, speakers use the borrowed term *mirritjjin* to refer to folk medicines.

The numbers of species identified in the Indigenous Australian languages discussed here are comparable with figures provided for other folk taxonomies in Berlin (1992). In Wubuy, Heath (1982) records around 250 names for plants and plant parts. In Anindhilyakwa, Waddy (1988) records around 197. In Ngalakgan, Merlan (1983) and my own fieldwork have recorded around 100 names for flora, but it is clear that this figure does not exhaust the flora terminology.

3.2 Animals and fish

The taxonomy of animals in Ngalakgan is shown in Figure 2. It is quite similar to that of trees. We observe a similar flat structure, with the majority of names corresponding to biological species. However, some important species (like macropods) do have a generic term which happens to correspond to a true biological generic (I argue below that this is accidental). There are several named superordinate

---

5. Kriol is the name given to the vernacular language spoken by the majority of Aboriginal people in the Top End and Kimberley regions (Sandefur 1979). It is an English-lexified creole that attained its present form in the early decades of the 20th century. It is now the biggest Aboriginal language, in terms of numbers of speakers.

classes: *gony* 'macropod', *jerrk* 'bird', *jeny* 'fish', *jamben* 'snake', *nardi* 'frog' and *janayh* 'goanna'.

One characteristic which distinguishes biological fauna from flora is the degree of polytypy: the extent to which genera divide into two or more contrasting species. Most fauna names correspond to what are biologically-speaking "monotypic generics". For instance, *dugurlah* 'ringtailed possum' (*Trichosurus vulpecula*) and *nyuluk* 'native cat' (*Dasyurus hallucatus*) are the only specific representatives of these genera in this region of Arnhem Land. In those cases where there are several species represented, there is evidence of "super-classing", prototypicality, and "skewing" between languages. For instance, we find skewing in the names applied to two species of *Cacatua* (cockatoo) – the White Cockatoo (*C. galerita*) and the Little Corella (*C. sanguinea* or *pastinator*) – both of which are common in the Top End. In Ngalakgan, the name *ngerrk* can be applied to both, but if the two are distinguished, then *ngerrk* applies specifically to *C. galerita*. In other Central Arnhem Land languages, according to Coleman (1994), it is *ngalalak* which is applied in this way, but it also refers specifically to the White Cockatoo (*C. galerita*).[6]

Despite the relative abundance of higher-order terminology in the domain of fauna, there is little to separate the lifeform category (e.g. *jerrk* 'bird') from the generic category (e.g. *janayh* 'goanna') apart from the analyst's biases, since there is little overlap in the sets of referents named by lifeforms and (true) generics. For instance, there are no generic names for classes of birds apart from the lifeform itself, and the folk generics (*sensu* Berlin) corresponding mostly to biological species. Indeed, most of the extant categories which happen to correspond to biological genera (like *gony* 'macropod', *janayh* 'goanna') can alternatively be regarded as names for lifeforms. Goannas and kangaroos both have movement and appearance characteristics that set them apart from other animates, much as birds are set apart by their characteristics as a separate lifeform.

Apart from these lifeform terms, which appear to be genuinely biological, there are also some functional superordinate terms. *Ray* can be applied to any small game animals such as birds and reptiles. The limits of the denotational range of *ray* are not clear, however. Macropods, when discussed as food items, are typically referred to as *gony* rather than *ray*, though they may also be referred to as *janggu* 'meat' after capture (as can any animals included in *ray*). And, using the same test that we applied to *barrakgarlh* 'spear (shaft)' above, we can show that, for instance, any edible species can be considered to be a "kind of" *janggu* 'meat'. Here though,

---

6. It is possible that there has been lexical restructuring in Ngalakgan, such that the original term for White Cockatoo has been replaced with a new term, which is onomatopoeic. In addition, this seems to be a regional difference. As in Ngalakgan, the *ngalalak ~ ngalalek* term is applied to the Little Corella in Jawoyn and Warray also (Mark Harvey, p.c.).

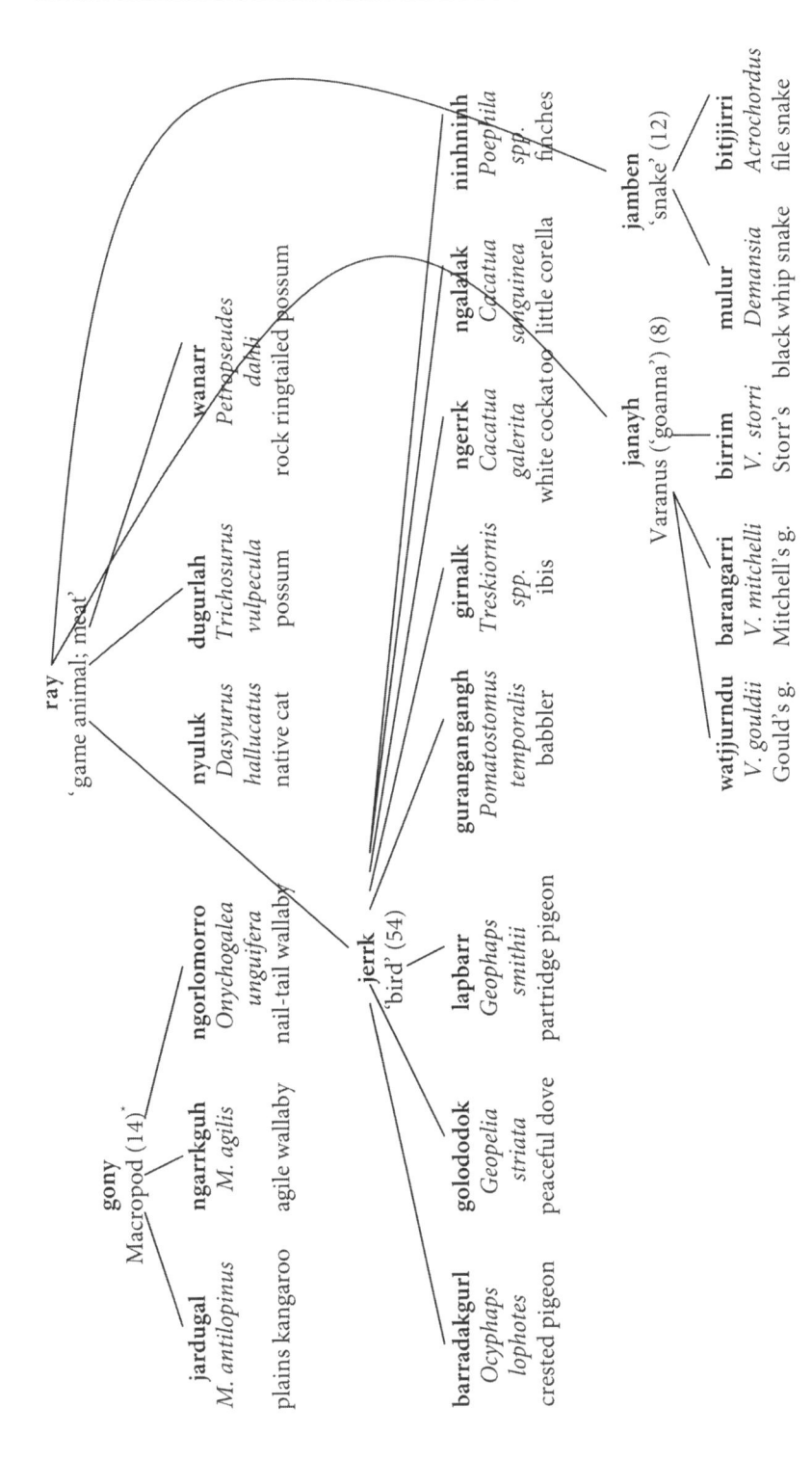

Chapter 11. Ethnobiological classification and the environment in Northern Australia 249

Figure 2. A fragment of the Ngalakgan folk taxonomy of terrestrial and avian vertebrates
*Numbers indicate approximate numbers of each class in the lexicon so far recorded

ray 'game animal; meat'

gony Macropod (14)*
- jardugal *M. antilopinus* plains kangaroo
- ngarrkguh *M. agilis* agile wallaby
- ngorlomorro *Onychogalea unguifera* nail-tail wallaby

- wanarr *Petropseudes dahli* rock ringtailed possum
- dugurlah *Trichosurus vulpecula* possum
- nyuluk *Dasyurus hallucatus* native cat

jerrk 'bird' (54)
- barradakgurl *Ocyphaps lophotes* crested pigeon
- golododok *Geopelia striata* peaceful dove
- lapbarr *Geophaps smithii* partridge pigeon
- gurangangangh *Pomatostomus temporalis* babbler
- girnalk *Treskiornis spp.* ibis
- ngerrk *Cacatua galerita* white cockatoo
- ngalalak *Cacatua sanguinea* little corella
- ninhninh *Poephila spp.* finches

janayh *Varanus* ('goanna') (8)
- watjjurndu *V. gouldii* Gould's g.
- barangarri *V. mitchelli* Mitchell's g.
- birrim *V. storri* Storr's

jamben 'snake' (12)
- mulur *Demansia* black whip snake
- bitjirri *Acrochordus* file snake

there are no superordinate biological categories which include *gony* but not *janggu*, and so the test we applied to *gu-got* 'paperbark' cannot be applied here to *janggu*. Intuitively however, *janggu* classifies animals in a different way to biological terms like *gony* 'kangaroo' and *jerrk* 'bird'. For instance, while we can ask questions such as 'what do birds eat?' (using the generic term *jerrk*) we can't ask this kind of question about *janggu*, though we should be able to if *janggu* were the same kind of thing as *jerrk* 'bird', that is, a biological entity (individual or kind). Whether this test can be applied to *ray* and similar terms in other Australian languages or not is not clear and deserves further investigation.

Taking the null hypothesis then, there are just two levels to the Ngalakgan fauna taxonomy: lifeforms and folk generics. The former name both "true" lifeforms, e.g. *jerrk* 'bird', as well as genera such as *Macropus* and *Varanus*, and potentially also functional labels such as *ray* 'game animal'. The folk generics in many cases name (biological) monotypic genera (e.g. *dugurlah* 'possum', *nyuluk* 'quoll'), but in some cases name species (e.g. *jardugal*, *ngarrkguh* – *M. antilopinus*, *agilis*, respectively). This portion of the Ngalakgan taxonomy then, behaves more like the typical folk taxonomies of foragers discussed in Berlin (1992). The status of the higher superordinate terms, such as *ray* is unclear. Not all animals appear to be regarded as kinds of *ray*, and hence this term does not satisfy the taxonomic criterion for an equivalent term such as "animal", but it does satisfy the taxonomic criterion for a subset of the term "animal".

The taxonomy of fish in Ngalakgan and other Indigenous Australian terminologies is rather different to that of both flora and non-aquatic fauna (Figure 3). In particular, the terms for fish are much less specific than are the terms for either animals or plants. The biological range of fish is similar to that of plants: Many genera are represented by several species. But the terminological characteristics of this domain in these languages are more like that of animals: Names are applied to biological genera, or even families, rather than species. I have represented this difference schematically in Figure 4; see Section 3.3 for further discussion.

When one examines this domain more closely, it is apparent that the denotational range of names is a function of the salience of the species in question. For highly salient species, like catfish, there is much more careful terminological distinction of species than for small, less important species such as *jirrbili* 'bonefish (herrings, anchovies)'.[7] This is what Berlin, Breedlove and Raven (1973) would predict.

---

7. The terminology applied to catfish is quite elaborate in many Arnhem Land languages (see Coleman 1994), but at present understudied in Ngalakgan and the other languages mentioned here.

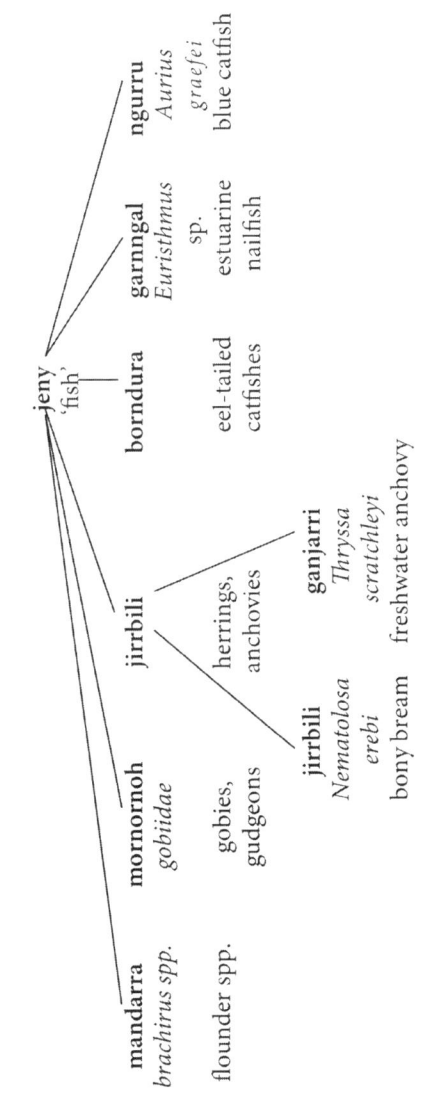

Chapter 11. Ethnobiological classification and the environment in Northern Australia 251

```
                           jeny
                           'fish'
   ┌──────────┬────────────┼────────────┬──────────┐
mandarra   mornornoh    jirrbili     borndura   garnngal      ngurru
brachirus spp. gobiidae              eel-tailed  Euristhmus   Aurius
                                     catfishes   sp.          graefei
flounder spp. gobies,                            estuarine    blue catfish
              gudgeons                           nailfish
              ┌──────────┬──────────┐
           jirrbili              ganjarri
           Nematolosa            Thryssa
           erebi                 scratchleyi
           bony bream  herrings, freshwater anchovy
                       anchovies
```

Figure 3. A fragment of the Ngalakgan folk taxonomy of fish

3.3 Summary: Ngalakgan folk taxonomy and the Berlin system

I now consider how well the data from Ngalakgan fit the Berlin system. What is immediately apparent is that different domains of life display different levels of specificity: trees are possibly the most specific, fish the least, with animals somewhere in between. Figure 4 represents this difference schematically.

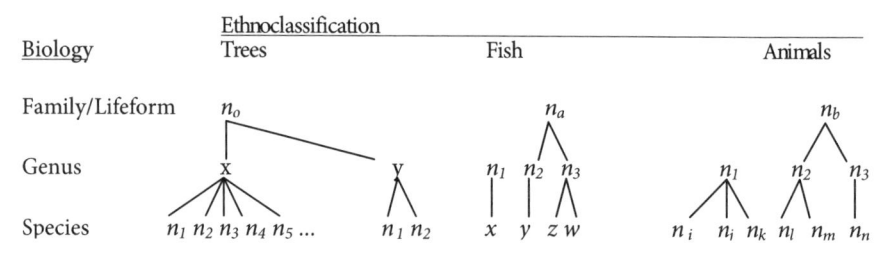

	Ethnoclassification		
Biology	Trees	Fish	Animals
Family/Lifeform	n_o	n_a	n_b
Genus	x y	n_1 n_2 n_3	n_1 n_2 n_3
Species	$n_1\ n_2\ n_3\ n_4\ n_5\ ...$ $n_1\ n_2$	x y z w	n_i n_j n_k n_l n_m n_n

Figure 4. Relationships between names, biological taxa and domains in Ngalakgan. Ethnoclassificatory domains range along the horizontal axis, biological ranks along the vertical axis. The variable n indicates names, variables x, y, z indicate (unnamed) biological taxa

In the domain of flora, there are just two lifeform terms, *darh* (or *jandah*) 'tree, stick' and *notjjo* 'grass'. The majority of names included as kinds of *darh* refer to species (or possibly small groups of species which are indistinguishable in appearance), as far as can be determined. Under the Berlin system, all these names in Ngalakgan would be regarded as folk generics. In many cases, these names do, in fact, refer to biologically monotypic genera, for example *mu-malbah* 'Ironwood' refers to the only species of *Erythrophleum*, and *gu-jalng* the only species of *Grevillea* in this part of the Top End, and hence, any attempt to distinguish "folk generic" from "folk specific" in these cases becomes vacuous. At the other end of the scale, the local species of *Eucalyptus*, *Melaleuca* and *Acacia* all have individual names, and none are collectively grouped under any superordinate names corresponding to any biological grouping, with the exception of the Paperbarks. I argue in Section 5 that these facts follow from the nature of the indigenous flora. In other cases, genera with a handful of closely related species, such as *Syzygium*, or *Ficus*, are nevertheless not labelled with a generic term, rather, all species are distinguished terminologically.[8]

There are 89 names in the Ngalakgan lexicon which are applied to plants. When we consider the biological denotation of these names, 38 refer to taxa which are most probably monotypic genera in this region, but 35 refer to taxa from

---

8. There are several species of *Syzygium* found in the Top End, at this point it is unclear whether some species are classed under one term in Ngalakgan and related languages.

biological genera which are securely polytypic, mostly from just a handful of large genera such as *Eucalyptus, Melaleuca* and *Acacia* (the remainder refer to taxa whose status as polytypic or monotypic I am unsure of). The percentages of names corresponding to biologically monotypic and polytypic genera in the Ngalakgan lexicon are roughly equal, at 40% each. Berlin (1992), following the work of systematic biologists such as Clayton (1972), proposes that in biological systems, scientific classification arrives at a constant of around 64% monotypic genera for plants. This means that what the Ngalakgan choose to name favours monotypy over polytypy. This pattern is predicted by Berlin (1992: 84–86). However, the actual system that we find in Ngalakgan and other Indigenous Australian languages is counter to his broader prediction that very high levels of polytypy, as is found in the genus *Eucalyptus* for instance, should strongly *disfavour* linguistic recognition of separate species of the genus. I discuss this difference further in the conclusion, and argue that the structure of flora found in the Australian environment does not lend itself to the kind of mapping procedure from biological system to linguistic system which Berlin proposes as a universal (1992: 85).

Beyond the lifeform terms, there are few good examples of names that refer to more than one species. Examples such as Ngalakgan *gu-got* 'paperbark', or Wubuy *arara* 'firestick (trees)' refer to groups of species with high functionality. These names do not distinguish genera or families so much as functions. They are associated in each case with specific activities. One says 'I'm going to look for some *gu-got*' with the intention of finding a specimen that can be used for one of the several purposes to which paperbark is put: wrapping food or babies, or making shelter; similarly with *arara*. In either case, what matters is not the identity of the particular species, but its usefulness for the activity in mind. As evidence for this, the Ngalakgan term *gu-got* is also applied to European-imported goods such as (writing) paper, rolling papers (for smoking), and paper money, suggesting that the focal meaning of this term is that of flat papery substances useful for some purpose, rather than a subset of a biological genus. Despite this, as discussed above in Section 3.1, *gu-got* can nevertheless be described as a kind of *darh* 'tree', and so it must be considered to be part of the biological taxonomy, albeit a term with a range that also encompasses denotata which are strictly speaking non-biological.

Unlike the domain of flora, many fish names refer to multiple biological species. Here again, the Berlin system would claim that these names are folk generics, that just happen to refer to biological genera, families or unrelated groups of fish which look or behave similarly (or in some cases are used for similar functions, such as bait).[9] They contrast in this respect with the denotation of tree names in

---

9. It is notable that Waddy (1988) finds many more examples of mismatches between Anindhilyakwa names and biological species in the domain of animates than in that of flora. In the

Ngalakgan. The question is: Why should the names for plants, and more particularly trees, be so specific in Australian languages? I return to this question in the conclusion, and argue that it is an effect of the nature of Australian flora itself.

It is also notable that size of group bears no relation to the existence of labelled categories. Easily the largest group of taxa is insects and arthropods. Yet most Aboriginal languages have very sparse terminology in this domain. Typically there are "lifeform" terms such as 'spider', 'grub', 'caterpillar', 'ant', 'butterfly/moth' which label the entire family or order. Individual genera, let alone species, are rarely named. By contrast, goannas do not form a particularly large group. There are 19 named species found in the NT. Yet generic terms for 'goanna' are not uncommon (e.g. Ngalakgan and Lardil both have one, though not Wubuy or Anindhilyakwa). Presumably, this difference is to be handled under some metric of "salience". I do not discuss this difficult issue further here, although in some cases it bears a relation to economic importance: Traditionally, goannas were important food items in every Aboriginal group in this region, insects were not.

The last observation to be made is that names are monomial at every level, even that of "variety" (as in the two varieties of paperbark commonly named by Arnhem Land groups). I now move on to examine this last point in greater detail, since it is one of the prime criteria used by Berlin (1992) to identify folk generics.

4 Characteristics of names for individuals and kinds

In this section we explore the nature of names for biological taxa in Ngalakgan and Wubuy. I will show that these names cannot be used as evidence for the folk taxonomic rank of their denotata, contra the proposals of Berlin (1992). Rather, names at all taxonomic levels are similar: They are simple, unanalysable names which cannot be compounded with other nouns in order to form more specific ("binomial") names for biological taxa. In this respect, the characteristics of names for biological taxa, which we find to be the norm in Australian languages, are quite different to those of English and many other languages.

In many respects, names for specific biological taxa in Australian languages have similar characteristics to names for persons and places. In fact, species names and place names are both sources of personal names. All three types of names are morphologically simple (that is, unanalysable): They do not consist of smaller

---

domain of flora, the correspondence between linguistic name and biological species is much more exact. The Wagiman system discussed in Liddy et al. (2006) however suggests that more careful botanical work would find instances where terminal folk taxa correspond to several (largely indistinguishable) species. Still, the reason for this common difference in the correspondence of folk taxa and scientific taxa in each domain (as in Figure 4) is worth exploring.

parts which have any recognisable meaning. Example (3) presents some examples of personal names from Ngalakgan people. All traditional personal names in Ngalakgan are taken from one of two sources: names for biological taxa, or names for places (or both).[10]

(3) Personal names in Ngalakgan:
Makgarndah (also the name for a Stringybark (*Eucalyptus*) sp.)
Golokgurndu (also a placename)
Nyuluk (also the name for 'native cat' (*Dasyurus* sp.), also a placename)

Like personal names in English, but unlike English names for biological taxa, these names cannot be directly modified. In English, names for biological genera can often be compounded with higher order generic terms, in order to delimit or constrain the reference of the primary lexeme itself:

(4) gum *tree* (any kind of *Eucalypt*), wattle *bird* (a kind of bird, *Anthochaera* spp. and related spp.), wattle *blossom*, acacia *gum* (exudate from *Acacia*), paperbark *container*

These kinds of constructions are never used in Ngalakgan and Wubuy. There are no examples of this kind (see Baker 2002a, 2002b for further discussion; I have capitalised proper names here where English would likewise use capitalised forms):

(5) a. **bigurr makgarndah*   'stringbark man'
        (i.e the man called 'Stringybark')
    b. **darh makgarndah*   'stringybark tree'
    c. **langga yawurlwarra*   'the billabong called Yawurlwarra'
    d. **gu-jerrk jendewerretj* 'willywagtail bird' (*Rhipidura leucophrys*)
    e. **langga jendewerretj*   'Willywagtail billabong'
    f. **mu-mirh jendewerretj*   'Willywagtail cave'
    g. **gu-gurndu jendewerretj* 'Willywagtail country' [sites associated with the Willywagtail totem]

In Australian languages generally, names for biological taxa are simple names, not complex names. They do not generally involve any element that labels superordinate taxa (such as the equivalent of *pine* or *oak*, to take a Northern Hemisphere example such as *white pine* or *pin oak*). In this respect, Australian languages such as Ngalakgan differ from many languages examined by Berlin, where the existence

---

10. I refer here to the personal names in traditional language which are "open" that is public. Persons also have a number of names which are more or less private or secret and which may be drawn from other domains of reference.

of structures like those in (5) is taken as criterial (in Berlin, Breedlove & Raven 1973) for the identification of rank in folk taxonomies. I quote here at length from Berlin (1992):

> In ethnobiological lexicons, the names for plant and animal taxa are of two basic structural types that can be referred to as *primary* and *secondary plant and animal names*. Each structural type can be distinguished on the basis of linguistic, semantic, and taxonomic properties.
> a. Linguistically, *primary plant and animal names* may be simple (e.g., *louse, frog, oak*), or complex (e.g., *skunk cabbage, forget-me-not, catfish*). In contrast, *secondary plant and animal names* (exemplified by words such as *sugar maple, large-mouthed bass*, and *Stellar's jay*) are always linguistically complex.
> b. Semantic and taxonomic criteria show linguistically complex primary names to be of two structural types, *productive* and *unproductive*. Productive forms include a constituent that labels a taxon superordinate to the form in question (e.g., *catfish, bluebird, bullfrog*). In contrast, none of the constituents of unproductive forms marks a category superordinate to the form in question (e.g. *prairie dog* is not a 'kind of *dog*', *silverfish* is not a 'kind of *fish*').
> c. *Secondary plant and animal names* are linguistically complex expressions, one of whose constituents indicates a category superordinate to the form in question (e.g., *red oak, fox terrier*). However, secondary forms differ from primary productive expressions in that the former occur, with predictable exceptions, only in contrast sets whose members share a constituent that labels the taxon that immediately includes them.
>
> **Generic taxa, and those lifeform and intermediate taxa that are labeled, are generally labeled by primary plant and animal names** (e.g. *snipe, woodcock, oak, redbud, jackass, cockroach, ironwood, breadfruit, tapeworm, bedbug, earwig, mudpuppy*, and *bullfrog*), **while, with specifiable and notable exceptions, subgeneric taxa are labeled by secondary names** (e.g. *blue spruce, spotted salamander, California quail* and *band-tailed pigeon*). (Berlin 1992: 27–28, my emphases)

Names for biological taxa in the Australian languages discussed here are equivalent to Berlin's "unanalysable primary lexemes" (Berlin 1992: 28–29). Moreover, as I show below, these names are primary lexemes at *every level*, even that of variety.

In particular, names for biological genera or lifeforms do not combine with other elements in order to form names for specific taxa. We do not find constructions such as those in (6), the analog of Berlin's "secondary names", being used in Ngalakgan or Wubuy to refer to biological taxa:

(6) a. **gony-ngurlyih*   'black kangaroo'
macropod-black
b. **janayh-nirriget*   'spotted goanna'
goanna-spotted

Ngalakgan and Wubuy do possess compounds of this type, involving names for biological taxa and adjectival modifiers, but compounds are never used to refer to "kinds", they only refer to individuals. The most typical compound consists of a generic noun, including those denoting lifeforms and non-terminal genera, and an adjectival predicate:

(7) a. *gony-ngolkgo*   'big kangaroo/wallaby'
    macropod-big
 b. *langga-ganyah*   'little billabong'
    lagoon-small
 c. *gurndu-yotjjong*   '"clear" (not sacred) country'
    country-not.sacred

Compounds like these do not name kinds (that is, taxa). The compound *gony-ngolkgo* does not refer to a particular *kind of* kangaroo (i.e. a taxon) which is big, it refers to a specific individual which happens to be big, but which may belong to any of the macropod species encompassed by the term *gony*. That is, compounds characteristically predicate contingent attributes, rather than necessary ones, of individuals.

Even in Australian languages which do allow (specific) biological terms to occur in compounded or phrasal nouns, such as Western Desert, these kinds of structures are never used as names of kinds (Cliff Goddard, p.c.). For instance, in Arrernte, specific terms such as *aherre* 'red kangaroo' (*Macropus rufus*) can occur in phrases with generics such as *kere* 'meat' to indicate that a species is being construed as potential prey in the current context (Wilkins 2000: 151):

(8) *Ikwere-nge*   *re-therre*   *perte-ke*   *anteme,*
    3sg.DAT-ABL   3dl-NOM   creep.up-PC   now
    kere   ***aherre***   *ikwere.*
    game/meat   red.kangaroo   3sg.DAT
    'After that, the two of them now crept up on the red kangaroo.'

Just as in Ngalakgan and Wubuy, these phrasal constructions refer to specific individuals, rather than kinds of things. There are no compounded or phrasal nouns of this type which refer to kinds. Terms for biological kinds are overwhelmingly monomial terms, just as in Ngalakgan and Wubuy.[11]

---

11. While it is the norm for biological names to be monomial in Australian languages, I am aware of two classes of exceptions. It is not unusual for Australian languages to have a small class of terms for biological taxa which are formally compounds. For instance, Warray (western Arnhem Land) has names such as *a-lany-bit-tu* 'MASC-tail-coloured-OBL' 'black-footed tree rat', *dum-dingding-u* 'eye-sticky-OBL' 'fish sp – oxyeleotris', literally, these are 'having coloured tail', 'having sticky eyes'. However, these always involve a body part and an adjective. Crucially, they

Some of the more salient animals in Australian languages commonly have names referring to gender or age specific forms. Even these names are monomial. The examples in (9) are taken from Wubuy:

(9) Gender/age specific names for animal taxa (Wubuy: Heath 1982)
  a. Antilopine wallaroo *M. antilopinus* (a kind of kangaroo; other macropod species have similar sets)
     arrjambal — male, or general term
     arndaalburru — female
     lhaanda — young
  b. Bandicoot *Isoodon* sp.
     warnkurag — male/general term
     jurrgurldumburl — female term
     barlwarl — young
  c. Sand goanna (*V. gouldii*)
     wardaabirr — large *V. gouldii*
     wilamawilama — smaller *V. gouldii*
  d. Barramundi (*Lates calcarifer*)
     yinggurlbandi — fully-grown
     ajarrgarlig — young

In short, the Berlin system can only be applied to the Indigenous Australian folk taxonomies under the assumption that the majority of terms are at the level of *folk generic*, even though they label species, or even in some cases varieties or sex- or growth stage-specific forms that are clearly subsumed under more general terms. The linguistic difference between folk taxonomies such as Australian English and the Indigenous Australian system remains unexplained, under the Berlin system.

By making the distinction between monomial and polynomial terms criterial for the distinction between folk generic and folk specific, Berlin is treating a linguistic distinction as a universal. Clearly, the distinction between monomiality and polynomiality cannot have this status.[12]

---

don't involve a biological hypernym (Mark Harvey, p.c.). Arrernte has a small class of similar compounds (John Henderson, p.c.). Secondly, some Australian languages require *classifiers* to precede nouns. In Kugu Nganhcara (Cape York: Johnson 1988), for example, one finds specific names based on phrases involving a classifier followed by the specific name itself, e.g. all fish names start with the classifier for fish *nga'a*. Since all nouns (including generic nouns) require a classifier, these examples do not weaken the generalisation that names for biological taxa are simple names, in Australian languages.

12. Berlin (1992) acknowledges that the polynomiality requirement cannot, in fact, be a universal, retreating from the position put in Berlin, Breedlove and Raven (1973). Nevertheless, he seems reluctant to let go of it, since he favourably quotes Hays (1979) who claims that the excep-

5 Conclusion: Why are the taxonomic systems of Aboriginal societies so different to that of English?

In this section I argue that the major reason why the Berlin system runs into difficulties in characterising the ethnobotanical systems of Indigenous Australia is due to the nature of the Australian flora itself. It is well-known that the Australian environment is unusual in being dominated for much of its extent by just a handful of genera, principally *Eucalyptus* (with over 800 named species), and *Acacia* (with over 1000 named species):

> The Australian flora is usually regarded as unique in the world, chiefly because it contains a high proportion of endemic genera and partly because two genera, *Eucalyptus* and *Acacia*, with a total of over 1000 species, dominate the vegetation over most of the continent. (Beadle 1981: 33)

Moreover, several of the most widely distributed and polytypic genera – *Eucalyptus* (including *Angophora* and *Corymbia*), *Melaleuca, Leptospermum, Lophostemon, Xanthostemon* and *Syzygium* belong to just one family: *Myrtaceae*.

All of the Aboriginal groups surveyed here (except the Western Desert and Arrernte people) have their traditional territories in the Top End region of the Northern Territory, roughly, that portion north of latitude 14°. This region is classified as "Tropical Eucalypt woodland/grassland" and is characterised by the following species, according to the National Vegetation survey (Commonwealth of Australia 2001):

> ... a mix of species *Eucalyptus tectifica* (Darwin box), *E. tetrodonta* (Darwin stringybark), *E. miniata* [Woollybutt], *Corymbia foelscheana, C. latifolia, C. flavescens, C. polycarpa, C. nesophila, C. clarksoniana, C. grandifolia, C. bleeseri, C. ferruginea, Erythrophleum chlorostachys* with an understorey of [various grasses of spp. *Sorghum, Triodia, Chrysopogon* etc.]

Two of these species, *E. tetrodonta* (Darwin Stringybark) and *E. miniata* (Woollybutt) are dominant across the whole of the Top End and Kimberley (Beadle

---

tions to the rule "should not be allowed to obscure the nature and significance of binomialisation as a commonly occurring pattern of folk nomenclature" (Hays 1979: 265, cited in Berlin 1992: 118). Clearly, at least in the Australian case, monomiality cannot be regarded as an exception to the rule. Rather, the rule is that names for biological referents are monomial, at every level. Within Australia, the exception is polynomiality. The only discussion of a case of this type that I have seen is McKnight (1999), who shows that the Lardil simultaneously use several distinct systems of classification. One of these (the ordinary language) has exclusively monomial names. Others (such as the secret initiates' language Demiin), use polynomial names. In the latter case, polynomiality is required because of the extremely impoverished lexicon of the language, leading to massive polynomiality throughout all domains of reference.

1981: 198). But all of the other dominant species belong to the same genus (*Eucalyptus*, or to the closely related subgenus *Corymbia*), with the exception of Ironwood (*Erythrophleum chlorostachys*), the only non-Eucalypt to have anything like the distribution of the Eucalypts in this environment.[13]

As to other species, Brock (1993: 13) characterises the environment of the tropical savannah woodlands thus:

> The most distinctive and wide-ranging eucalypt community in northern Australia ... is dominated by *Eucalyptus tetrodonta* and *E. miniata*, either singly or in combination. Smaller trees in the understorey are patchily distributed e.g. *Erythrophleum chlorostachys*, *Terminalia ferdinandiana*, *T. grandiflora*, *Acacia* spp., *Planchonia careya*, *Buchanania obovata*, *Xanthostemon paradoxus* and *Syzygium suborbiculare*.

It would seem then, that the most natural place to look for "fundamental biological discontinuities" is at the species level, in many cases, in Australian ecosystems. This is because the locally dominant species in almost every Australian ecosystem are drawn from just a handful of genera. Because these species are "dominant", they are impossible to ignore. They are therefore cognitively "salient" for the purposes of naming. In addition, because these dominant species belong to just a handful of genera, the most salient discontinuities just happen to be at the species level rather than the generic level. In other words, I would claim, the individual species belonging to large polytypic genera such as *Eucalyptus*, *Acacia*, *Melaleuca*, and *Ficus* are cognitively equivalent, in terms of the local biological discontinuities, to species such as *Erythrophleum chlorostachys* which locally just happens to be a monotypic genus.

Such a system is not one with which Berlin appears to be familiar, since he explicitly proposes that in families and genera with large numbers of members, it is highly unlikely that individual species will be given simple names:

> At the extreme end of this continuum, families become increasingly dense in that there are large numbers of genera, some of which are monotypic but many of which are further subdivided and encompass several or many closely related

---

13. There is some dispute over the internal classification of what was formerly known as the genus *Eucalyptus* and closely related *Angophora*. Before the publication of Hill and Johnson (1995), the species named as *Corymbia* spp. here were all classified as *Eucalyptus*. Since Brooker (2000), they can again be referred to as *Eucalyptus*, depending on the source cited. Species from all three subgenera share many characteristics, such that many Australians find individual species difficult to distinguish. Notably, the subgenera *Corymbia* does not correspond well to any named groups in either the Australian English folk taxonomy nor in any Aboriginal taxonomies examined here. In this respect it contrasts with *Angophora*, which has a corresponding folk botanical term 'Apple' in Australian English.

species. Taxa comprising families with this structure will share many characters and will be the least distinctive because the gaps separating them have narrowed even further. *The internally diversified polytypic genera complicate the perceptual scene even further. The likelihood of each individual species receiving a separate, "distinctive name", sensu Bartlett, in the folk system is lowest for these perceptually similar classes of organisms*. More generally, one might argue that biologically recognised taxa of any rank showing low levels of polytypy should be more likely candidates for linguistic recognition in a system of ethnobiological classification than taxa showing high levels of polytypy ... (Berlin 1992: 85; my emphasis)

However, such a system, where the species belonging to large, internally-diversified polytypic genera and families are individually named, is exactly what we find to be typical of the Australian folk taxonomies of plants.

We may now consider, in the Australian context, how useful would be a taxonomic system based on the biological generic level, as it is in English-based folk taxonomies. It would seem that names based on the rank of genus would serve little useful purpose in identifying "fundamental biological discontinuities" in the perception of the natural world. More importantly perhaps, the nature of the natural environment in Australia is such that the folk scientist would never begin by naming the genus of *Eucalyptus*, because there are so many distinctive species of the genera that the most natural place to name 'salient discontinuities' is at the species level.

What makes this more plausible is the fact that, in the Roper at least, the various species of Eucalypts are relatively distinct, because 'species in mixed stands commonly belong to different subgenera' (Beadle 1981: 82). The subgenera of eucalypts (for which see Pryor & Johnson 1971) are distinguishable partly on the basis of the bark characters (Beadle 1981: 84) which are used in the Australian English folk taxonomy to distinguish subgroups, even though they have little taxonomic value for biology. The differences between Eucalypts may therefore be perceptually greater than the differences between, say, local species of Maple and Pine in Europe and North America.

Despite the differences between English-based folk taxonomy, as in Table 1, and the Indigenous Australian systems, the Australian environment has also affected the structure of the Australian English taxonomy of Eucalypts. Australian English distinguishes several subgroups of Eucalypts with monomial names (*gum, stringybark, ironbark, peppermint, ash* etc.), see Figure 5. These names are simple, since they cannot ordinarily be combined with a generic term (*stringybark gum, *ironbark gum, *peppermint gum, *ash gum are all infelicitous in Australian English). In Berlin's terms then, they appear to be folk generics rather than folk specifics. For one thing, monomiality is a characteristic of folk generics in many languages. And for another, many of these subgroups, such as *box* and *peppermint ash*, can be further subdivided into what seem to be folk specifics: *yellow box* and *white box, narrow-leaved peppermint ash* and *mountain ash*, respectively. Given the diversity and dominance of Eucalypts in almost every part of the continent, this is a virtual given.

What the Indigenous and the non-Indigenous Australian folk taxonomies have in common then, is an apparent need to distinguish salient discontinuities in the genus Eucalypt below the generic level. This makes both systems distinct from the English-base systems found elsewhere and by Berlin as a virtual standard.

I take this pattern in Australian English as evidence for the position advanced here: that the botanical environment of Australia is sufficiently distinct from the typical European environment so as to demand a different taxonomic strategy from the inhabitants of that environment, whether Indigenous or non-Indigenous. It appears the Australian flora is also distinct from that of the tropical environments studied by Berlin and associates, presumably because none of them are dominated to the same degree by large, internally diverse genera such as *Eucalyptus* and *Acacia*. It remains to be seen whether environments which are similar to the Australian one have comparable effects on folk taxonomic structure.

The structure of ethnobiological classification among Aboriginal societies raises the question of whether the folk taxonomic class "genus" is in fact as universal, or salient, as Berlin has claimed (cf. Brown 1986). The evidence of those Australian languages for which we have data indicates that the prototypical taxon among plants is at biological species rank. To claim that these folk taxa correspond to the folk genera found in other ethnoclassificatory systems is simply to obscure the nature of the differences between them. Terms corresponding to biological generic taxa are ill-developed in the available descriptions of Indigenous Australian folk taxonomies. In many cases, hypernymic terms for groups of species do not, in fact, refer to biological genera at all, but either to lifeforms or to named classes derived from some other kind of classificatory system, with a functional basis ("edible plants", "game animals"). Indeed, the evidence for taxonomic structure in Aboriginal groups for which we have good descriptions is rather sparse, beyond the inclusive categorisation of a subset of the flora and fauna into lifeform and/or functional categories.

Finally, the evidence from Indigenous Australian groups shows rather clearly that the dominance of local flora by species from large, diverse genera such as *Eucalyptus* can have a significant impact on the structure of folk taxonomies, both Indigenous and non-Indigenous. Further work on the relationship between folk taxonomy and the biological environment should enable us to determine how robust this effect is in other human societies.

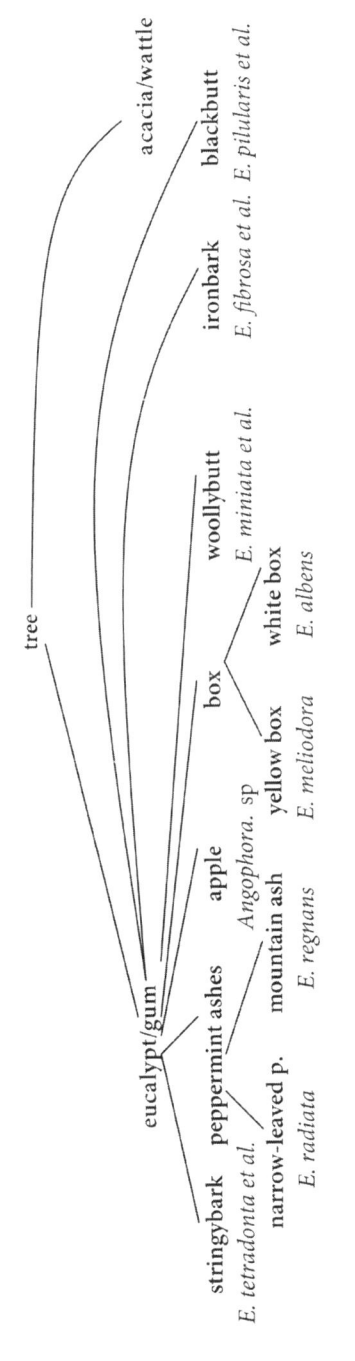

Chapter 11. Ethnobiological classification and the environment in Northern Australia 263

```
                                            tree
                                             |
        ┌────┬──────┬──────┬─────┬─────┬─────┴─────┬──────────┬──────────────┐
   eucalypt/gum                                                           acacia/wattle
        │
 ┌──────┼─────────┬──────────┬────────┬─────────┬──────────┬──────────┐
stringybark  peppermint ashes   apple      box      woollybutt  ironbark   blackbutt
E. tetradonta et al.   │    Angophora. sp            │      E. miniata et al.  E. fibrosa et al.  E. pilularis et al.
         ┌─────┴──────┐                     ┌───────┴────┐
   narrow-leaved p.  mountain ash      yellow box    white box
     E. radiata        E. regnans       E. meliodora    E. albens
```

Figure 5. A fragment of the Australian English folk taxonomy of Eucalypts

Abbreviations

ABL	ablative	OBL	oblique
DAT	dative	PC	past continuous
dl	dual	PP	past punctual
INT	interrogative clitic	REL	relational
MASC	masculine noun class	S	subject
NEUT	neuter noun class	s/sg	singular
NOM	nominative	VEG	vegetable noun class

Acknowledgements

This chapter is based partly on fieldwork carried out in Ngukurr, Urapunga and Numbulwar communities, thanks to the Ngalakgan and Nunggubuyu people there who contributed their knowledge, in particular Didamain Uibo, Langayina and Anne Rami, and †*Nyulpbu*, †*Golokgurndu*, and †*Gerrepbere*. Fieldwork on Wubuy was supported by two University Research Grants from the University of New England. I would like to thank two anonymous reviewers for their extensive comments which greatly improved the chapter. Thanks also to Cliff Goddard, Mark Harvey, John Henderson, Karan Jones, Nick Reid, Andrea Schalley, Ian Smith and Glenn Wightman for discussion of the ideas presented here. Naturally responsibility for any errors remains my own.

References

Baker, Brett. 2002a. How referential is agreement? The interpretation of polysynthetic disagreement morphology in Ngalakgan. In Nicholas Evans & Hans-Jürgen Sasse (eds.), *Problems of polysynthesis* [Studia Typologica 4], 51–86. Berlin: Akademie.

Baker, Brett. 2002b. Let's go to where her backbone is: Placenames in the Roper. In Luise Hercus, Flavia Hodges & Jane Simpson (eds.), *The land is a map: Placenames of Indigenous origin in Australia*, 103–130. Canberra: Pandanus Books/Pacific Linguistics.

Beadle, Noel C. W. 1981. *The vegetation of Australia*. Stuttgart: Fischer.

Berlin, Brent. 1992. *Ethnobiological classification: Principles of categorization of plants and animals in traditional societies*. Princeton, NJ: Princeton University Press.

Berlin, Brent, Dennis E. Breedlove & Peter H. Raven. 1973. General principles of classification and nomenclature in folk biology. *American Anthropologist* 75. 214–242.

Brock, John. 1993. *Native plants of northern Australia*. Chatswood, NSW: Reed.

Brooker, Ian. 2000. A new classification of the genus *Eucalyptus* L'Hér. (*Myrtaceae*). *Australian Systematic Botany* 13. 79–148.

Brown, Cecil H. 1986. The growth of ethnobiological nomenclature. *Current Anthropology* 27. 1–18.

Clayton, William Derek. 1972. Some aspects of the genus concept. *Kew Bulletin* 27. 281–287.

Coleman, Carolyn. 1994. Comparative word lists from Central Arnhem Land languages (Electronic files). Darwin: Department of Education.

Commonwealth of Australia. 2001. Australian native vegetation assessment. Canberra: National Land and Water Resources Audit. URL, downloaded 30 March 2005, http://audit.deh.gov.au/ANRA/vegetation/docs/native_vegetation/nat_veg_contents.cfm.

Cruse, David. 1986. *Lexical semantics*. Cambridge: CUP.

Dixon, Robert M. W. 1977. *A grammar of Yidiny*. Cambridge: CUP.

Goddard, Cliff & Arpad Kalotas. 1985. *Punu: Yankunytjatjara plant use*. Alice Springs, NT: Institute for Aboriginal Development.

Hays, Terence E. 1979. Plant classification and nomenclature in Ndumba, Papua New Guinea Highlands. *Ethnology* 18. 253–270.

Heath, Jeffrey. 1978. Linguistic approaches to Nunggubuyu ethnobotany and ethnozoology. In Lester Hiatt (ed.), *Australian Aboriginal concepts*, 40–55. Canberra: Australian Institute of Aboriginal Studies.

Heath, Jeffrey. 1982. *Nunggubuyu dictionary*. Canberra: Australian Institute of Aboriginal Studies.

Hill, Ken D. & Lawrie A. S. Johnson. 1995. Systematic studies in the Eucalypts 7. A revision of the bloodwoods, genus Corymbia (*Myrtaceae*). *Telopea* 6(2–3). 185–504.

Johnson, Steve. 1988. The status of classifiers in Kugu Nganhcara nominals. *Aboriginal Linguistics* 1. 198–203.

Liddy, Lenny Gappuya, Lulu Dalppalngali Martin, Joe Galwaying Huddlestone, Lena Jululuk (Liddy), Helen Imorrotjba Liddy, Clara Gumbirtbirtta McMah, George Jabarlgarri Huddlestone, Mark Harvey & Glenn Wightman. 2006. *Wagiman plants and animals: Aboriginal knowledge of flora and fauna from the mid Daly River area, northern Australia* (Northern Territory Botanical Bulletin 30). Darwin: Dept. of Natural Resources, Environment and the Arts and Diwurruwurru-jaru, Katherine.

McKnight, David. 1999. *People, countries, and the Rainbow Serpent*. Oxford: Oxford University Press.

Merlan, Francesca. 1983. *Ngalakan grammar, texts, and vocabulary*. Canberra: Pacific Linguistics.

Merlan, Francesca. 1998. *Caging the rainbow: Places, politics and Aborigines in a north Australian town*. Honolulu: University of Hawai'i Press.

Pryor, Lindsay D. & Lawrie A. S. Johnson. 1971. *A classification of the Eucalypts*. Canberra: Australian National University.

Rosch, Eleanor. 1978. Principles of categorization. In Eleanor Rosch & Barbara B. Lloyd (eds.), *Cognition and categorization*, 28–49. Hillsdale, NJ: Erlbaum.

Sandefur, John R. 1979. *An Australian creole in the Northern Territory: A description of Ngukurr-Bamyili dialects*, Part 1 [Work papers of SIL-AAB, B3]. Darwin: Summer Institute of Linguistics.

Waddy, Julie. 1988. *The classification of plants and animals from a Groote Eylandt Aboriginal point of view*. Vols. 1 & 2. Darwin: Australian National University North Australia Research Unit.

Wilkins, David. 2000. Ants, ancestors and medicine: A semantic and pragmatic account of classifier constructions in Arrernte (Central Australia). In Gunther Senft (ed.), *Systems of nominal classification*, 147–216. Cambridge: CUP.

CHAPTER 12

Events masquerading as entities
Pseudorelative perception verb complements in Mawng (Australian) and Romance languages*

Ruth Singer

In Mawng, an Australian Aboriginal language of North-west Arnhem land, perception verbs take a complement clause that is identical in form to a relative clause. Similar "pseudorelative" complement clauses are also used with perception verbs in Romance languages and linguists have puzzled over why languages would express events using a form typically used for entities. I argue that the development of the pseudorelative complement clause in these unrelated languages is the result of common functions of perception verb complements in discourse cross-linguistically. Perception verbs are often used to introduce new participants and situations from the viewpoint of an existing discourse referent.

1   Introduction

This study looks at an unexpected convergence in the expression of perception in Mawng and in some Romance languages such as French. Mawng is a non-Pama Nyungan language of the Iwaidjan language family. Both Mawng and some Romance languages have a type of perception verb complement clause that is identical in form to a relative clause – usually called the pseudorelative (Dik & Hengeveld 1991; van der Auwera 1985). The fact that the pseudorelative formally

---

*   The Mawng data here are from my own fieldwork apart from those examples noted as sourced from Hewett et al. (1990). Those with the code 'C+H' are from Capell and Hinch (1970) and those with the code HH were recorded and/or transcribed by Heather Hinch. Many thanks to Warruwi Community Inc. for supporting this research and Nita Garidjalalug in particular for working with me on this topic. This study has benefited greatly from input by Nicholas Evans, Rachel Nordlinger, Alice Gaby, two anonymous reviewers and attendees at the International Language and Cognition Conference (ILCC) 2004. Special thanks to one reviewer who suggested some structural changes.

resembles a relative clause means that perception of an event is effectively expressed like perception of an entity. The occurrence of the pseudorelative in these unrelated languages suggests that there may be some universal tendencies favouring its development. This study argues that rather than originating from biological universals of sensory perception, the development of the pseudorelative in both language families is the result of common functions of perception verb complements in discourse. Perception verb complements can be used to introduce new discourse referents and new situations through the perspective of an existing discourse referent. There are clear parallels between the use of Mawng and French pseudorelatives in discourse. The fact that the pseudorelative is a fairly rare type of perception verb complement in all the languages that it occurs in supports the theory that it has a specialised discourse status.

Perception can be categorised into three basic types. Perception of an entity involves the use of an object complement as in (1).

(1) *He saw the chicken.*

Immediate perception of an event requires the use of a clausal complement as in (2).

(2) *He saw the chicken cross the road.*

The idea of "immediate perception" is that the experiencer immediately perceives the described event while it is taking place, thus the tense, aspect and mood (TAM) of the complement clause is dependent on the TAM of the matrix clause.

The third main type of perception is mental perception of a proposition. This type of perception is typically encoded by mental state predicates such as *know* but may be encoded by visual and aural perception predicates as they are often metaphorically extended to mental perception. In (3) the visual perception predicate *see* is used with a proposition complement to express mental perception of a proposition.

(3) *He saw that the chicken had been hit by a car.*
(He saw it dead by the side of the road but did not witness it being hit).

Dik and Hengeveld (1991) discuss the semantic differences between the three types of perception described above and their structural correlates in various languages.[1] The contrast between perception of an entity versus perception of an event is important to the nature of pseudorelatives. The distinction between immediate perception of an event and mental perception of a proposition is relevant to describing the difference between Mawng pseudorelatives and Romance pseudorelatives. Both events that are immediately perceived and those that are expressed as propositions will be referred to as "event complements". Where it is necessary to

---

1. I use the term "event" where they use "State of Affairs".

contrast the two types of complements, what is immediately perceived will be referred to as "immediate perception of an event".

Strong patterns in the encoding of perception are found cross-linguistically. There are two main topics that have dominated typological work on perception verb complements. The first is the correspondence between certain semantic distinctions and the syntax of complementation of perception verbs (Dik & Hengeveld 1991; Givón 1980; Viberg 1984). The second topic that has been widely investigated cross-linguistically is the apparently universal tendency for metaphorical extension from the domain of sensory perception to the domain of cognition (Evans & Wilkins 2000; Sweetser 1990; Vanhove & Gaume 2005). This second topic is a minor theme in this study, which concerns itself mainly with the question of why an unusual structure like the pseudorelative would occur in unrelated languages.

In the following section some basic properties of Mawng are introduced and then the three types of complement clauses that occur with perception verbs are described. The formal syntactic structure of complementation in Mawng is not a focus of this study, which looks mainly at the semantic and discourse properties of pseudorelatives. After a detailed account of the three types of complement clause in Mawng, I turn to the Romance pseudorelative, pointing out similarities and differences to the Mawng pseudorelative. Then I develop a functional account of the Mawng pseudorelative. Parallels between the structure of focus sentences and pseudorelatives suggest that pseudorelatives function primarily to express a particular information structure. In this section I develop a theory that Mawng pseudorelatives place focus on the subject of the complement clause as Lambrecht (2002) argues for French pseudorelatives. I then draw parallels with work that has been done on Korean relative clauses and perception verb complements and argue that although the subject of a pseudorelative complement is in focus, the predication in a pseudorelative complement is an asserted rather than presupposed. The unusual form of the pseudorelative results from cognitive constraints on introducing new referents and simultaneously making new predications of them (Lambrecht 1994).

2 An introduction to some relevant features of Mawng

Mawng is part of the Iwaidjan language family which is spoken in an area on the coast east of Darwin in the Northern Territory, Australia. Mawng has about three hundred speakers and is still being acquired by children. Figure 1 shows the area in which Mawng was traditionally spoken, which includes a section of the coast and the two islands North Goulburn Island and South Goulburn Island.

Mawng has five genders. The genders and their articles are listed in Table 1 on the next page.

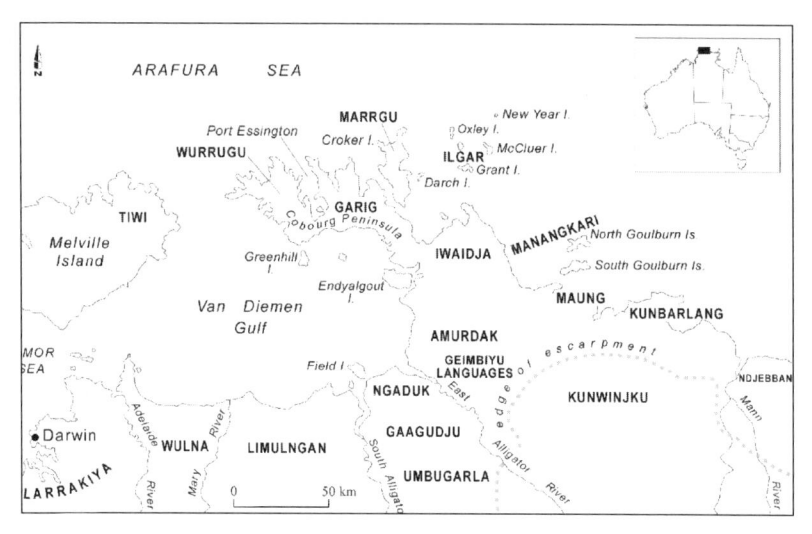

Figure 1. Location of Mawng and nearby languages in the northern part of the Northern Territory. Source: Evans (2000). Note Maung = Mawng

Note that the article *ta* is used for both Land and Edible genders. Gender agreement in all its manifestations is blocked for human plural referents because there are special plural forms for humans which do not indicate gender. If a given form is glossed for gender and has a human referent it should be understood to be singular. Number is not usually indicated for nonhuman referents.

Table 1. Mawng's five genders

ja	MA	Masculine
jita	FE	Feminine
ta	LL	Land gender
mata	VE	Vegetation gender
ta	ED	Edible gender

2.1 The Mawng verb

Mawng verbs cross-reference one or two arguments through the use of a verb prefix. Verbal cross-referencing only indicates gender for third person referents.[2] The transitive verb in (4) shows cross-referencing of a first person singular subject and a third person feminine object.

---

2. The distinction made for transitive subjects is somewhat reduced: Only masculine vs. nonmasculine gender are distinguished. The abbreviation GEN is used for the category "non-masculine".

(4) *Nginy-purru-n.*
    1sg/3FE-know-NP
    'I know her.'

Use of noun phrases to refer to arguments of the verb is optional if the identity of the argument is recoverable from the context or unimportant.

Semitransitive verbs are verbs which only cross-reference their subject but subcategorise for a second argument which is optionally encoded by an oblique pronoun that follows the verb directly. The verb *-alyu* 'hear, feel' encodes the experiencer as the subject and the entity which is the source of the sound as an oblique object as shown in (5).

(5) *K-e-lyu-ø   ngaw.*
    PR-3MA-hear-NP   3GEN.OBL[3]
    'He heard her.'

Complement taking perception predicates may be semitransitives like *-alyu* 'hear/feel' or transitives like *-aya* 'see'. Perception is understood here to include both predicates of sensory perception and cognition. In addition to semitransitive verbs and regular transitives, some of the perception verbs discussed in this study show lexicalised agreement. Lexicalised agreement is an unusual phenomenon found in one fifth of Mawng verbs. It is best understood as the exploitation of the morphological resources usually used in cross-referencing arguments to construct new senses of a verb. The senses created through lexicalised agreement may subcategorise for different sets of arguments. For example, some complement taking perception verbs show Land gender object agreement when they take an event complement. The verb *-wurru* 'think, know' shows the expected masculine object agreement when it is used to mean 'know a person' in (6).

(6) *Punyi k-ini-wurru-n   ja   marryun.*
    father PR-3MA/3MA-think-NP   MA   boy
    'Father is thinking about the boy.' (Hewett et al. 1990)

When *-wurru* 'think, know' occurs with an event complement it shows Land gender object agreement as in (7).

(7) *Ngungpurrun   angku-wurru-ning   [ta   awu-yama-ngung].*
    maybe   3pl/3LL-think-PC   LL   3pl-work-PC
    'They might have been thinking about the work they were doing.'
    (Reciprocals3 031)

---

3. Note that the oblique pronoun also only has a masculine vs. non-masculine gender distinction.

The complement taking verbs -*miyarma* 'want' and -*mulu* 'want to go/do' also show lexicalised Land object agreement when they take event complements. This evidence might suggest that complement clauses are treated syntactically as Land gender which would not be surprising as Land gender is associated with events, thought and speech in diverse ways.[4] However, most transitive verbs that take complement clauses do not alternate between productive agreement and Land gender object agreement like -*wurru* 'think', -*miyarma* 'want' and -*mulu* 'want to go'. For example, the verb -*aya* 'see' has productive object agreement in (8) although it takes an event complement. The matrix verb object agreement cross-references the feminine subject of the complement clause.

(8) *Iny-aya-ntung   ta   iny-arra-ngung   parak.*
    3MA/3FE-see-PC   LL   3FE-go2-PC   AWAY
    'He was watching her walking away.' (Reciprocals3 047)

We cannot predict which verbs will take a Land gender object with an event complement. While -*mulu* 'want to go', -*miyarma* 'want' and -*wurru* 'think/know' have Land gender object agreement when they take a propositional complement, -*aya* 'see' always has canonical agreement. There is not space here for a detailed discussion of lexicalised agreement.[5] The important points to note are:

a. Lexicalised agreement is a widespread phenomenon in Mawng, not restricted to complement taking predicates.
b. Lexicalised agreement patterns are specific to particular lexical items and not predictable from syntactic considerations alone.
c. Lexicalised agreement is only related to argument structure indirectly, through verb sense.

3   The three types of complement clauses in Mawng

3.1   Unmarked complement clauses

The most common type of complement clause lacks any special marking and can occur with any type of complement taking predicate. The complement clause simply follows the complement taking predicate as in (9).

---

4. The fact that events are usually treated as Land gender has probably led to the use of the article *ta* in *ta* complement clauses. See Singer (2006) for further discussion of the semantic basis of Mawng genders.
5. Lexicalised agreement is discussed in detail in Singer (2006).

(9) *Ng-alyu-ngan [a-miraw-ning pata warra kamumu].*
    1sg-hear-pp 3pl-sing-pc PL 3pl women
    'I heard the women singing.' (Hewett et al. 1990)

Note that within unmarked complement clauses the argument noun phrases and the predicate may occur in any order. In (9) the subject noun phrase *pata warra kamumu* 'the women' follows the predicate while in (10) the subject noun phrase precedes the predicate in the complement clause.

(10) *Y-alyu-ngan ja warranyngiw i-wararrke-nang.*
     3MA-hear-pp MA child 3MA-cry-pc
     'He heard a child crying.' (Giant2 010)

3.2 Nominalised complement clauses

The other two types of complement clause that occur in Mawng are nominalised complement clauses. Nominalisation in Mawng is a type of *syntactic* nominalisation similar to that found in Tibeto-Burman languages (Genetti 2006). Syntactic nominalisation is not a process deriving a verbal noun from a verb but a process that makes an entire clause into a nominal.[6] In Mawng nominals include nouns, adjectival nominals and some adverbs. As in Tibeto-Burman languages, nominalised clauses are used as relative clauses, complement clauses and independent clauses in Mawng. Mawng nominalised clauses always begin with an article which is then directly followed by the verb.[7] The Mawng article does not encode definiteness or specificity but rather nominality in general.[8] It is only ever found directly before verbs as part of a nominalisation. The use of the article to nominalise Mawng clauses parallels the use of noun class prefixes to nominalise clauses in Ngan'gityemerri (Reid 1990).

3.2.1 The 'ta' nominalised complement clause

The *ta* nominalised clause is nominalised using the Land gender article *ta*. The *ta* nominalised complement clause has only been recorded with a subset of all complement taking predicates. An example of a *ta* complement encoding immediate perception of an event is shown in (11).

---

6. So Thompson and Longacre (1985) refer to this type of nominalisation as *clausal nominalisation*.
7. Compare with the freer word order in unmarked complement clauses.
8. See Singer (2006) for more on the Mawng article.

(11) Pa   aw-alyu-ngan   ta   ma-warlkanyi-ny.
     P.SEQ   3pl-hear-PP   LL   3VE-fall-PP
     'They heard him fall.' (Giant1 010)

Ta complement clauses can also encode a proposition as shown in (12).

(12) Kayirrk   kung-purru-n   [ta   aw-ura-n-pi   Manawan].
     now   2sg/3LL-know-NP   LL   3pl-go1-PP-TWDS   place.name
     'You know now that they went to Maningrida.' (C+H Text 4: 3)

The article *ta* has a wide range of functions.[9] It is used for Edible and Land gender and with first or second person referents. It also occurs with temporal adverbs, temporal adverbial clauses[10] and locational clauses.

3.2.2   The pseudorelative complement clause

While *ta* complements have only been found with a subset of complement taking verbs, pseudorelatives in turn occur only with a subset of those complement taking predicates which take *ta* complements. A pseudorelative complement clause is shown in brackets in (13) below.

(13) La   naka   ngarrung-purru-n   [ja   naka
     and   DEM.S.MA   1pl.ex/3LL-know-NP   MA   DEM.S.MA[11]
     ja   k-i-maju-ø].
     MA   PR-3MA-die-NP
     'Because we know that someone has died.' (HH Text 2: 16)

---

9. There are many similarities between the use of *ta* and the particle *ga-na* in Marra (Heath 1981). The particle *ga-na* is formally related to the neuter class article *n-ga-na* and is used for first and second persons, subordinate clauses and is also used in focus constructions. The Land and Edible genders in Mawng can be considered to roughly correspond to the neuter class in Marra.

10. Hale (1976) drew attention to the fact that many Australian languages have a single type of subordinate clause which can be either interpreted as a temporal adverbial clause or a relative clause. The result of this is that we might find a sentence that could be interpreted either as 'I saw the emu while it was drinking' or 'I saw the emu which was drinking'. Mawng does not have this ambiguity because temporal adverbial clauses always take the article *ta* whereas the article used with relative clauses varies depending on the gender of its head. In addition relative clauses usually have a head noun, while temporal adverbial clauses only very occasionally have a temporal adverb as a head.

11. This masculine demonstrative 'that' can be used to refer to new participants in addition to given participants.

Note that the complement clause in (13) differs in two ways from a *ta* complement clause. Firstly the article used to nominalise it is the masculine article *ja*. Secondly the nominalised clause is preceded by a "head" noun which also has this article. Pseudorelative complement clauses and relative clauses are formally identical. Both types of clause are nominalised by an article which varies in gender according to the "head".[12] An example of the verb *-wurru* 'think, know' with a real relative clause as entity object is shown in (14) for comparison, note the masculine object agreement in *-wurru*.

(14) *Ngi-wurru-n   [ja   arrarrkpi [ja   ati-ma-ny   parak*
     1sg/3MA-know-NP MA   man   MA   3MA/3ED-take-PP   AWAY
     ta   kurnpi]].
     ED   green.plum
     'I know the man who took the green plums.' (Complement1 096)

We can clearly distinguish pseudorelative complements from relative clauses because *-wurru* 'think, know' has lexicalised Land gender object agreement when it takes an event complement. Example (14) cannot be interpreted as 'I know that the man took the green plums' because of the masculine object agreement in *-wurru*. Similarly, the clause shown in brackets in (13) must be a pseudorelative complement because if it was a relative clause *-wurru* 'think, know' would have masculine object agreement. The alternation that *-wurru* undergoes between canonical and lexicalised agreement shows that pseudorelative complements are event complements rather than a type of object argument.

The key features of the Mawng relative clause are that the head noun always precedes the relative clause and both head and relative clause are preceded by an article agreeing with the head in gender and number. The relative clause functions much like an adjectival nominal. The head of a relative clause can have a wide range of grammatical roles both within the relative clause and within the matrix clause. One key way in which the Mawng pseudorelative differs from the relative clause is that the "head" of a pseudorelative is always the subject of the complement clause predicate. This restriction is also found in Romance pseudorelatives.

Sight verbs seem to be the most common complement taking predicates to occur with Romance pseudorelatives[13] but they do not take pseudorelative complements in Mawng. The verbs *-alyu* 'hear, feel' and *-wurru* 'think, know' are the most common verbs found with pseudorelative complements. These two verbs may seem an odd couple as from a European viewpoint we might expect 'see' and

---

12. This noun is a real head in relative clauses but not in pseudorelatives.
13. Judging from examples of pseudorelatives given in the literature.

'hear' or 'see' and 'know' to pattern together syntactically. In fact in Mawng the verbs for 'hear, feel' and 'think, know' show more similarities. Only *-alyu* 'hear, feel' and *-wurru* 'think, know' can take propositions as complements while *-aya* 'see' cannot. This supports Evans and Wilkins (2000) finding that hearing rather than sight is more often lexicalised as the pathway to the acquisition of knowledge in Australian languages. In Mawng, it is not possible to say something like Example (3): *He saw that the chicken had been hit by a car* because sight is not grammaticalised as a basis for making deductions.[14]

We have already seen that *-alyu* is a semitransitive verb which can take an oblique object to encode an animate source of a sound and that it can occur with both unmarked complement clauses (Example 9) and *ta* complement clauses (Example 11). In addition to being the translation equivalent for 'hear', *-alyu* is also used to express passive tactile perception. An example of *-alyu* being used in this way is shown in (15).

(15) Malany la   aw-alyu-ng   [ta   kunak   ta   an-jirrngu-nang]
     [so then]   3pl-feel-PC   LL   ground LL   3LL-shake-PC
     pata   ngakngak.
     PL   bird.type
     'Then the Ngakngak birds felt the ground shaking.' (AM Text 1: 19)

Although the complement clause in (15) is nominalised by the article *ta* it is a pseudorelative complement rather than a *ta* complement. The article *ta* is used because the "head" of the pseudorelative *-kunak* 'ground' – is a Land gender nominal. The article occurs twice: once before the head and then again before the nominalised clause, whereas in a *ta* complement clause the article only occurs once at the start of the clause. An interesting feature of (15) is that the subject noun phrase *pata ngakngak* follows the pseudorelative complement. Relative clauses are found clause finally. The occurrence of the subject NP after the complement clause in (15) is indicative of the closer bond between the complement taking predicate and the pseudorelative, than a predicate and a relative clause.

Example (15) encodes immediate perception of an event whereas (16) encodes mental perception of a proposition because it is not possible to actually hear people 'wanting'.

---

14. I am discussing syntax and grammaticalisation only here. There is nothing wrong with making inferences in Mawng based on what you can see, but this is not done through complementation. We could say instead: 'This chicken is squashed. It must have been hit by a car.'

(16) La   naka[15]   y-alyu-ngan   pu   [pata arrarrkpi
     and DEM.S.MA   3MA-hear-PP   3pl.OBL   PL   people
     pata angku-mulu-ning   kiyap].
     PL   3pl/3LL-want.to.go-PC fish(MA)
     '(He went down to the shore) Because he heard that some people were thinking of going fishing.' (AM Text 1: 48)

Note that an oblique object pronoun can co-occur with an event complement as in (16). The function of the oblique pronoun with *-alyu* 'hear' when it takes a complement clause is still unclear. For example in (17) the oblique pronoun *nuyu* 'him' does not seem to encode the source of the sound but rather the subject of the complement clause.

(17) Ng-alyu-ngan   nuyu   ta   i-murnangani-ny-ka.
     1sg-hear-PP   3MA.OBL   LL   3MA-return-PP-H
     'I heard of the fact that he returned.' (C+H: 102)

Example (16) is difficult to translate for two reasons, but it is an interesting, complex example worth discussing. Firstly, the verb *-mulu* 'want to go' does not have an exact translation equivalent in English. The verb has lexicalised agreement for a Land gender object so it behaves like a syntactically intransitive predicate with the goal complement *kiyap* 'fish'.[16] Secondly, the use of 'hear' with a *that* complement in the English translation to (16) implies that the subject of the matrix clause, a serpent, heard from somebody else that a group of people were going fishing. In fact the serpent heard one person calling out to some others to come fishing and thus deduced that the group was about to go towards the shore. The problem in finding an adequate translation is due to the fact that when 'perception of a proposition' is encoded by *hear* in English there is an implicature that the proposition was obtained through an intermediary passing on information.[17] This implicature does not exist in Mawng as hearing is grammaticalised as a pathway to the acquisition of knowledge.

---

15. This demonstrative has a discourse function here, providing a logical link between this sentence and the next. *Because* the snake heard that the people were going fishing, he headed to the shore to eat them. Note that *naka* has the same function in (13). The occurrence of *naka* functioning as a logical connective in both examples provides some evidence that pseudo-relatives are typically used for strong assertions.

16. Goal complements like *kiyap* 'fish' occur with intransitive predicates.

17. In addition to the three types of perception I outlined earlier, Dik and Hengeveld (1991) add a fourth type: 'perception of a speech act' which is the type of complement in the English translation.

In summary, there are three types of complement clause in Mawng. The unmarked complement clause type is found with a wide range of verbs. A subset of these take a *ta* complement. A subset of those verbs which take a *ta* complement and express perception can also take the pseudorelative complement. Givón (1980) describes many languages in which differences in the form of perception verb complements correspond to the distinction between immediate perception of an event versus perception of a proposition. Interestingly, all three types of Mawng complement clause can be used for both these types of complements.

4   Pseudorelatives in French and Mawng

There are a number of ways to express perception of an event in French. A complement clause with an infinitive verb can be used as in (18).

(18) French
J'ai   vu   [Paul   fumer].
I have   seen Paul   smoke
'I have seen Paul smoke.' (van der Auwera 1985: 219)

Another option is to use a complement clause marked with the complementiser *que* 'that' as in (19).

(19) French
J'ai   vu   [que   Paul   fumait].
I have   seen that   Paul   smoked
'I have seen that Paul smoked.' (van der Auwera 1985: 219)

A further possibility is to use the pseudorelative as in (20).

(20) French
J'ai   vu   [Paul   qui   fumait].
I have   seen Paul   who   smoked
'I have seen Paul smoking.' (van der Auwera 1985: 220)

Note that in (20) the noun *Paul* follows the perception verb, and is followed by the complementiser *qui*. Example (20) does not mean 'I saw Paul who was smoking', or 'I saw the Paul who smokes' (as opposed to some other person named Paul). It can only mean that I perceived an event, namely Paul smoking. Like the Mawng pseudorelative, the French pseudorelative can only occur with a small number of perception verbs and even with these verbs it has a very restricted distribution.

In (20) the verb in the pseudorelative complement has past tense. A pseudorelative complement can also have present tense as in (21).

(21) French
Marie voit [Roger qui mange les pommes].
Marie sees Roger who eat the apples
'Mary sees Roger eating the apples.' (Noonan Forthcoming)

Note that the tense of the French pseudorelative is always the same as that of the matrix clause, whereas relative clauses are not dependent on their matrix clause for tense (Barron 1999). In (20) both matrix and complement clause predicates are in the past tense and in (21) both matrix and complement clause predicates are in the present tense. French pseudorelatives are only ever used to encode immediate perception of an event and cannot encode propositions, unlike Mawng pseudorelatives.

Pseudorelatives in Romance languages can take a proper noun as their head, which is not possible for restrictive relative clauses (Dik & Hengeveld 1991).[18] An example of a French relative clause is shown in (22) for comparison.

(22) French
Je le connais, celui [qui a écrit ce livre].
I him know him who has written that book
'I know him, the one who has written that book.' (van der Auwera 1985: 224)

Nonrestrictive relative clauses can take a much wider range of heads, including proper nouns. However the intonation pattern is different between matrix clauses and their relative clauses and matrix clauses and their pseudorelative complements. There is a greater intonation break between relative clauses and their matrix clause.[19]

The pseudorelative is also a feature of the Romance languages Italian, Spanish, Catalan and Rumanian (Barron 1999). Example (23) shows an Italian pseudorelative while (24) shows a Spanish pseudorelative.

(23) Italian
Leo ha visto [Clio che mangiava la pizza].
Leo saw Clio who was eating the pizza
'Leo saw Clio eating the pizza.' (Barron 1999: 12)

---

18. It is possible to use a proper noun as the head of a relative clause if the referent of the proper noun is unclear. For example: (i) *I bumped into the Paul who smokes* (here a relative clause is used to distinguish between two possible Pauls).

19. Observed by Anna Wierzbicka for French (pers. comm.). Barron (1999) also notes this contrast for Italian pseudorelatives and relative clauses. There is a lack of descriptive work on the intonation of pseudorelatives. Work similar to that done by Winkler (1997) for secondary predicates would probably have interesting results.

(24) Spanish
Oigo a   [Maria que toca   la guitarra].
 I   hear Maria who is playing the guitar
'I hear Maria playing the guitar.' (van der Auwera 1985: 223)

French, Spanish and Italian pseudorelatives all share the following properties (Barron 1999; Dik & Hengeveld 1991; van der Auwera 1985):

1. Only a small subset of verbs expressing perception and discovery can take pseudorelative complements.
2. Immediate perception of an event is encoded but not perception of a proposition.
3. Perception must be of an observable process, rather than simply a state.

Further afield, Noonan (Forthcoming) reports that the pseudorelative occurs in Lori, an Iranian language, but does not give any examples. In Section 6 I discuss some recent work on structural parallels between internally headed relative clauses and a particular type of perception verb complement in Korean (Kim Forthcoming; Yang 1994).

The pseudorelative complement is the least common type of complement clause of the three that occur in Mawng. Even those perception verbs that can take a pseudorelative take *ta* complement clauses much more frequently. The status of the pseudorelative in Romance languages seems to be similar (van der Auwera 1985). The main difference between the distribution of the Mawng pseudorelative and the Romance pseudorelatives is that Romance pseudorelatives are restricted to sentences encoding immediate perception of an event (Barron 1999) whereas Mawng pseudorelatives can be propositions. So in Romance languages cognition predicates never take pseudorelative complements, whereas *-wurru* 'think, know' does take pseudorelative complements in Mawng.

The pseudorelative is an unusual structure, as it is initially unclear why a minor type of perception verb complement should resemble a relative clause. The appearance of pseudorelatives in Mawng adds weight to those accounts of Romance pseudorelatives which seek to explain its form in functional terms as the formal similarities between the languages are minimal. In the next sentence I look at structural parallels between focus sentences and relative clauses in French and Mawng. These suggest that common discourse strategies have led to the appearance of the pseudorelative in typologically distant language groups.

5. Relative clauses and focus sentences

Pseudorelative complements present a mismatch between form and function. We expect events to be expressed as clauses while entities are expressed as nominals. Yet the pseudorelative looks like a complex NP but encodes an event. Interestingly, the pseudorelative is not the only relative clause-like element that does not actually encode an entity. In both French and Mawng, we find a relative clause-like element is part of special focus sentences. Lambrecht (2002) discusses the occurrence of a relative clause-like element in some French cleft constructions. These are basically similar to English cleft sentences like that in (25) which also have a relative clause-like element.

(25) *It was him [who killed the bus driver].*

Schachter (1973) shows that formal similarities between focus constructions and relative clauses are extremely common crosslinguistically.[20] In Mawng, the main argument focus construction[21] is similar to a French or English cleft construction apart from the fact that it is a nonverbal sentence. Examples of these focus constructions are shown in shown in (26) and (27).

(26) "A   nuka   [ja   ini-wu-ng   [ja   nuka   ja
     ah   DEM.P.MA   MA   3MA/3MA-kill-PP   MA   DEM.P.MA   MA
     manya]]."
     dead.person
     "Ah, this is the one who killed the dead man." (HH Text 2: 74)

In (26) the outer bracket delimits the relative clause like element, while the inner brackets identify an object NP within the relative clause like element.

(27) *Nakapa   [ja   awuni-wa-ny   kani-pa   Weyirra].*
     DEM.NV.MA   MA   3MA/3pl-eat-PP   here-EMPH1   place.name
     'That's the one that ate them at Weyirra.' (AD Text 16: 22)

The major formal difference between pseudorelatives and focus sentences is that the subject of focus sentences occurs without an article. The initial "head" of a pseudorelative has an article, which links it to the relative clause-like part through gender agreement and marks the entire constituent as being a subordinate clause

---

20. Merlan (1981) finds similar structural parallels between subordinate clauses and focus sentences in some Northern Australian languages.
21. I use Lambrecht's (1994) definition of "argument focus construction" here.

rather than an independent focus sentence.[22] The use of relative clause-like elements in Mawng focus sentences points to a possible motivation for the unexpected form of pseudorelative complements; pseudorelative complements may have a different information structure to other complement clause types.

6   Towards a discourse-based account of the Mawng pseudorelative

Perception verb complements provide a means for new situations and participants to be introduced into a narrative through the perspective of a protagonist. So while the subject of focus sentences is usually given, the subject of pseudorelatives is usually new. This suggests that the two constructions have a different information structure. However, Lambrecht (2002) notes some similarities between these two structures in French which can explain the link in Mawng. He points out that both cleft constructions and pseudorelative complement clauses have a similar information structure in that the shared entity argument is the focus of the main clause but the topic of the subordinate clause. In addition, he argues that pseudorelative complements could potentially violate a universal cognitive constraint on introducing a new referent into the discourse whilst simultaneously making a predication of it.[23] He claims that this problem is avoided through the use of a complex sentence construction. Lambrecht's explanation goes some way to explaining the use of Mawng pseudorelatives in discourse.

It is worth having another look at example (16) at this point. This example clearly introduces a new referent into the discourse whilst simultaneously making a predication on it.

(16)   *La   naka   y-alyu-ngan   pu   [pata   arrarrkpi*
      and   DEM.S.MA   3MA-hear-PP   3pl.OBL   PL   people
      pata angku-mulu-ning   kiyap].
      PL   3pl/3LL-want.to.go-PC   fish(MA)
      '(He went down to the shore) Because he heard that some people were thinking of going fishing.' (AM Text 1: 48)

In the story from which (16) is taken, *Yinkarnarrk* – a rainbow serpent – is sleeping when he hears something. The section of text that follows (16) describes how a man called *Natimpala* had gone down to the shore to check the tide and then

---

22. Parallels between non-verbal clauses and nominals are found in many languages, see for example Woodbury (1985).

23. Lambrecht (1994) refers to this constraint as the 'Principle of the separation of reference and relation'.

called out to the rest of his group to hurry up and set their nets before the tide went down. Through perceiving the man calling out, the rainbow serpent deduces that a group of people are heading to the shore, so he heads there and eats them. It is difficult to get an interpretation involving this type of deduction when using the English verb *hear* with a complement clause. This makes it difficult to translate (16) into English. A less literal but more natural English translation would take a form like that in (28).

(28) *He found out [that there were some people [who were about to go fishing]]*.

In order to construct this more natural translation of (16) we had to change the perception verb because *hear* has different properties to *-alyu*. Since both the referent and the predication in the complement clause are new, the referent and the predication are expressed in the form of a noun with a relative clause-like element in the English translation too. This shows that there are strong similarities not only between Mawng and French but also English in the way that new referents can be introduced and predications made on them.

There is one problem with the link that has been made between relative clauses, focus sentences and pseudorelative complements in French and Mawng. The predication in a focus sentence like (25) or (26) is always presupposed whilst the predication in pseudorelatives is an assertion. In English, we find a contrast between restrictive relative clauses like (29) in which the predication is presupposed and nonrestrictive relative clauses like (30) in which the predication is asserted.

(29) *I asked the woman [who lives down the hall] for some sugar.*

(30) *(Where did you get that sugar?) I just bumped into a woman [who gave me some sugar].*

Mawng relative clauses can also be restrictive or nonrestrictive relative clauses. An example of a relative clause with a restrictive meaning was given in (14). An example of a relative clause with a nonrestrictive meaning is shown in (31) below.

(31) *Awuni-ma-ny-apa   pata   arrarrkpi*
      3MA/3pl-get-PP-EMPH1 3pl   Aboriginal
      [*pata marrik ngawun-purru-ø pata wi-ngurlaj*].
      3pl   NEG   1sg/3pl-know-I1 3pl   3pl-name
      'He got those aboriginal people, whose names I don't recall.' (AD Text 7: 4)

Relative clauses in Mawng can contain predications that are either presupposed or asserted. This may explain why relative clause-like forms are used both in focus sentences and as pseudorelative complements.

It was mentioned in Section 4 that in Korean there is also a formal correspondence between a type of relative clause and a type of perception verb complement.[24] Korean has both internally headed and externally headed relative clauses and there one type of perception verb complement in Korean which is formally identical with the internally headed relative clause type (Kim Forthcoming). Yang (1994) demonstrates that the predication in internally headed relative clauses is an assertion. So the type of relative clause which is formally identical to the perception verb complement type in Korean is the one which can be an assertion. In addition to the parallels found between the encoding of perception verb complements in Mawng and Romance languages we find parallels in Korean.

Mawng pseudorelatives contain assertions and their subject is new and in focus so they are more like independent clauses which have whole sentence focus more than argument focus sentences. There is no particular form for whole sentence focus in Mawng. Perhaps for this reason, the form of argument focus sentences has been co-opted into performing the function.[25] Alternatively we could see focus sentences and pseudorelatives as two different developments of the relative clause construction in Mawng. Relative clauses can contain either presupposed or asserted predications. The use of a relative clause-like element in focus sentences has developed from the restrictive functions of relative clauses while the use of a relative clause-like element as a complement clause has developed from the nonrestrictive functions of relative clauses.

One aspect of Mawng pseudorelatives that has not yet been explained is the presence of logical operators in all three examples of pseudorelatives discussed. Examples (13) and (16) begin with *la naka* and (15) begins with *malany la*, logical operators used to indicate a causal link between the events in the sentence they occur in and an event mentioned either before or after that sentence. These logical operators are fairly common but it seems more than a coincidence that they occur

---

24. Another language which shows similarities to Mawng in its complementation patterns is Tsez (Polinsky 2000). In Tsez the matrix verb agrees in gender with its complement clause. There is a default gender used for agreement with a complement clause that has unmarked predicate focus. This parallels the use of the article *ta* in *ta* complement clauses, which seem to have unmarked predicate focus. In Tsez, if an absolutive NP within the complement clause is the topic, then the matrix verb agrees in gender with that argument. This is similar to the variation we find in the gender of the article used to nominalise pseudorelative complements in Mawng. In both languages a default gender is used for complement clauses with unmarked information structure while the gender is controlled by a particular argument of the complement clause when the complement clause has a marked information structure. The difference is that the variable agreement in Tsez is in the matrix verb whereas in Mawng it is in the articles that nominalise the complement clause.

25. Or perhaps the argument focus construction and the sentence focus construction once had the same form, as they do in many languages (Lambrecht 1994).

in all three examples. The presence of these logical operators may be due to the use of pseudorelatives to make particularly strong assertions that have a key role in the development of a narrative.

7 Conclusions

The most common structure used for complementation in Mawng is extremely simple; two linked clauses with no special marking. However, it is possible to encode complementation in very complex ways. There are two types of nominalised complement clauses – *ta* complements and pseudorelatives. In addition to this a number of complement taking predicates show lexicalised agreement for those senses which take clausal complements. This alternation between canonical and lexicalised agreement was shown to be a lexico-semantic process although it might appear to be syntactic. Lexicalised agreement in *-wurru* 'think, know' shows that the pseudorelative is syntactically an event complement clause rather than an entity object.[26]

The pseudorelative which has been studied in the most detail is the French pseudorelative. Romance pseudorelatives differ from Mawng pseudorelatives in that they can only encode immediate perception of an event and the pseudorelative clause is dependent on the matrix clause for tense. Mawng pseudorelatives can encode perception of an event or perception of a proposition and the pseudorelative clause tense can vary from that of the matrix clause. Thus French has greater restrictions on the types of predications that can be encoded by pseudorelative complements. This could be viewed as a limitation on the complexity of new situations that can be introduced simultaneously with new referents. It was also noted that there are differences between the way in which sight and hearing can be construed as pathways to the acquisition of knowledge in French and Mawng. Syntactic possibilities show that while sight can be contrued as a means for acquiring knowledge in French, hearing fulfills this function in Mawng.

The pseudorelative has bamboozled linguists for decades because it takes the form of an entity but encodes an event. However the similarity between the form of the complement clause and an entity argument is superficial and is related instead to the use of relative clause-like elements in constructions such as focus sentences. The link between focus sentences and pseudorelatives is their information structure – they put focus on a referent whilst simultaneously making a predication of it. The differences between the two constructions is that the referent of a

---

[26] This excludes analyses of the Mawng pseudorelative as an entity object with some type of secondary predication of it.

focus sentence is usually given whilst the referent of a pseudorelative complement clause is usually new. In addition, the predication in a focus sentence is usually presupposed while the predication in a pseudorelative complement is asserted. Focus sentences and pseudorelatives are argued to have developed from different types of relative clauses.

Mawng pseudorelatives have many similarities with pseudorelatives in Romance languages despite the great typological differences between the languages. Lambrecht (2002) argues that there is a universal cognitive constraint on introducing a new referent into discourse while making a predication on it. This constraint calls for specialised complex sentence constructions like those complementation structures involving pseudorelatives. The common functions of perception verb complements in discourse have led to a convergence in both form and function in many different languages. The convergence in form exists *within* each language: between relative clauses and pseudorelatives. The convergence in function exists across languages as diverse as Mawng, Romance languages and Korean.

Abbreviations

1	first person	MA	Masculine gender
1PL.EX	first person plural exclusive	NEG	negative preverbal particle or prefix
1PL.IN	first person plural inclusive	NP	non-past tense suffix
2	second person	NV	far/nonvisible
3	third person	OBL	oblique pronoun
AWAY	postverbal directional particle	P	proximal
DEM	demonstrative[27]	PC	past continuous suffix
ED	Edible gender	pl	plural
EMPH1	emphatic suffix for nominals, backgrounding suffix/postverbal particle for verbs	PL	plural article
		PP	past punctual suffix
		PR	present tense prefix
F	future tense form of verbal prefix	S	near speaker/middle distance
FE	Feminine gender	sg	singular
GEN	Non-masculine gender	SEQ	gloss used for the conjunction *la* when it is linking clauses but not translatable as *and* or *but*
H	hither directional suffix		
LL	Land gender	TWDS	postverbal directional particle (towards)
LOC	locative preposition	VE	Vegetation gender

---

27. Demonstratives are glossed with three symbols. The second symbol distinguishes the four paradigms: P (proximal), S (near speaker/middle distance), G (given) and NV (far/nonvisible). These are very rough approximations of their spatial functions. The discourse functions of the demonstratives are not fully understood as yet.

References

Auwera, Johan van der. 1985. The predicate relatives of French perception verbs. In Alide Machtelt Bolkestein, Casper de Groot & J. Lachlan Mackenzie (eds.), *Predicates and terms in Functional Grammar*, 219–234. Dordrecht: Foris.

Barron, Julia. 1999. Perception, volition and reduced clausal complementation. Manchester: University of Manchester PhD thesis.

Capell, Arthur & Heather E. Hinch. 1970. *Maung grammar*. The Hague: Mouton de Gruyter.

Dik, Simon C. & Kees Hengeveld. 1991. The hierarchical structure of the clause and the typology of perception-verb complements. *Linguistics* 29. 231–259.

Evans, Nicholas. 2000. Iwaidjan: A very un-Australian language family. *Linguistic Typology* 4. 1–20.

Evans, Nicholas & David Wilkins. 2000. In the mind's ear: The semantic extensions of perception verbs in Australian languages. *Language* 76(3). 546–592.

Genetti, Carol. 2006. Complementation and complementation strategy in Dolakha Newar. In Robert M. W. Dixon & Alexandra Y. Aikhenvald (eds.), *Complementation and complementation strategies: A cross-linguistic typology* [Explorations in Linguistic Typology 3], 137–158. Oxford: OUP.

Givón, Talmy. 1980. The binding hierarchy and the typology of complements. *Studies in Language* 4(3). 333–377.

Hale, Kenneth. 1976. The adjoined relative clause in Australia. In Robert M. W. Dixon (ed.), *Grammatical categories in Australian languages*, 78–105. Canberra: Australian Institute of Aboriginal Studies.

Heath, Jeffrey. 1981. *Basic materials in Mara: Grammar, texts, and dictionary*. Canberra: Pacific Linguistics.

Hewett, Heather E., Anne Dineen, David Stainsby & Robyn Field. 1990. Maung dictionary project, ASEDA. http://coombs.anu.edu.au/SpecialProj/ASEDA/ASEDA.html.

Kim, Min-Joo. Forthcoming. Internally headed relatives parallel direct perception complements. In Mutsuko Endo Hudson, Peter Sells & Sun-ah Jun (eds.), *The Japanese/Korean Linguistics Conference* 13. Stanford CA: CSLI.

Lambrecht, Knud. 1994. *Information structure and sentence form: Topic, focus, and the mental representations of referents*. Cambridge: CUP.

Lambrecht, Knud. 2002. Topic, focus, and secondary predication. The French presentational relative construction. In Claire Beyssade, Reineke Bok-Bennema, Frank Drijkoningen & Paola Monachesi (eds.), *Romance languages and linguistic theory 2000. Selected papers from 'Going romance' 2000, Utrecht, 30 November – 2 December*, 171–212. Amsterdam: John Benjamins.

Merlan, Francesca. 1981. Some functional relations among subordination, mood, aspect and focus in Australian languages. *Australian Journal of Linguistics* 1(2). 175–210.

Noonan, Michael. Forthcoming. Complementation. In Timothy Shopen (ed.), *Language typology and syntactic description*. 2nd edn. Cambridge: CUP.

Polinsky, Maria. 2000. Variation in complementation constructions: Long distance agreement in Tsez. In Kaoru Horie (ed.), *Complementation*. 60–90. Amsterdam: John Benjamins.

Reid, Nicholas. 1990. Ngan'gityemerri: A language of the Daly River Region, Northern Territory of Australia. Canberra: Australian National University PhD thesis.

Schachter, Paul. 1973. Focus and relativization. *Language* 49(1). 19–46.

Singer, Ruth J. 2006. Agreement in Mawng: Productive and lexicalised uses of agreement in an Australian language. Melbourne: University of Melbourne Phd thesis.

Sweetser, Eve. 1990. *From etymology to pragmatics: Metaphorical and cultural aspects of semantic structure*. Cambridge: CUP.

Thompson, Sandy A. & Robert E. Longacre. 1985. Adverbial clauses. In Timothy Shopen (ed.), *Language typology and syntactic description* 3, 171–205. Cambridge: CUP.

Vanhove, Martine & Bruno Gaume. 2005. Sensory and cognitive perception in a crosslinguistic perspective: A semantic and lexical analysis. *Association for Linguistics Typology* VI. Padang, Sumatra, 21–25 July 2005.

Viberg, Åke. 1984. The verbs of perception: A typological study. In Brian Butterworth, Bernard Comrie & Östen Dahl (eds.), *Explanations for language universals* [Linguistics 21]. 123–132. Berlin: Mouton de Gruyter.

Winkler, Suzanne. 1997. *Focus and secondary predication*. Berlin: Mouton de Gruyter.

Woodbury, Anthony C. 1985. Noun phrase, nominal sentence, and clause in Central Alaskan Yupik Eskimo. In Johanna Nichols & Anthony C. Woodbury (eds.), *Grammar inside and outside the clause*, 61–88. Cambridge: CUP.

Yang, Byong-Seon. 1994. Morphosyntactic phenomena of Korean in Role and Reference Grammar: Psych-verb constructions, inflectional verb morphemes, complex sentences, and relative clauses. Buffalo: State University of New York PhD thesis. Published in 1998 as *Role and Reference Grammar Kaylon (Introduction to Role and Reference Grammar)*. Seoul: Hankuk Publishers.

CHAPTER 13

Word and construction as units of categorization

The case of change predicates in Estonian*

Renate Pajusalu and Ilona Tragel

The functions of four Estonian core verbs – *jääma* 'remain', *minema* 'go', *saama* 'get' and *tulema* 'come' – as change-of-state predicates are discussed. The selection of change verbs in Estonian depends on whether the change is conceived of as negative or positive.

Can we claim that the Estonian data show that there is a category of negative/passive change, expressed by the verb *jääma* in change-of-state constructions or that there is a category in Estonian covering both meanings of *jääma*: 'continuation' and 'negative change'? If we accept the claim that category is represented by the word – the data do seem to support the second view. Various constructions keep the different senses of a polysemous verb apart: constructions, just as lexemes, have categorizing power.

1 Introduction: Word, category, polysemy, construction

Most speakers would claim that categories are typically expressed by means of words. What categories, then, are expressed by polysemous words? The most frequent words in a language tend to be polysemous as their high frequency results from their potential to express a large number of situations, events, relations, etc. The frequent uses of such words lead to new analogies, new functions and new meanings. Several of such words have been "worn out" to such an extent that they are now part of grammar rather than lexicon. The grammaticalization theory explains the emergence of grammatical units in language with some words expressing certain types of relations recurring so frequently that they get shortened and/or affixed to other types of words occurring in the adjacent position, eventually

---

* This study is supported by Estonian Science Foundation grants No. 5813, 6510.

lose their lexical independence and become grammatical elements (Heine & Kuteva 2002). There is, however, a whole range of words which, although they seem to have the potential to develop into grammatical units, have not undergone these developments. In this study we focus on some Estonian frequent verbs, which express change and have, in many cases, highly schematic meanings but which have nevertheless retained their status as independent words. We have dealt with these kinds of words in a larger research project, in which we call them 'core words' (see for example Tragel 2001). If we regard language as a whole, grammar intertwined with vocabulary, these words appear to form the "core" of language. Most of these items have features of semantic primitives (Wierzbicka 1996) – our study, however, is concerned with the words central to the Estonian language, and we do not claim such words are universal.

Defining the independent meaning of a core verb is not a straightforward task. Nor is it easy to capture the range of categories represented by each of these verbs. No semantic description, even a fairly comprehensive one as far as the lexical senses of a word are concerned, can encompass the wide selection of grammatical functions that the verbs express. A cross-linguistic comparison of the functions shows a degree of variation. Some languages express the relations denoted by lexemes in Estonian through grammatical elements. For example, according to *the World Lexicon of Grammaticalization*, the source concept REMAIN is expressed in Portuguese by means of the durative auxiliary verb *ficar*, used to refer to an event that is in progress at reference time, meaning 'keep on doing', 'be doing' (Heine & Kuteva 2002: 255), while the corresponding Estonian verb *jääma* 'remain' is definitely part of the lexicon rather than grammar.

Can we reasonably assume, then, that a speaker combines all meanings of a polysemous word to form a single category corresponding to the word? How do the grammatical functions of a frequent word affect its lexical meaning? Or – assuming there are no clear-cut borders between categories – if a word represents several categories, would the speaker of the language perceive the categories as conceptually closer to one another than if the meaning patterns were different? That is, would the fact that the verb *jääma* in Estonian means both 'change' and 'continue, remain' imply that CHANGE and CONTINUATION are somehow closer concepts for a speaker of Estonian, compared with languages where there is no such polysemy?

Such category "mergers", however, do not seem to be a particularly convenient solution for language users. The case of Estonian change verbs (*jääma* 'remain', *saama* 'get', *minema* 'go', *tulema* 'come'), considered in more detail below, shows that if a word comes to represent a very wide spectrum of senses, the various meanings are likely to become associated with certain restricted contexts (constructions), which helps the speakers to keep the different uses apart. So the various subcategories of meaning and function are represented by the different constructions in (1) (the constructions are discussed in more detail below).

(1) a. *jää-b*   *haige-ks*
       remain-3SG ill-TRANS
       'fall ill' (NOM-change-construction)
    b. *jää-b*   *teh-a*
       remain-3SG do-INF
       'remain to be done' (V3+INF-construction)
    c. *jää-b*   *tege-ma*
       remain-3SG do-SUP
       'stay to do, go on doing' (V+SUP-construction)
    d. *jää-b*   *tege-ma-ta*.
       remain-3SG do-SUP-ABE
       'remain undone' (V+SUP-ABE-construction)

As Eve Sweetser has pointed out: "We are only gradually coming to the full realization that grammatical constructions, like lexical items, not only have meaning but offer fascinating evidence about human conceptual structure" (1997: 116).

Studying the motivation behind meaning extensions and shifts will, thus, provide information about the potential of the particular category: What are the analogies and other mechanisms through which semantic shifts are realized; are there any restrictions on use as to the degree of abstraction (assuming that most verbs have originally denoted well-defined activities of human beings or animals – see e.g. Heine 1997).

Finding such motivation is, however, a difficult task as we are concerned here with very frequent language items expressing very general categories (deeply rooted in our language and mind) with a highly schematic meaning and are, therefore, extremely demanding as to the metalanguage used in description.

2   Expressing change in Estonian: An overview

Change in situations is one of the most important observations in human cognition. To some extent, change is implicit in all sentences with event predicates. If a boy runs across the street, his location is changed; if a field has been sown with grain, the field changes from empty to sown, etc. Taking this argument further, we can also claim that the sentence *The girl was reading a book* expresses a change from ignorance to knowledge and that *The child jumped into the water* expresses a change from a dry to a wet state. In this study, however, we will consider only inherent change constructions, in which change is a natural part of the situation or event described and we do not need any complex reasoning processes to reach the conclusion that a change has taken place. To borrow Frawley's definition of inchoatives: the verbs which describe "entry into a new state from an old state, or the crossing of the boundary of one state into another" (Frawley 1992: 190). From the perspective of time intervals, inchoatives code a "transition from one interval to another, or the crossing of the lower bound of the interval of the new state" (Frawley 1992: 191). We will thus focus on expressions explicitly describing the change in some aspect of the subject. The subject is typically the grammatical subject; in impersonal sentences, the subject may be left implicit.

In Estonian, such situations are described by five verbs (the verb *muutuma* 'change' and the core verbs *jääma* 'remain', *saama* 'get', *minema* 'go', *tulema* 'come'), and a large number of monolexemic verbal derivations. Adding a suffix (in most cases *-stu* or *-ne*) to a stem denoting state is a very productive derivational mechanism in Estonian (see e.g. Kasik 1996: 70–76). *Haige-stu-ma* 'fall ill', for example, has been derived from the nominal stem *haige* 'a sick person' by adding affix *-stu* and *pakse-ne-ma* 'get fatter' from the stem *paks* 'fat' by adding affix *-ne*. Such verbs often have analytic or polylexemic counterparts, formed by means of the verb *muutuma* 'change' or constructions involving one of the four core verbs listed above. *Haigestuma* is synonymous with *haigeks jääma*, lit. 'remain ill', *paksenema* is synonymous with *paksuks muutuma*, lit. 'change fat' or *paksuks minema*, lit. 'go fat', depending on the context. Analytic constructions tend to be preferred in informal language in particular.

The selection of the change predicates thus poses an interesting problem also from a contrastive perspective. Choosing the correct verb for an analytic construction (*muutuma* 'change', *jääma* 'remain', *saama* 'get', *minema* 'go' or *tulema* 'come') causes significant problems for learners of Estonian as a foreign language.

3   Change-of-state constructions in Estonian

3.1   The formation of change-of-state constructions

As the examples with the verb *jääma* 'remain' (1a-1d) show, the meanings of a polysemous verb can be determined by the construction. In this section, we give a more detailed analysis of the constructions formed with the verbs *jääma* 'remain', *saama* 'get', *minema* 'go' and *tulema* 'come' in their change-of-state senses.

There are 14 grammatical cases in Estonian. The first three cases (the nominative, the genitive and the partitive) are formed largely through stem changes; the remaining 11 cases by adding a suffix. In this article, we refer to the cases listed in

Table 1 (for a more comprehensive description of the case system in Estonian, see Erelt 2003: 32–43).

Table 1. Some Estonian Cases

Case	Abbreviation	Suffix	Function
Nominative	NOM	– (unmarked base form)	
Illative	ILL	*-sse*	Motion into something
Elative	ELAT	*-st*	Motion out of something
Allative	ALL	*-le*	Motion onto a surface (in its locative function)
Translative	TRANS	*-ks*	Change into something
Abessive	ABE	*-ta*	Absence of something

The constructions involve, besides nouns, some state adverbials denoting the transfer into a state. There is a group of state adverbs (ADV) in Estonian which vary in form, depending on whether an entity is in a state or is entering a state. Several of such adverbs are formed by means of the suffix *–le*, such as *elevi-le* '(get) excited' (*elevi-l* '(be) excited') but there are exceptions, such as *norgu* '(get) depressed' (*norus* '(be) depressed').

3.2 NOM-change-construction and ELAT-change-construction

The two main change-of-state constructions in Estonian are the NOM-change-construction and, with the verbs *saama* 'get' and *tulema* 'come', the ELAT-change-construction (Pajusalu 1994; Pajusalu et al. 2004). As the word order is quite flexible in Estonian, the components do not necessarily follow the same order as given in the construction formula.

NOM-change-construction
In NOM-change-constructions the change experiencer is in the nominative case; the resulting state is in the translative or in the allative case or expressed by a state adverbial.

    NOM-TRANS–construction (cf. Example 2):
    [[NPnom]   [Vchange]   [NPtrans]]
    [[change experiencer] [change-of-state verb] [resulting state]]
    NOM-ADV–construction (cf. Example 3):
    [[NPnom]   [Vchange]   [AdvP]]
    [[change experiencer] [change-of-state verb] [resulting state]]

NOM-ALL/ILL construction (cf. Example 4)
[[NPnom]   [Vchange]   [NPall/ill]]
[[change experiencer]   [change-of-state verb]   [resulting state]]

(2) a. *Mees saa-b terve-ks.*
       man get-3SG well-TRANS
       'The man gets well.'
    b. *Mees jää-b haige-ks.*
       man remain-3SG ill-TRANS
       'The man falls ill.'

(3) a. *Poiss jää-b norgu.*
       boy   remain-3SG depressed
       'The boy gets depressed.'
    b. *Tüdruk lähe-b elevi-le.*
       girl   go-3SG excited-ALL
       'The girl gets excited.'

(4) a. *Ilm lähe-b vihma-le.*
       weather go-3SG rain-ALL
       'The weather is turning rainy.'
    b. *Haige tule-b teadvuse-le.*
       patient come-3SG consciousness-ALL
       'The patient is regaining consciousness.'
    c. *Naine jä-i mõtte-sse.*
       woman remain-3SG.PST thought-ILL
       'The woman became thoughtful.'

ELAT-change-construction
The change experiencer is in the elative.

[[NPelat]   [Vsaama/tulema]   [NPnom]]
[[change experiencer]   [change-of-state verb]   [resulting state]]

(5) a. *Tüdruku-st saa-b kirjanik.*
       girl-ELAT get-3SG writer
       'The girl will become a writer.'
    b. *Poisi-st tule-b kuulus teadlane.*
       boy-ELAT come-3SG famous scientist
       'The boy will be a famous scientist.'

All these constructions consist of three members. If the word order is neutral, the first position is occupied by the CHANGE EXPERIENCER in the nominative or, in case of the verbs *saama* 'get' and *tulema* 'come', in the elative (i.e. not the grammatical subject), followed by the change-of-state verb *jääma* 'remain', *saama* 'get', *minema* 'go', *tulema* 'come' or *muutuma* 'change'. The third component of the construction is the RESULTING STATE – a lative state adverbial (see Erelt et al. 1995: 92) in the form of an adverb or a NP in the translative or a locative case in the NOM-change-construction; a NP in the nominative in the ELAT-change-construction. The verb *muutuma* 'change' requires a translative RESULTING STATE and can thus be used only in the NOM-change-construction. All three components are mandatory, except in case of change in weather conditions (*läheb vihmale* 'It's going to rain', *jääb vaikseks* 'It's quieting down') or agentless impersonal sentences.

In the NOM-change-construction, the basic three-member schema may be complemented by the PREVIOUS STATE (NP-ELAT) – especially with the verb *muutuma* 'change'. Temporal and spatial adverbials may also be added.

(6) Patsi̬ent **muutu-s** kahvatu-st punetava-ks.
    patient change-3SG.PST pale-ELAT red-TRANS
    'The patient turned from pale to red.'

Both change-of-state constructions can be used also with other verbs. The NOM-change-construction can include almost any change-implying verbs.

(7) a. Mets **kasva-s** suure-ks.
       forest grow-3SG.PST big-TRANS
       'The forest grew high.'
    b. Poiss **trügi-s** esimese-ks.
       boy push-3SG.PST first-TRANS
       'The boy pushed his way past the others and got to the front.'

A similar construction can be used in sentences expressing causality: The CHANGE EXPERIENCER is the grammatical object and a CAUSER is added as the grammatical subject. *Tegema* 'do, make' is a core verb frequently occurring in causal constructions.

[[NPnom]   [Vchange]   [NPelat]   [NP]]
[[causer] [change-of-state verb] [change experiencer] [resulting state]]

(8) a. Kuulsus **tee-b** tema-st narri.
       fame do-3SG 3SG.ELAT fool.GEN
       'Fame is making a fool of him.'
    b. Tema-st **teh-ti** staar.
       3SG do-PASS.PST star
       'She was made a star.'

The use of the core verbs *jääma* 'remain', *saama* 'get', *minema* 'go' and *tulema* 'come' provides a clear example of construction meaning: The verbs have different meanings in other contexts. In addition to the two basic constructions, there are, however, a number of borderline cases in which it is difficult to draw a line between the change-of-state and other meanings of the verbs. Some of such cases will be discussed briefly below. In some cases, these verbs may have senses similar to change-of-state meanings in some other constructions but these cannot be regarded as prototypical.

The verb *muutuma* 'change' differs from the four core verbs occurring in change-of-state constructions in that it is neutral as to the mode of change. *Muutuma* 'change' is not considered here in more detail as it is not a core verb and is not as polysemous as the other verbs discussed here.

As the study focuses on the characteristics of change process, different interpretations of the CHANGE EXPERIENCER (individual and role reading, i.e. whether the change involves a particular individual or a set of individuals; see Sweetser 1997) will not be discussed either. All the verbs under consideration here can be assigned both interpretations, at least in some contexts, which supports the claim that polylexemic change predicates allow a role reading.

4   The change-of-state senses of Estonian core verbs

In the following section of the chapter, we will focus on the change-related meanings of four Estonian core verbs (about Estonian core verbs see Tragel 2003). As pointed out above, there are at least four frequent Estonian verbs (besides the verb *muutuma* 'change') expressing change in certain constructions: *jääma* 'stay, remain', *saama* 'get, receive', *minema* 'go' and *tulema* 'come'. The most productive change-related construction is the NOM-change-construction, which, subject to certain semantic restrictions, can be used with three of the four verbs, as will be shown below.

4.1   *Jääma* 'remain'

The verb *jääma* has at least two central meanings – 'remain, stay, continue (doing something)' and 'change' – which, being somewhat contradictory, may appear at first glance an illogical case of polysemy. This leads easily to ambiguity if sentences are taken out of context: In the sentences below, we do not know whether the girl underwent a change or maintained a particular condition. In most cases, however, such contextless sentences tend to be given a change interpretation. If *jääma* 'remain' does refer to the continuation of a state, the sentence describes a situation which may have changed but did not.

(9) a. *Tüdruk jä-i haige-ks.*
girl remain-3SG.PST ill-TRANS
'The girl fell ill. / The girl continued to be ill.'
b. *Tüdruk jä-i norgu.*
girl remain-3SG.PST depressed
'The girl became depressed. / The girl continued to be depressed.'
c. *Tuul jä-i nõrga-ks.*
wind remain-3SG.PST weak-TRANS
'The wind weakened. / The wind remained weak.'

If the RESULTING STATE is expressed by an adjective in the comparative form, only a change reading is possible:

(10) *Tuul jä-i nõrge-ma-ks.*
wind remain-3SG.PST weak-COMP-TRANS
'The wind got weaker.'

Jääma 'remain' typically expresses the following kinds of change in the NOM-change-construction:

1. (of animate referents) falling ill, getting weaker (i.e. changes regarded as having a negative impact on the EXPERIENCER's well-being). In this sense, *jääma* 'remain' is used with the resulting states *haigeks* 'ill-TRANS', *viletsaks* 'weak-TRANS', *nõrgaks* 'weak-TRANS', *rasedaks* 'pregnant-TRANS', *vanaks* 'old-TRANS', *norgu* 'depressed', *kõhnaks* 'thin-TRANS', *purju* 'drunk', etc.

(11) *Mees jä-i haige-ks.*
man remain-3SG.PST ill-TRANS
'The man fell ill.'

2. (of animate referents) getting more passive: e.g. with the resulting states *vait* 'silent', *rahulikuks* 'calm-TRANS', *mõttesse* 'thoughtful-TRANS', etc.

(12) *Tüdruk jä-i mõtte-sse.*
girl remain-3SG.PST thought-ILL
'The girl became thoughtful.'

3. (of inanimate referents) getting smaller or emptier: e.g. with the resulting states *tühjaks* 'empty-TRANS', *väikseks* 'small-TRANS', *nõrgaks* 'weak-TRANS', *lühikeseks* 'short-TRANS'.

(13) Vii-si-n   möobli   välja ja   tuba   jä-i
     bring-PST-1SG furniture out   and room   remain-3SG.PST
     tühja-ks.
     empty-TRANS
     'I took the furniture out and the room became empty.'

In some cases, change is expressed in such a way as if it had occurred with an inanimate entity, even though the change experiencer was actually a human being and the entity itself remained the same:

(14) a. Kleit   jä-i   väikse-ks.
         dress remain-3SG.PST   small-TRANS
         'The dress got too small.'
     b. Voodi   jä-i   lühikese-ks.
         bed   remain-3SG.PST   short-TRANS
         'The bed got too short.'

The borderline cases include the construction [[V*jääma*] [V-SUP]]. If the verb in the infinitival form denotes a state or a passive activity, such construction is ambiguous (if used out of context) between two readings: 'change into a new state' and 'continuation of an existing state':

(15) Poiss   jä-i   maga-ma.
     boy   remain-3SG.PST   sleep-SUP
     'The boy fell asleep. / The boy went on sleeping.'

The only possible interpretation associated with an active verb is 'continuation' – to imply change (the beginning of an event), the speaker has to use some other verb, such as *hakkama* 'start' (cf. *Tüdrukud hakkasid tantsima* 'The girls started to dance'):

(16) Tüdruku-d   jä-i-d   tantsi-ma.
     girl-PL   remain-PST-3PL   dance-SUP
     'The girls stayed on dancing.'

Change is negative also in such constructions as *ilma jääma* 'to be left without' and *jääma* + [V-SUP-ABE/NP-ABE], as shown in the following examples. As these are essentially negative constructions, there is always some kind of opposition involved: typically between a statement and an earlier assumption. In Example (17a), the speaker has had some reason to believe that the boy gets the money and the book. Such cases can perhaps be analyzed in terms of positive assumptions becoming negative. The same applies to Example (17b): Here the speaker has reasonably expected the book to be read.

(17) a. *Poiss jä-i* **ilma** *raha-ta.*
  boy remain-3SG.PST without money-ABE
  'The boy was left without the money.'
 b. *See raamat jä-i* **luge-ma-ta.**
  This book remain-3SG.PST read-SUP-ABE
  'The book was left unread.'

4.2 Minema 'go'

Minema (stem variants *mine-*, *lähe-* and *läks-*) denotes change in the following three prototypical cases:

1. (of animate referent) involuntary change in mental or physical condition, particularly towards a state of increased agitation (except in case of illness or illness-like conditions, when the verb *jääma* 'remain' is used):

(18) a. *Ta läks närvi.*
  3SG go.3SG.PST nervous
  'He became nervous.'
 b. *Ta läks punase-ks.*
  3SG go.3SG.PST red-TRANS
  'He became red.'
 c. *Süda läks pehme-ks.*
  heart go.3SG.PST soft-TRANS
  'His heart softened.'
 d. *Kala külje-d läksi-d heleda-ma-ks.*
  fish.GEN side-PL go.PST-3PL light-COMP-TRANS
  'The sides of the fish became lighter.'

2. changes of inanimate referents (i.e. changes in which there is no intent on the change experiencer's part), particularly weather conditions. This group may include subjectless sentences:

(19) a. *Taevas läks pilve.*
  sky go.3SG.PST cloud-ILL
  'The sky clouded over.'
 b. *Ilm läks sooje-ma-ks.*
  weather go.3SG.PST warm-COMP-TRANS
  'The weather became warmer.'
 c. *Vesi läks kuu-ma-ks.*
  water go.3SG.PST hot-COMP-TRANS
  'The water got hot.'

d. *Elu läks   raske-ma-ks.*
   Life go.3SG.PST hard-COMP-TRANS
   'Life became harder.'
e. *Lähe-b pimeda-ks.*
   go-3SG dark-TRANS
   'It's getting dark.'

3. (of inanimate referent) change involving increase if the opposite process of decrease is denoted by the verb *jääma* 'remain'. The most typical resulting state is *tugeva-ma-ks* 'stronger-COMP-TRANS' (with *jääma*, *nõrge-ma-ks* 'weaker-COMP-TRANS'). This group provides an example of how the selection of verbs is influenced by the lexical structure of the language as the use of the construction is, at least partly, motivated by the lexical opposition:

(20) a. *Vihm läks   tugeva-ma-ks.*
        rain go.3SG-PST strong-COMP-TRANS
        'The rain became heavier.'
     b. *Vihm jä-i   nõrge-ma-ks.*
        rain remain-3SG.PST weak-COMP-TRANS
        'The rain became softer.'

(21) a. *Lärm läks   tugeva-ma-ks.*
        noise go.3SG.PST strong-COMP-TRANS
        'The noise increased.'
     b. *Lärm jä-i   nõrge-ma-ks.*
        noise remain-3SG.PST weak-COMP-TRANS
        'The noise quietened.'

Minema 'go' can occur in the NOM-change-construction with a RESULTING STATE in the allative (e.g. *ilm läheb sooja-le* 'the weather is getting warmer-ALL', *nägu läheb naeru-le* 'he is smiling', *läheb tuisu-le* 'there's going to be a storm'), similarly to *tulema*, the other motion verb denoting change (see Section 4.4).

In a way, *minema* 'go' expresses change most explicitly, compared with the other three core verbs analyzed in the study, as, unlike *jääma* 'remain' and *saama* 'get', *minema* 'go' is often interchangeble with *muutuma* 'change'. There is, however, a clear distinction in formality: *minema* 'go' sounds much more colloquial (22a) than *muutuma* 'change' (22b).

(22) a. *Ilm   läks   sooje-ma-ks.*
        weather go.3SG.PST warm-COMP-TRANS
        'The weather became warmer.'

b. *Ilm* **muutu-s** *sooje-ma-ks.*
   weather change-3SG.PST warm-COMP-TRANS
   'The weather became warmer.'

4.3 Saama 'get'

Saama 'get' occurs in both the NOM-change-construction and the ELAT-change-construction. The use of *saama* 'get' in these constructions is, however, subject to certain restrictions. The ELAT-change-construction appears to be questionable with an adjectival RESULTING STATE as an adjective does not usually occupy the position of the grammatical subject. The construction with a nominative CHANGE EXPERIENCER is normally not used in cases in which the change cannot be considered the result of purposeful action on the CHANGE EXPERIENCER's part, as in (23e).

(23) a. *Tüdruk* **sa-i** *kuulsa-ks.*
       girl get-3SG.PST famous-TRANS
       'The girl became famous.'
   b. ?*Tüdruku-st* **sa-i** *kuulus.*
       girl-ELAT get-3SG.PST famous
       'The girl became famous.'
   c. *Poiss* **sa-i** *arsti-ks.*
       boy get-3SG.PST doctor-TRANS
       'The boy became a doctor.'
   d. *Poisi-st* **sa-i** *arst.*
       boy-ELAT get-3SG.PST doctor
       'The boy became a doctor.'
   e. ?*Poiss* **sa-i** *kurjategija-ks.*
       boy get-3SG.PST criminal-TRANS
       'The boy became a criminal.'
   f. *Poisi-st* **sa-i** *kurjategija.*
       boy-ELAT get-3SG.PST criminal
       'The boy became a criminal.'

Consequently, both constructions are possible in case of a NP RESULTING STATE, expressing the goal of intentional purposeful action.

Typical uses of *saama* in the NOM-change-construction include the following:

1. (of animate referent) change resulting from intentional purposeful action. This use of *saama* 'get' is related to the modal meaning of *saama* 'can', describing the agent's ability to overcome difficulties and achieve a desired goal.

(24) a. *Sa-i-n   selle   töö   kiiresti teh-tud.*
       get-PST-1SG this.GEN work   quickly   do-PTCP
       'I managed to do the work quickly.'
   b. *Sa-i-me   aja   jooksul   sõbra-ks.*
       get-PST-1PL time.GEN during   friend-TRANS
       'As time went on, we managed to become friends with him.'

2. (of animate referent) change leading to a positive development. Positive evaluation seems to play an even more significant role in the selection of *saama* as the change predicate, compared with the purposeful action criterion – becoming famous, for example, may be unintentional, and yet the verb *saama* 'get' is used. In most cases, however, intention and positive evaluation are closely connected as no one would purposefully aspire to a negative state.

(25) a. *Poiss sa-i   kuulsa-ks.*
       boy   get-3SG.PST   famous-TRANS
       'The boy became famous.'
   b. *Laps   sa-i   lõpuks terve-ks.*
       child get-3SG.PST finally healthy-TRANS
       'Finally the child made a recovery.'

The positive evaluation criterion would also explain the use of *saama* 'get' to refer to changes in a person's age in a neutral, non-evaluative way. By contrast, the use of *jääma* 'remain' implies a negative evaluation.

(26) a. *Vanaisa   sa-i   87-aastase-ks.*
       grandfather get-3SG.PST   87 year-TRANS
       'Grandpa turned 87.'
   b. *Vanaisa   jä-i   äkki   vana-ks.*
       grandfather remain-3SG.PST   suddenly   old-TRANS
       'Grandpa has aged suddenly.'

3. (of inanimate referents) positive change resulting from purposeful human action:

(27) a. *Mõte   sa-i   teo-ks.*
       idea   get-3SG.PST act-TRANS
       'The idea was realised.'
   b. *Tee   sa-i   tuttava-ks.*
       road   get-3SG.PST familiar-TRANS
       'The road became familiar.'
   c. *Asi   sa-i   selge-ks.*
       thing get-3SG.PST clear-TRANS
       'The thing became clear.'

Saama 'get' often appears in the change-of-state construction *valmis saama* 'get ready' – the selection of the verb *saama* 'get' here is not surprising as it is mostly due to human action that something gets ready or completed. The expression, however, can also refer to the ripening of grain and berries – a possible motivation here is 'positivity' in the widest sense of the word, covering purposefulness and increase, as well as positive evaluation.

(28) *Vili   sa-i   valmis.*
     grain get-3SG.PST ripe
     'The grain ripened.'

The changes expressed by *saama* 'get', however, vary in nature and can be explained by the above-mentioned categories only partly. The following sentence, for example, sounds quite natural in Estonian, although the change involved is definitely negative and does not result from any purposeful action:

(29) *Lapse-d   sa-i-d   märja-ks   ja   musta-ks.*
     child-PL get-PST-3PL wet-TRANS and dirty-TRANS
     'The children got wet and dirty.'

4.4   *Tulema* 'come'

Tulema 'come' is a less frequent change-of-state verb, compared with the other verbs analysed here. In certain contexts, however, the verb definitely implies change. These sentences represent the NOM-change-construction, with the RESULTING STATE mostly in the allative (or, in some cases, in the translative). Such changes are also motivated metaphorically: The RESULTING STATE is seen as the goal of the CHANGE EXPERIENCER's motion. So in the examples below, a sick person "comes" into the space of consciousness, the Opposition into the space of power, the deception from the domain of secrecy to that of openness.

(30) a. *Haige   tul-i   teadvuse-le.*
        patient come-3SG.PST consciousness-ALL
        'The patient regained consciousness.'
     b. *Opositsioon tul-i   võimu-le.*
        opposition come-3SG.PST power-ALL
        'The Opposition came to power.'
     c. *Pettus   tul-i   avaliku-ks.*
        deception come-3SG.PST public-TRANS
        'The deception came to light.'

Tulema 'come' is sometimes used also in the ELAT-NOM-construction, referring in particular to acquiring a professional qualification or the skills needed for some occupation. In this domain of changes, *tulema* 'come' is almost synonymous with *saama* 'get'.

(31) a. *Tema-st   tuleb   uurija.*
3SG-ELAT come-3SG reseacher
'He will become a researcher.'
b. *Selle-st   tule-b   suur jama.*
this-ELAT come-3SG big trouble
'This is going to bring about much trouble.'

4.5 Change verbs: A summary

The change-of-state meanings of *jääma* 'remain', *saama* 'get', *minema* 'go' and *tulema* 'come' are not the primary meanings for any of the four verbs. Clearly, the verbs do not form a well-established system – which is not surprising, assuming that the predicates have acquired the change-related senses in the course of a grammaticalization process.

As change predicates, all the four verbs are strongly linked to constructions: They acquire the change-of-state meaning in a restricted number of environments. Looking at the data, it may appear that there are no regularities whatsoever and that, for example, learners of Estonian as a foreign language should simply be provided with lists of words that occur with each of the four predicates. It nevertheless seems to be the case that a native speaker is able to make a semantic distinction between the verbs, even though it is not possible to make four sentences that would differ only with respect to the change predicate: Compared with the others, *tulema* 'come' is subject to stricter selectional restrictions.

In most cases, a particular change-of-state verb is associated with a particular type of change and the categorization system of the language as if provides the speaker with a ready-made option. For example, only (32a) can be used to describe a situation in which someone falls ill, while (32b)–(32d) are unacceptable.

(32) a. *Mees jä-i   haige-ks.*
man remain-3SG.PST ill-TRANS
'The man fell ill.'
b. **Mees sa-i   haige-ks.*
man get-3SG.PST ill-TRANS
c. **Mees läks   haige-ks.*
man go.3SG.PST ill-TRANS

d. *Mees **tul-i**   **haige-ks**.
    man   come-3SG.PST ill-TRANS

In some cases, however, the speaker is allowed more flexibility to choose how to describe a situation. Between the sentences given in Example (33), a native speaker of Estonian perceives the following differences: in (33a) (*jääma* 'remain') Mari's state is conceived of as becoming more passive; in (33b) (*saama* 'get') Mari's retirement is regarded as a positive change – she does not have to work any longer; (33c) (*minema* 'go') is neutral in these respects. The fact that retirement can be described as a positive event (33b) predisposes (33a) and (33c) to a negative interpretation: The speaker did not select the verb *saama* 'get' – consequently, the retirement was not wished for.

(33) 'Mari retired.'
   a. Mari **jä-i**   *pensioni-le*.
       Mari remain-3SG.PST pension-ALL
   b. Mari **sa-i**   *pensioni-le*.
       Mari get-3SG.PST   pension-ALL
   c. Mari **läks**   *pensioni-le*.
       Mari go.3SG.PST   pension-ALL

It is easier to make up sentence pairs with two different change verbs. Examples (34a)–(34b) and (35a)–(35b) all concern weight-related changes. Examples (34a) and (35a) are common, neutral expressions, motivated apparently by the knowledge (today perhaps slightly old-fashioned) that people lose weight as a result of an illness, while gaining weight is a natural process. Examples (34b) and (35b) are not very common and emphasize the person's effort to change her weight: In Example (34b), the girl has probably been dieting; in Example (35b), she has made a conscious attempt to put on weight.

(34) 'The girl became thin.'
   a. Tüdruk **jä-i**   *kõhna-ks*.
       girl   remain-3SG.PST thin-ALL
   b. Tüdruk **sa-i**   *kõhna-ks*.
       girl   get-3SG.PST   thin-TRANS

(35) 'The girl became fat.'
   a. Tüdruk **läks**   *paksu-ks*.
       girl   go.3SG.PST   fat-TRANS
   b. Tüdruk **sa-i**   *paksu-ks*.
       girl   get-3SG.PST   fat-TRANS

While admitting that there are many exceptions (particularly in case of the verb *saama* 'get'), we would like to draw the following conclusion: *jääma* 'remain' expresses (various kinds of) negative change, *saama* 'get' a positive change (with regard to purposefulness and evaluation), and *minema* 'go' a change towards a state of agitation in case of an animate referent and a positive change (with regard to quantity) in case of an inanimate referent. *Tulema* 'come' occurs less frequently as a change-of-state verb and is motivated primarily by its central meaning of deictic motion (in most cases, towards a positive state).

5   Principles for categorizing change in Estonian

The discussion above has shown that change can typically occur towards one of the two poles that can be referred to as the positive and the negative end of a scale. Positivity and negativity here relate to three domains:

1. Quantity (increase-decrease) (cf. *jääma* 'remain' and *minema* 'go');
2. Purposefulness, activity (passive-active): as regards making efforts but also e.g. mental agitation (as opposed to the norm) (*jääma* 'remain' and *saama* 'get');
3. Evaluation of the state of the human being from the EXPERIENCER's point of view (improve-deteriorate) *jääma* 'remain' and *saama* 'get'.

These domains are obviously interrelated. Consider, for example, the construction *jääb haigeks* 'falls ill-TRANS': Falling ill relates to the negative poles in all three domains (in the domain of quantity, the strength decreases; in the domain of activity, the person becomes more passive and from the EXPERIENCER's point of view, illness is obviously always given a negative evaluation).

Why the three domains form such a system can be explained in terms of the metaphor theory by Lakoff and Johnson (1980): The cognitively salient image schema UP-DOWN has metaphorical extensions (partly metonymically motivated) in all the three domains. Evidence from many languages has shown that (1) MORE IS UP; LESS IS DOWN, (2) ACTIVE IS UP; PASSIVE IS DOWN, and (3) GOOD IS UP; BAD IS DOWN (see e.g. Barcelona 2000). Thus all the three domains have the same orientation and they are logically associated with the same scale.

The scalar nature of change provides an explanation for the fact that in a number of cases the selection of the change verb seems to be motivated by lexical oppositions (see e.g. Cruse 1986). Lexical opposition is similarly based on scalarity and relates to the same cognitive schema. Such opposition is clearly inherent in the following cases:

a. *haigeks jääma* 'fall (lit. 'remain') ill-TRANS' – *terveks saama* 'get well-TRANS'
b. *nõrgemaks jääma* 'get weaker-TRANS' – *tugevamaks saama* 'get stronger-TRANS' (of a human being); *tugevamaks minema* (of e.g. weather conditions, lit. 'go stronger-TRANS')

The existence of oppositions is central to the categorization of change as it implies a choice between at least two verbs in each case. By choosing one, the speaker rejects the other. All cases in which change is expressed by *jääma* 'remain' involve the rejection of the verb *saama* 'get', implying an active role for the EXPERIENCER. These choices may be established in language but there are also cases in which the speaker has to make a deliberate choice in each instance (34) and (35).

Change is described in language mainly from the AGENT's or the EXPERIENCER's point of view: The selection of change predicates depends on whether an agent or a patient has an active or a passive role in the change or whether the change is evaluated as negative or positive.

The EXPERIENCER's position may be taken up by an inanimate entity which, in fact, undergoes no change whatsoever. What changes is the human agent or rather their relationship with the inanimate entity. The situation is categorized, however, as if the change was experienced by the inanimate object involved (36) which, if taken literally, is downright wrong – neither the dress nor the road do undergo any changes.

(36) a. *Kleit jä-i väikse-ks.*
    dress remain-3SG.PST small-TRANS
    'The dress got too small.'
  b. *Tee sa-i tuttava-ks.*
    road get-3SG.PST familiar-TRANS
    'The road became familiar.'

The change is perceived by the human agent; in (36a), the person cannot fit in the dress any longer; in (36b), the road has been taken several times before and the speaker has become familiar with it.

Change is expressed by polysemous words and the change-of-state meaning is realized through constructions: Without the existence of such well-established constructions, it would be fairly complicated to understand in which meaning a given verb is being used. While the Estonian language, with its relatively large number of cases – 14 – provides very good opportunities for the emergence of such constructions, change (from the perspective of resultativeness) has been analysed as a typical construction meaning also in languages with no morphologically marked cases (e.g. Goldberg 1995). As has been mentioned above, research on the cognitive status and categorizing power is still at an early stage.

The most problematic case is presented by the verb *jääma* 'remain'. Can we claim that for speakers of Estonian there is a category of negative/passive change, expressed by the verb *jääma* 'remain' in change-of-state constructions or that there is a category in Estonian covering both meanings of *jääma*: 'continuation' and 'negative change', as suggested by the identity of form?

While we do not have the means to provide a conclusive answer to this question, it seems that for a speaker of Estonian 'negative change' is closer to 'continuation', compared with speakers of languages which do not have a similar case of polysemy.[1] Tuomas Huumo has written about the counterpart of *jääma* 'remain' in Finnish (closely related to Estonian) that although the verb itself does not appear to express change (unlike the Estonian verb, the Finnish verb carries no explicit change-of-state meaning), the apparently static meaning of the word paradoxically does imply change: There has been a possibility for change but it has not been realized (Huumo 2007). Similarly, Estonian *jääma* 'remain' in the continuation sense suggests a change in assumptions: The speaker has expected that a situation may change but it has not. This means that change and continuation may be of a less contradictory nature than they appear to be and not as mutually exclusive within a single category.

6 Conclusion

In this study, we discussed the functions of four of the top-frequency and most polysemous verbs (core verbs) of Estonian – *jääma* 'remain', *minema* 'go', *saama* 'get' and *tulema* 'come' – as change-of-state predicates. We found that the selection of change verbs in Estonian depends on whether the change is conceived of as negative or positive (on the scales of quantity or activity and, to a certain extent, evaluation). Within positive changes, a further distinction is drawn between active purposeful changes and involuntary changes. So we may say that in Estonian, the categorization of change is based on a scale of positive-negative change. Positive change is categorized in terms of an increase in quantity or activity, evaluated as positive by human beings. Negative change, by contrast, is categorized in terms of a decrease in quantity or activity, evaluated as negative.

Various constructions help to keep the different senses of a polysemous verb apart as constructions have categorizing power. Interpretation in terms of lexemes and constructions may lead to different category structures: E.g. in case of *jääma* 'remain', CHANGE and CONTINUATION are covered by the same category (or two categories with fuzzy borders) at the level of the lexeme, while at the level of

---

1. Similar polysemy is also found in Germanic languages (Rosenthal 1984).

the construction, there is a clearer distinction as two readings are possible only in one type of construction.

Abbrevations

1, 2, 3	person	NOM	nominative
ABE	abessive	PL	plural
ADV	adverb	PST	past tense
COMP	comparative	PTCP	participle
ELAT	elative	SG	singular
ILL	illative	SUP	supine
INF	infinitve	TRANS	translative

References

Barcelona, Antonio. 2000. *Metaphor and metonymy at the crossroads. A cognitive perspective.* Berlin: Mouton de Gruyter.

Cruse, David A. 1986. *Lexical semantics.* Cambridge: CUP.

Erelt, Mati. 2003. *Estonian language* [Linguistica Uralica. Supplementary Series 1]. Tallinn: Estonian Academy Publishers.

Erelt, Mati, Reet Kasik, Helle Metslang, Henno Rajandi, Kristiina Ross, Henn Saari, Kaja Tael & Silvi Vare. 1995. *Eesti keele grammatika II. Süntaks* [Estonian Grammar II. Syntax]. Tallinn: Eesti Teaduste Akadeemia Keele ja Kirjanduse Instituut.

Frawley, William. 1992. *Linguistic semantics.* Hillsdale, NJ: Lawrence Erlbaum.

Goldberg, Adele E. 1995. *Constructions: A construction grammar approach to argument structure.* Chicago, IL: The University of Chicago Press.

Heine, Bernd. 1997. *Cognitive foundations of grammar.* Oxford: OUP.

Heine, Bernd & Tania Kuteva. 2002. *World lexicon of grammaticalization.* Cambridge: CUP.

Huumo, Tuomas. 2007. Force dynamics, fictive dynamicity and the Finnish verbs of 'remaining'. *Folia Linguistica. Acta Societatis Linguisticae Europaeae* 41(1/2). 73–98.

Kasik, Reet. 1996. *Eesti keele sõnatuletus* (Estonian derivation). Tartu: Tartu Ülikooli eesti keele õppetooli toimetised 3.

Lakoff, George & Mark Johnson. 1980. *Metaphors we live by.* Chicago, IL: The University of Chicago Press.

Pajusalu, Renate. 1994. *Muutumisverbid eesti keeles ja nende vasted soome keeles* (Change predicates in Estonian and their counterparts in Finnish) [Lähivertailuja 8; Oulun yliopiston suomen ja saamen kielen laitoksen tutkimusraportteja 40], 83–97. Oulu: Oulun yliopisto.

Pajusalu, Renate, Ilona Tragel, Ann Veismann & Maigi Vija. 2004. *Tuumsõnade semantikat ja pragmaatikat.* Tartu: Tartu Ülikooli üldkeeleteaduse õppetooli toimetised 5.

Rosenthal, Dieter. 1984. *Studien zur Syntax und Semantik des Verbs 'bleiben' unter besonderer Berücksichtigung des Niederdeutschen und Niederländischen.* Göteborg: Acta Universitatis Gothoburgensis.

Sweetser, Eve. 1997. Role and individual interpretations of change predicates. In Jan Nuyts & Eric Pedersen (eds.), *Language and conceptualization,* 116–136. Cambridge: CUP.

Tragel, Ilona. 2001. On Estonian core verbs. In Ilona Tragel (ed.), *Papers in Estonian cognitive linguistics* (Publications of the Department of General Linguistics 2), 145–169. Tartu: Tartu University Press.

Tragel, Ilona. 2003. *Eesti keele tuumverbid* [Estonian core verbs] (Dissertationes Liguisticae Universitatis Tartuensis 3). Tartu: Tartu University Press.

Wierzbicka, Anna. 1996. *Semantics: Primes and universals.* Oxford: OUP.

CHAPTER 14

Categories and concepts in phonology
Theory and practice

Helen Fraser

The first part of this chapter brings together some ideas about the role of words and concepts that are widely agreed in theories of language and cognition, and suggests it would be reasonable to expect these ideas to be applied to the words and concepts used within those theories. The second part argues that this is not always the case. Theorists sometimes use words and concepts in a way that is at odds with their own theories about language and cognition. An explanation for this is offered, and a method for detecting and correcting problems that arise from it is proposed. The focus is phonology, and its application in human (as opposed to computational) domains, such as pronunciation teaching.

1 The role of concepts

One of the most widely agreed ideas in the disciplines that study language and cognition is that naive realism is wrong. Naive realism is the doctrine that a word's meaning is the thing it refers to (its referent). According to naive realism the meaning of the word *dog*, for example, can be given by pointing at a dog. Pointing can indicate a word's meaning in certain informal situations, but referential theories of meaning have been discredited at least since the time of Saussure, the "father of modern linguistics" (Ellis 1994; Harris 1981; Macnamara 1982; Wells 1993).

The best known problem with naive realism (Chapman 2000; Fromkin & Rodman 1974) is that there is not a one to one relationship between meanings and referents. Words can have different meanings ('senses') even though they refer to the same thing (*evening star* and *morning star*, *thunder* and *lightning*), or the same meaning even though they refer to different things (the meaning of the word *dog* remains the same even when it is used to refer to different individual dogs). Words can even have meaning when they refer to something that does not exist at all (*the present king of France, unicorn*).

A more serious problem is that pointing at something does not by itself indicate what the word means. If I point at a dog, how can you be sure I intend the particular meaning that *dog* happens to have, rather than the meaning *dog's head* or *black dog* or *poodle* or *quadruped*, or *running*, or even *loyalty*, or *smelly*?

The view that has replaced naive realism (for the most part, sophisticated realism will be mentioned below) is that there is a level between words and reality, and that words refer not directly to reality but to this intermediate level. Though the existence of such an intermediate level has been agreed for some time, the detailed understanding of its nature, and terminology to refer to it, has changed considerably over time (Gardner 1985; Jahoda 1993; Joseph, Love & Taylor 2001; Leahey 1980). At one stage, when theorists sought to avoid reference to the unobservable individual mind, it was understood via behaviour or usage (Palmer 1976). When the mind came to be acknowledged, it came to be referred to as the level of mental representation. This term however has considerable theoretical "baggage" (Fraser 1992; Shanon 1993). The ordinary word 'concept' conveys the intended meaning clearly without need for technical definition or hedging. Partly thanks to work in Cognitive Linguistics, "concept" is now returning to wider use in theoretical discussion (Croft & Cruse 2004; Goddard 1998; Murphy 2002), and is the term we will use here to refer to the "something" that lies between words and reality.

2   What is a concept?

Though the existence and role of concepts is agreed, an agreed definition of what exactly a concept is is harder to find. However, we can set out several characteristics of concepts that are generally accepted (Murphy 2002).

First, a concept is distinct from the reality behind it: The concept of a dog is something different from a dog. This is often captured by saying that concepts are "abstract" with respect to reality. We will come back to this term "abstract" in more detail, but it is worth pausing here to specify which meaning of "abstract" is intended. Often a concept is said to be abstract when the reality behind the concept is intangible. This is its usage in the traditional term "abstract noun", according to which *happiness* is abstract, because you cannot touch happiness. Other times, the word 'abstract' is used of the concept itself, to mean that it is formed through abstraction from reality. Abstraction is a process whereby we notice (or "draw out", as in the etymological meaning of abstract) aspects of reality (whether tangible or not) that are salient or relevant to us at that time and in that context. It is this latter sense of "abstract" that is relevant throughout this paper.

Second, while some concepts relate to universally observable aspects of reality, and some may be innate, most concepts, even those we consider very basic, are learned through complex processes of socialisation and education within a particular language and culture (Bloom 2000). Whereas once it was thought that differences among languages arose from use of different words to "label" established "bits of reality", one of Saussure's major contributions was his insistence that languages differ not just in their signifiers (words), but also in what is signified (concepts). Following the work of Whorf (Carroll 1956; Lee 1996), study of a wide range of "exotic" languages made it clear that different languages "carve up" reality into concepts in different ways.

Third, even within a language, concepts are context dependent. Things do not fall into one category once and for all, but can be conceptualised in different ways in different contexts. For example *tomato* falls into the category *fruit* in botanical contexts but into the category *vegetable* in (most) culinary contexts; whether something is a *cup* or a *mug* depends not on its shape alone but also on the context in which is appears (Labov 1973). It is quite natural for people to move between different conceptualisations of the same "bit of reality" as they move between different contexts. Thus a dog can be conceptualised as, say, a *dog*, or an *animal*, or a *poodle*, or a *pet*, or *Canis familiaris*, in appropriate contexts.

Taken together these characteristics mean that concepts are not only distinct from reality, they are not even "mappings" of aspects of reality onto another level. Thus a concept cannot be fully defined by enumerating physical or formal features of the reality behind it. Although we might informally define "dog" by listing the features of a dog ('has four legs and says woof', or 'has such and such DNA structure'), and although formal analysis of concepts into binary features can be useful in some contexts, definition of concepts in terms of features can never be fully complete. At best, it works within an agreed context with agreed constraints on its interpretation (Polanyi 1966).

The complex relationship between reality and concepts has come to be understood through the idea that a concept embraces a *category* of things. A category is a set of things (not necessarily physical things of course: events, properties of things, emotions and other non-physical things are also included) that are grouped together as being "the same" regardless of physical differences. Defining "category" precisely is a challenge, and has been a focus of attention in the cognitive sciences for some time. Wittgenstein (1958/1974) suggested members of a category share a "family resemblance" rather than any particular set of physical features. More recent theory suggests that a category can be defined in terms of a prototype, with "prototypical" members at the centre of the category and more "peripheral" members around an often "fuzzy" boundary, e.g. a canary is a prototypical bird whereas an ostrich or a penguin is a more peripheral member of the category bird (Lakoff 1987; Taylor 1989).

3 What about words?

From the discussion so far it is clear that as well as being distinct from reality, concepts are also distinct from words: The word *dog* is different from the concept *dog*. Just as concepts are not "mappings" of reality, so words are not "mappings" of concepts. The same or very similar concepts can be lexicalised with different words, or the same word can be used with different meanings, depending on the context. Through homonymy, synonymy and the like, the relationship between words and the concepts they refer to is many-to-one, and context dependent. But what is a word? From the foregoing discussion it is clear that a word is a label or term or representation or symbol for a concept.

Through the use of words people are able not just to have concepts but to think about concepts. Having words for concepts gives the powerful ability to compare and contrast concepts, and create new concepts by abstraction of salient similarities and differences in their parts or properties. For example, by comparing faces, we can build up new concepts of their parts, such as *nose*, *eye*, *chin*, and so on. By comparing objects, we can build up new concepts of their properties, such as *red* and *blue*, *square* and *round*, etc. By comparing these new concepts, we can come to yet more abstract concepts such as *colour* or *shape*. Through processes like these we can end up with concepts at varying levels of abstractness.

4 Why study concepts?

One reason to seek a good understanding of the nature of concepts arises from the position they occupy on the intermediate level described above. It is often said that concepts mediate our understanding of reality. What we experience is not raw reality, but reality filtered through our concepts. In order to understand reality itself, then, we have to find a way to get behind or beyond our concepts of it, to be able to say 'it seems this way, but in reality it is this way'. Doing this requires an ability to distinguish between concept and reality, and to put the concepts to one side so as to consider the reality.

Systematising and formalising this process of setting aside our own viewpoint is the basis of scientific discovery. Consider the concept of sunrise. The concept involves an understanding of the sun revolving around the earth, rising in the east and setting in the west. In order to understand the reality, we have to set the concept of sunrise aside and consider what is happening from a point of view other than our own. If we do that, obviously, we find that in reality it is the earth that revolves around the sun.

Of course, as the great scientists recognise, our ability to do this "setting aside" is limited, and scientific understanding is inevitably constrained to some extent by cultural context and point of view (Chalmers 1982; Feynman 1986; Field & Mawer 1998; Schuster 1994). Nevertheless, the continuing attempt to achieve this kind of detachment is fundamental to scientific endeavours of all kinds. The more rigorously we can make the distinction between our concepts and the reality behind them, the more accurate will be our theories in the natural sciences.

Another reason it is important to understand concepts is that it is concepts, not definitions, that give us the real meanings of words. A word (take *democracy* for example) can easily be given a definition, but if we want to find out what it really means to the people who use it, we need to undertake a more careful analysis of the concept behind the word. Using this approach, linguists have given a great deal of attention to the different concepts embodied in the words of different cultures (e.g. Wierzbicka 1997).

The most important reason to seek a good understanding of concepts, however, is that it is our concepts of reality, not reality itself, that drive our behaviour. Consider a person being threatened by attack from a tiger. The person will naturally feel fear, and behave accordingly. It seems obvious that the tiger causes the fear, and thus the behaviour. It is not difficult to demonstrate, though, that it is not the tiger itself that causes the fear but the person's concept of the tiger. If the tiger is about to attack, but the person doesn't know it is there, the person will feel no fear. Even if the person sees the tiger they will not feel fear if they do not conceptualise it as dangerous (say through ignorance of the real nature of tigers, or through confidence in their ability to deflect attack in some way).

Though it is easy to demonstrate in principle that concepts drive behaviour, the idea that particular behaviours are driven by concepts can be a bone of contention. Most people are ready enough to accept that other people's behaviour is driven by concepts rather than reality – but much less inclined to accept the same of their own behaviour. To tell someone who fears attack by a tiger that their fear is caused not by the tiger but merely by their concept of the tiger is to risk making them very annoyed.

The reason is the word *merely*. The idea that behaviour is driven by concepts not by reality seems to imply that the concepts are illusions, "all in the mind", and that the behaviour they drive is in some way irrational or unjustified. This is not a valid inference from the statement, however. Certainly some of our concepts are inaccurate reflections of reality, or even illusions. Many of our concepts on the other hand are very accurate reflections of reality, as evidenced by our continued survival as individuals and as a species, and as pointed out by sophisticated realists (Gibson 1966; Millikan 1984). Nevertheless a concept is something distinct from reality.

5. Theorising concepts

We use reasoning based on recognition of the characteristics and role of concepts frequently and naturally in everyday life. For example, we recognise that the same behaviour can get a person labeled *terrorist* in one context and *freedom fighter* in another. Everyday reasoning about behaviour often involves reference to concepts ('The tourist got the rash because he had no concept that grass could be dangerous', 'Kids roam the street because our society is losing its concept of family'). We know that different words (*foetus, unborn baby*), though technically synonyms, embody different concepts in a way that can affect attitudes and behaviour (Elgin 1999). If we hear a movie is "great", we want to know who thinks so before accepting the review. We readily dismiss a theory that links an ancient culture's use of the symbol "I" with the concept "eye", on the grounds that the concept of "I" and its relationship to "eye" depends on a context and viewpoint which would not have been available in the ancient culture.

The cognitive sciences aim to systematise and extend our understanding of language and cognition. Concepts, as we have seen, are fundamental to both language and cognition, and the cognitive sciences clearly require some kind of theory of concepts. This in turn requires a concept of concepts, taking us into the realm of metatheory.

It would seem reasonable to expect that the concept of concept used in developing this metatheoretical understanding would take into account what is known about concepts in general, as described above. However, ensuring this is more difficult than might at first be imagined. This is where the philosophical method of phenomenology is very useful (Bolton 1979; Fraser 1992; Magee 1987; Passmore 1968; Roche 1973; Spiegelberg 1982; Spurling 1977).

Phenomenology is not well known in the cognitive sciences these days, though it has been highly influential on the thinking we take for granted in our era (Magee 1987; Passmore 1968) – especially the widespread acceptance of the three-way distinction between words, concepts and reality discussed above. Unfortunately phenomenology is often misrepresented as being merely a way of talking about subjective experience. Even more unfortunately, it is often equated with the more extreme versions of postmodernism, which assert that subjective experience is all there is (Lecercle 1990; Sarup 1988). Phenomenology does emphasise the role of experience, in the sense that it insists on recognition for the level of concepts which mediates between us and reality. But it never does this without an entirely equal emphasis on the role of reality in making concepts what they are.

A good way to understand the way phenomenology sees this relationship between concept and reality is via analogy with the potter and the clay. According to this analogy, reality is the clay, the person conceptualising reality is the potter, and the concept is the pot. The potter has a great deal of influence over the clay, in the sense of being able to sculpt it into many forms. Clearly though this can only ever be influence, not total control. The nature of the clay contributes to the nature of the pot. No potter can make a pot with no clay at all, or turn clay into a silk shirt.

Just as both the clay and the potter are essential contributors to the pot, so both reality and the person conceptualising it are essential contributors to the concept. That is why saying that fear of a tiger is caused by the person's concept of the tiger does not mean the fear is caused by a mere illusion. A concept is the product of conceptualisation *of* reality not a creation out of nothing.

None of this is difficult to accept. It can even seem obvious, given the well agreed points discussed above. However its implications can be hard to follow with consistency – and the phenomenologists have an explanation for this.

6 The Natural Attitude

One of the phenomenologists' most useful concepts is that of the Natural Attitude (Spiegelberg 1982). The Natural Attitude is our tendency to behave as though words refer to reality, rather than to concepts of reality. The Natural Attitude is similar to naive realism, but it is not an "ism" or philosophical doctrine, to be asserted or opposed. Rather it is a mode of thinking – an attitude we can choose to take or not to take to things that we do or experience. The term *Natural Attitude* emphasises that it is indeed entirely natural, and not especially naive. Normal life would be unthinkable without it. In order to engage in projects, we need to behave as if our concepts of reality are reality. Distinguishing concept and reality requires us to step outside the Natural Attitude, and use a different mode of thinking – a reflective mode. This reflective mode cannot be achieved while actively engaged in a project or endeavour.

An example might clarify. Recall the concept of sunrise. The scientific discovery that the earth revolves around the sun doesn't cause us to lose the concept of sunrise. In everyday life, we live in the Natural Attitude, and continue to see the sun as rising in the east and setting in the west. In a reflective mode, we take an attitude of detachment, and know that the earth really revolves around the sun. We can move easily between these two attitudes.

The problem is it is not always so easy to maintain an attitude of detachment. Even after the incident is over, the person being threatened by a tiger is not so keen to detach from the situation sufficiently to attribute the fear to a concept, as the Natural Attitude would insist it should be, rather than to the tiger. Indeed it is not so many centuries since an attitude of detachment was lacking in regard to the concept of sunrise, as Galileo found to his cost. We see then that the Natural Attitude can cause problems for theories, by making it difficult to keep the three levels of word, concept and reality distinct, to get "behind" words to the concepts they relate to, and "behind" concepts to the reality they relate to. We saw an example earlier in the ambiguity of the term abstract that results from confusion about whether it is the concept, or the reality behind the concept, that is abstract.

Phenomenology is not so much a doctrine as a simple but powerful method for achieving this "getting behind", and disentangling the three levels of word, concept and reality when they inevitably get confused.

7   A method of analysis

The phenomenological method involves explicit recognition of and focus on the idea that a concept – any concept – is a product, not a self-existing entity. Clay pots do not "just happen", and neither do concepts. The existence of a pot presupposes prior processes such as moulding and firing clay. The existence of a concept presupposes prior processes of conceptualisation, such as abstraction and categorisation.

If we want to analyse or study clay pots, we can classify them in many different ways. For example, we can consider the materials they are made of, or their size and shape, or the place they come from, or the techniques of their creation. Each of these is valid – depending on our purposes or goals at the time. The same is true of concepts. It is perfectly possible to classify concepts according to the nature of the reality they relate to (their "abstractness" in the traditional sense) or in any of many other ways. However the phenomenologists emphasise the value, when studying the role of concepts in cognition, of classifying concepts according to the kinds of processes that have been involved in their creation, how they got to be what they are (their abstractness in the sense being developed here). In order to do this we need to look at two further presuppositions of the existence of a concept.

First, just as the processes of creating a pot presuppose a "someone" who has carried out the processes of moulding and firing, so the processes of creating a concept presuppose a "someone" who has carried out the processes of abstraction and conceptualisation. Even if we don't know who made the pot, we are sure someone did; and we can say certain things with a certain degree of confidence about that someone. So it is with the someone who creates a concept.

Second, just as the existence of a pot presupposes the prior existence of a "something" from which it is made, exactly the same is true of concepts. Every concept is a concept of something – not necessarily something tangible, but something we can experience in reality. (This is the idea behind Brentano's original phenomenological concept of intentionality [Chisholm 1960], quite different from the common usage of the same word in cognitive science – see further discussion and references in Fraser 1992.) Although we cannot objectively describe reality, we can make inferences about the nature of the reality behind a concept in much the same way as we can make inferences about the nature of the clay from which a pot was created.

The problem in analysing concepts is that the Natural Attitude makes it difficult to be sure whether we are talking about a concept, or about the reality behind the concept, or about a word that represents the concept. The phenomenological method therefore involves asking what we might call Framework Questions of the terms we use. For example:

- What concept lies behind this term?
- What 'bit of reality' lies behind this concept?
- What kind of person can have this concept?
- What prior concepts does that person need to have?
- In what context does that "bit of reality" have to occur to be conceptualised in this way?

It is interesting to note that these questions simply make explicit and systematise the processes of reasoning we use informally every day, whenever we need to distinguish one person's use of a word from another's (recall the *eye/I* and other examples above). In everyday life, however, we use these processes haphazardly, slipping in and out of the Natural Attitude. The phenomenological method helps us formalise our thinking and apply it consistently, even when the Natural Attitude threatens to lead us into error.

Use of the Framework Questions gives us a tool for understanding the term "abstract" and specifying the relative abstractness of concepts, by foregrounding the fact that though the term "abstract" is used as an adjective, it is really a participle. It presupposes someone's prior activity of abstracting, or "drawing out" salient aspects of reality in much the same way as the term *thrown pot* presupposes someone's prior activity of throwing a pot on a wheel.

The Framework Questions would readily reveal, for example, that for someone to understand the concept *Canis familiaris*, a prior concept of *dog* would very likely need to be in place. Additional acts of abstraction beyond those required for the concept *dog* are required to establish the concept *Canis familiaris*. This means *Canis familiaris* is a more abstract concept than *dog*. Concomitantly, *dog* is a more "basic" concept than *Canis familiaris*, in a sense that is in accord with though somewhat different from the "basic concepts" of Cognitive Linguistics (Lakoff 1987; Langacker 1987).

8 Metalanguage

We have seen that the cognitive sciences require a metatheory with a concept of *concept*, and discussed the measures that are necessary to ensure that this concept of concept is used in ways which do not contradict our own theories about concepts and conceptualisation.

Linguistic theories use language to talk not just about the external world, but also about language itself, through use of a metalanguage. Of course the terms of such a metalanguage are words like any other words. They refer not to reality but to concepts of reality, with all that entails. It would be reasonable to expect that our theories of language should take into account all we know about words and concepts from our scientific study of language and cognition. Unfortunately this is not always easy to ensure – due, again, to the Natural Attitude.

To avoid succumbing to inappropriate use of the Natural Attitude, it is not enough just to create rigorous definitions of the terms of the metalanguage. It is essential to make a rigorous analysis of the meanings the terms have in the contexts in which they are used (i.e. of the concepts behind the words). Though it may seem strange to those outside the discipline, this is rather rare in Linguistics. Wierzbicka (1998) undertakes a project of analysing the meaning of a number of key words in linguistic theory, such as *word, sentence, clause,* and so on. However her project does not include terms for units below the level of the word. A similar project is needed in relation to phonological terms.

9 Phonological terms

Phonological terms are words for concepts of parts of words: *syllable, phoneme, letter, feature, stress, fricative, coronal, lenition,* and so on. Clearly these terms are words like any other words, and refer not to reality but to concepts, with all that entails. Again perhaps surprisingly to outsiders to the discipline, this has not been a focus of attention in mainstream phonology, which traditionally defines phonological terms as collections (whether as lists, or complex "feature geometries") of physical or formal features, in a way that might be considered "naive realism" in a different context.

A move towards understanding phonological terms in the light of theories of conceptualisation and categorisation has been taken within the field of Cognitive Linguistics. For example, several scholars (Lakoff 1987; Langacker 1987; Mompeán 2002; Nathan 1996) have noted that phonemes are better understood as categories of sounds, in the sense developed above, than as sets of sounds that share physical or formal features. This has triggered valuable developments in theory (Taylor 2002).

However, I suggest the implications of the insight that phonological terms are words like any others may be considerably greater than has so far been realised.

To see this it is useful to think explicitly about phonological terms as words. In this way we can see the situation with phonological terms as identical to that we have discussed above in relation to pots, dogs, etc. Any one "bit of phonological reality" can be conceptualised in a number of different ways (for example in terms of spelling, words, morphemes, syllables, features, phonemes, and so on) some of which are more basic and some more abstract. It is clear we need to ask the Framework Questions of the terms to sort out the appropriate hierarchy of abstractness. Before we can answer the Framework Questions in relation to phonological terms, we need to rehearse briefly (see Fraser 2004a, 2004b for more detail) some facts about these terms which are very well established in psycholinguistics (Berko Gleason 2005) but not widely known outside this discipline.

10   Acquisition of phonological terms

Children can discriminate different speech sounds from earliest infancy (Gerken & Aslin 2005), but it is not till the age of around 12 months that they learn to use sounds as words, and name their concepts of things that are salient to them in their experience. At this stage, however, they have no metalinguistic awareness – they can use words, but have no concepts of words as such. It is generally not till the age of four that children can even identify a word as distinct from the thing it names (Gombert 1992).

Once they have the concept of *word*, children still have little awareness of the distinction between the sound of a word and its meaning (Byrne 1998). Further abstraction is needed before they can focus on the sound as distinct from the meaning so as to compare the sound of different words, and yet more abstraction is needed before they can divide the sound of a word into parts. At this early stage, these parts are not individual "sounds" in the adult sense. The child starts by conceptualising large or salient parts of words such as rhymes, or the beginnings of words (Treiman 1993), according to the specific characteristics of their own language.

Many speakers of many languages never develop phonological awareness beyond this level. Those who go on to acquire literacy however must learn to conceptualise and name individual sounds in a more explicit and systematic way, in order to attach orthographic symbols to them. Much evidence suggests that this process of acquiring literacy radically changes a person's concepts of the sound of speech, and that, without literacy, people do not have even concepts, let alone words, for individual sounds (Coulmas 1989; Linell 1988; Olson, Torrance & Hildyard 1985; Read et al. 1986). As part of the process of acquiring literacy, they develop such concepts in a manner that is not only specific to the language they speak, but to the writing system they learn. This means that the phonological concepts of people from different language and literacy backgrounds can be radically different (Strange 1995) in ways that are often not fully appreciated outside the discipline of psycholinguistics (Fraser 2001).

In relation to alphabetic writing systems this process is called the development of phonemic awareness. However it is important to note that what is gained is not awareness of a full systematic set of phonemes (units of sound which contrast in a particular language). That requires much more sophisticated metalinguistic processing: as anyone who has taught first year linguistics will know, even highly literate adults generally have poor phonemic awareness (Scarborough et al. 1998).

All that is needed for alphabetic literacy is a concept of a "sound" as something that can be represented with a letter (Byrne 1998). Understanding this principle allows simple words to be "sounded out". Of course, reading does not really work through a sounding out process (Just & Carpenter 1987). This is just an intermediate stage of conceptualisation that bootstraps the child into literacy. Very soon, fluent reading processes take over and words are recognised globally in a way that seldom requires analysis down to the level of individual phonemes.

Nevertheless, literacy education involves explicit instruction in the idea that letters or other symbols stand for pre-existing sounds. This can at first be confusing for children as it is true only to a very limited extent – as we have seen, individual sounds are abstractions from words, not components of words. Normally however children quickly gain an implicit understanding of how reading really works, and have no need to question the idea that letters stand for sounds. The whole process encourages a Natural Attitude view, common to most literate adults, that letters really represent actual sounds of the words they spell, whereas in fact they represent concepts of sounds, in the context of prior understanding of words.

Most people's metalinguistic development stops at this stage. However some (probably including many readers of the current volume) go on to learn phonemic transcription (generally not without some difficulty) and form a more systematic concept of phonemes as distinct from letters. Of these, a small proportion go further, again usually with some difficulty, to understand that phonemes do not actually sound the same every time they occur (the /a/ in *bat* is phonetically different from the same phoneme in *bad*). This allows them to develop a concept of allophones (variant pronunciation of phonemes in different positions in words) as distinct from phonemes, and recognise that orthography relates not directly to allophones but to phonemes. Even fewer progress, via recognition that allophones allow only very limited description of the complex continuous phonetic reality of speech, to the more sophisticated concepts of "real" phonetics. Finally, a vanishingly small number of people combine this with the understanding of theoretical phonology needed to conceptualise relationships between all these levels (Fraser 1997).

11 Abstractness of phonological terms

What we have just done is set the stage for a hierarchy of abstractness of various phonological terms according to the processes of abstraction that are required to create the concepts behind them. This hierarchy can be explored by answering the Framework Questions for each phonological term, such as *word*, *syllable*, *phoneme*, and so on.

Consider for example, the term *phoneme*. This term refers to a particular way of conceptualising speech. The "something" behind the concept is "raw speech". The "someone" who can have this concept is a sophisticated language user with alphabetic literacy and some training in linguistics. Prior concepts required include a concept of *word*, *letter*, and a considerable degree of metalinguistic awareness.

In answering the questions for a range of terms like this, it becomes clear that the concept of a word, though abstract, is far less abstract than concepts of parts of words. The concepts of letters and spelling are more abstract than the concept of word, and the concept of phoneme is more abstract again. Any phonetic concepts are far more abstract than the concept of phoneme, with the more "accurate" or sophisticated phonetics the most abstract of all (further detail on this is available in Fraser 2004a).

This view of the relative abstractness of phonological terms makes good sense in terms of the view of conceptualisation and lexicalisation we have explained in some detail above. Compelling as it is when built up from first principles like this, however, this view is highly unorthodox in relation to standard phonological theory.

Generally it is taken for granted that phonetics represents the real sound of speech. There is considerable variation in the sophistication of what is understood by "phonetics". Many people believe phonemic transcription is "phonetics", while those with greater training in linguistics are increasingly aware of more and more phonetic detail. The most sophisticated theorists (Laver 1994) acknowledge that any phonetic representation is inevitably somewhat abstract with respect to the reality of speech. However, it is universally understood that a phonetic representation is the least abstract view of speech, closest to the reality of actual speech sounds. Phonological concepts are universally agreed to be more abstract than phonetic concepts, and orthography is considered so abstract, or distant from the reality of speech sounds, as to be barely worth considering in scientific discussions of speech.

How can this view that phonetic terms refer to the reality of speech coexist with the equally widely accepted view that words refer not to reality but to concepts of reality? This coexistence can be attributed to the Natural Attitude. Linguists have been prominent contributors to the understanding of concepts and their role in cognition outlined above, but it remains difficult for us, while engaged in the "project" of theorising, to retain the reflective attitude needed to recognise the terms of our own theories as words like those we study with our theories.

12 Implications for theory

What does all this mean? Should we dismiss theories that assume phonetic representation to be less abstract than phonemic, and supplant them with phenomenological theory? Of course not. To do so would be to presume a degree of reality for a particular concept of "abstract" that would fly in the face of everything that has been said so far. We would be getting trapped by the Natural Attitude in a horribly ironic way. What it means is that we should use a hierarchy of abstractness and other theoretical commitments that suit our purposes in a particular context. The Framework Questions can be very useful in working this out.

Linguistics is a very broad discipline, encompassing a wide range of theoretical and practical contexts. Rather than assuming an implicit and unanalysed view of the relative abstractness of phonological terms will be valid for all those contexts, we should explicitly choose a hierarchy that is appropriate to the particular context in which we work and the particular goals we seek to achieve – just as we use different methods of studying pots according to whether we are interested in their physical characteristics, their provenance, or whatever.

Much of linguistics has a descriptive aim, seeking to understand the structure of language, how it changes, and the typological relationships between individual languages, in a way that is not primarily concerned with the cognitive processing of language. The Framework Questions reveal, for example, that these branches of study tend to presuppose languages, rather than speakers, as the Subject of change (for example, it is common to speak of languages evolving, or of phonemes merging and splitting, rather than of people changing the way they speak). In this context that is not a problem, and the traditional hierarchy of abstractness is entirely appropriate, allowing as it does succinct reference to characteristics of languages, and prediction (at least post facto) of relationships among them.

Other branches of linguistics turn more to questions of the processing of languages by users. Some of these have the explicit goal of creating computer-based implementations of linguistic theories, either for the practical value of the computer systems themselves, or on the grounds that this method provides the best way to test theories. Computer implementations by their nature require the traditional hierarchy of abstractness, with phonetics at the bottom, and it makes sense to carry this into linguistic theories in contexts where it is appropriate to accept an analogy between the human mind/brain and a computational device.

There are contexts however where this analogy between human cognition and computation is not a helpful one. If we move into such a context, we must surely be free to choose a hierarchy of abstractness, and other theoretical commitments, to suit that context, without being constrained by a sense that theories from the computational context represent reality and should not be interfered with. Rather than being forced to apply theoretical concepts developed in a different context, we need to find or develop concepts more appropriate for this new domain of theory.

Such a change of context occurs when we apply linguistic theory directly to humans without the computational analogy – for example when teaching literacy or pronunciation. In these contexts the traditional hierarchy is quite inappropriate. To use it involves attributing concepts to subjects that they simply could not have. This is much the same kind of error as attributing the concept of the letter "I" to a culture without alphabetic writing. Of course the obvious rejoinder is that concepts involved in subconscious processing of speech are different: If someone knows how to form English plurals, they "must" have some concept of the difference between voiced and voiceless consonants, even if it is only an implicit one, with psychological, rather than real, reality. It is certainly useful for linguists to describe the behaviour of language users as if they had those concepts. This way of speaking allows efficient accounts of and predictions of behaviour. However this cannot be what is really happening inside people's heads. It conflicts strongly with the view that all words relate to concepts rather than to reality. A term like *voiced consonant* must refer to a concept, not to an implicit concept, and cannot refer to reality, even psychological reality. Of course people without the "voiced consonant" concept can form English plurals – but they do so on the basis of observation of similarities and differences among words, not on the basis of a concept of "voiced consonant" (Hannam, Fraser & Byrne 2007).

13 Implications for practice

Teaching second language pronunciation is a good example of such a human context, in which the traditional hierarchy of abstractness is not appropriate. This may explain why pronunciation teaching has so often been considered difficult or even impossible (Celce-Murcia, Brinton & Goodwin 1996; Fraser 2000; Macdonald 2002).

If someone with no training in phonology has the task of teaching pronunciation, the Natural Attitude inclines them to think pronunciation is obvious, well represented by spelling, except for a few irregularities like *cough/bough*. They may expect their students to learn by repeating a pronunciation model. When this is unsuccessful, as it often is, they ascribe the problem to some defect in the learner – they cannot hear properly, or their muscles are "frozen". They may give up, or try to help by using a multimedia program that purports to "show speech as it really is", via acoustic or articulatory representations. Surprising as it often seems to those not experienced in teaching pronunciation, even to the learners themselves, this does not generally help much.

If someone with training in phonology with the mainstream hierarchy of abstractness has the task of teaching pronunciation, they may be inclined to teach the basic phonemes and stress patterns of the language, and the rules for putting them together. This can of course be useful in certain contexts, but can have the unfortunate result that students can recite the rules of phonology – in pronunciation that violates those very rules.

The problem with both methods is that they attempt to operate on a level that is highly abstract from the point of view of the students, and not affecting the concepts that actually drive their pronunciation. From the perspective developed above, teaching pronunciation is a matter of changing behaviour, which is driven by concepts. People from different language and literacy backgrounds have radically different phonological concepts driving their pronunciation (Strange 1995). The difficulty in learning pronunciation is that people generally have very little ability to name their phonological concepts. They are stuck in the Natural Attitude, assuming that the terms of their writing system, if any, provide an accurate view of phonological reality.

If the teacher is aware of this, pronunciation teaching is not particularly difficult – certainly not impossible. It is simply a matter of helping learners change their pronunciation behaviour by accessing and changing their phonological concepts (Fraser 2001), using principles of concept formation and modification widely understood in educational psychology (Lefrancois 1994; Williams & Burden 1997).

The interesting thing is that many teachers through experience and intuition actually use concept formation techniques to help students effectively with pronunciation. However their work is not theorised in this way. Both theoretical and practical accounts of second language pronunciation (Archibald 2000) accept the traditional hierarchy uncritically.

A useful analogy to understand the difference in these approaches sees the conceptual approach as being like designing road signs, while mainstream theory is like drawing maps of roads. In designing maps the aim is to give an accurate representation of the location, direction and surface of the roads. In designing road signs the aim is to create a representation that is instantly understandable to drivers, conveying just the information they need in that moment to help them anticipate road conditions and drive safely. In other words, their aim is to affect the level of concepts which drive behaviour in a very immediate way, with the minimum need for explicit learning and analysis.

A great deal of research goes into designing road signs. Till now very little research has examined what types of metalinguistic communication are appropriate to different kinds of learners in different contexts.

14 Conclusion

We have covered a lot of ground in this discussion, in the belief that it is useful occasionally to step back and consider the connections between philosophy, metatheory, theory and application in a broader context. Particularly in the case of linguistics, it can often be surprising how much disparity there is between our treatment of language in the theories we develop, and our underlying assumptions about the language we ourselves use in developing those theories. This is by no means to invalidate theories based on those underlying assumptions, but rather to let us see those assumptions for what they are, and provide an opportunity to consider developing theories from a different theoretical base.

Acknowledgements

As well as the ILCC audience and two anonymous reviewers, I would like to thank members of the University of New England's Language and Cognition Research Centre for discussion of a seminar-style precursor to this chapter, and José-Antonio Mompeán-González for particularly helpful comments on a prior draft.

References

Archibald, John (ed.). 2000. *Second language acquisition and linguistic theory*. Oxford: Blackwell.
Berko Gleason, Jean. 2005. *The development of language*, 6th edn. Boston, MA: Pearson Education.
Bloom, Paul. 2000. *How children learn the meanings of words*. Cambridge, MA: The MIT Press.
Bolton, Neil. 1979. Phenomenology and psychology: Being objective about the mind. In Neil Bolton (eds.), *Philosophical problems in psychology*, 158–175. London: Methuen.
Byrne, Brian. 1998. *The foundation of literacy: The child's acquisition of the alphabetic principle*. Hove: Psychology Press.
Carroll, John B. (ed.). 1956. *Language, thought, and reality: Selected writings of Benjamin Lee Whorf*. Cambridge, MA: The MIT Press.
Celce-Murcia, Marianne, Donna M. Brinton & Janet M. Goodwin. 1996. *Teaching pronunciation: A reference for teachers of English to speakers of other languages*. Cambridge: CUP.
Chalmers, Alan. 1982. *What is this thing called science?* Buckingham: Open University Press.

Chapman, Siobhan. 2000. *Philosophy for linguists: An introduction.* London: Routledge.
Chisholm, Roderick M. 1960. *Realism and the background of phenomenology.* Glencoe: Free Press.
Coulmas, Florian. 1989. What writing means for linguistics. In Florian Coulmas (ed.), *The writing systems of the world*, 267–273. Oxford: Basil Blackwell.
Croft, William & D. Alan Cruse. 2004. *Cognitive linguistics.* Cambridge: CUP.
Elgin, Suzette Haden. 1999. *The language imperative: How learning languages can enrich your life and expand your mind.* Cambridge, MA: Perseus.
Ellis, John M. 1994. *Language thought and logic.* Evanston IL: Northwestern University Press.
Feynman, Richard. 1986. *Surely you're joking, Mr Feynman! Adventures of a curious character* (as told to Ralph Leighton and edited by Edward Hutchings). London: Unwin.
Field, Laurie & Giselle Mawer. 1998. *Introducing workplace training: The new roles.* Sydney: NSW Department of Education and Training.
Fraser, Helen. 1992. *The subject of speech perception: An analysis of the philosophical foundations of the information-processing model of cognition.* London: Macmillan.
Fraser, Helen. 1997. Phonology without tiers: Why the phonetic representation is not derived from the phonological representation. *Language Sciences* 19(2). 101–137.
Fraser, Helen. 2000. *Coordinating improvements in pronunciation teaching for adult learners of English as a second language.* Canberra: Commonwealth of Australia, Department of Education Training and Youth Affairs. http://www-personal.une.edu.au/~hfraser/docs/HF_ANTA_REPORT.pdf.
Fraser, Helen. 2001. *Teaching pronunciation: A handbook for teachers and trainers.* Sydney: TAFE NSW Access Division. http://www.dest.gov.au/ty/litnet/docs/Teaching_Pronunciation.pdf.
Fraser, Helen. 2004a. Constraining abstractness: Phonological representation in the light of color terms. *Cognitive Linguistics* 15(3). 239–288.
Fraser, Helen. 2004b. Representing speech in practice and theory. In William Hardcastle & Janet Beck (eds.), *A figure of speech: A festschrift for John Laver*, 93–128. New Jersey, NJ: Lawrence Erlbaum.
Fromkin, Victoria & Robert Rodman. 1974. *An introduction to language.* New York, NY: Holt, Rinehart and Winston.
Gardner, Howard. 1985. *The mind's new science: A history of the cognitive revolution.* New York, NY: Basic Books.
Gerken, Lou Ann & Richard N. Aslin. 2005. Thirty years of research on infant speech perception: The legacy of Peter W. Jusczyk. *Language Learning and Development* 1(1). 5–21.
Gibson, James J. 1966. *The senses considered as perceptual systems.* Boston: Houghton Mifflin.
Goddard, Cliff. 1998. *Semantic analysis: A practical introduction.* Oxford: OUP.
Gombert, Jean-Emile. 1992. *Metalinguistic development.* Hemel Hempstead: Harvester Wheatsheaf.
Hannam, Rachel, Helen Fraser & Brian Byrne. 2007. The sbelling of sdops. Preliterate children's spelling of stops after /s/. *Reading and Writing* 20(4). 399–412.
Harris, Roy. 1981. *The language myth.* London: Duckworth.
Jahoda, Gustav. 1993. *Crossroads between culture and mind: Continuities and change in theories of human nature.* Cambridge, MA: Harvard University Press.
Joseph, John E., Nigel Love & Talbot J. Taylor. 2001. *Landmarks in linguistic thought II: The western tradition in the twentieth century.* London: Routledge.

Just, Marcel & Patricia A. Carpenter. 1987. *The psychology of reading and language comprehension*. Boston, MA: Allyn and Bacon.
Labov, William. 1973. The boundaries of words and their meanings. In Charles. N. Bailey & Roger W. Shuy (eds.), *New ways of analyzing variation in English*, Vol. 1, 340–373. Washington, DC: Georgetown University Press.
Lakoff, George. 1987. *Women, fire and dangerous things: What categories reveal about the mind*. Chicago, IL: University of Chicago Press.
Langacker, Ronald. 1987. *Foundations of cognitive grammar*. Stanford CA: Stanford University Press.
Laver, John. 1994. *Principles of phonetics*. Cambridge: CUP.
Leahey, Thomas H. 1980. *A history of psychology: Main currents in psychological thought*. Upper Saddle River, NJ: Prentice Hall.
Lecercle, Jean-Jacques. 1990. *The violence of language*. London: Routledge.
Lee, Penny. 1996. *The Whorf theory complex: A ciritical reconstruction*. Amsterdam: John Benjamins.
Lefrancois, Guy. 1994. *Psychology for teaching*, 8th edn. Belmont, CA: Wadsworth.
Linell, Per. 1988. The impact of literacy on the conception of language: The case of linguistics. In Roger Säljö (ed.), *The written world: Studies in literate thought and action*, 41–58. Berlin: Springer.
Macdonald, Shem. 2002. Pronunciation: Views and practices of reluctant teachers. *Prospect* 17(3). 3–15.
Macnamara, John. 1982. *Names for things*. Cambridge, MA: The MIT Press.
Magee, Bryan. 1987. *The great philosophers*. London: BBC Books.
Millikan, Ruth Garrett. 1984. *Language, thought, and other biological categories: New foundations for realism*. Cambridge, MA: The MIT Press.
Mompeán, Jose-Antonio. 2002. *The categorisation of the sounds of English: Experimental evidence in phonology*. Murcia: University of Murcia PhD dissertation.
Murphy, Gregory L. 2002. *The big book of concepts*. Cambridge, MA: The MIT Press.
Nathan, Geoffrey. 1996. Steps towards a cognitive phonology. In Bernard Hurch & Richard Rhodes (eds.), *Natural phonology: The state of the art*, 107–120. Berlin: Mouton.
Olson, David, Nancy Torrance & Angela Hildyard (eds.). 1985. *Literacy language and learning: The nature and consequences of reading and writing*. Cambridge: CUP.
Palmer, Frank R. 1976. *Semantics: A new outline*. Cambridge: CUP.
Passmore, John. 1968. *A hundred years of philosophy*. Harmondsworth: Pelican.
Polanyi, Michael. 1966. *The tacit dimension*. New York, NY: Doubleday.
Read, Charles, Yun-Fei Zhang, Hhong-Yin Nie & Bao-Qing Ding. 1986. The ability to manipulate speech sounds depends on knowing alphabetic writing. *Cognition* 24. 31-44.
Roche, Maurice. 1973. *Phenomenology, language and the social sciences*. London: Routledge and Kegan Paul.
Sarup, Madan. 1988. *An introductory guide to post-structuralism and postmodernism*. New York, NY: Harvester Wheatsheaf.
Scarborough, Hollis S., Linnea C. Ehri, Richard K. Olson & Anne E. Fowler. 1998. The fate of phonemic awareness beyond the elementary school years. *Scientific Studies of Reading* 2. 115–142.
Schuster, John. 1994. *The scientific revolution: An introduction to the history and philosophy of science*. Wollongong: University of Wollongong.

Shanon, Benny. 1993. *The representational and the presentational: An essay on cognition and the study of mind.* New York, NY: Harvester Wheatsheaf.

Spiegelberg, Herbert. 1982. *The phenomenological movement: A historical introduction.* The Hague: Martinus Nijhoff.

Spurling, Laurie. 1977. *Phenomenology and the social world: The phenomenology of Merleau-Ponty and its relation to the social sciences.* London: Rouledge and Kegan Paul.

Strange, Winifred (ed). 1995. *Speech perception and linguistic experience: Issues in cross-language research.* Baltimore, MD: York.

Taylor, John R. 1989. *Linguistic categorisation: Prototypes in linguistic theory.* Oxford: Clarendon.

Taylor, John R. 2002. *Cognitive grammar.* Oxford: OUP.

Treiman, Rebecca. 1993. *Beginning to spell: A study of first-grade children.* New York, NY: OUP.

Wells, George Albert. 1993. *What's in a name? Reflections on language magic and religion.* Chicago, IL: Open Court.

Wierzbicka, Anna. 1997. *Understanding cultures through their key words: English, Russian, Polish, German, Japanese.* New York, NY: OUP.

Wierzbicka, Anna. 1998. Anchoring linguistic typology in universal human concepts. *Linguistic Typology* 2(2). 141–194.

Williams, Marion & Robert L. Burden. 1997. *Psychology for language teachers: A social constructivist approach.* Cambridge: CUP.

Wittgenstein, Ludwig. 1958/1974. *Philosophical investigations.* Oxford: Basil Blackwell.

CHAPTER 15

You can run, but:

Another look at linguistic relativity

Roger Wales

Eight verbs of motion were performed by actors and recorded using a 3-dimensional infrared system (point-light system). These recordings were presented to two sets of participants, one native English speaking, the other Spanish, to make force-choice judgments of which verb the performance represented. General descriptions of each verb were compiled based on their prominent characteristics. These general definitions were used as a means for comparison of incorrect judgments. Results show that the verbs for which errors are made have a number of overlapping structural characteristics. The relevance of this to our understanding of how meanings in language are expressed and understood is discussed in the context of discussions of "linguistic relativity".

1   What's the argument?

The question of how language influences the way we think has exercised our human minds for as long as there are written records. It certainly seems to be the case that most of us assume a connection between the ways in which we speak and the ways we think. The fact that the way we most typically express our thought processes through language seems to make the connection a natural one. At that level of generalisation the connection seems unexceptionable. A more specific and contentious possibility is raised when we consider the proposition that the way our specific language allows some things to be expressed constrains our capacity to think about those things. When the latter possibility is raised the discussion becomes decidedly lively! It seems also that the academic motives for proposing this form of the connection can be rather varied. For some it is simply an expression of abstract possibility: Something along the lines of, if the human species and thus the human mind is essentially unitary, how can something like the accident of ones native language significantly constrain (even determine) the way we think? On the other hand, for some, the proposal of linguistic relativity is more about expounding and glorying in the diversity of human kind. Another more recent tack seems to be that the existence of linguistic relativity may be a pointer to the non-existence of language universals (of course the latter is contingent on how the claims for language universals are expressed). Given the diversity of issues associated with the topic, it is perhaps acceptable to reconsider some of them, despite some committed scholars appearing to believe that the issue is now beyond dispute (e.g. Levinson's expressive call, "Enough is enough!" [2003a]; other extended discussions include Bowerman & Levinson 2001; Gentner & Goldin-Meadow 2003; Gumperz & Levinson 1996; Hickmann 2003; Levinson 2003b; Lucy 1992; Nuyts & Pederson 1997).

Note in the subsequent discussion the hypothesised relation is stated in different terms as between "language" (in its many forms) and "thought", "thinking", "cognition" etc. Nothing in the literature, apart from the fact of variation in term, seems to be at stake with respect to the hypothesised relation. (It may be revealing that such variation does not seem to carry any theoretical consequences but that is a matter which will not be explored further here.) What is important to emphasise, in contrast to other approaches, is a more explicit commitment to considering the issues in terms of processing. Many of the other approaches tacitly, and in some cases explicitly, anchor the discussion to relations between semantic and conceptual entities. The thrust of such discussion seems to be to determine if and when such semantic categories can be distinguished from conceptual ones. This is a much discussed issue. Many have taken the view that, at least on the basis of intuition, we have concepts for which there are no semantic expressions. Given the difficulty/impossibility of referring to such concepts without the semantic categories, it is doubtful if such contrasts can be sustained (see for example, Lyons 1977). Rather our approach is to consider the essence of the problem as the ways, if any, by which linguistic entities affect conceptual processes. The emphasis is on processing, and not just representational categories.

Part of the problem seems to lie in exactly *what* is being claimed here. Many of the differences between one proponent and another seem to reflect as much a difference in how the issues are defined as what the data are that support or deny them. So, what's the question?

The issues can be laid out in a preliminary way as follows:
1. There's a difference between Languages A and B.
2. Are the differences about the same thing? (What are the criteria? If they are not about the same thing, what's the basis for comparison? Are we dealing with speech; with some aspect of grammatical structure; with the way that a

semantic domain "carves nature at its joints", to use Francis Bacon's famous expression; with the way interactive communication takes place? The more different the domains of comparison are the harder to know what to make of any processing differences.)
3. There's a difference in the processing (in perception, memory, problem solving, or interpersonal communication) of users of Languages A and B.
4. Is this processing difference in relation to habitual thought or possible thought?
5. So???

You will notice that this schema already indicates where some of the variation in theoretical discussion and attendant data may come from. At the heart of this way of laying out the issues is the fact that while the proposal of linguistic relativity starts from a description of structural difference of some kind this difference is merely the starting point. Much of the rest of the issues rests not on claims or counter claims about structural difference but processing difference. And it is surely critical to consider exactly where the processing effects are located. Otherwise subsequent claims about the consequences of the processing differences are likely to still be contentious to say the least. But of all the issues that concern us regarding how to interpret such processing differences as may be found, is the one relating to whether the locus of the constraints is with habitual or possible thinking. The point here is critical. It is certainly not uninteresting to find that language structures of whatever kind affect patterns of habitual thinking. However with respect to the stronger claim that is often invited by the linguistic relativity hypothesis, it is the constraint on *possible* thought patterns which is concentrated upon. Apart from anything else, this distinction is obviously central to the impact linguistic relativity might have on our conceptions of human kind.

Before we get to examine a sample of the sorts of data that are thought to be relevant to evaluating the status of linguistic relativity, we should first consider a few of the methodological considerations which have informed the discussion of this topic to date.

First, there are issues of correlation. Much of the evidence adduced to support one position or another rests on the logic of correlation. That is, what is the degree of association between one side of the equation (language) and the other side (thought)? Although this aspect in itself is unexceptionable, there are some problems with how it is sometimes applied.

The problem of circularity: It is famously difficult (some might say impossible) to completely dissociate the definition of the categories of language from those of thinking. One way of trying to do this is to reduce as much as possible the influence of one relative to the other. But it is often more or less impossible to eliminate the possibility that the way that one has been defined rests, at least in part, on the way the other has been. If there is any suggestion of that then the interaction which may be observed is arguably a consequence of the overlap in definition. One of the motivators of the work on this topic by the likes of Brown and Lenneberg (1954) and Lenneberg and Roberts (1956), was to find a domain which allowed a degree of independent definition of language and of thought. The categories which seemed to allow this were the colour ones, since they could be specified independently by reference to their physical attributes (usually, saturation, brightness and wavelength). It is sometimes asserted that this move was motivated by the exigencies of experimental psychology, but long before the same proposal had been sketched by Bertrand Russell (1927), even if he didn't sully his hands with the subsequent experimental work. Be that as it may, the need to dissociate the parameters of language definition from thought processes is surely essential if the issue of linguistic relativity is to be addressed in a way that does not beg questions about circularity.

There is another problem with how the results of many studies in this area are presented. The claims are said to show an "influence" from one domain on the other, which while not conclusive, are "suggestive". Suggestive of what? That the results are inconclusive? That there is no demonstrable relation between the two? No. The suggestion usually invites the conclusion that there is a demonstrable connection, but for more conclusive evidence we'll have to wait for another day! The discussion after the data presentation proceeds merrily along as if that other day has already arrived.

The other area of concern is that in which scholars invite from such data the inference that the connection involves causality. The conditions on showing causality seem to me to rest on showing not simply that there is some (interesting) connection between language and habitual thought, but that the latter is determined by the language. As we know (and any first year statistics student should be able to tell you) correlations are not acceptable grounds for claims about causality, precisely because of the circularity in the observed interdependence. The causality is just as able to proceed in the opposite direction. Thus nothing in itself hangs on finding (even suggestive) correlations. More is needed in order to mount the argument for causal relations.

2 The role of positive and negative instances

One of the things which are indicative in this area is the kind of evidence that is thought suggestive. It is almost always "positive", that is, it is taken to support the hypothesis that the connection exists between language and thought. However, it is worth noting that in scientific terms what is often (usually?) more revealing is the existence of negative evidence: that is, where the data points to a lack of relation. It would be more compelling to find those cases where the correspondence between language and thinking did *not* exist. Yet this is rarely the motivation in the reported studies. So it is at least as interesting to ask questions which not only ask, why do we get different effects when we do, but also, why do we not get effects when we don't?

Of related interest are questions to do with where the variance comes from? That is, given that there is often considerable variation in the way in which participants respond in different tasks, it is perhaps critical to try and explain what the sources of variation might be rather than assuming that all the variation is due to the correspondence or otherwise between language and thinking. Given this question, it is also relevant to ask, can the variation be manipulated? This is of particular concern if one of the sources of variation is task demands that are not intrinsic to the language/cognition relationship.

Let us consider some of the issues as they occur in a variety of examples drawn from the literature on the topic. Note, this is not an exhaustive review, which is beyond the scope and length of this chapter. Rather the examples are chosen to give some sense of the scatter and range of studies which have been used to try and address the relationship. They are certainly of wider scope than the criteria which have been asserted by such as Lucy (1992) as needing to be met to allow the relation to be systematically studied. But these criteria have the appearance of being self-serving with respect to their intended conclusions. For example, the position is taken that no domain of language, such as colour, should be considered whose explanatory underpinnings may be physiologically determined. This sort of argumentation reads like the elimination by fiat of those areas of study which might provide a contradictory result to that looked for. The range selected here should help to indicate that a wider domain of possible interaction can be looked at than the traditional areas of temporal expressions (the focus of Whorf's original [1956] discussions), colour, or spatial expressions. They should also point to some of the practical issues that have been sketched above. In the light of the differences in these studies, data will then be presented which were collected to evaluate one central aspect of the linguistic relativity hypothesis.

3 Examples

Early children's language is often the focus of studies in this area. This is hardly surprising since if there were to be a fundamental interaction between language and other cognitive processes this is surely somewhere where we might expect to find it. Later we will comment on results found from infants, but for the present let us briefly look at one aspect of preschool children's ability: Differences with demonstratives (expressions which are deictic, that can be interpreted relative to the speaker and hearer's location in the context of utterance). Working with Michael Garman, Patrick Griffiths and Beatrice Clayre, this was part of a crosslinguistic study of English, the Dravidian language Tamil, and a tribal language of Sarawak Lun Bawang (Wales 1974; Wales, Garman & Griffiths 1976). The point of studying the children's ability in simple experimental tasks to handle the expressions in their own languages, was that these languages differ with respect to the explicitness with which they express the relation between speaker and hearer's location. The children were tested in tasks where they acted out with one doll, instructions from another doll. These instructions were of the form: 'jump here', or 'jump there' with variations in the relative positions of the dolls. There was a pronounced difference in the precision with which the children in these three groups dealt with the instructions using demonstratives. These differences were in the order Lun Bawang, best, Tamil in the middle, English least good. This is consistent with the degree of explicitness with which the languages express the relation between speaker and hearer. Thus there seems to be an indication that the degree to which the language is explicit in its expression of a given relationship the easier it is for children to operate with that distinction. (Note also that this addresses one of Lucy's [1992] understandable concerns, which is that such studies should not be oriented to those aspects which are inherently easier to express in English than comparable languages.) It is, however, worth noting that while there were clear respects in which the demonstrative system in the three languages differed and found correlated behavioural differences, the same was not true of the system of comparatives. The Lun Bawang children and the Tamil children operated at the same level with spatial comparatives as the English children despite marked differences between the languages. In fact with Lun Bawang the advice originally from a linguist expert in the area, was that to do such studies in Lun Bawang would be a waste of time given the paucity of this aspect of their linguistic system! So, one result each way!

Another tack is demonstrated by a study by Yoshimi Harsel (Harsel & Wales 1987). This examined the scanning strategies of primary school children whose native language was either Japanese or Australian English. The children showed that the strategies they used in problem solving tasks were influenced by the orthographic conventions associated with each language. It is hard to argue that this sort of effect is intrinsic to the language/cognition relationship, yet it follows much the same interpretative logic involved in many studies in this domain.

One of the most interesting set of studies of language difference effects on categorisation have been reported by Choi and Bowerman (1991), and Bowerman and Choi (2001). They contrasted the ways in which prepositional structures in Korean and English expressed relations between items. They show a striking contrast in the way the two languages partition the world. This difference is glossed in terms like containment versus closeness of fit. They further show that this sort of difference is constraining the speakers responses as early as three years old. These demonstrations are among the most compelling provided for showing the effects of different language structures on categorisation processes. Bowerman and Choi (2001) are careful to qualify the conclusions they draw, although they seem to believe (with considerable reason) that their results provide a challenge to those who question linguistic relativity.

While in no way intending to set aside this challenge, there are issues here about the interpretation of differences in developmental strategies. Consider the Paris based studies on infant speech perception (Christophe, Mehler & Sebastián-Gallés 2001; Mehler, Christophe & Ramus 2000; Ramus & Mehler 1999; Ramus, Nespor & Mehler 1999). Consider in particular the studies done by Ramus with neonates. The infants using the non-nutritive sucking technique (whereby the babies' sucking rate is an index of the attention to auditory stimuli), discriminate French or Japanese from English or German, but not from each other. This is even true if the speech stimuli are re-synthesised so as to replace each consonant with an 's' and each vowel with an 'a' and the pitch contour is manipulated so that no "intonational" information remains other than the stress pattern. These discriminations, note, are shown by the children within hours of birth. Either the children acquired them in the womb, or from immediate imprinting. In another couple of months, Christophe has shown that the children are then able to discriminate between French and Japanese. The interest in this is of course that the stress patterns of French and Japanese are similar, both being more "syllable timed" while those of English and German are "stress timed". (French and Japanese differ in that the latter is also moraic, but this difference is not sufficient to distract the children in the discrimination task.) Now it seems most likely that the interpretation of such results is not to claim that they show the stress patterns of a language "determining" the categorisation of speech sounds but rather disposing the child first to attend to those aspects which are familiar. Perhaps this sort of interpretation applies not only to speech data but also to the interpretation of semantic categories, even if the latter are arguably more complex? Of course, to extrapolate from such studies with speech perception to propositional content is at this stage purely speculative. However, note that Crain, Goro and Minai (In press) report children as young as two years handling quantifiers in different languages in similar ways, despite structural differences between the adult usage in these languages.

Another area which has excited a deal of interest with respect to linguistic relativity is that concerning spatial descriptions. A key component of this interest is contrasting ways in which spatial descriptions can be expressed in different languages. The focus of the contrast is between what we may call "egocentric" versus "non-egocentric" systems. In some it is said the only way to describe spatial relations is in relative terms, such as *right, left, in front of* etc. That is "egocentric". In contrast there are languages where the expressions are absolute/cardinal such as *east, south* etc. That is "non-egocentric". Levinson (2003b) and his colleagues have extensively studied such differences, and found that where the language only allows, say, a non-egocentric set of spatial descriptions, the way that people who use such a language remember a given array is fundamentally influenced by the descriptive system inherent to that language. While there is no doubt about the intrinsic interest in such data, their interpretation is less transparent than might first appear. This is especially true of the methods used in these studies which seem not to control for the role of rehearsal and hence the influence of the linguistic encoding processes the participants have used. The latter does not invalidate the results but it does suggest that they are best taken to support the influence of language on habitual thinking, not on what is possible.

Although not directly comparable with these studies, Anna Filipi and I (2004) have recently been looking at related issues in the uses of egocentric versus non-egocentric expressions in English discourse. English of course allows either mode of expression. We have been looking at how speakers communicate with each other in an Australian version of the "Edinburgh Map Task" (Millar et al. 1994). In this task, one person has to guide the other to draw a route through a series of landmarks only some of which they have in common on their respective maps. Speakers are influenced by whether they know their interlocutor and the strategies which either partner commits to. These can vary between route internal or external perspectives, whether the person is communicating as if they are inside the landscape or outside looking in. Within these options speakers can vary between a number of versions that we have characterised as "survey", "gaze", "no perspective" or "default". The details can be found in Filipi and Wales (2004). The relevant point is not simply that speakers can vary in their locutions but that they vary within the task in ways that are plainly not *ad hoc*. While it is not always clear why they are shifting from an egocentric to a non-egocentric mode, or vice versa, there seem to be discourse constraints placed on which variant is more appropriate. This sort of result indicates that some of the concern about the relation between language structure and language use is going to be a product of discourse constraints. If this is taken as correct, as it surely must be given the wealth of growing data on discourse processes, then this in turn is likely to impact on the evaluation of data said to demonstrate relations between language use and other cognitive processes.

As indicated above, because of the influence of Whorf's work, one of the linguistic domains particularly associated with the linguistic relativity hypothesis is the effect of the way languages differ in the ways they express temporal information. Whorf (1956) himself was concerned to explore the consequences of differences in the tense and aspectual system of some languages. Another, perhaps more immediately accessible domain for examining these differences, are the emphases provided by spatial metaphors for time. One particularly interesting series of studies of this kind is provided by Boroditsky (2000) and colleagues. Specifically they looked at the differential effect between English and Chinese of such metaphors. English predominantly uses the horizontal dimension to express linguistically the passage of time, whereas Chinese concentrates attention on the vertical dimension. In initial experimental studies the participants were quicker in making judgments in the dimension associated with their native language. However the difference between the English and Chinese participants essentially disappeared when the English group was first trained for a fairly short period on making the judgments in the vertical dimension. This result is consistent with the view that the processing differences are a product of habitual association with the categories of the native language, but that the latter are not determining factors in the speakers' capacity to perceive/think/respond.

All this suggests that perhaps we need to consider not only the complexities of theoretical relation between language and cognition, but also task constraints. The literature is replete with examples of the importance of this aspect in interpreting our studies. The task constraints may be as direct as the need to control for the effect of memory in the interval between initial construal of the situation and subsequent testing. This is an old problem which caused some memory researchers back in the sixties and seventies to require of their participants that they do such things as count backwards, out loud, in threes, from a large number. The point of this sort of arcane procedure was to inhibit the possibility that the participants might be rehearsing what they were trying to remember. For our present purposes the issue is less that rehearsal itself might be taking place as that the form of this rehearsal is likely to privilege the form of encoding of the original situation. This of course is likely to be a linguistic encoding, and so make results which point to a "language" effect less than compelling. A number of otherwise interesting studies are open to this complaint.

A different set of task constraints is indicated by the ease with which experimenters' intentions may be misconstrued by their respondents. Among examples of such effects can be listed the ways young children may interpret situations in ways which suggest that they cannot "appropriately" understand them. Donaldson (1978) surveys a number of such examples. One elegant demonstration she refers to is that of Martin Hughes demonstration of early "egocentricity". The standard result to that point had been the claim by Piaget and Inhelder (1947/1956) that in the famous Three Mountains task, children who were not yet "concrete operational" thinkers (typically about seven years of age) failed to take another person's perspective. Hughes showed that children no older than three could take the perspective say of a 'naughty boy' hiding from a 'policeman'. Clearly presenting the problem to children in a context they could relate to had a startling effect on their revealed cognitive capacities.

A different set of examples is provided by the stream of studies by Michael Cole and colleagues (Cole 1999; Cole & Scribner 1974; Cole et al. 1971; Lave 1988) showing that in different cultures, including different contexts within our "own", people could appear to either fail or succeed in certain tasks precisely as a function of whether the task demands were contextualised in such a way that they were either relevant or not to their culture. A related set of results were reported by Henle (1962) showing that normal people scarcely failed in their interpretations of syllogisms when these had been constructed to be interpretable in the respondent's normal life contexts. What was even more compelling was Henle's demonstration that when an "error" was made it always followed from the respondents changing the premises, not failing in the relevant inference. (This has overtones of the results with very young children of Crain, Goro and Minai [In press], showing that the logic underlying the children's understanding of linguistic connectives is already well formed, and it is not language specific.)

This of course then raises concerns about the role of possible biological constraints. The role of experimental studies of colour terms and their motivation has already been referred to. Subsequently Berlin and Kay (1969) transformed the way this domain was considered. By considering a wide array of languages they advanced two key postulates: That despite appearances to the contrary regarding how languages referred to the colour spectrum, there were very general (universal?) constraints on what counted as best (focal) instances of any given basic colour term (one that was exclusively utilised for colour descriptions); and that if we knew the number of basic colour terms a language might have, we could predict with some accuracy what domains they referred to (start with a brightness difference; then a partial ordering of hue contrasts). While details of their proposals have been refined (and a few instances contradicted) the essential elements of the proposal have stood the test of time. It is important to note that the proposal only refers to "basic colour terms" and not to the range of ways in which languages can and do refer to colour. In the latter sense the domain of colour seems as much to support relativity as used to be traditionally argued (e.g. by Russell 1927). Into this mix we should point also to the sorts of effects as Conklin (1955) long ago reported, namely the way in which some cultural contexts could change the way in which colour terms might be interpreted. It is also relevant here to note Lucy's argument that in those areas where there are physiological correlates (as is obviously the case with colour perception as spelled out by such as De Valois & Abramov 1966; De Valois, De Valois & Mahon 2000) it may be inappropriate to look for lack of correspondence between language and cognition. This argument of Lucy's seems perverse when we consider that it depends on our lack of knowledge of the physiological underpinnings of behaviour. Is the argument that there are significant aspects of our behaviour that can not have a physiological account associated with them? Surely not.

To return to the Berlin and Kay proposals, they are paralleled by Ekman's (1982) studies of the recognition of facial emotion. In the early sixties, standard texts (e.g. Woodworth & Schlosberg 1954) pointed to the lack of correspondence between not only cultures but also many people within a culture, in the reliability of the recognition of both the colour and facial emotion domains. With the advent of Berlin and Kay, and Ekman's research it became clear that this variability could be shown to have a robust underpinning of culturally independent processes. Again, it seems the issue is one of how the empirical question is asked, not just what the "results" are.

Let us briefly broaden the consideration of biological constraints in what is perceived as culturally diverse behaviour. We might focus on some implications of evolutionary theory. Although it is probably not useful to speculate about the detailed relevance of evolution to many aspects of language and language behaviour, it is perhaps relevant to consider how aspects of evolutionary theory have been applied to other domains of apparent behavioural diversity. One example of this, among many, is that provided by the exposition of Potts and Short (1999) on the relationship between sexual apparatus and associated social structure. The nature of the social structure correlates closely with the size of the male sexual organs. In crude summary this equates to: If the genitals are relatively small the social group is close (e.g. gorillas), if they are large, the behaviour is more promiscuous (e.g. chimpanzees). What appears to be considerable variation, and is, becomes explicable as the interrelationships between nature and nurture become clear. Consistent with a mid-nineteenth century speculation of Darwin's, this analysis shows the interdependence of the organic and the social. It would be a bold person indeed who claimed that either direction of the interdependence was causal! This example should perhaps serve as a warning about the nature of interpretations that are "sensible", in any situation where we are dealing with interactive relationships, as we are with linguistic relativity.

4   Point-light displays

Let us turn now to the experimental study that is the heart of this chapter. It utilises a technique called point-light displays. It is a technique which was first reported by a French doctor, Marey (for an excellent review of the literature on the use of these point-light displays see Verfaillie 2000). The technique rose to prominence as a result of ground breaking applications commenced by Johansson (1973, 1975, 1977). It essentially entails attaching a light source to each main juncture of the body – the ankle, knee, hip, shoulder, wrist, elbow – and to ensure that the body is not perceived as beheaded, the forehead. If an array of these dots of light are seen in static mode, and without knowledge of the source, they are often seen as if simply a random dot array. If however, they are seen in motion, the inevitable and immediate impression is of a person moving. This dynamic perception has become the substance of many studies of "biological motion". Much has been done with this technique establishing for example, the possibility of distinguishing the gender of the person to whom the lights are attached, or if the person picks up and throws a object in this condition, the perceiver can make a remarkably accurate estimate of the weight of the object and how far it may have been thrown. There are now good grounds also for supposing that there are specific parts of the brain which are particularly involved in the processes of perceiving biological motion (e.g. Oram & Perrett 1994). It is this technique that was utilised for the studies to be reported here.

5 Verbs of motion

The domain of language which this experiment addressed was verbs of motion. An early study of the complex set of Dutch verbs of motion had been conducted using as part of the array of methods available, point-light displays, by Levelt, Schreuder and Hoenkamp (1978). Their study was inevitably difficult given the complexity of applying the technique in those days. Today it is possible to use computer controlled software operating with LEDs as the "light" sources, and thus the technique is much more amenable to relatively easy manipulation.

The study of verbs of motion has become a very pertinent area for discussing linguistic relativity in recent years in particular stimulated by the typological analyses of Talmy (1985). In short, Talmy subcategorises languages with respect to their verbs of motion into two classes:
- Satellite framed: manner and path distinct (as in English, *ran to x*);
- Verb framed: path dominant (*enter, ascend*: borrowings in English from Romance languages where such constructions are dominant).

Such differences themselves encourage considering the possibility that they will be reflected in the thinking of the native speakers of languages of the two types. This interest is reinforced by the fact that these verbs not only involve semantic but syntactic properties which move the focus of study to a sphere that is often overlooked in the concentration of effort on the semantic/conceptual properties of single lexical items that are largely nominal. They are also obviously spatial in scope, which connects with studies that have concerned themselves with other linguistic entities that interact with the spatial/perceptual domain. Of the studies that have looked at the consequences of these different language types the following three are representative. Slobin (1996) has used data particularly from written sources (published novels and the like) to show striking differences in the verb forms used to express motion. These differences are in the direction that Talmy's typological analysis would lead one to expect. Slobin is however, careful to make clear that his interpretation of such data does not lead him to deterministic conclusions. He postulates a way of talking about such relations in terms of "language for speaking" (or given the focus of his basic data, this should perhaps be said to be "language for writing", a distinction which may be of some importance). What is clear from Slobin's study though is that in so far as the data are consistent with differences between the languages it is with respect to their habitual use, not their necessary linguistic/conceptual options.

Papafragou, Massey and Gleitman (2002) with a more directly interventionist experimental design contrasting Greek and English (as Slobin contrasted Spanish and English) found data that they interpret as not supporting the language difference/conceptual difference relation that might have been predicted on the grounds of the typological differences (although it should be noted that their reported data are not as conclusive on this point as the authors seem to suppose).

An interesting study by Finkbeiner et al. (2002) also contrasted Spanish and English, with speakers describing the movements of abstract pictorial figures. In their first study they found the typologically expected differences between the language users. However, when they controlled for memory effects, preventing rehearsal, the differences between the two language groups disappeared.

Our basic study was first conducted with English (see Wales, Webster & Lusher 2003, for details of methods and analyses). The study involved two components:

a. in a laboratory setting which allowed acting out the verbs, using infra-red point-light recordings of the movements (four participants, two of each gender, recording their best versions of each verb twice); and
b. asking perceptual judgments of twenty seven participants through forced choice decisions, with associated ratings of degree of certainty. These judgments were given on seeing in series each of the two versions of each verb of each actor, presented in random order.

The verbs chosen for the second part of the study were those deemed to be most representative of human locomotion without the ambiguity of other legitimate forms of interpretation. For example the verb *jump* was excluded since it is not clear if it is describing locomotion from A to B, or say, jumping on the spot. Of course there is a degree of judgment here by the experimenters which can be said to be relatively arbitrary. For example, the verb *hop* was included in the target verb set despite the fact that it also can be interpreted as hopping on the spot! But it was included so as to have a contrast to otherwise two-legged locomotion, and also to see if the effect of its low lexical frequency had any effect on its perceptual salience. The target set of verbs included *hop*, and also *walk, stroll, shuffle, shamble, run, jog* and *sprint*. Other verbs recorded at the acting stage such as *jump* (or *gallop*, eliminated from the target set because it was not associated primarily with human locomotion) were used in a practice set to familiarise participants in the perceptual judgment part of the study with the experimental requirements.

The basic results are presented in Table 1.

Table 1. Percentages of incorrect judgments for each English verb
(Error rates <5% are not reported)

	sprint	*run*	*jog*	*shuffle*	*hop*	*amble*	*stroll*	*walk*
sprint		14						
run	91		95					
jog		86		51				
shuffle						39		
hop								
amble				23			71	12
stroll				12		42		85
walk				10		18	26	

A number of the results were of interest; not all the verbs were equally well recognised. Overall, the correct judgment of verbs was 58.55% and a marked variance was noted. The order and percentages of correct judgments were *hop* (100%), *jog* (73%), *run* (73%), *walk* (73%), *sprint* (60%), *shuffle* (48%), *stroll* (43%) and *amble* (34%). This provides some indication of how easily each of the verbs was recognised. The order and percentage of the frequency of verbs nominated by the participants was *run* (16.9%), *jog* (15.8%), *walk* (13.2%), *hop* (12.7%), *stroll* (12.6%), *amble* (11.3%), *shuffle* (9.3%) and *sprint* (8.2%). Errors in judgments (a term of convenience to describe the mismatch between the judgement and the actors' intentions) were seen as resulting from confusion in judgments of verbs that perhaps have similar characteristics, with patterns of errors providing an insight to the conceptual groupings of these verbs. Incorrect judgments and their percentages for each verb are presented in Table 1. Considering these data indicates that *hop* is a verb on its own, with 100% correct identification, although still with some erroneous assignments from other target verbs also. Of the rest however it can be seen that the verbs cluster into two groups, one of which is centred on *walk*, and includes *stroll*, *shuffle*, and *amble*. The other is centred on *run*, and includes *jog* and *sprint*. There were two ways in which the data were further analysed. Analyses of correct and incorrect judgments were conducted and while most verbs had one predominant incorrect answer, the verbs *amble* and *shuffle* showed a number of incorrect alternatives. Temporal and structural analyses into the salient features of the actors' performances of all verbs were conducted and provided an insight into the particular characteristics that allow a verb to be recognised.

General descriptions of each verb were compiled based on their prominent characteristics. The two dimensions by which the *walk* and *run* sets of verbs are distinguished are the relative speed of the locomotion and whether the feet are typically on the ground at the same time or not. It is worth noting that with respect to the first criterion, velocity, this is strictly relative since the differential effect can be observed with very different rates of movement by different people. Other characteristics on which the acting out of the verbs differed included such features as head and arm movements. These general definitions were used as a means for comparison of incorrect judgments. Results show that the verbs for which errors are made have a number of overlapping structural characteristics. Additionally, the two verbs with the highest number of errors had characteristics more in line with the incorrectly chosen verb than with the verb intended by the actor (for details see Wales, Webster & Lusher 2003). The study demonstrates that reliable information about the nature and content of lexical interpretations of action verbs is available in the actions used to perform them. This is obviously of relevance to our understanding of how meanings in language are expressed and understood.

The issue of interest here is whether these interpretations are particular to English (and perhaps languages that are typologically like it in regard to verbs of motion) or whether languages which seem very different in their verbs of motion induce different perceptual commitments in their speakers. This was looked at by repeating exactly the same procedures and recorded point-light displays, but using Spanish as the target language. The materials for this part of the study were prepared by Dr Lilit Thwaites of the La Trobe University Spanish program. (The key Spanish "equivalents" are listed with Table 2.) Obviously given the linguistic materials which led Talmy to postulate a different typological description for languages such as Spanish, the materials for this part of our study were not single lexical items. However, does the difference in this "language for speaking", to use Slobin's terminology, result in a different set of perceptions/categorisations of the point-light displays? At least we would expect that the ordered relations even in the error patterns might be different from those of the English cohort. This part of the study was conducted with half a dozen native speakers of Spanish (with a small number we might also expect less interpretable variance, but in fact this was not the case).

Table 2. Percentages of incorrect judgments for each Spanish verb*
(Error rates <5% are not reported)

	Target verb							
	sprint	*run*	*jog*	*shuffle*	*hop*	*amble*	*stroll*	*walk*
sprint		44						
run	80		95	19				
jog	13	56		35				
shuffle	7					28		
hop								
amble				6			70	
stroll				13		28		100
walk				23		45	26	

* correr a toda prisa	'sprint'	saltar a la pata coja	'hop'
correr	'run'	vagar	'amble'
hacer footing	'jog'	pasear	'stroll'
andar arrastrando los pies	'shuffle'	andar	'walk'

If the data in Table 2 are examined they clearly have the same distributional pattern as in Table 1. The inclusion of path information in the verb, with less or no emphasis on manner, does not dispose the perceiver to see the displays in a way that is intrinsically different from those whose dominant verbal mode separates the manner from the path. To all intents and purposes the perceivers seem to be the same regardless of their native language. This, of course, does not mean that the semantic differences in the two verbal types are irrelevant. Simply, that the differences do not determine how the user of the language perceives the world of relevant actions. Looked at from a biological perspective this is not a surprising result.

6 What can we conclude?

We completely agree with Lucy's dictum regarding relativity (Lucy 1996: 37): "A full account must identify the properties of natural language which make diversity possible and give it a crucial role in cultural life." It would be ridiculous to suggest that the discussion and data presented here succeed in this noble endeavour. But what they may serve to do is point to some key aspects of such an endeavour that have arguably been under-represented in discussions of the topic to date. The following points may serve as a summary of these key aspects presented above:

1. Observing cases of influence between language and cognition is a starting point, not an end point.
2. Linguistic relativity is not equivalent to linguistic diversity. It has to do with process, not simply representations (and thus is only indirectly relevant to arguments about universals). This is not of course to deny the fascinating possibility that a contributor to language change may precisely be a shift to avoid some of the consequential constraints of "habitual" thinking induced by language structure.
3. To study process we need to be explicit about processing variables. For example, relevant aspects of perception, memory and task construal are as pertinent as those about relations between representations. In fact some of the concerns about relative representational consequences risk being tautological in their scope.
4. Describing processes involves taking biological constraints as seriously as we do social constraints. A more dynamic context may well shift the locus of interpretation. It seems schizoid to assume that descriptions in this as in any area of human behaviour are to be found that ignore to the point of violation, species relevant contexts.
5. Looking at the interplay of linguistic and cognitive effects includes noting both where there are and where there are not effects. As our discussion has highlighted, there seem to be many cases that point to some sort of linguistic relativity. And there are many that do not. A more fruitful direction for theoretical development would appear to be the explanation of when both positive and negative instances are to be accounted for.
6. Returning to the starting distinction between habitual and possible thought processes, the following questions remain to be addressed: If there are apparent interactions between language and other cognitive processes are these indicators of the familiar modes of thinking which follow from the emphases invited by the structures of the speaker's language, or are they constraints on what is cognitively possible? Are there ways in which interactive effects can be shifted? If so, then they are unlikely to be consistent with interpretations of determination. When and why is it difficult to make the shift from habitual effects? When is it impossible to make those shifts? Only when answers are demonstrably available to these questions will arguments about linguistic determination be worthy of sleep loss.

Acknowledgements

I am indebted to Kate Webster and Dean Lusher for their help with the point-light studies, and to Lilit Thwaites for her help with the Spanish expressions. Kerrie Delves also provided considerable scribal help. I am grateful to each of them.

References

Berlin, Brent & Paul Kay. 1969. *Basic color terms: Their universality and evolution.* Berkeley, CA: University of California Press.
Boroditsky, Lera. 2000. Metaphoric structuring: Understanding time through spatial metaphors. *Cognition* 75(1). 1–28.
Bowerman, Melissa & Soonja Choi. 2001. Shaping meanings for language: Universal and language-specific in the acquisition of spatial semantic categories. In Bowerman & Levinson (eds.), 475–511.
Bowerman, Melissa & Stephen C. Levinson (eds.). 2001. *Language acquisition and conceptual development.* Cambridge: CUP.
Brown, Roger & Eric Lenneberg. 1954. A study in language and cognition. *Journal of Abnormal and Social Psychology* 49. 454–462.
Choi, Soonja & Melissa Bowerman. 1991. Learning to express motion events in English and Korean: The influence of language-specific lexicalization patterns. *Cognition* 41. 83–121.
Christophe, Anne, Jacques Mehler & Nuria Sebastián-Gallés. 2001. Perception of prosodic boundary correlates by newborn infants. *Infancy* 2. 385–394.
Cole, Michael. 1999. Culture-free versus culture-based measures of cognition. In Richard J. Sternberg (ed.), *The nature of cognition*, 645–664. Cambridge, MA: The MIT Press.
Cole, Michael, & Sylvia Scribner. (eds.). 1974. *Culture and thought: A psychological introduction.* New York, NY: Wiley.
Cole, Michael, John Gay, Joseph A. Glick & Donald W. Sharp (eds.). 1971. *The cultural context of learning and thinking.* New York, NY: Basic Books.
Conklin, Harold. 1955. Hanunoo color categories. *Southwest Journal of Anthropology* 11. 339–344.
Crain, Stephen, Takuya Goro & Utako Minai. In press. Hidden units in child language. In Andrea C. Schalley & Drew Khlentzos (eds.), *Mental states. Vol.1: Evolution, function, nature* (Studies in Language Companion Series 92). Amsterdam: John Benjamins.
De Valois, Russell L. & Israel Abramov. 1966. Color vision. *Annual Review of Psychology* 17. 337–362.
De Valois, Russell L. Karen K. De Valois & Luke E. Mahon. 2000. Contribution of S opponent cells to color appearance. In *National Academy of Sciences of the United States of America* 97(1). 512–517.
Donaldson, Margaret. 1978. *Children's minds.* London: Fontana.
Ekman, Paul (ed.). 1982. *Emotion in the human face.* Cambridge: CUP.
Filipi, Anna & Roger J. Wales. 2004. Perspective-taking and perspective-shifting as socially situated and collaborative actions. *Journal of Pragmatics* 36. 1851–1884.
Finkbeiner, Michael, Janet Nicol, Delia Greth & Kumiko Nakamura. 2002. The role of language in memory for actions. *Journal of Psycholinguistic Research* 31(5). 447–457.

Gentner, Dedre & Susan Goldin-Meadow (eds.). 2003. *Language in mind*. Cambridge, MA: The MIT Press.

Gumperz, John J. & Stephen C. Levinson (eds.). 1996. *Rethinking linguistic relativity*. Cambridge: CUP.

Harsel, Yoshimi & Roger J. Wales. 1987. Directional preference in problem solving. *International Journal of Psychology* 22(2). 195–206.

Henle, Mary. 1962. On the relation between logic and thinking. *Psychological Review* 69(4). 366–378.

Hickmann, Maya. 2003. *Children's discourse: Person, space and time across languages*. Cambridge: CUP.

Johansson, Georg. 1973. Visual perception of biological motion and a model for its analysis. *Perception and Psychophysics* 14. 201–211.

Johansson, Georg. 1975. Visual motion perception. *Scientific American* 232(6). 76–88.

Johansson, Georg. 1977. Studies on visual perception of locomotion. *Perception* 6. 365–376.

Lave, Joan. 1988. *Cognition in practice: Mind, mathematics and culture in everyday life*. New York, NY: CUP.

Lenneberg, Eric & John Roberts. 1956. The language of experience: A study in methodology. Memoir 13, Supplement to *International Journal of American Linguistics* 22.

Levelt, Willem J. M., Robert Schreuder & Edward Hoenkamp. 1978. Structure and use of verbs of motion. In Robin N. Campbell & Philip T. Smith (eds.), *Recent advances in the psychology of language*, 137–162. New York, NY: Plenum Press.

Levinson, Stephen C. 2003a. Language and mind: Lets get the issues straight! In Gentner & Goldin-Meadow (eds.), 25–46.

Levinson, Stephen C. 2003b. *Space in language and cognition: Explorations in cognitive diversity*. Cambridge: CUP.

Lucy, John A. 1992. *Language diversity and thought: A reformulation of the linguistic relativity hypothesis*. Cambridge: CUP.

Lucy, John A. 1996. The scope of linguistic relativity: An analysis and review of empirical research. In Gumperz & Levinson (eds.), 37–69.

Lyons, John. 1977. *Semantics*. Cambridge: CUP.

Mehler, Jacques, Anne Christophe & Franck Ramus. 2000. How infants acquire language: Some preliminary observations. In Alec Marantz, Yashusi Miyashita, & Wayne O'Neil (eds.), *Image, language, brain: Papers from the first mind-brain articulation project symposium*, 51–75. Cambridge, MA: The MIT Press.

Millar, Bruce, Julie Vonwiller, Jonathan Harrington & Philip Dermody. 1994. The Australian national database of spoken language. *International Conference on Acoustics, Speech and Signal Processing* 94(1). 97–100.

Nuyts, Jan & Eric Pederson. 1997. *Language and conceptualization*. Cambridge: CUP.

Oram, Michael W. & David I. Perrett. 1994. Response of anterior Superior Temporal Polysensory (STPa) neurons to "Biological Motion" stimuli. *Journal of Cognitive Neuroscience* 6. 99–116.

Papafragou, Anna, Christine Massey & Lila Gleitman. 2002. Shake, rattle, 'n' roll: The representation of motion in language and cognition. *Cognition* 84. 189–219.

Piaget, Jean & Bärbel Inhelder. 1947/1956. *The child's conception of space*. Translated from the French by F. J. Langdon & J. L. Lunzer. London: Routledge & Kegan Paul.

Potts, Malcolm & Roger Short. 1999. *Ever since Adam and Eve: The evolution of human sexuality*. Cambridge: CUP.

Ramus, Franck & Jacques Mehler. 1999. Language identification with suprasegmental cues: A study based on speech resynthesis. *Journal of the Acoustical Society of America* 105(1). 512–521.

Ramus, Franck, Marina Nespor & Jacques Mehler. 1999. Correlates of linguistic rhythm in the speech signal. *Cognition* 73(3). 265–292.

Russell, Bertrand. 1927. *An outline of philosophy*. London: Allen & Unwin.

Slobin, Dan I. 1996. Two ways to travel: Verbs of motion in English and Spanish. In Masayoshi Shibatani & Sandra A. Thompson (eds.), *Grammatical constructions: Their form and meaning*, 195–219. Oxford: Clarendon.

Talmy, Leonard. 1985. Lexicalization patterns: Semantic structure in lexical forms. In Timothy Shopen (ed.), *Language typology and syntactic description*, 57–149. Cambridge: CUP.

Verfaillie, Karl. 2000. Perceiving human locomotion: Priming effects in direction discrimination. *Brain and Cognition* 44. 192–213.

Wales, Roger J. 1974. The child's sentences make sense of the world. In Francois Bresson & Jacques Mehler (eds.), *Les problemes actuels de psycholinguistique* (Current Problems of Psycholinguistics). Paris: Centre Nationale de la Recherche Scientifique.

Wales, Roger J., Michael Garman & Patrick Griffiths. 1976. More or less the same: A markedly different view of children's comparative judgements in three cultures. In Roger J. Wales & Edward C. T. Walker (eds.), *New approaches to language mechanisms*, 29–54. Amsterdam: North Holland.

Wales, Roger J., Kate E. Webster & Dean S. Lusher. 2003. Another look at verbs of motion. Paper presented at the *9th Australian/5th International Cognitive Science Conference*, July 2003.

Whorf, Benjamin L. 1956. *Language, thought and reality: Selected writing of Benjamin Lee Whorf*. Cambridge, MA: The MIT Press.

Woodworth, Robert S. & Harold Schlosberg. 1954. *Experimental psychology*, 2nd edn. New York, NY: Holt, Rinehart & Winston.

Name index

A
Abramov, Israel 340
Ackerman, Brian P. 192
Aebischer, Verena 30
Amberber, Mengistu 29
Ameka, Felix 14–16, 50
American Psychiatric Association 136
Ames, Roger T. 113
Apresjan, Jurij 63–65, 70, 71, 74, 76, 77
Archibald, John 326
Arciuli, Joanne 6, 7, 215, 216, 218, 221, 226, 227, 229, 234, 235
Aslin, Richard N. 321
Astington, Janet W. 192
Auwera, Johan van der 267, 278–280

B
Baayen, R. Harald 216
Bacon, Francis 333
Baillargeon, Renee 193
Baker, Brett 7, 8, 246, 255
Banfield, Ann 151, 152
Barcelona, Antonio 309
Baron-Cohen, Simon 136, 137
Barrington, Graham 4, 5
Barron, Julia 279, 280
Bartlett, Frederic C. 149
Beadle, Noel C. 259, 261
Bekerian, Debra A. 97
Bellugi, Ursula 137
Berko Gleason, Jean 321
Berlin, Brent 7, 56, 239–242, 247–256, 258–262, 340, 341
Berman, Ruth A. 145, 150–153, 173, 176, 177, 181, 182, 185, 187
Bishop, Dorothy V. M. 138
Black, Maria 216, 235
Bloom, Paul 313
Bock, Kathryn 214–216, 226
Boland, Julie E. 214
Bolton, Neil 316
Boroditsky, Lera 339

Boscolo, Pietro 150, 153
Boucher, Jerry D. 19
Bowerman, Melissa 174, 175, 188, 332, 336, 337
Boym, Svetlana 79, 80
Braine, Martin D. 213
Brasseur, Judith 192
Breedlove, Dennis E. 239, 240, 250, 256, 258
Brewin, Chris R. 97
Briggs, Jean L. 18
Brinton, Donna M. 325
Brock, John 260
Broderick, Victor K. 206
Brooker, Ian 260
Brotherson, Anna 54
Brown, Cecil H. 262
Brown, Roger 334
Bruder, Gail 151
Bruner, Jerome 12, 137
Bugenhagen, Robert D. 14
Burden, Robert L. 326
Burusphat, Somsonge 180, 181
Buttrick, Samuel 209
Byrne, Brian 321, 322, 325

C
Cacciari, Cristina 192, 206
Capell, Arthur 267
Capps, Lisa 137–139
Carlson, Stephanie M. 208
Carpenter, Patricia A. 322
Carroll, John B. 313
Cassidy, Kimberley W. 214
Celce-Murcia, Marianne 325
Chafe, Wallace 145
Chalmers, Alan 315
Chandler, Michael 208
Chao, Yuan-Jen 111
Chapman, Siobhan 311
Chappell, Hilary 14, 17, 114
Chater, Nick 214
Chen, Tong 115
Chiat, Shula 216, 235
Chisholm, Roderick M. 318

Choi, Soonja 174, 336, 337
Chomsky, Noam 41
Christiansen, Morten H. 214
Christophe, Anne 337
Cisotto, Lerida 150, 153
Clark, Herbert H. 189, 209
Classen, Constance 128
Clayton, William Derek 253
Clements, Wendy A. 208
Cohen, Donald J. 134
Cole, Michael 340
Coleman, Carolyn 242, 248, 250
Colston, Herbert L. 5, 6, 192, 193, 199, 205, 206
Coltheart, Max 217, 218
Commonwealth of Australia 259
Conklin, Harold 340
Couturat, Louis 42
Crain, Stephen 337, 340
Croft, William 312
Cruse, David Alan 240, 246, 306, 312
Cupples, Linda 6, 7, 215, 216, 218, 221, 226, 227, 229, 234, 235

D
D'Andrade, Roy 81
Danesi, Marcel 109
Dasher, Richard B. 119
Davis, Sally M. 215
De Valois, Karen K. 340
De Valois, Russell L. 340
DeFrancis, John 111, 116
Denny, Peter J. 47
Dessaix, Robert 61
Diener, Ed 30
Dijk, Teun van 145
Dik, Simon 267–269, 277, 279, 280
Dixon, Robert M. W. 244
Donaldson, Margaret 339
Douglas, Joan D. 192
Dritschel, Barbara H. 97
Duchan, Judith F. 151

Dunn, Judith 135

E
Eco, Umberto 103
Ekman, Paul 18, 341
Elgin, Suzette Haden 316
Ellis, John M. 311
Enfield, N. J. 14, 18
Erelt, Mati 293, 295
Evans, Nicholas 119, 265, 269, 270, 276

F
Fabb, Nigel 145
Fehr, Berverley 12
Feynman, Richard 315
Field, Laurie 315
Filipi, Anna 338
Finkbeiner, Michael 343
Flavell, Eleanor R. 192
Flavell, John H. 192
Folk, Jocelyn 214
Folstein, Susan 136
Fortescue, Michael 23, 74, 81
Fraser, Helen 9, 312, 316, 319, 321–323, 325, 326
Frawley, William 292
Frith, Uta 136, 137
Fritz, Anna S. 208
Fromkin, Victoria 311
Fudge, Erik 217

G
Gardner, Howard 312
Garman, Michael 336
Gaume, Bruno 269
Genetti, Carol 273
Gentner, Dedre 175, 332
Gerken, Lou Ann 321
Gibbs, Raymond W. 192, 193, 205, 206
Gibson, James J. 315
Givón, Talmy 269, 278
Gladkova, Anna 2, 3, 22
Gleitman, Lila 343
Goddard, Cliff 2, 11–14, 16–20, 22, 23, 25, 26, 35, 39, 40, 46, 47, 62, 63, 66–68, 81, 86, 87, 114, 239, 242, 257, 312
Goldberg, Adele E. 307
Goldin-Meadow, Susan 175, 332
Goldman, Susan 150
Gombert, Jean-Emile 321
Goodwin, Janet M. 325
Gopnik, Alison 207

Goro, Takuya 337, 340
Graumann, Carl F. 151
Green, Francis L. 192
Grice, Paul H. 209
Griffiths, Patrick 336
Grimes, Joseph E. 145
Gumperz, John J. 175, 332

H
Hala, Suzanne 208
Hale, Ken 16, 274
Hall, David 113
Hall, Edward 109
Hannam, Rachel 325
Happé, Francesca 135
Harkins, Jean 11, 17, 18, 86
Harré, Rom 18
Harris, Roy 311
Harsel, Yoshimi 336
Harvey, Mark 248, 258
Hasada, Rie 25
Hays, Terence 258, 259
Heath, Jeffrey 239, 242, 244, 245, 247, 258, 274
Heider, Karl G. 19
Heine, Bernd 290, 291
Hengeveld, Kees 267–269, 277, 279, 280
Henle, Mary 340
Hewett, Heather E. 267, 271, 273
Hewitt, Lynne 151
Hickmann, Maya 145, 179, 182–184, 188, 332
Hildyard, Angela 321
Hill, Ken D. 260
Hinch, Heather E. 267
Hinds, John 145
Hix, Hollie R. 208
Hoenkamp, Edward 342
Holland, Nancy 18
Hoogewerf, Rupert 115
Hopper, Paul J. 176
Huumo, Tuomas 308

I
Inhelder, Bärbel 339

J
Jackendoff, Ray 41
Jahoda, John E. 312
Ji, Shaojun 145
Jimenez, Beatrice C. 192
Joanisse, Mark F. 216, 234
Johansson, Georg 342
Johnson, Lawrie A. S. 260, 261

Johnson, Mark 113, 306
Johnson, Michael D. 205
Johnson, Nancy S. 149
Johnson, Steve 258
Johnston, Judith R. 174
Jones, Rhys 56, 57
Joseph, Robert 136
Joseph, John E. 312
Just, Marcel 322

K
Kaczmarek, Aleksandra 188
Kallmeyer, Werner 151
Kalotas, Arpad 239, 242
Kanchanawan, Nitaya 180, 181
Karlsson, Susanna 16, 22, 23, 66–68
Kasik, Reet 292
Kay, Paul 56, 340, 341
Kehres, Jennifer 137
Keller, Shauna B. 199, 205
Kelly, Michael H. 214–221, 225–227, 234
Kim, Min-Joo 280, 284
Kirkpatrick, John 18
Kitayama, Shinobu 18
Klima, Edward S. 137
Koenig, Jean-Pierre 180, 181
Kuiper, Melissa S. 193
Kuntay, Aylin C. 188
Kuteva, Tania 290
Kvavilashvili, Lia 95, 97

L
Labov, William 137, 145, 158, 313
Lakoff, George 113, 306, 313, 319, 320
Lambrecht, Knud 269, 281, 282, 284, 286
Langacker, Ronald 319, 320
Lave, Joan 340
Laver, John 323
Leahey, Thomas H. 312
Lecercle, Jean-Jacques 316
Lee, Iksop 87
Lee, Penny 11, 313
Lee, Yosep 99
Lefrancois, Guy 326
Leibniz, Gottfried Wilhelm 2, 3, 38–41, 46
Lenneberg, Eric 334
Levelt, Willem J. M. 342
Levinson, Stephen C. 174, 175, 188, 332, 338

Levorato, Maria D. 192, 206
Levy, Robert 18
Li, Naicong 151
Li, Ping 176
Liddy, Lenny Gappuya 240, 242, 245, 254
Linell, Per 321
Linton, Marigold 95
Locke, John 46
Longacre, Robert E. 145, 273
Losh, Molly 137–139
Love, Nigel 312
Loveland, Katherine 137
Lucariello, Joan 157
Lucy, John A. 332, 335, 346
Luksaneeyanawin, Sudaporn 180
Lusher, Dean S. 343, 345
Lutz, Catherine A. 18
Lyons, John 332

M
Macdonald, Shem 325
Macnamara, John 311
MacWhinney, Brian 181
Magee, Bryan 316
Mahon, Luke E. 340
Makeeva, Irina 77
Mandler, George 95, 97
Mandler, Jean M. 149
Markus, Hazel Rose 18
Masjid, Asifa 175
Massey, Christine 343
Mawer, Giselle 315
Mayer, Mercer 138, 177, 178
McGivern, Robert 151
McKnight, David 240, 242, 259
Meehan, Betty 56, 57
Meepoe, T. Amy 180
Mehler, Jacques 337
Melčuk, Igor 64, 71
Merlan, Francesca 239, 247, 281
Merleau-Ponty, Maurice 129
Millar, Bruce 338
Millikan, Ruth Garrett 315
Minai, Utako 337, 340
Monaghan, Padraic 214
Morris, Joanna 216, 234
Morris, Robin 214
Moses, Louis J. 208
Muansuwan, Nuttanart 180, 181
Murphy, Gregory L. 312
Mushin, Ilana 151–153

N
Nathan, Geoffrey 320
Nespor, Marina 337
Nippold, Marilyn 192
Noonan, Michael 279, 280
Norbury, Courtenay F. 138
Nordqvist, Åsa 152
Nuyts, Jan 332

O
O'Banion Varma, Keisha 150
O'Brien, Jennifer 205, 206
Ochs, Elinor 135, 137
Olson, David R. 192, 321
Oram, Michael 342
Ortony, Andrew 193
Ots, Thomas 129
Owen, Stephen 112, 119
Ozonoff, Sally 136

P
Padučeva, Elena 64
Pajusalu, Renate 8, 9, 293
Palmer, Frank R. 312
Palmer, Gary 11
Papafragou, Anna 343
Passmore, John 316
Peel, Bettina 192
Peeters, Bert 17
Pennington, Bruce F. 136
Pesmen, Dale 25
Perner, Josef 192, 208
Perrett, David I. 342
Piaget, Jean 174, 339
Piepenbrock, Richard 216
Pinker, Steven 213
Polanski, Virginia G. 206
Polanyi, Michael 313
Polinsky, Maria 284
Pollard, David 112
Potts, Malcolm 341
Proxorov, Urij 79
Pryor, Lindsay D. 261

Q
Quinn, Naomi 18

R
Ramsey, Robert S. 87
Ramus, Franck 337
Raven, Peter H. 239, 240, 250, 256, 258
Read, Charles 321
Reid, Nicholas 273
Reilly, Judy S. 137, 151

Repacholi, Betty M. 207
Rijn, Hedderik van 216
Roberts, John 334
Roche, Maurice 316
Rodman, Robert 311
Rogers, Sally J. 136
Rosaldo, Michelle Z. 18
Rosch, Eleanor 3, 7, 241
Rosenthal, Dieter 308
Rumelhart, David E. 149
Russell, Bertrand 334, 340
Russell, James A. 12, 136
Ryan, Marie-Laure 158

S
Sandefur, John R. 247, 265
Sanders, Jose 151, 163
Sapir, Edward 1, 10, 12, 85
Sarup, Madan 316
Scarborough, Hollis S. 322
Schachter, Paul 281
Schank, Roger C. 95
Scherer, Klaus R. 30
Schlosberg, Harold 341
Schmidt, Todd P. 180
Schreuder, Robert 209, 342
Schuster, John 315
Schwartz, Theodore 18
Scribner, Sylvia 340
Sebastián-Gallés, Nuria 337
Sellen, Abigail J. 94
Selman, Robert L. 151
Sereno, Joan A. 214, 226
Shanon, Benny 312
Sharp, Diana 150
Shirai, Yasuhiro 176
Shore, Bradd 18
Short, Roger 341
Shweder, Richard A. 18
Sigman, Marian 137
Singer, Ruth 8, 272, 273
Slobin, Dan I. 145, 150–153, 173–177, 181, 182, 185, 187, 188, 343, 345
Smith, Annette 140, 149
Smith, Carlotta S. 180
Solomon, Olga 134, 135, 137, 138
Solomon, Robert 62
Spence, Donald P. 95
Spiegelberg, Herbert 316, 317
Spooren, Wilbert 151
Spurling, Laurie 316
Sternin, Iosif 79
Stirling, Lesley 4, 5, 145

Strange, Winifred 322, 326
Strömqvist, Sven 177, 179
Suh, Eunkook M. 30
Sullivan, Kate 137–139, 208
Summerfield, Angela B. 30
Sweetser, Eve 109, 127, 128, 269, 291, 296
Synott, Anthony 109

T
Tager-Flusberg, Helen 136–138
Talmy, Leonard 342, 343, 345
Taylor, Catherine L. 192
Taylor, John R. 313, 320
Taylor, Marjorie 192
Taylor, Talbot J. 312
Thepkanjana, Kingkarn 180
Thompson, Sandra A. 273
Thurber, Christopher 137, 138
Tolstoy, Leo 72
Tomlin, Russell 145
Torrance, Nancy 321
Tragel, Ilona 8, 9, 290, 296
Traugott, Elizabeth C. 119
Travis, Catherine 14, 17
Treiman, Rebecca 321
Tunali, Belgin 137

U
Uryson, Elena 64

V
Vanhove, Martine 269
Verfaillie, Karl 341
Verhoeven, Ludo 177, 179
Verrekia, Laura 216, 234
Viberg, Åke 23, 110, 269
Vinge, Louise 109
Volkmar, Fred R. 134
Vosniadou, Stella 193

W
Waddy, Julie 240, 242, 247, 253
Wales, Roger 9, 10, 336, 338, 343, 345
Waletzky, Joshua 137, 145, 158
Wallbott, Harald G. 30
Webster, Kate E. 343, 345
Wegner, Daniel M. 97
Weist, Richard M. 188
Wells, George Albert 311
West, Stephen H. 129
White, Geoffrey M. 18
Whorf, Benjamin Lee 1, 10, 41, 42, 59, 174, 313, 335, 338
Wiebe, Janet 150
Wierzbicka, Anna 2, 3, 11–16, 18, 21, 22, 25, 30, 39, 40, 43–47, 53, 57, 58, 62–64, 66, 71, 77, 78, 80, 85, 86, 103, 114, 115, 279, 290, 315, 320

Wilkins, David P. 119, 247, 257, 269, 276
Williams, Marion 326
Wimmer, Heinz 192
Winkler, Suzanne 279
Winner, Ellen 192, 193, 206, 208
Winograd, Eugene 95
Winskel, Heather 5
Wittgenstein, Ludwig 313
Woodworth, Robert S. 341
Wysocka, Jolanta 188

X
Xunzi 109

Y
Yang, Byong-Seon 280, 284
Yang, Lien-Sheng 111
Yangklang, Peerapat 181
Ye, Zhengdao 2, 4, 111, 114, 116, 129
Yoon, Kyung Joo 2, 4, 25, 27, 28, 86, 87, 108
Yu, Ning 113, 114

Z
Zaliznjak, Anna 65, 73, 80
Zamora, Anita 151
Zevin, Jason 216, 234
Zlatev, Jordan 181
Žolkovskij, Alexander 64, 71
Zubin, David A. 151

Language index

A
Amharic 39
Anindhilyakwa 240, 242, 247, 253, 254
Arrernte 175, 247, 257–259
Australian English 8, 242, 244, 258, 260–263, 336

B
Burarra 3, 37, 56–58

C
Catalan 279
Chinese 2, 4, 14, 15, 30, 39, 109–129, 179, 180, 182–184, 186, 187, 339

D
Dutch 342

E
English 1–4, 6, 7, 9–19, 21–31, 35, 37–39, 42, 44–46, 48, 49, 57, 58, 61–81, 86–88, 90, 94, 95, 98, 103, 104, 110, 111, 114, 118, 126, 173–177, 179, 182, 183, 187, 213–235, 240, 242, 244, 254, 255, 258–262, 277, 281, 283, 325, 331, 336–339, 342–345
Estonian 8, 289–308
Ewe 14, 16, 17, 39, 50

F
Finnish 308
French 17, 18, 30, 128, 179, 267–269, 278–283, 285, 337, 341

G
German 15, 18, 25, 30, 173, 177, 179, 182, 183, 187, 245, 337
Greek 343
Guugu-Yimidhirr 175

H
Hebrew 173, 177, 179, 182, 183, 187

I
Italian 279, 280

J
Japanese 17, 25, 39, 336, 337

K
Korean 2, 4, 11, 24, 25, 27, 28, 31, 85–105, 108, 174, 269, 280, 284, 286, 336
Kriol 247
Kugu Nganhcara 258

L
Lao 14, 39
Lardil 240, 242, 254, 259
Latin 128
Lori 280
Lun Bawang 336

M
Malay 11, 14, 15, 17–21, 24–27, 31, 39
Mandarin Chinese 14, 17, 109–129, 179, 180, 182–184, 186, 187
Mawng 8, 267–286
Mbula 14, 39

N
Ngalakgan 7, 239–264
Nunggubuyu 239, 242

P
Polish 3, 14, 15, 18, 38–40, 49

R
Romance languages 8, 9, 267–269, 275, 279, 280, 284–286, 342
Rumanian 279
Russian 2, 3, 22, 25, 39, 61–81

S
Samoan 17
Scandinavian languages 67
Spanish 9, 10, 14–16, 39, 173, 177, 179, 182, 183, 187, 279, 280, 331, 343, 345, 346
Swedish 11, 22–24, 67

T
Tamil 336
Thai 5, 173, 180–188
Turkish 173, 177, 179, 182, 187

U
Ulwa 16

W
Wagiman 240, 242, 245, 254
Western Desert 242, 257, 259
Wubuy 7, 239, 244–247, 253–258

Y
Yankunytjatjara 15, 39, 242
Yolngu Matha 17

Subject index

A
absolute systems 175
abstract concepts 42, 43, 80, 113, 121, 122, 125, 126, 312, 314, 319, 321, 323, 324
abstraction 9, 291, 312, 314, 318, 319, 321–323
actors 145, 147, 148, 331, 343–345
agglutinating 88
attentional flexibility 133, 157
autism 4, 5, 133–171
autistic children 4, 136, 138

B
back-translation 12, 30
basic concepts 65, 312, 319
basic emotions 13, 18, 19, 21
basic level categories 7, 241, 242
basic syntactic frames 13, 15, 17
basic words 27, 37, 45, 62, 67, 77, 78, 88, 112
beginning 55
belief 2, 3, 13, 20, 22, 27, 61, 65, 68, 71, 73–80, 113, 192, 208, 210
binomial names 239, 241, 254
biological motion 342
bodily experience 110, 113, 114
body/mind dichotomy 4, 110, 113, 129
bottom 53, 54
bottom-up approach 209

C
caretaker 5, 187
categorisation 2, 6–8, 37, 65, 86, 214, 227, 235, 262, 289–310, 318, 320, 336, 337, 345
causal connective 5, 184–186
causal relations 145, 150, 154, 334
causal structure 150, 160
causality 137, 138, 149, 151, 295, 334
change of state 9, 289–310
Childhood Autism Rating Scale (CARS) 139
children's stories 135, 138, 140, 145, 150, 152
chwuek- 86, 88, 89, 98–100
chwuekha- 2, 4, 85, 86, 88–90, 98–104
circularity 333, 334
Clinical Evaluation of Language Fundamentals (CELF) 139
coding 8, 103, 137, 138, 145, 151, 153, 177, 183, 187, 196–201, 269, 280, 284, 338, 339
cognition 2, 4–7, 11, 12, 38, 40, 45, 51, 59, 61, 62, 65, 80, 86, 88, 94, 103, 109–132, 133, 134, 153, 173–190, 191–193, 205, 207, 209, 241, 269, 271, 291, 311, 316, 318, 320, 324, 325, 332, 335, 336, 339, 340, 347
cognitive constraint 8, 269, 282, 286
cognitive development 5, 192, 193, 203
cognitive experience 85, 104, 109, 110
cognitive linguistics 25, 85, 113, 312, 319, 320
cognitive processes 11, 62, 96, 103, 127, 135, 141, 161, 335, 338, 347
cognitive scenario 18, 21
cognitive science 2, 3, 9, 11, 13, 17, 25, 29, 31, 61, 62, 65, 86, 313, 316, 319, 320
cognitive state 6, 91, 104, 109, 110, 137
cognitive structure 4, 7, 8
colour 3, 37, 45, 46, 50, 56–58, 241, 314, 335, 340, 341
colour terms 340
complement 8, 15–17, 22, 67–69, 71, 77, 92, 93, 95, 102, 111, 119–121, 267–288
complement clauses 267–288
complementation 14, 269, 276, 284–286
computer games 158
concepts 2, 3, 9, 11–13, 21, 25, 28, 29, 31, 37, 39, 41–59, 61–65, 80, 85–88, 90–105, 109, 113, 114, 121, 122, 124–126, 129, 136, 174–176, 290, 311–330, 332
conceptual metaphor 110, 113, 114, 192
conceptual prime/primitive 3, 4, 39, 40, 61, 85
conceptual system 40, 85, 109, 110, 112–114, 129
conceptualisation 47, 49–51, 85, 86, 103, 128, 130, 173, 174, 317, 318, 320, 322, 323
concrete concepts 42, 43, 45
connectives 5, 155, 179, 181–188, 340
construction meaning 296, 307
constructions 8, 9, 16, 42, 63, 67, 68, 71, 72, 74, 77, 89, 255–257, 274, 281, 282, 284–286, 289–310, 342
corpus 31, 66 –68, 77, 87, 111, 218
culturally familiar stories 144

D
deictic 150, 151, 306, 336
developmental disorder 134, 136
developmental process 151, 174
dimensions 48, 52, 54, 331
direct speech 137, 143, 151–153, 156, 159
discourse 8, 137, 145, 150, 151, 179, 199, 267–269, 277, 280, 282, 286, 338
discourse analysis 133–135, 150
disyllables 6, 7, 213–237
DSM-IV 136

E
early development view 191–193, 207
Edinburgh Map Task 338
egocentric 78, 337–339

emotional state 101, 103, 104, 151, 154
empirical 3, 5, 7, 12, 37–40, 59, 63, 80, 103, 108, 191, 208, 214, 215, 341
end 53–56
entity 9, 27, 214, 250, 267–288, 293, 298, 307, 318, 332, 343
episode boundaries 145, 149
episodic macrostructure 4, 5, 133, 135, 145, 149, 159
ethnocentrism 1–4, 11, 31, 80, 86
ethnopsychological construct 13, 24, 25, 29
evaluation 137, 158
event 21, 26, 35, 39, 40, 92, 93, 102, 108, 145, 147, 150, 173, 176, 177, 179–182, 185, 187, 214, 267–269, 271, 272, 275–281, 284, 285, 289–292, 298, 305, 313
evolutionary theory 341
executive control 4, 5, 136, 137, 160
experience 8, 12, 18, 23, 29, 30, 31, 51, 58, 85, 86, 95, 103, 104, 109, 110, 113, 114, 116–121, 124–130, 138, 176, 179, 202, 205, 206, 208, 316
experience-near concept 29
experimental studies 135, 339–341
expressive framing 133, 151
extreme case formulation 197, 198, 200–203

F

facial emotion 341
familiar children's stories 135, 140, 152
features 134, 135, 149, 150, 151, 152, 160, 173, 214, 242, 269, 275, 313, 320, 321, 345
figurative language 5, 6, 191–212
figurative language comprehension 191–194, 206, 207
figurative language development 5, 191–212
flashbacks 97
focus sentence 269, 280–286
folk generic 239–242, 248, 250, 252–254, 258, 261
folk taxonomy 7, 8, 239–244, 247, 249–252, 254, 256, 258, 260–263

genus 241, 242, 244, 252, 253, 260–262

G

global 56, 133, 136, 137, 145, 149, 151, 157, 159, 160
global coherence 145, 149
grammatical category 6, 7, 213–237
grammaticalisation 276, 289, 304
gustatory experience 118–120, 124–128

H

habitual thoughts 333, 334, 338, 347
hands 47–52
happiness studies 30
high 48, 53
higher-functioning 4, 136, 138, 139
hyperbole 5, 6, 191, 194–207

I

I believe 22, 38, 78
I believe that 22, 23, 78, 79
ideophones 50
imperative 89, 91, 94
imperfective aspect 176, 177, 180, 182, 183, 185, 186
imperfective-perfective 173, 176–178, 180, 186
infant speech perception 337
inflation 197–201, 203, 205
information structure 269, 282, 284, 285
inhibitory control 133, 157
input language 174, 175, 188
insider perspective 12, 31
intellectual disability 136
intransitive 89, 277
involuntary retrieving 95, 96, 104

K

Kid Pix 142, 145
kiek-, 86, 88, 89, 98–100
kiekha-, 2, 4, 85, 86, 88–100, 102–104
knowledge 3, 6, 15, 22, 23, 61, 92, 95–97, 135, 140–144, 151, 153, 155, 156, 159–161, 193, 210, 276, 277, 285

knowledge state management 5, 135, 140–144, 153, 158

L

language acquisition 6, 105, 173, 174, 179, 183, 184, 187, 188, 193, 213
language delay 136
language development 5, 6, 139, 152, 173–190, 191–212
language disorder 134, 139
language-for-speaking 343, 345
LASPOM 6, 191, 208–210
late development view 5, 6, 192, 205–207
lexical stress 7, 213–221, 226, 227, 232–235
lexicalised agreement 271, 272, 275, 277, 285
lexicon 6, 11, 12, 14, 21, 29, 41–44, 85, 87, 249, 252, 253, 256, 259, 289, 290
linguistic relativity 9, 10, 173–175, 331–350
linguistics 25, 41, 61, 65, 85, 113, 311, 312, 318, 320, 323, 324, 327
local perspective 157, 160
locative terms 174
long 38, 45, 46, 48, 49, 50, 52, 53, 54, 55, 56
low 48, 53

M

memory 4, 9, 11, 29, 85–107, 119, 333, 339, 343, 347
mental processes 69, 85, 103, 104, 119, 124, 125
mental space 176
mental states 1, 2, 3, 5, 11, 12, 13, 17, 29, 30, 31, 62, 65, 75, 76, 77, 78, 81, 85, 103, 104, 109, 111, 120, 124, 127, 133, 136, 137, 138, 150, 152, 155, 157, 159, 160, 268
metalanguage 1, 2, 4, 11–35, 39, 61–64, 85–87, 104, 105, 108, 110, 114, 291, 320
metaphor 98, 110, 112–114, 192–194, 205, 206, 303, 306, 339
metarepresentational thought 192
metatheory 316, 320, 327

Subject index

mind 1–4, 6, 11, 13, 24–29, 31, 37, 38, 40, 41, 45, 51, 59, 86, 110, 113, 129, 191, 208–210, 291, 312, 325, 331
mind-blindness 4, 136, 159,
mind-popping 95
monomial 7, 239, 241, 242, 254, 257–259, 261
morphosyntactic 35, 40, 85, 86, 88, 160
Moscow School of Semantics (MSS) 3, 61–63, 76

N
naïve realism 9, 311, 312, 317, 320
narrative production 6, 141, 145, 150, 152
narrative structure 147
Natural Attitude 9, 317, 319, 320, 322, 324–326
naturalistic methodologies 135
naturalistic production 5, 191, 206
neologisms 143, 153
nominalisation 26, 273
nominalised complement clauses 273, 285
nonverbal IQ 139
noun 213–237, 244, 245, 257, 258, 273–275, 279, 283, 312
noun stems 88, 89
NSM (Natural Semantic Metalanguage) 1–4, 12–15, 17, 18, 24, 28, 29, 31, 38–43, 57–59, 62–70, 80, 86, 87, 104, 108, 110, 114, 115, 129
NSM descriptions 31

O
obligatoriness 182, 185
obligatory 173, 175–177, 179, 180, 182, 187, 188
onomatopoeia 137, 151, 152, 159
oral narratives 133, 134
orthography 7, 213, 216–219, 227, 233, 234, 322, 323

P
pagination 147
parts 24–28, 42, 48–50, 52, 55, 56, 120, 255, 314, 321
perception 6, 8, 9, 45, 46, 110, 111, 124, 129, 150, 191, 208, 209, 242, 261–288, 333, 337, 340, 342, 345, 347

perfective aspect 176, 177
perspective 4, 9–12, 16, 58, 104, 114, 129, 133, 135–137, 150–153, 157, 159–161, 268, 282, 291, 338–340
pervasive development disorder 139
phenomenology 26, 316, 318
phonemic awareness 322
phonetics 322–324
phonological terms 320, 321, 323, 324
physical properties 38, 46, 50
place 93, 145, 214, 254, 255, 318
polysemy 48, 50, 289, 290, 296, 308
population 134, 138, 139, 150
Post Traumatic Stress Disorder 97
predicate 3, 5, 8, 9, 64, 98, 104, 119, 152, 160, 180, 257, 268, 271–277, 279, 280, 285, 287, 289, 291, 292, 296, 302, 304, 307–310
primes 2–4, 11–17, 21–24, 29, 31, 35, 37, 39, 40, 42–47, 52–54, 61, 63, 70, 76, 104, 105, 108
primitives 2, 4, 61– 65, 76, 85, 87, 104, 108, 114, 128, 290
processing 6, 9, 136, 145, 215–218, 234, 235, 322, 324, 325, 332, 333, 339, 347
processing variables 347
progressive 91, 92, 177, 178, 180
pronunciation 311, 322, 325, 326
proposition 22, 74, 80, 268, 274, 276–280, 285
propositional attitude 2, 3, 61–83
prospective 94
pseudorelative complement clauses 267, 274, 275, 282
psycholinguistics 209, 235, 321, 322
punctuation 141, 143, 152, 195, 199

Q
qualitative analysis 133, 134, 139, 160

R
reader theatre 140, 149, 152, 154

reading 145, 209, 217, 218, 229, 234, 235, 296, 297, 298, 309, 322
rectangular 38, 49
relation 5, 42, 145, 150, 154, 177, 182–188, 214, 289, 334, 338, 345, 347
relative clause 5, 184–186, 267–269, 273–276, 279–286
relative systems 175
remember 11, 86, 88, 95, 103
repetition 137, 141, 151
reported speech 141, 152, 155, 156
reported thought 155, 156
retellings 135, 139, 140, 142, 149, 150, 152–159
retrieving 91–97, 99–102, 104
rhetorical question 197, 198, 201, 203
round 38, 45, 46, 48–50, 52, 314

S
satellite-framed languages 176, 342
scanning strategies 336
scenario 18, 21, 31, 121
SEE (semantic primitive), 14, 37, 39, 46, 114
semantic molecules 43–45, 52–54, 115
semantic space 174
sense 4, 109, 115, 120, 127–129
sensory experience 23, 109, 110, 113, 114, 119, 127, 128
sensory perception 268, 269, 271
sentence construction 217, 229–233, 282, 286
serialisation 181, 185, 186
shape 3, 37, 45–50, 52–55, 241, 314, 318
short 48, 52, 53
simultaneity 176, 179
situation 27, 70–72, 74, 94, 96, 154, 176, 177–180, 186, 188, 195, 197, 198, 267, 268, 282, 285, 289, 291, 292, 297, 304, 305, 307, 308, 339
smell 17, 110, 128
spatial 145, 147, 149, 174, 175, 286, 295, 335–339, 343
spatial domain 173, 174, 176, 188, 343

speakers 1–4, 6–9, 23, 24, 37, 38, 40, 42–45, 50, 58, 79, 80, 85, 87, 89–104, 120, 150, 152, 153, 174–176, 179, 185, 187, 191, 194–202, 204, 207, 210, 213, 215, 216, 228, 239, 242, 245–247, 269, 289, 290, 298, 304, 305, 307, 308, 321, 324, 336–339, 342, 343, 345, 346, 347
speech act 42–44, 277
story comprehension 138, 141
suffixes 88, 89, 91, 92, 216, 292, 293
syllogisms 340
syntax 63, 87, 108, 138, 269, 276

T
task 9, 134, 135, 141, 150, 153, 155, 157, 159–161, 175, 197, 200, 204, 208, 215–217, 219, 229–235, 336–340, 347
task constraints 339
temporal 5, 16, 56, 67, 95, 104, 145, 147, 149, 151, 155, 173, 177–188, 274, 295, 335, 338, 345

temporal domain 173, 176–179, 182, 186
The Three Billy Goats Gruff 135, 139, 140, 143, 146, 147, 154, 157, 158, 169–171
The Three Little Pigs 135, 139, 140, 142, 146–148, 153, 155, 165–168
theories of autism 4, 133–135
Theory of mind 6, 136, 137, 151, 152, 159, 191, 192, 207–209
THINK (semantic primitive) 11, 12, 14–17, 21–23, 29, 61, 64–69, 80, 104, 114
thinking-for-speaking 5, 173, 175, 176, 185, 188
titles 116, 145, 146, 157, 158, 160
top 53, 54
top-down 209
TOUCH (semantic primitive) 37, 46, 128
transitive 89, 91, 98, 270–272
translation 11, 12, 18, 30, 105, 114, 129, 277, 283
typically developing 138, 145, 150, 153

typological analyses 342, 343

U
universal concepts 39
universality 63–65, 67, 79, 85, 174

V
verbs 2, 8–10, 13, 15, 17, 22, 23, 29, 67, 77, 86, 88–90, 92, 99, 103, 104, 152, 177, 181, 213–237, 267–288, 289–310, 331, 342–346
verb-framed languages 176, 342
verbs of motion 9, 10, 300, 331, 342, 345
volition 90, 91, 93
voluntary retrieving 104

W
weak central coherence 4, 136, 137, 149, 160
wide 48
word beginnings 7, 213, 217–237, 321,
word endings 7, 216–218, 221, 226, 227, 229, 234, 235

Table of contents of volume 1

Preface		VII
List of contributors		IX
1.	Mental states: Evolution, function, nature *Drew Khlentzos and Andrea C. Schalley*	1
2.	Lithic design space modelling and cognition in *Homo floresiensis* *Mark W. Moore*	11
3.	"As large as you need and as small as you can": Implications of the brain size of Homo floresiensis *Iain Davidson*	35
4.	*Homo* on Flores: Some early implications for the evolution of language and cognition *Michael J. Morwood and Dorothea Cogill-Koez*	43
5.	Evolving artificial minds and brains *Pete Mandik, Mike Collins and Alex Vereschagin*	75
6.	Multi-agent communication, planning, and collaboration based on perceptions, conceptions, and simulations *Peter Gärdenfors and Mary-Anne Williams*	95
7.	The modal-logical interpretation of the causation of bodily actions *Hiroyuki Nishina*	123
8.	Do we access object manipulability while we categorize?: Evidence from reaction time studies *Anna M. Borghi, Claudia Bonfiglioli, Paola Ricciardelli, Sandro Rubichi and Roberto Nicoletti*	153
9.	Speaking without the cerebellum: Language skills in a young adult with near total cerebellar agenesis *Alessandro Tavano, Franco Fabbro and Renato Borgatti*	171

10.	Ontologies as a cue for the metaphorical meaning of technical concepts *Helmar Gust, Kai-Uwe Kühnberger and Ute Schmid*	191
11.	Anti-realist assumptions and challenges in philosophy of mind *Drew Khlentzos*	213
12.	Vagueness, supertranslatability, and conceptual schemes *Arcady Blinov*	233
13.	Visual representation in a natural communication system: What can signed languages reveal about categorisation across different modes of representation? *Dorothea Cogill-Koez*	247
14.	Hidden units in child language *Stephen Crain, Takuya Goro and Utako Minai*	275

Name index	295
Subject index	299
Table of contents of Volume 2	303

Studies in Language Companion Series

A complete list of titles in this series can be found on the publishers' website, *www.benjamins.com*

97   DOLLINGER, Stefan: New-Dialect Formation in Canada. Evidence from the English modal auxiliaries. xxii, 355 pp. *Expected January 2008*
96   ROMEO, Nicoletta: Aspect in Burmese. Meaning and function. xv, 289 pp. *Expected January 2008*
95   O'CONNOR, Loretta: Motion, Transfer and Transformation. The grammar of change in Lowland Chontal. 2007. xiv, 251 pp.
94   MIESTAMO, Matti, Kaius SINNEMÄKI and Fred KARLSSON (eds.): Language Complexity. Typology, contact, change. xiv, 340 pp. + index. *Expected January 2008*
93   SCHALLEY, Andrea C. and Drew KHLENTZOS (eds.): Mental States. Volume 2: Language and cognitive structure. x, 362 pp.
92   SCHALLEY, Andrea C. and Drew KHLENTZOS (eds.): Mental States. Volume 1: Evolution, function, nature. 2007. xi, 304 pp.
91   FILIPOVIĆ, Luna: Talking about Motion. A crosslinguistic investigation of lexicalization patterns. 2007. x, 182 pp.
90   MUYSKEN, Pieter (ed.): From Linguistic Areas to Areal Linguistics. vii, 274 pp. + index. *Expected February 2008*
89   STARK, Elisabeth, Elisabeth LEISS and Werner ABRAHAM (eds.): Nominal Determination. Typology, context constraints, and historical emergence. 2007. viii, 370 pp.
88   RAMAT, Paolo and Elisa ROMA (eds.): Europe and the Mediterranean as Linguistic Areas. Convergencies from a historical and typological perspective. 2007. xxvi, 364 pp.
87   VERHOEVEN, Elisabeth: Experiential Constructions in Yucatec Maya. A typologically based analysis of a functional domain in a Mayan language. 2007. xiv, 380 pp.
86   SCHWARZ-FRIESEL, Monika, Manfred CONSTEN and Mareile KNEES (eds.): Anaphors in Text. Cognitive, formal and applied approaches to anaphoric reference. 2007. xvi, 282 pp.
85   BUTLER, Christopher S., Raquel HIDALGO DOWNING and Julia LAVID (eds.): Functional Perspectives on Grammar and Discourse. In honour of Angela Downing. 2007. xxx, 481 pp.
84   WANNER, Leo (ed.): Selected Lexical and Grammatical Issues in the Meaning–Text Theory. In honour of Igor Mel'čuk. 2007. xviii, 380 pp.
83   HANNAY, Mike and Gerard J. STEEN (eds.): Structural-Functional Studies in English Grammar. In honour of Lachlan Mackenzie. 2007. vi, 393 pp.
82   ZIEGELER, Debra: Interfaces with English Aspect. Diachronic and empirical studies. 2006. xvi, 325 pp.
81   PEETERS, Bert (ed.): Semantic Primes and Universal Grammar. Empirical evidence from the Romance languages. 2006. xvi, 374 pp.
80   BIRNER, Betty J. and Gregory WARD (eds.): Drawing the Boundaries of Meaning. Neo-Gricean studies in pragmatics and semantics in honor of Laurence R. Horn. 2006. xii, 350 pp.
79   LAFFUT, An: Three-Participant Constructions in English. A functional-cognitive approach to caused relations. 2006. ix, 268 pp.
78   YAMAMOTO, Mutsumi: Agency and Impersonality. Their Linguistic and Cultural Manifestations. 2006. x, 152 pp.
77   KULIKOV, Leonid, Andrej MALCHUKOV and Peter de SWART (eds.): Case, Valency and Transitivity. 2006. xx, 503 pp.
76   NEVALAINEN, Terttu, Juhani KLEMOLA and Mikko LAITINEN (eds.): Types of Variation. Diachronic, dialectal and typological interfaces. 2006. viii, 378 pp.
75   HOLE, Daniel, André MEINUNGER and Werner ABRAHAM (eds.): Datives and Other Cases. Between argument structure and event structure. 2006. viii, 385 pp.
74   PIETRANDREA, Paola: Epistemic Modality. Functional properties and the Italian system. 2005. xii, 232 pp.
73   XIAO, Richard and Tony McENERY: Aspect in Mandarin Chinese. A corpus-based study. 2004. x, 305 pp.
72   FRAJZYNGIER, Zygmunt, Adam HODGES and David S. ROOD (eds.): Linguistic Diversity and Language Theories. 2005. xii, 432 pp.
71   DAHL, Östen: The Growth and Maintenance of Linguistic Complexity. 2004. x, 336 pp.
70   LEFEBVRE, Claire: Issues in the Study of Pidgin and Creole Languages. 2004. xvi, 358 pp.

69 TANAKA, Lidia: Gender, Language and Culture. A study of Japanese television interview discourse. 2004. xvii, 233 pp.
68 MODER, Carol Lynn and Aida MARTINOVIC-ZIC (eds.): Discourse Across Languages and Cultures. 2004. vi, 366 pp.
67 LURAGHI, Silvia: On the Meaning of Prepositions and Cases. The expression of semantic roles in Ancient Greek. 2003. xii, 366 pp.
66 NARIYAMA, Shigeko: Ellipsis and Reference Tracking in Japanese. 2003. xvi, 400 pp.
65 MATSUMOTO, Kazuko: Intonation Units in Japanese Conversation. Syntactic, informational and functional structures. 2003. xviii, 215 pp.
64 BUTLER, Christopher S.: Structure and Function – A Guide to Three Major Structural-Functional Theories. Part 2: From clause to discourse and beyond. 2003. xiv, 579 pp.
63 BUTLER, Christopher S.: Structure and Function – A Guide to Three Major Structural-Functional Theories. Part 1: Approaches to the simplex clause. 2003. xx, 573 pp.
62 FIELD, Fredric: Linguistic Borrowing in Bilingual Contexts. With a foreword by Bernard Comrie. 2002. xviii, 255 pp.
61 GODDARD, Cliff and Anna WIERZBICKA (eds.): Meaning and Universal Grammar. Theory and empirical findings. Volume 2. 2002. xvi, 337 pp.
60 GODDARD, Cliff and Anna WIERZBICKA (eds.): Meaning and Universal Grammar. Theory and empirical findings. Volume 1. 2002. xvi, 337 pp.
59 SHI, Yuzhi: The Establishment of Modern Chinese Grammar. The formation of the resultative construction and its effects. 2002. xiv, 262 pp.
58 MAYLOR, B. Roger: Lexical Template Morphology. Change of state and the verbal prefixes in German. 2002. x, 273 pp.
57 MEL'ČUK, Igor A.: Communicative Organization in Natural Language. The semantic-communicative structure of sentences. 2001. xii, 393 pp.
56 FAARLUND, Jan Terje (ed.): Grammatical Relations in Change. 2001. viii, 326 pp.
55 DAHL, Östen and Maria KOPTJEVSKAJA-TAMM (eds.): Circum-Baltic Languages. Volume 2: Grammar and Typology. 2001. xx, 423 pp.
54 DAHL, Östen and Maria KOPTJEVSKAJA-TAMM (eds.): Circum-Baltic Languages. Volume 1: Past and Present. 2001. xx, 382 pp.
53 FISCHER, Olga, Anette ROSENBACH and Dieter STEIN (eds.): Pathways of Change. Grammaticalization in English. 2000. x, 391 pp.
52 TORRES CACOULLOS, Rena: Grammaticization, Synchronic Variation, and Language Contact. A study of Spanish progressive -ndo constructions. 2000. xvi, 255 pp.
51 ZIEGELER, Debra: Hypothetical Modality. Grammaticalisation in an L2 dialect. 2000. xx, 290 pp.
50 ABRAHAM, Werner and Leonid KULIKOV (eds.): Tense-Aspect, Transitivity and Causativity. Essays in honour of Vladimir Nedjalkov. 1999. xxxiv, 359 pp.
49 BHAT, D.N.S.: The Prominence of Tense, Aspect and Mood. 1999. xii, 198 pp.
48 MANNEY, Linda Joyce: Middle Voice in Modern Greek. Meaning and function of an inflectional category. 2000. xiii, 262 pp.
47 BRINTON, Laurel J. and Minoji AKIMOTO (eds.): Collocational and Idiomatic Aspects of Composite Predicates in the History of English. 1999. xiv, 283 pp.
46 YAMAMOTO, Mutsumi: Animacy and Reference. A cognitive approach to corpus linguistics. 1999. xviii, 278 pp.
45 COLLINS, Peter C. and David LEE (eds.): The Clause in English. In honour of Rodney Huddleston. 1999. xv, 342 pp.
44 HANNAY, Mike and A. Machtelt BOLKESTEIN (eds.): Functional Grammar and Verbal Interaction. 1998. xii, 304 pp.
43 OLBERTZ, Hella, Kees HENGEVELD and Jesús SÁNCHEZ GARCÍA (eds.): The Structure of the Lexicon in Functional Grammar. 1998. xii, 312 pp.
42 DARNELL, Michael, Edith A. MORAVCSIK, Michael NOONAN, Frederick J. NEWMEYER and Kathleen M. WHEATLEY (eds.): Functionalism and Formalism in Linguistics. Volume II: Case studies. 1999. vi, 407 pp.

41 DARNELL, Michael, Edith A. MORAVCSIK, Michael NOONAN, Frederick J. NEWMEYER and Kathleen M. WHEATLEY (eds.): Functionalism and Formalism in Linguistics. Volume I: General papers. 1999. vi, 486 pp.
40 BIRNER, Betty J. and Gregory WARD: Information Status and Noncanonical Word Order in English. 1998. xiv, 314 pp.
39 WANNER, Leo (ed.): Recent Trends in Meaning–Text Theory. 1997. xx, 202 pp.
38 HACKING, Jane F.: Coding the Hypothetical. A comparative typology of Russian and Macedonian conditionals. 1998. vi, 156 pp.
37 HARVEY, Mark and Nicholas REID (eds.): Nominal Classification in Aboriginal Australia. 1997. x, 296 pp.
36 KAMIO, Akio (ed.): Directions in Functional Linguistics. 1997. xiii, 259 pp.
35 MATSUMOTO, Yoshiko: Noun-Modifying Constructions in Japanese. A frame semantic approach. 1997. viii, 204 pp.
34 HATAV, Galia: The Semantics of Aspect and Modality. Evidence from English and Biblical Hebrew. 1997. x, 224 pp.
33 VELÁZQUEZ-CASTILLO, Maura: The Grammar of Possession. Inalienability, incorporation and possessor ascension in Guaraní. 1996. xvi, 274 pp.
32 FRAJZYNGIER, Zygmunt: Grammaticalization of the Complex Sentence. A case study in Chadic. 1996. xviii, 501 pp.
31 WANNER, Leo (ed.): Lexical Functions in Lexicography and Natural Language Processing. 1996. xx, 355 pp.
30 HUFFMAN, Alan: The Categories of Grammar. French lui and le. 1997. xiv, 379 pp.
29 ENGBERG-PEDERSEN, Elisabeth, Michael FORTESCUE, Peter HARDER, Lars HELTOFT and Lisbeth Falster JAKOBSEN (eds.): Content, Expression and Structure. Studies in Danish functional grammar. 1996. xvi, 510 pp.
28 HERMAN, József (ed.): Linguistic Studies on Latin. Selected papers from the 6th International Colloquium on Latin Linguistics (Budapest, 23–27 March 1991). 1994. ix, 421 pp.
27 ABRAHAM, Werner, T. GIVÓN and Sandra A. THOMPSON (eds.): Discourse, Grammar and Typology. Papers in honor of John W.M. Verhaar. 1995. xx, 352 pp.
26 LIMA, Susan D., Roberta L. CORRIGAN and Gregory K. IVERSON: The Reality of Linguistic Rules. 1994. xxiii, 480 pp.
25 GODDARD, Cliff and Anna WIERZBICKA (eds.): Semantic and Lexical Universals. Theory and empirical findings. 1994. viii, 510 pp.
24 BHAT, D.N.S.: The Adjectival Category. Criteria for differentiation and identification. 1994. xii, 295 pp.
23 COMRIE, Bernard and Maria POLINSKY (eds.): Causatives and Transitivity. 1993. x, 399 pp.
22 McGREGOR, William B.: A Functional Grammar of Gooniyandi. 1990. xx, 618 pp.
21 COLEMAN, Robert (ed.): New Studies in Latin Linguistics. Proceedings of the 4th International Colloquium on Latin Linguistics, Cambridge, April 1987. 1990. x, 480 pp.
20 VERHAAR, John W.M. S.J. (ed.): Melanesian Pidgin and Tok Pisin. Proceedings of the First International Conference on Pidgins and Creoles in Melanesia. 1990. xiv, 409 pp.
19 BLUST, Robert A.: Austronesian Root Theory. An essay on the limits of morphology. 1988. xi, 190 pp.
18 WIERZBICKA, Anna: The Semantics of Grammar. 1988. vii, 581 pp.
17 CALBOLI, Gualtiero (ed.): Subordination and Other Topics in Latin. Proceedings of the Third Colloquium on Latin Linguistics, Bologna, 1–5 April 1985. 1989. xxix, 691 pp.
16 CONTE, Maria-Elisabeth, János Sánder PETÖFI and Emel SÖZER (eds.): Text and Discourse Connectedness. Proceedings of the Conference on Connexity and Coherence, Urbino, July 16–21, 1984. 1989. xxiv, 584 pp.
15 JUSTICE, David: The Semantics of Form in Arabic. In the mirror of European languages. 1987. iv, 417 pp.
14 BENSON, Morton, Evelyn BENSON and Robert F. ILSON: Lexicographic Description of English. 1986. xiii, 275 pp.
13 REESINK, Ger P.: Structures and their Functions in Usan. 1987. xviii, 369 pp.
12 PINKSTER, Harm (ed.): Latin Linguistics and Linguistic Theory. Proceedings of the 1st International Colloquium on Latin Linguistics, Amsterdam, April 1981. 1983. xviii, 307 pp.
11 PANHUIS, Dirk G.J.: The Communicative Perspective in the Sentence. A study of Latin word order. 1982. viii, 172 pp.

10 DRESSLER, Wolfgang U., Willi MAYERTHALER, Oswald PANAGL and Wolfgang Ullrich WURZEL: Leitmotifs in Natural Morphology. 1988. ix, 168 pp.
9 LANG, Ewald and John PHEBY: The Semantics of Coordination. (English transl. by John Pheby from the German orig. ed. 'Semantik der koordinativen Verknüpfung', Berlin, 1977). 1984. 300 pp.
8 BARTH, E.M. and J.L. MARTENS (eds.): Argumentation: Approaches to Theory Formation. Containing the Contributions to the Groningen Conference on the Theory of Argumentation, October 1978. 1982. xviii, 333 pp.
7 PARRET, Herman, Marina SBISÀ and Jef VERSCHUEREN (eds.): Possibilities and Limitations of Pragmatics. Proceedings of the Conference on Pragmatics, Urbino, July 8–14, 1979. 1981. x, 854 pp.
6 VAGO, Robert M. (ed.): Issues in Vowel Harmony. Proceedings of the CUNY Linguistics Conference on Vowel Harmony, May 14, 1977. 1980. xx, 340 pp.
5 HAIMAN, John: Hua: A Papuan Language of the Eastern Highlands of New Guinea. 1980. iv, 550 pp.
4 LLOYD, Albert L.: Anatomy of the Verb. The Gothic Verb as a Model for a Unified Theory of Aspect, Actional Types, and Verbal Velocity. (Part I: Theory; Part II: Application). 1979. x, 351 pp.
3 MALKIEL, Yakov: From Particular to General Linguistics. Selected Essays 1965–1978. With an introduction by the author, an index rerum and an index nominum. 1983. xxii, 659 pp.
2 ANWAR, Mohamed Sami: BE and Equational Sentences in Egyptian Colloquial Arabic. 1979. vi, 128 pp.
1 ABRAHAM, Werner (ed.): Valence, Semantic Case, and Grammatical Relations. Workshop studies prepared for the 12th International Congress of Linguists, Vienna, August 29th to September 3rd, 1977. xiv, 729 pp. *Expected Out of print*